Seeking Justice

The Judging of Supreme Court Nominees

Michael Comiskey

University Press of Kansas

Published by the University Press of Kansas (Lawrence, Kansas 66049), which was
organized by the Kansas Board of Regents and is operated and funded by Emporia State
University, Fort Hays State University, Kansas State University, Pittsburg State
University, the University of Kansas, and Wichita State University

Library of Congress Cataloging-in-Publication Data

Comiskey, Michael.
    Seeking justices : the judging of Supreme Court nominees / Michael Comiskey.
        p. cm.
    Includes bibliographical references and index.
    ISBN 0-7006-1346-3 (cloth : alk. paper) — ISBN 0-7006-1347-1 (pbk : alk. paper)
    1. United States. Supreme Court. 2. Judges—Selection and appointment—United
States. 3. Law and politics. I. Title.
    KF8742.C63 2004
    347.73'2634—dc22

                                                                        2004013285

British Library Cataloguing-in-Publication Data is available.

Printed in the United States of America

10 9 8 7 6 5 4 3 2

Contents

Acknowledgments

I owe more debts for the completion of this project to more people than I can possibly recall.

I wish to thank the Pennsylvania State University for a sabbatical to begin this book, and for subsequent, periodic partial relief from the normal teaching duties.

Scholars who offered advice on portions of the manuscript or other assistance, some as reviewers for the University Press of Kansas, some as discussants of portions of this book presented at conferences, and some simply as interested and generous colleagues, include Sheldon Goldman, D. Grier Stephenson Jr., Tinsley Yarbrough, Henry Abraham, Fred I. Greenstein, Mark Silverstein, Mary Mattingly, Lauren Bell, Robert A. Katzmann, Priscilla Zotti, Robert E. O'Connor, Beau Breslin, Mark Kessler, and Barbara Perry.

Faculty at my home institution who made useful comments on parts of the manuscript or rendered other assistance include Richard Ball, Elaine Barry, Beverly Peterson, and Evelyn Pluhar-Moravetz.

I offer my sincerest apologies to anyone I have forgotten to mention.

I contributed all of the shortcomings of this book.

To the Faculty of Penn State Fayette

1

Introduction: Contrasting Perspectives on the Confirmation Process

On July 1, 1987, President Ronald Reagan nominated Judge Robert H. Bork of the United States Court of Appeals for the District of Columbia to replace the retiring Justice Lewis F. Powell of the United States Supreme Court. Powell had been a universally acknowledged swing vote on the Court for the previous fifteen years. Bork's conservative jurisprudence and unquestionable professional credentials made him perhaps the ideal figure to implement the Reagan Administration's "plan to have the federal judiciary carry . . . [its] conservative social agenda and a free market economic philosophy into the next century."[1] Liberal forces, equally aware of Bork's potential to transform constitutional law, launched a massive, furious attack on the nominee's ideology. After a bitter struggle lasting nearly four months, the Senate rejected Bork's nomination by a vote of fifty-eight to forty-two.

The president, after vowing to choose another nominee whom Bork's opponents "would object to just as much" as Bork, nominated Judge Douglas H. Ginsburg, a forty-one-year-old federal appeals court judge with eleven months' experience on the bench, whose legal philosophy was far less clear than Bork's but was heavily influenced by the free market–oriented "law and economics" movement.[2] After Ginsburg's nomination was withdrawn after allegations of relatively recent marijuana use, the president nominated and the Senate happily confirmed a perceived moderate conservative, Judge Anthony Kennedy of the Ninth Circuit Court of Appeals.

In 1990, the first President Bush sidestepped conservative pressure to avenge Bork's defeat when he nominated little-known New Hampshire Supreme Court Justice[3] David H. Souter, whose unknown views gave rise to the sobriquet "stealth nominee." To the surprise of nearly everyone, Souter went on to become one of the Court's most liberal justices.[4]

The following year, Bush nominated an African American, Judge Clarence Thomas of the federal Court of Appeals for the District of Columbia, to replace the ardently liberal Justice Thurgood Marshall. Marshall was the Court's first African American justice, a longtime crusader for civil rights, and an icon of the American left. Color aside, Thomas was Marshall's opposite in every way. A hard-edged forty-three-year-old conservative who opposed affirmative action, Thomas had earlier fought a running battle with congressional Democrats who had accused him of failing to enforce antidiscrimination laws during his one year as Assistant Secretary of Education for Civil Rights (1981–82) and eight years as chairman of the Equal Employment Opportunity Commission (EEOC, 1982–1990), where he allegedly retaliated against agency whistle-blowers. Thomas had also traded insults with congressional Democrats and leaders of the mainstream civil rights organizations and taken to the conservative lecture circuit before joining the federal bench to espouse conservative political and legal dogmas, attack his ideological foes, and praise Colonel Oliver North of Iran-Contra fame. Just days before the scheduled Senate vote on his nomination, Thomas was accused of sexual harassment by Anita Hill, a former subordinate at the Department of Education and the EEOC. His already tense confirmation proceedings then became a public spectacle that repelled virtually everyone. After only a short delay occasioned by the accusations, the Senate confirmed Thomas fifty-two to forty-eight.[5]

The years spanning the Bork (1987) and Thomas (1991) nominations spawned a flood of journalistic and scholarly commentary on the High Court confirmation process, most of it critical. This literature fell generally into two schools, designated throughout this work as the legalist and the political schools. Although both were critical of the confirmation process, they offered nearly opposite diagnoses of the flaws in the process and the measures needed to correct them.

The legalist school held that the obsessive scrutiny of nominees' character, qualifications, and—especially—politicolegal views by hostile senators, the news media, and the many interest groups active in the confirmation process had heightened conflict over nominations, produced excessive publicity that distorted the legitimate purposes of the confirmation process (and was often obsessed with scandal and conflict), excessively politicized the process, and induced presidents to nominate undistinguished legal figures with short and uncontroversial paper trails who could win confirmation easily. Adherents of this school, although not entirely of one mind, suggested various reforms to bring about a less political, less sensational confirmation process. Generally, they advocated a greater emphasis on nominees' professional legal credentials, less (or no) emphasis on nominees' politcoconstitutional ideologies, a lesser role for outside interest groups, and a general depublicizing of the process by, for example, ceasing the live telecasts of the Senate Judiciary Committee's confirmation hearings.[6]

Writers in the second, political, school focused mainly on the Senate's inability to get most nominees to reveal their beliefs on legal issues, so that senators could give or withhold informed consent to nominations, and emphasized the president's ability to place nearly anyone of his choosing on the Court and thereby exert excessive influence over the development of constitutional law.

Their suggested reforms centered around greater presidential consultation with the Senate before the president chooses a nominee, more effective questioning of nominees at Senate confirmation hearings, requiring nominees to give more candid testimony as a condition of their confirmations, securing greater ideological balance on what had become an increasingly conservative Court after the late 1960s, and generally placing a higher burden of proof on the president and the nominee to prove the nominee's suitability for a justiceship.[7]

The opposing legalist and political streams of commentary on the confirmation process were accompanied by a set of more positive accounts of the process, most of them in book form and authored by political scientists. Although many political scientists' studies of the process were highly empirical and descriptive,[8] some political scientists offered some evaluation of the process. Like commentators in the political school, these analyses generally describe and defend the "political" nature of the confirmation process since its inception (including senatorial examination of nominees' ideologies)[9] and defend the open, participatory nature of the modern confirmation process.[10] But unlike writers in the political school, they are unconcerned with the Senate's supposed inability to learn enough about nominees' ideologies or to prevent excessive presidential influence over the appointment of justices and the development of constitutional doctrine, trusting in a robust confirmation process to prevent these outcomes. Most of these works, however, concentrate more on the development of the confirmation process than the adequacy of its present mode of operating,[11] or open windows only on selected aspects of the confirmation process, such as failed nominations[12] or presidents' efforts to sell their nominees to the Senate.[13]

Fervor over the confirmation process for High Court nominees subsided in President Bill Clinton's first two years, largely as a result of his purposeful selection of two relatively pragmatic and (only) moderately liberal nominees: Judges Ruth Bader Ginsburg in 1993 and Stephen G. Breyer in 1994 (the only two Supreme Court nominations Clinton would make). But the last six years of Clinton's tenure and the first term of President George W. Bush saw a renewal of ideological combat over these presidents' lower court nominees. In Clinton's last six years, Democrats repeatedly charged the Republican-held Senate with delaying consideration of the president's judicial nominees for ideological reasons, a charge Republicans denied.[14] The pace of judicial confirmations was, however, sufficiently slow to prompt Chief Justice William H. Rehnquist, a conservative Republican, to call for more and speedier Senate votes—whether favorable or otherwise—on the president's judicial nominees.[15]

For several reasons, the stage seemed set for a return to the tumultuous High Court confirmation politics of the Reagan and first Bush presidencies during the first term of President George W. Bush: the president proved to be substantially more conservative than his father[16]; the Senate was divided by shifting, razor-thin margins[17]; the president's first years in office saw the occurrence of repeated conflicts—including Senate filibusters—over the president's lower court nominees[18]; Senate Democrats vowed not to be "steamrolled" into approving highly conservative judicial nominees at any level[19]; and the president appeared likely to make multiple Supreme Court nominations as a result of the age of several sitting justices[20] and the widespread belief that two of the oldest justices, Chief Justice Rehnquist and Justice Sandra Day O'Connor, would like to have a Republican president choose their successors.[21]

As of this writing (early 2004), conflict over High Court appointments had not resumed because it could not: to the surprise of nearly all Court watchers, no justice retired between January 2001 and early 2004. But the arguments over the proper criteria for Senate evaluation of Supreme Court nominees, the role of interest groups and the media in the process, the legal abilities of contemporary appointees, the Senate's ability to learn enough about nominees' ideologies, the president's ability to pack the Court, and many related issues will almost certainly recur.

Although this book is not intended as an apology for the modern confirmation process for U.S. Supreme Court nominees, it conveys a generally positive picture of that process. Like other books by political scientists, it rejects most legalist criticisms of the confirmation process and affirms the political school's endorsement of an open, highly visible, ideological process for evaluating nominees to the nation's highest court. It differs from those other works of political scientists by the unusual directness and detail with which it approaches these tasks, and by its similarly thorough explanation of why the political school's fears of presidential dominance over the appointment of justices and, by extension, the development of constitutional law, are exaggerated. It also differs from other books by political scientists by evaluating the confirmation process comprehensively, rather than emphasizing selected aspects of it, such as its historical development, presidents' efforts to win confirmation for their nominees, or the causes of failed nominations. And evaluation of the process is not confined to the final chapter, but occurs throughout the book, as the major concerns of the legalist and political schools are examined in sequence.

THE MODERN CONFIRMATION PROCESS

Subsequent chapters will present the legalist and political critiques of the confirmation process in greater detail, in tandem with the evidence adduced to evaluate them. Here it is necessary to describe those features of the modern process essential to understanding both the process and the positive and negative perspectives it has generated.

The confirmation process for U.S. Supreme Court nominees, like virtually all processes of American government, has undergone tremendous change in more than two hundred years. Any attempt to provide a thorough history of the process in one chapter would inevitably produce a superficial duplication of more thorough accounts by others.[22] Certain features of the modern confirmation process for Supreme Court nominees are nonetheless so prominent, so salient in debates about the process, or so different from what went before that delineation of those features is vital to an understanding of the modern confirmation process and the disagreements surrounding it.

IDEOLOGY AS THE SUPREME FACTOR

This book uses Elena Kagan's useful shorthand definition of judicial ideology as a person's "understanding of the role of courts in our society, the nature of and values embodied in our Constitution, and the proper tools and techniques of interpretation, both constitutional and statutory."[23] Conflict over Supreme Court nominations has always reflected competing ideologies and interests pertaining to the allocation of power and the direction of public policy.[24] But as other factors that were once of considerable importance gradually diminished, ideology emerged in the latter half of the twentieth century as the nearly exclusive focus of confirmation politics.

In the nineteenth century, "The Supreme Court . . . was regarded much like [any other] political institution, the membership of which, senators believed, should be geographically dispersed and politically reliable."[25] Before the Circuit Court of Appeals Act of 1891 relieved the justices of all circuit-riding duties, nearly every Supreme Court nominee was from the same circuit as the departing justice.[26] Although politics in the larger sense of the term was the primary source of failed nominations in that period, the confirmation process of the time was notable for its inclusion of politics in the less noble senses of the term. The Senate of the latter nineteenth century at least occasionally rejected nominees on the bases of regionalism (when presidents ignored the regional norms of the time), personal rivalry, patronage, and raw partisanship.[27] But as Reconstruction ended and the Civil War receded into distant memory, temporarily dominant war-related issues—such as fidelity to the Union and to Republican Reconstruction policies—diminished, and "sectional and partisan rivalries"[28] eased as well.

At the same time, "the Court's standing improved steadily, in large part because of changes in its workload and in perceptions of the judge's role."[29] These "changes in its workload" included a tripling of the High Court's docket between 1870 and 1890,[30] which helped persuade Congress to eliminate the justices' circuit-riding duties in 1891. This elimination greatly diminished the connection between the circuits and the justices, who were thereafter less and less seen as representatives of the circuits. Presidents were then freer to nominate justices with diminished attention to geography, and opposition to nominees on the basis of regional considerations declined and lost much of its legitimacy.[31]

The altered "perceptions of the judge's role" reflected the rise of legal formalism, which held that judges are, or should be, neutral decision givers whose rulings emerge with almost mathematical determinism from a process of mechanistic legal reasoning. This conception of the judge's role did not, of course, eliminate political evaluations of nominees. But it did at least diminish their frequency and legitimacy.[32]

These changes in institutional arrangements and beliefs, along with the passing of the Civil War–related issues, inclined the Senate to defer to presidential prerogative in Supreme Court appointments. Senators' "political interference in the selection process was generally scorned. Confirmation of qualified judges was perceived as a welcome expression of nationalism and nonpartisanship."[33] The result was an unprecedented seventy-five-year period of relative harmony in Supreme Court appointments, with only one reject-ed nomination out of forty-six between 1894 and 1968.[34]

Cracks in this era of good feeling appeared after the Supreme Court's ruling in *Brown v. Board of Education* (1954), which banned legally required segregation of the races. Although pre-*Brown* nominees had given Senate tes-timony only intermittently, every nominee in the several years after *Brown* appeared before the Senate Judiciary Committee and faced questions from conservative Southern Democrats on the nature of the Constitution (fixed or evolving), and in particular, the nominee's thoughts on *Brown*.[35]

The Warren Court did not, however, stop its alleged liberal activism with *Brown*. It loosened prohibitions against obscenity, forced the controversial one-man–one-vote doctrine on reluctant states, raised the wall of separation between church and state to ban prayers in public schools, and greatly expanded the rights of criminal suspects and defendants. The effect of these decisions was twofold: "a broadening of the substantive content of the rights guaranteed" by the Constitution—as well as other, unlisted rights—and "their application to every state, county, city and crossroads in the land. Critics and supporters alike of these new rights-centered public policies by necessity converged on the Supreme Court."[36]

Two such convergences are particularly relevant for our purposes. The first occurred in the confirmation proceedings for Justice Abe Fortas, the lib-eral Democratic protégé of President Lyndon Johnson whom Johnson sought to elevate to chief justice in 1968. At his confirmation hearings, as Mark Silverstein has described them, conservatives "placed the burden of [the Warren Court's] fifteen years of decision making directly on the shoulders of one man,"[37] scoring the nominee for the Warren Court's record on obsceni-ty, voting rights, federalism, and criminal justice, including one pro-defen-dant decision from 1957—eight years before Fortas joined the Court.[38]

The second convergence occurred in the presidential campaign of 1968. School desegregation, school prayer, obscenity, criminal justice, and the Court itself became major issues, and candidates Richard Nixon and George Wallace promised to nominate "strict constructionists" who would reverse the Court's direction.[39] The results of that election made it clear that the Democratic party had lost the electoral stranglehold it had enjoyed in the South since the Civil War and the national electoral majority it had enjoyed since the New Deal realignment of the 1930s. But no nationwide realignment occurred in 1968, and the Republicans did not gain a national majority. As a result, Nixon became the first new president since 1848 to face both a House and Senate controlled by the opposite party.[40]

When Nixon nominated predictably conservative figures for the

Supreme Court, they met with equally predictable (and twice successful) opposition: nominees Clement Haynsworth and G. Harrold Carswell were rejected by votes of 55–45 and 51–45, respectively. Carswell's professional qualifications were widely questioned, and both nominees faced serious questions about their ethics, issues that likely provided the marginal votes required to reject them. But the bulk of the opposition was ideological, coming in both cases from Democrats and liberal Republicans.[41] And Nixon's 1971 nomination of William H. Rehnquist for associate justice was confirmed sixty-eight to twenty-six after an ideologically inspired struggle. Rehnquist would face, and win, a similar struggle after his nomination by President Reagan to be chief justice in 1986.[42]

The rejections of Haynsworth and Carswell led to the appointment of Justice Harry Blackmun, who surprised everyone by becoming one of the Court's more liberal justices. And Nixon also nominated Lewis F. Powell, an only moderately conservative figure who quickly became the Court's most obvious swing vote.

The ideological tug-of-war between Nixon and a more liberal Democratic Senate produced a middle-of-the-road Court that nonetheless exacerbated the nation's ideological divisions on some major issues. The Burger Court, named for another Nixon appointee—the moderately conservative Chief Justice Warren E. Burger (1969–1986)—approved court-ordered busing for school desegregation[43]; upheld racial preferences for minorities in schools, workplaces, and the awarding of government contracts[44]; and, above all, mandated legal abortion on demand in the first six months of pregnancy in all fifty states.[45] Add to these developments the Reagan Administration's determined efforts to roll back not only the liberal holdings of the Warren and Burger eras but also federal regulatory powers unquestioned since the New Deal,[46] and the result was a near-complete breakdown of the constitutional consensus that prevailed in America from the New Deal to the 1960s. (An exception to this consensus was the fight over desegregation in the 1950s and 1960s, which roiled mainly the South.) It is therefore no surprise that the nominations of William Rehnquist (for chief justice) in 1986, Antonin Scalia that same year, Robert Bork in 1987, and Clarence Thomas in 1991 were overtly ideological, as was the opposition to Rehnquist, Bork, and Thomas (at least until charges of sexual harassment emerged against Thomas).[47]

Thus did consideration of nominees' ideologies become the openly predominant focus of confirmation politics. Legalist writers have often attacked the legitimacy of senators' ideological evaluations of, and ideological opposition to, judicial nominees. This legitimacy is the subject of Chapter 2.

RENEWED INTENSITY OF CONFLICT

A conspicuous feature of the history of High Court confirmations is the fluctuating level of conflict. The first three presidents—Washington, Adams, and Jefferson—experienced only one rejected nomination of the nineteen they made (Washington's nomination of John Rutledge to be chief justice in 1795). Their other eighteen nominations won Senate approval within a week of their submission to the Senate.[48]

The second rejected nomination was that of Alexander Walcott, made by President James Madison in 1811. This rejection marked the start of an eighty-year period of frequent conflict over High Court nominees. Eighteen of the next sixty-three nominations—over one-fourth of the total—went down to defeat, the last of these being Grover Cleveland's nomination of Wheeler H. Peckham in 1894.[49]

The period 1894 to 1968 saw a remarkable about-face from the preceding eighty years. Only one nomination out of forty-six was rejected in those seventy-four years—that of Hoover nominee John J. Parker in 1930.[50]

The rejection of President Lyndon Johnson's nomination of his friend, Justice Abe Fortas, for chief justice in 1968 ushered in a renewed era of higher conflict. In the twenty-six years from 1968 to 1994, four of eighteen nominations were rejected—those of Fortas (1968), Clement Haynsworth (1969), G. Harrold Carswell (1970), and Robert Bork (1987). The Senate also failed to act on Johnson's nomination of Homer Thornberry to replace Fortas as associate justice in 1968 (since Fortas's blocked promotion meant that his seat had not become vacant). One other nomination was withdrawn (that of Reagan nominee Douglas Ginsburg in 1987), and there were major struggles over three other nominations—those for William H. Rehnquist (for associate justice in 1971 and chief justice in 1986) and Clarence Thomas (in 1991).

Commentators in the legalist school have expressed several concerns about the origin and allegedly harmful consequences of this renewed conflict: (1) that it is media driven and preoccupied with scandal; (2) that it diverts attention from the professional qualifications of nominees; (3) that it reflects and furthers the "overpoliticization" of the confirmation process; (4) that it delegitimizes the three branches of government in the public mind; and (5) that it induces presidents to nominate undistinguished but uncontroversial figures who can win confirmation. Concerns of this sort are the subject of Chapters 3 and 4.

PREPONDERANT PRESIDENTIAL INFLUENCE OVER HIGH COURT APPOINTMENTS

Despite the heightened frequency of conflictual nominations starting in the late 1960s, several factors afford presidents a preponderant influence over Supreme Court appointments. First, the president can choose an individual from a bevy of qualified candidates, but the Senate, once the president selects a nominee, can only react to the president's choice. The president therefore sets the agenda for the ensuing confirmation process, and in politics, the agenda-setter has an inherent advantage in determining the outcome. Second, barring any unforeseen problem with the nominee's record on ethics, a president can normally count on senators of his party to support the nominee out of party loyalty and their probable affinity for the nominee's ideology. Third, as Alexander Hamilton correctly predicted in *The Federalist,* senators sometimes vote to confirm a nominee not truly to their liking because they realize the president could nominate someone worse.[51] And fourth, perhaps out of respect for the office of the presidency (another factor Hamilton foresaw),[52] or possibly as a legacy of the relatively quiescent period from 1894 to 1967, many senators of both parties still adhere in principle to a presumption in favor of a nominee's confirmation, affording the president the benefit of any doubts about the nominee that are not plainly disqualifying. Senators of both parties expressed their belief in this principle of deference as late as the 1990s.[53]

Perhaps the clearest example of continuing senatorial deference to the president was the 1990 confirmation of David Souter. Souter was not a distinguished nominee. His judicial career included little or no experience in dealing with the federal statutory and constitutional questions that preoccupy the U.S. Supreme Court. His views on those questions were a mystery. Although he was often described as displaying a scholarly bent, his published scholarship consisted of one article—a tribute to a fellow New Hampshire Supreme Court justice.[54] In Souter's courtly manner and in his temperate Senate testimony, some senators found either reassurance or disappointment that Souter was no agenda-driven conservative. But the consensus view of him after his confirmation hearings was that of a conservative of some unknown intensity, still largely the "stealth nominee" he appeared to be when nominated. The enigmatic nominee nonetheless won confirmation by a vote of ninety to nine.[55]

There are signs, however, that senatorial adherence to deference as a matter of principle eroded amid the ideological schism and combat starting in the late 1960s. One sign of that erosion is the simple increase in opposition to presidential nominations since that time. The principle of senatorial deference is bound to decline in a period of eroding constitutional consensus as more senators are asked to support nominees with what these senators view as unpalatable constitutional ideologies. In addition, the Senate's extraordinary inquiry into charges of sexual harassment against nominee Clarence Thomas served to subvert the principle of senatorial deference. After the seemingly inconclusive hearings on those charges, many Democratic senators made floor statements explicitly repudiating the notion that the Senate owes the president or a nominee any deference or benefit of the doubt,[56] a position most Republican senators would almost certainly embrace in the case of a troubled Democratic nominee.

Despite this development, the presidency will almost certainly retain its primacy over High Court appointments because of the president's ability to choose a nominee, the support of the president's party in the Senate, and the willingness of senators of the opposite party to support nominees they find acceptable, if not truly desirable. This primacy has prompted some proponents of the political critique of the confirmation process to charge that presidents can pack the Court with ideological soul mates and acquire excessive influence over future developments in constitutional law, a charge examined in Chapter 7.

MORE DETAILED SCRUTINY OF NOMINEES

A natural accompaniment to the Senate's overriding interest in nominees' politicolegal ideologies is what Henry Abraham has called the Senate's "augmenting tendency to pay closer, and more protracted, attention to nominated candidates"[57]—primarily to their political and legal beliefs, but also to their professional credentials and ethical records, especially if these latter subjects offer a cover to what is really ideological opposition.[58]

The intense interest in nominees' ideologies results directly from universal recognition of the Court's undoubted power over public policy and the inevitable influence of a nominee's preferences regarding the allocation of political power and the content of public policy on his or her future votes as a justice.[59] As nominee Anthony Kennedy openly acknowledged in his written questionnaire for the Senate Judiciary Committee in 1987, "It is a fact . . . not a perception, that courts have become more active in the public dialogue and in policy making than at any other time in our constitutional history. This expanded role of the courts tends to erode the boundaries of judicial power, and also threatens to permit the individual biases of the judge to operate."[60]

Whatever constraining force precedent and the requirements of legal reasoning may exert, these individual biases do in fact operate, as common observation and the political science literature both demonstrate.[61]

Before the late 1960s, Senate examination of Supreme Court nominees was often remarkably casual by today's standards. Senate hearings normally took one day, or two at the most. They were held by only a subcommittee of the Senate Judiciary Committee until the 1940s. There were no hearings at all for nominees James F. Byrnes in 1941, Wiley Rutledge in 1943, and Harold Burton in 1945. (Byrnes and Burton were sitting senators when nominated.)[62] Only four nominees testified at their hearings before nominee testimony became routine with the first post-*Brown* nominee, John Marshall Harlan II, in 1955.[63] Even after *Brown,* Senate hearings and nominee testimony were usually cursory. As late as 1969, Warren Burger, nominee for chief justice, was the only witness at his one-hour, forty-minute confirmation hearing.[64]

This casual mode of operation would soon become a thing of the past. At Carswell's five-day confirmation hearings in 1970, senators heard from five outside interest groups, confronted the nominee with a verbatim transcript of a racist speech he had given as a candidate for a state legislative seat in 1948, and caught him dissembling about his role in privatizing a public golf course in 1956 to prevent the facility's desegregation.[65] In 1987, senators thoroughly questioned Robert Bork for five days—Senator Edward Kennedy even played back an audiotape of damaging remarks Bork had made at a college seminar two years earlier—then took testimony from seventeen interest groups over seven more days.[66] In 1991, senators quizzed nominee Clarence Thomas for five days about his record on equal employment issues, his public speeches, his beliefs on abortion, the role of natural law and original intent in constitutional interpretation, the existence of property rights, his criticisms of prominent civil rights leaders, and his praise of Colonel Oliver North, among numerous other matters.[67] They then heard from representatives of forty-three interest groups, for and against the nomination, over three more days (before the sexual harassment charges produced a final three days of hearings).[68]

The Senate's habit of scrutinizing nominees more closely is evidenced by the increasing length of the hearings transcripts. From 1930 to 1949, they averaged 42 pages; from 1950 to 1969, 264 pages; since 1970, 1,117 pages.[69] This growth is not due solely to the increased number of controversial nominations starting in the late 1960s; the hearings transcripts for five relatively recent noncontroversial nominees (O'Connor, Kennedy, Souter, Ginsburg, and Breyer) average 819 pages. And the Senate took testimony from an average of fourteen groups for these five nominations, compared to eleven and five for the earlier controversial nominations of Haynsworth and Carswell, respectively.[70]

The Senate is not alone in conducting intensified scrutiny of High Court nominees. In addition to an FBI background check, the American Bar Association Committee on the Federal Judiciary evaluates every nominee's written judicial opinions and published articles and examines every nominee's professional record for relevant experience, professional competence, and judicial temperament.[71] More tellingly, perhaps, interest groups from across the political spectrum examine every aspect of a nominee's record, sometimes hiring a law firm for the purpose.[72]

Finally, the news media investigate a nominee's personal and professional history to a much greater degree than in the past. When President Johnson nominated Abe Fortas for chief justice in 1968, reporters from *Time* magazine and the *New York Times* helped uncover Fortas's close personal and political ties to Johnson that continued even after Fortas joined the Supreme Court as associate justice in 1965.[73] And in 1991, reporters from *Newsday* and National Public Radio, acting on tips from senators or staffers, worked overtime to locate Anita Hill and force her into going public with her charges of sexual harassment against Clarence Thomas.[74]

Despite these seemingly thorough examinations, commentators in the political school have often expressed the concern that senators learn little about nominees' ideologies, or little that they can act on, and are therefore unable to give or withhold informed consent to High Court nominations. Chapter 6 examines this concern.

A MORE OPEN PROCESS

The intensified scrutiny of nominees now takes place in a glare of publicity vastly different from the closed proceedings of the past. The openness and deliberate pace of the modern process, combined with the proliferation of interest groups in the latter twentieth century,[75] also provide public opinion and numerous groups access to, and influence on, the confirmation process.

Until 1913, senators were not popularly elected and were therefore insulated to a large degree from public opinion. Secretive Senate procedures further insulated the confirmation process from observation and influence by the public and other interests. "Public confirmation hearings were virtually nonexistent prior to the 1916 Brandeis nomination,"[76] and hearings—usually brief—continued to be held in private until the 1950s.[77] Until 1929, Senate debate on all nominations was held in closed session unless two-thirds of the Senate voted to open the debate. In that year, the Senate adopted the modern rule: confirmation debates would be open unless a majority of senators voted to close them.[78] Moreover, public opinion polls did not exist until the 1930s, rendering difficult the transmission to senators of public sentiment (to the extent the public could have any informed opinion about matters normally handled so privately).

The speed with which the Senate processed High Court nominations— between 1894 and 1967, it almost invariably confirmed them—also hindered both the formation of public opinion and the possibility of meaningful interest group input. Nominations of that era typically came to a Senate vote within a month after the president made them, often within a few days.[79] (And they necessarily passed through the Senate Judiciary Committee even faster.) Because of the closed and expeditious—almost hasty—nature of the process, neither interested members of the public nor relevant groups had the time or opportunity to study a nominee's record, then mobilize and influence the Senate. Hence public opinion and the positions of organized interests—if these things existed at all—were simply not a factor in Senate consideration of the vast majority of nominations.

Today, at least in the case of controversial nominations, "The confirmation process is a distinctly public affair, with all of its participants grappling with each other for public support."[80] The confirmation hearings begin several weeks or more after the president submits the nomination, providing the news media with plenty of time to investigate and report on the nominee. Interest groups have time to analyze a nominee's record, gauge public opinion on the nomination, take a position, form coalitions with other groups, mobilize their members, rally public support for their position, and lobby senators directly and through grassroots campaigns. At the televised confirmation hearings, the nominee, the ABA Committee, scholars, and interest groups will present their analyses and their arguments for or against the nomination. The president will make public remarks on the nominee's behalf, and various White House operatives will attempt to influence press coverage of the nomination and sway the public, to garner interest group support for the nominee, and to guide the nominee through the Senate.[81] The whole process culminates in the Senate floor debate and vote televised by C-SPAN. The contrast from the quick, closed process of the past could hardly be greater.

Writers in the legalist school have often lamented the openness and high public visibility of modern High Court confirmation proceedings. They believe variously that this openness and visibility (1) permit the media to create scandal out of nominees' personal or professional peccadilloes; (2) allow outside interest groups to conduct political campaigns for or against nominees; (3) introduce public opinion into what should be an elite-centered process; (4) inflate the importance of the Senate's public hearings in the confirmation process; (5) place a premium on political gamesmanship and the way participants in the process appear on television; and (6) distort the confirmation proceedings by encouraging senators to posture, to confront nominees, or to focus their inquiries into nominees' positions on particular issues—positions senators either misunderstand or distort for political effect—rather than make a considered judgment on the nominees' professional credentials, integrity, and judicial temperament. The result, in short, is an overpoliticization of the confirmation process by the media, single-minded issue groups, and senators. Chapter 3 examines these claims.

GREATER INVOLVEMENT BY THE WHITE HOUSE

One actor whose increased involvement in the confirmation process merits a separate discussion is the president. The White House is the prime mover behind every nomination, and many White House efforts on behalf of nominees take place off the public stage. It may be surprising that significant White House involvement has become routine only in recent decades. Presidents, after all, have always sought confirmation for their nominees. But there was little for presidents and their aides to do in earlier eras when most nominations were confirmed or rejected within a short time, with little involvement by anyone outside the Senate.

The modern executive's exertions for confirmation result directly from changes in the confirmation process. First is the higher level of conflict over nominations since the late 1960s, and the president's consequent need to make greater efforts on behalf of nominees. Second, the much closer scrutiny of nominees over a longer time span by a larger number of actors inevitably raises more questions about nominees, questions that must be answered or otherwise contained to maximize the probability of confirmation. Third is the benefit from having public support for a nominee,[82] which necessitates the cultivation of the public either directly or through intermediaries such as interest groups or the mass media.[83] In the case of a controversial nominee such as Clarence Thomas, these efforts may effectuate a confirmation strategy that is quite extensive and sophisticated.[84]

Every administration gives every nominee a refresher course in constitutional law led by specialists in the Justice Department, has every nominee study videotapes of adroit Senate testimony by previous successful nominees, and holds mock confirmation hearings for each nominee—dubbed "murder boards" for the tough questions the "senators" hurl at the nominee— all to prepare the nominee to make a good impression at the real Senate hearings.[85] Administration "handlers," or better yet, a senator close to the nominee, will escort the nominee to a courtesy call with any senator who wishes to meet the nominee,[86] and administration officials and other support personnel may be stationed in Senate offices during the confirmation hearings to monitor the hearings, do response research, and feed the administration's spin on the hearings to the media.[87]

Finally, although the president oversees the execution of the confirmation strategy, and he and the White House Office of Congressional Liaison lobby senators privately, the president will make public statements on behalf of the nominee, a tactic that presidents seldom used until President Reagan's efforts on behalf of Robert Bork. (Well into the twentieth century, it was thought unseemly for presidents to make public political pleas on behalf of what were supposedly apolitical judicial nominations.)[88] Presidential abandonment of this "apolitical" norm comports with the more frequent conflict over High Court nominations in a Senate characterized both by senators' increased individual autonomy and their polarization into two opposing ideological blocs.

INDIVIDUAL AUTONOMY AND IDEOLOGICAL POLARIZATION IN THE MODERN SENATE

In the latter half of the twentieth century, two seemingly divergent but coexisting developments altered the environment of the Senate: in the words of political scientist Burdett Loomis, "the unlikely combination of individualism and partisanship."[89] On the one hand, senators gained increased individual autonomy. As party discipline weakened, senators were freer than ever to defy the party leadership and vote as they pleased. Assisted by larger staffs, senators became policy entrepreneurs, free to generalize or to specialize in policy areas of their choice and exert significant influence over issues outside the jurisdictions of their committees. Even the most junior senators took an active part in floor action and received important committee and subcommittee assignments, including subcommittee chairmanships. Respect for individual senatorial prerogatives became the norm.[90]

At the same time, however, the Senate became increasingly polarized along liberal/Democratic and conservative/Republican lines. As the regional realignment proceeded in the South, conservative Southern Democrats were largely replaced by conservative Republicans. And the number of liberal to moderate Republican senators, mainly from the northeast and northwest, dwindled as well. By the 1990s, there were "simply fewer moderates and liberals within the Republican party and fewer moderates and conservatives within the Democratic party."[91] As a result, "ideology and partisanship [were] increasingly aligned. Being conservative and being Republican [went] together," as did "being liberal and being Democratic."[92]

The growing ideological separation of the two parties produced an increase in both party-line voting (the percentage of the time that a majority of one party opposes a majority of the other on roll-call votes) and party unity scores in the Senate (the percentage of party-line votes on which an average Democrat or Republican votes with his or her party). From the early 1970s to the late 1990s, the percentage of party-line votes rose from about 40 percent to about 60 percent, peaking at over 75 percent in both houses in 1995, when the Republicans took control of the House and the Senate and made the Contract with America their agenda.[93] Since 1993, President Clinton's first year in office, party unity scores have fluctuated around an all-time high of nearly 90 percent.[94] Members of the same party, out of ideological inclination and choice, marched increasingly in lockstep even as they gained the freedom to go their own ways.

As in earlier times, the outcome of close votes in the Senate often depends on the ideological moderates in both parties. There are just many fewer of them than in the past. Thus, when presidents nominate relatively controversial figures for the Supreme Court, the Senate vote on the nomination is likely to follow party lines, with the outcome in close cases riding on the votes of a small number of moderates in both parties.

DIVIDED GOVERNMENT

Increased ideological conflict and party-line voting pose special problems for presidents when added to another development: the vastly greater incidence of High Court nominations made during periods of divided government, when the president faces a Senate majority of the opposite party. From 1897 to 1954, only two of thirty-six nominations were made during periods of divided government. The lone unsuccessful nomination of that period occurred in 1930, under unified Republican control of the White House and the Senate. From 1954 to 1994, fifteen of thirty-one nominations—approximately half—occurred under divided government, including four of the six unsuccessful nominations of that period. (The total of six includes the aborted nominations of Homer Thornberry in 1968 and Douglas Ginsburg in 1987.[95]) It is therefore not surprising that quantitative analyses have identified divided government as a risk factor for rejection of a nomination.[96] Despite the perils posed by the combination of divided government and increased partisanship, modern presidents facing opposition-controlled Senates have occasionally made provocative Supreme Court nominations. Among the clearest examples are those of Carswell, Bork, Douglas Ginsburg, and Clarence Thomas, all discussed in Chapter 3.[97]

It is within the evolution of the confirmation process as presented in this chapter that subsequent chapters examine these confirmation struggles, as well as less contentious confirmations and the contrasting perspectives on the confirmation process that these events have engendered.

PLAN OF THE BOOK

Chapters 2 to 4 examine three of the most prominent claims of the legalist school. Chapter 2 analyzes and rejects the claim that senators have no constitutional authority to evaluate Supreme Court nominees on the basis of their politicolegal ideologies. Chapter 3 examines the legalist claim that zealous investigations into nominees' ideologies, participation in the confirmation process by groups outside the Senate, the intrusive publicity attending modern High Court nominations, and other factors have distorted the confirmation process, generated excessive conflict, and overpoliticized the process.

Chapter 4 uses a survey on the quality of the Court's twentieth-century justices, administered to two hundred seventy-five scholars in the field of constitutional law and politics, to test the legalist claim that the modern preoccupation with nominees' ideologies has induced presidents to nominate second-tier figures with little-known and therefore uncontroversial views whose unspectacular legal abilities threaten to produce a mediocre Court. Although the results of the survey are subject to several caveats, and both great and near-great justices will likely continue to grace the Court, the survey results and common observation of modern confirmation politics require us to allow the possibility that the modern confirmation process may produce outstanding justices less often than in the past.

Chapter 5 revisits the confirmation of Justice Clarence Thomas, whose confirmation proceedings repelled observers of all stripes and whose ranking in the survey in Chapter 4 places him among the worst justices of the last century. The chapter concludes that Thomas's confirmation resulted from the overpowering politics of race, combined with a lack of political courage and ethics by many senators, rather than from flaws in the confirmation process per se.

Chapters 6 and 7 analyze major claims of the political school. Chapter 6 examines the concern that senators often fail to learn enough about nominees' politicolegal beliefs to give or withhold informed consent to their nominations, and therefore senators give these nominations insufficient scrutiny. Although there is support for this claim, the analysis finds the concern much overstated. Chapter 7 analyzes doctrinal developments during the Rehnquist Court of the late twentieth and early twenty-first centuries to test the oft-stated worry that despite increased opposition to nominees in recent decades, skillful presidents can pack the Court.

Chapter 8 summarizes the book's analyses of the legalist and political schools and reviews some of the most prominent proposals for reform of the confirmation process.

2

The Senate's Constitutional Role in the Confirmation Process

Legalist critics of an overly political confirmation process have often argued that senators have no constitutional or electoral mandate to examine nominees' legal ideologies, defined in the previous chapter as their "understanding of the role of courts in our society, the nature of and values embodied in our Constitution, and the proper tools and techniques of interpretation, both constitutional and statutory."[1] Of course, the constitutional text is silent regarding the criteria senators are to use in evaluating nominees' fitness for the Court, stating only that "[The president] shall nominate, and by and with the Advice and Consent of the Senate, shall appoint . . . Judges of the supreme Court."[2]

The Founders said little about the qualities judges should possess and how the Senate should evaluate them, except that judges should possess some undefined "merit."[3] Yet as the following pages show, there are clear indications that many of the Framers did countenance ideological scrutiny of nominees—or at the least would not have been surprised by it. Nor, despite the claims of some authors, is there anything in Alexander Hamilton's writings in *The Federalist* to indicate that senators should not undertake such scrutiny. Ideological scrutiny of Supreme Court nominees also, somewhat paradoxically, enhances the Court's legitimacy and is implicit in the philosophy and structure of the constitutional democracy the Founders created. And recent nominees have seldom, despite frequently expressed concerns, improperly prejudged contentious legal issues by revealing how they will vote in future cases while responding to senators' questions at their confirmation hearings.

THE INTENT OF THE FRAMERS

Although the Founders said little about desirable judicial qualities, they vigorously debated at the Federal Convention the merits of two alternative means of judicial appointment. One group, led by James Wilson of Pennsylvania and, initially, Alexander Hamilton of New York, believed the president should hold the sole power of appointment. Hamilton soon left this group, proposing on June 5, 1787, less than a month after the convention convened, that justices be nominated by the president and approved or rejected by the Senate.[4] An opposing group led by Roger Sherman and Oliver Ellsworth of Connecticut argued for senatorial appointment of the justices.

Advocates of purely presidential appointment made three arguments. First, the president would be less corruptible than a body of men such as the Senate.[5] Second, the president, representing the whole nation, would have greater knowledge than senators of persons fit to serve.[6] Third, the president, as an individual, would bear clearer responsibility in the event of a bad nomination than would the Senate as a collective body.[7] Supporters of senatorial appointment disputed the first two of these claims and said little in response to the third.[8]

Alongside these seemingly genuine differences over the most appropriate appointer, conflicting preferences over the appointments clause became entangled with the conflicting interests of the large and small states and, at least in the minds of some Framers, the northern and southern states.[9] On July 16, 1787, the adoption of the Great Compromise changed the basis of representation in the Senate from unequal representation based on population to the equal representation of all states. Within a few days, the large states, which hoped to supply most future presidents, lined up in favor of presidential appointment of judges in votes taken at the convention, whereas the smaller states voted for appointment by the Senate, in which they would have an equal vote.[10]

On July 18, the convention rejected by a vote of six states to two a motion to give the entire judicial appointment power to the president. Pennsylvania and Massachusetts, two of the larger states, supplied the only votes for the motion.[11] On July 21, the convention voted six to three to reject a motion granting the nomination power to the president and a veto power to the Senate. Another large state, Virginia, joined Pennsylvania and Massachusetts in supporting the proposal.[12] Later that day, the six smaller states that defeated this proposal voted to give the entire appointment power to the Senate, with the same three larger states in opposition.[13] The Senate's plenary power to appoint judges remained in the draft constitution almost to the convention's end. In early September, the Committee of Eleven, created to resolve lingering disputes and composed of one delegate from each state then represented at the convention, proposed the advice and consent procedure that the convention approved unanimously on September 7.

Further evidence of the influence of state rivalries in the appointment debates comes from the remarks of participants in those debates. At least five delegates argued for or against various modes of appointment on the grounds that a particular mode would favor one state or one group of states over another (specifically, the larger versus the smaller states, the northern versus the southern, or the state where the Founders thought the future national capital would sit).[14] James Madison, for instance, participated in this debate when he stated, perhaps indiscreetly, that his plan to give the president preponderant influence over appointments would prevent domination of the appointment process by smaller and northern states (and thereby benefit Madison's home state of Virginia, the only large southern state).[14] Oblique evidence of the importance of divergent state and regional interests comes from George Mason of Virginia, who found it "his duty to differ from his colleagues in their opinions and reasonings on this subject." He went on to say that the mode of appointing judges would have little impact on "the difference of interest between the Northern and Southern [states]," thereby implying that at least some of "his colleagues" thought it would.[15]

Additional evidence on this score comes from later statements by delegates to the Federal Convention at the ratifying conventions in Connecticut and North Carolina, where they reported that the Senate had been given a role in making appointments to keep the larger states from dominating the process. Joseph Harris, writing in the 1950s, called these statements "an afterargument in defense of the Constitution," and maintained that the appointments clause was a compromise between delegates who favored a strong executive and those who feared one.[16] Although Harris is no doubt correct in part,[17] he overlooks most of the evidence of conflicting state and regional interests cited above.

What does this history tell us about the intended role of the Senate in the judicial appointment process? Given the differences of opinion among the Framers on this question, it is clear, first, that there was no single intent of the Framers. Second, the preference of the more numerous smaller states for purely senatorial appointment implies that a majority of the states, if not of the delegates, intended the Senate to exercise great discretion—if it could not have the entire power—in naming judges. Delegates from these states would resist any senatorial role or range of criteria for senators to consider that was less than that of the president. Third, the Founders' own behavior implies that they could hardly have been surprised to find senators judging nominees by the same political and economic interests that guided themselves in the battle over the appointment power. It is clear from their generally skeptical view of human nature and the many barriers against political abuse they placed in the Constitution that they did not trust future generations to behave in a more high-minded way than they themselves did.

Could a delegate from a small state have contemplated that his state's senators would willingly participate in the appointment of a Court of "meritorious" justices drawn entirely from the large states? Did the delegates from the southern states think their senators would or should permit the president and the Senate to appoint a Court made up entirely of "well-qualified" Northerners? These things are hardly likely. The battle over the appointment power was largely an effort to secure appointments and future Supreme Court decisions favorable to the delegates' home states. In other words, it was a battle over the future justices' politics. And if the Founders countenanced the evaluation of nominees based on their likely positions on state or interregional issues, would they have ruled out opposition to a nominee by a senator who believed the nominee held a misguided view of the Constitution or dangerous beliefs about vital issues? It is impossible to imagine that they did. But if they somehow did so, they must have been sorely disappointed and surprised at the behavior of their contemporaries in the Senate of the 1790s who rejected George Washington's nomination of John Rutledge for chief justice in 1795 and began a long tradition of opposing nominees for personal, regional, and political reasons. The leader of the opposition to Rutledge was none other than Alexander Hamilton, a leading advocate of executive power, the originator of the Advice and Consent procedure, and according to some writers, the proponent of a nonpolitical confirmation process.[18]

The permissibility of examining nominees ideologically is also implicit in the view taken by those Framers who felt that appointment by the president alone would give too much power to one person. John Rutledge—perhaps ironically, in view of his later rejection by the Senate—articulated this objection most clearly. According to Madison's notes of the Convention, "Mr. Rutlidge [sic] was by no means disposed to grant so great a power to any single person. The people will think we are leaning too much towards monarchy," a position echoed by Oliver Ellsworth.[19]

The use of ideological criteria by senators is implied by, or at least consistent with, the concern that the president could acquire too much power if he alone were to determine who—and what views—would predominate on the Court. Given the great power of the modern Supreme Court, a power the Founders could hardly have foreseen, a modern American who shared the Framers' concern over excessive executive power (and they almost assuredly did not foresee the power of the modern presidency) would be impelled to take the view that senators who find the ideology of the president and his nominee objectionable should subject the nominee to careful ideological scrutiny with a real possibility of rejection on ideological grounds.

In short, the prolonged debate over the appointments clause at the Constitutional Convention was highly political, animated in part by the conflicting interests of the thirteen states and in part by a fear that the absence of a strong senatorial role would give the president too much influence over the Court. There is no reason to think that the Framers believed, or would have believed had they given the question more thought, that future appointment proceedings would be any different.

Coda: Alexander Hamilton in *The Federalist*

Before closing this discussion of the Founders' views, it is necessary to dissect what may be the most common legalist argument that ideological scrutiny of nominees contravenes the Founders' intentions: an argument gleaned from statements in Hamilton's *Federalist* 76. These statements are often used in an attempt to show the intention of *all* of the Founders that the Senate play a nonideological role in judicial appointments.[20] Aside from the dubious extrapolation from Hamilton's views to those of "the Founders," the argument rests on a misreading of *Federalist* 76. Nowhere does that essay advocate a nonideological role for the Senate. To the contrary, it indicates that Hamilton saw ideological review of nominees as proper in order to prevent presidential domination of the judiciary.

The argument is that Hamilton "maintained that there was in reality no essential difference between the power to nominate and the power to appoint."[21] The evidence for this argument is Hamilton's statements in consecutive paragraphs of Number 76 that "There can . . . in this view, be no difference between nominating and appointing," and "It is also not very probable that [the president's] nomination would often be overruled."[22]

These statements do not imply that Hamilton believed in the passive or nonideological review of nominees. His remark that there was "no difference between nominating and appointing" is often taken out of context. He made this statement because, as he explained in the very next sentence of Number 76, "[E]very advantage to be expected from [presidential appointment] would, in substance, be derived from the power of *nomination* . . . proposed to be conferred upon him. . . . The same motives which would influence a proper discharge of his duty in one case [appointment] would exist in the other [nomination]."[23] Thus, Hamilton was saying only that the president would take as much care while nominating as he would if he had the entire appointment power. He was making no statement about the role the Senate should play in reviewing nominees.

Hamilton offered two justifications for his second contention—that the Senate would not often reject nominees. First, the same president would usually make the next nomination, and the Senate would therefore have no assurance that it would like the next nominee any more than the first one. Second, senators would be inclined to defer to the president's choice out of respect for the office of the presidency and a reluctance to stigmatize the rejected nominee.[24] But nothing in the first of these factors implies that senators should not engage in ideological inquiry. It implies only that senatorial rejection of a nominee on the basis of ideological or other grounds may do the Senate little good (a conclusion that downplays the possibility that the president will compromise with the Senate and nominate a figure more to the Senate's liking, as several modern presidents have done).[25] And the likelihood of senatorial deference to the president's choice suggests only that in practice senators would give presidents the benefit of the doubt on whatever criteria senators choose to employ in voting on nominees. It does not tell us what those criteria should be. In short, as Charles Black has pointed out, Hamilton was merely making a *prediction* that the Senate would seldom reject a nominee, not a normative statement about the role the Senate *should* play.[26]

Hamilton also thought that rejections by the Senate would be infrequent because

> The possibility of rejection would be a strong motive to care in proposing. . . . [The president] would be both ashamed and afraid to bring forward . . . candidates who had no other merit than that of coming from the same State [as the president], or of being in some way or other personally allied to him, *or of possessing the necessary insignificance and pliancy to render them the obsequious instruments of his pleasure.*[27]

This passage implies two things. First, to secure the benefits of presidential nomination as Hamilton saw them, the possibility of rejection by the Senate would have to be a real one. Second, and more importantly, the last portion of this passage clearly implies that Hamilton was concerned about securing the judiciary's independence from the president. He revealed a similar concern in *Federalist* 77, where he criticized the appointment process in his own state of New York, which lacked legislative review of the governor's choice, because it "advance[d] . . . persons whose chief merit is their devotion to [the governor's] will."[28]

It is striking that Hamilton, the Convention's foremost advocate of executive power, expressed concern that Supreme Court justices would too faithfully mirror the president's "will." Hamilton's concern about presidential control of the judiciary implies that to preserve judicial independence, senators must give consideration to nominees' independence of mind and patterns of thought. Although one can draw a useful distinction between a nominee's manner of thinking and the conclusions the nominee reaches, there is clearly a connection between the two. At the very least, inquiry into a nominee's thought patterns inevitably pulls the inquirer within the shadow of the nominee's beliefs about current legal issues and the relationship between the nominee's beliefs and those of the president.

In conclusion, Hamilton's writings in *The Federalist* do not support the claim that he thought ideological review of nominees unnecessary or improper, or that the Senate should be a passive partner in the appointment of judges.[29] Moreover, although Hamilton's views are not a proxy for those of the Founders, his concern for judicial independence leans toward the opposite view and comports well with the views of those Framers who feared presidential domination of the other branches. The desire to prevent domination by any single person, group, or branch of the government was a paramount goal of the Founders and illuminates much about the Constitution's philosophy and structure. The next two sections consider more closely the Senate's role in the confirmation process in light of that goal and the constitutional structure to which it gave rise.

POLITICAL REVIEW OF SUPREME COURT NOMINEES IN A CONSTITUTIONAL DEMOCRACY

The American constitutional system is a constitutional democracy that combines democratic elements, whose core principle is majority rule, with constitutionalism, or limits on what the majority may do.[30] Perhaps the best-known constitutional or undemocratic elements are those we associate with the federal judiciary. The power of judicial review is the best-known example of an antidemocratic practice in the Constitution as it operates today. Not surprisingly, the democratic and antidemocratic elements in the system coexist uneasily. This uneasy coexistence led Ruth Bader Ginsburg, while serving as a federal appellate judge, to speak of "the tension between judicial supremacy [or judicial review] and democratic theory."[31]

Legalist commentators on the confirmation process sometimes write as though courts may counter the elected branches of government, but that it is improper or dangerous for the majoritarian elements of the system to check the guardians of the Constitution in the judicial branch. This view is mistaken. To maintain a constitutional democracy, the democratic elements—principally Congress and the president in the federal government—and the constitutional elements—in particular, the unelected federal judiciary—must exist in some sort of balance. The Founders did not advocate a "judgocracy" in which unelected judges run amok any more than they favored majoritarian tyranny. Nor would contemporary Americans want such a system. Checks and balances run in all directions, from the presidency and Congress to the courts and vice versa. Hence Robert Bork was wrong to declare that "it is not our constitutional form of government" for the Senate to "influence Supreme Court decisions in a variety of areas."[32] In a constitutional *democracy*, democratic and undemocratic elements interact in a "constitutional dialogue"[33] over the Constitution's meaning.

Equally mistaken is the related view that although senators might have some appropriate substantive input into the selection of justices, the people they represent do not. Justice Antonin Scalia has expressed a view along these lines: "[W]e are . . . having a plebiscite on the meaning of the Constitution every time a justice is nominated, and that's crazy."[34] Perhaps the clearest expression of this view is Judge Alex Kozinski's critique of the impact of public opinion on senators' voting on nominees Robert Bork and Clarence Thomas:

> We don't live in a direct democracy, we live in a representative one. It is based . . . on the principle that . . . there are things in government that should not be decided by the rabble, because it does not always operate rationally.
>
> What we saw with Bob Bork was an intrusion of direct democracy into a representative process. It was very troubling. . . .
>
> The Constitution is an anti-democratic instrument. It is a check on absolute and direct democracy. We have built this structure in order to avoid the adverse effect of direct democracy.[35]

The problem with this view is that it seeks representative democracy without the representation. This position is especially hard to defend since the enactment of the Seventeenth Amendment, which gave the power to elect senators to the people, whom senators are intended to represent. It is not for elected elites (who are not normally elected on the basis of whom they will place on the Supreme Court)[36] and Supreme Court justices alone to determine what the Constitution means. Stephen Carter eloquently stated the value of democratic participation in the constitutional dialogue when he wrote that "[A] broadly held public view, consistent over time, might . . . carry important truths for a Court that acts ultimately in the people's name."[37]

The difficulty is to inject a democratic element into the appointment process for Supreme Court justices while preserving a large measure of independence for the Court. The significant number of countermajoritarian High Court rulings in recent times demonstrates that the modern confirmation process is largely successful in preserving the Court's freedom of action. Among other countermajoritarian decisions, the Supreme Court has ruled since 1990 that: burning an American flag is protected speech[38]; state-enacted term limits for Congress members are unconstitutional[39]; Congress may not criminalize possession of a gun near a school[40]; the ban on public school prayers extends to graduations and sporting events[41]; Congress may not outlaw putting "indecent" materials on the Internet, where children might find them[42]; and Congress may not ban the production or possession of "virtual" child pornography that uses young-looking adults or computer images rather than actual children in its production.[43]

Martin Redish has cited the great independence of the Supreme Court to justify a democratic check at the appointment stage: "[I]t is for the very reason that the judiciary is so independent after appointment" that ideological review of nominees is "necessary as the only political majoritarian check" on the Supreme Court.[44] Redish was correct to note the shortage of checks on the justices. But one can make an even stronger argument for careful ideological review of nominees by noting that although other majoritarian checks are available, they strike most Americans today as so high-handed and threatening to judicial independence that they have been used only sparingly—if at all—in modern times.

The first such power is the impeachment and removal of justices. This method of checking the Supreme Court has been tried only once, in 1804, when the House impeached Justice Samuel Chase, an ardent Federalist, for abusing his powers as a trial court judge to punish members of the opposite party, the Jeffersonian Republicans.[45] Since Chase's acquittal in 1805, Congress has made no serious attempt to remove a justice for delivering objectionable opinions.[46]

A second means of democratically checking the Court is to change the number of justices by legislation. Congress has not exercised this power since 1869, when the number of justices was set at nine. So great is the modern reluctance to change the Court's size that even in the midst of a national emergency, the Great Depression, an overwhelmingly Democratic Congress rejected President Franklin Roosevelt's attempt to enlarge the Court and reverse the Court's decisions striking down key parts of the New Deal.[47]

A third method of democratically checking the Court is Congress's authority to withdraw certain types of cases from the Court's appellate jurisdiction.[48] In modern times, congressional attempts to curtail the jurisdiction of the federal courts have had a bifurcated history. On the one hand, Congress has repeatedly declined to use this court-stripping power to stymie the Supreme Court after it handed down unpopular rulings on several salient issues. In the 1950s, Congress rejected an attempt by conservatives to eliminate the Court's appellate jurisdiction over cases involving state action against suspected subversives. In 1968, the Senate rejected a provision that would have eliminated the authority of the federal courts to review state court decisions on the admissibility of confessions in criminal trials.[49] In the 1970s and 1980s, Congress rejected curbs on the Court's jurisdiction in cases involving abortion, busing, and school prayer.[50] Among the opponents of these efforts was the father of modern conservatism, Senator Barry Goldwater, who called these measures a "frontal assault on the independence of the courts" and "a dangerous blow to the foundations of a free society."[51]

On the other hand, in 1996 the Republican 104th Congress enacted legislation curtailing the federal courts' authority to hear successive habeas corpus appeals of state prison inmates. That Congress inserted a number of less visible court-stripping provisions into assorted bills signed by President Bill Clinton, including measures to block some class-action suits brought by poor people and immigrants (both legal and illegal), and to prevent federal court review of rulings unfavorable to such groups.[52]

Senator Goldwater identified the principal danger of court stripping as a democratic check on the courts: it is a "frontal assault on the independence of the courts [and] a dangerous blow to the foundations of a free society."[53] The victims of these assaults, when they are successful, will be precisely those who are disdained by societal majorities and unable to defend themselves in a majoritarian political system. David Cole has identified this threat in explaining why decisions on abortion, busing, and school prayer have survived the assaults while judicial protection of other interests has not: "In the 1980s, the targets [of court-stripping efforts] were controversial court decisions in areas where a lot of powerful people were arrayed on both sides. . . . [In the 1990s] the targets were immigrants, prisoners, and the poor—people who don't vote or can't vote."[54]

A second problem with curtailing the jurisdiction of the Supreme Court is that it would make the lower federal courts or the state supreme courts the final arbiter of federal constitutional questions. One possible consequence of this radical devolution of power is that the Constitution will end up meaning one thing in one jurisdiction and another thing in another jurisdiction, with no mechanism for reconciling the conflicting interpretations. A final hazard of court-stripping measures is that the courts—and ultimately the Supreme Court—may judge the constitutionality of such measures. If neither side backs down, thereby risking a damaging loss of credibility, there may be no way out of a debilitating constitutional crisis.

Curtailing the federal courts' jurisdiction need not always, on balance, be harmful. One can make a plausible argument that in some cases it may promote the efficient administration of justice or even enhance judicial authority. For instance, by restricting federal court jurisdiction over multiple petitions for habeas corpus from death-row and other inmates who have exhausted their regular course of appeals, Congress limited the ability of some inmates to file repetitious petitions that could indefinitely delay the implementation of a sentence. Nonetheless, in the late nineteenth and early twentieth centuries, as the prestige of the Supreme Court and an understanding of the need for judicial independence grew, court stripping, along with impeaching justices and changing the number of justices, generally fell into low regard.[55]

A fourth means of democratically checking the Supreme Court is the power to reverse the Court's decisions by constitutional amendment. One practical limitation on this method is that it is very difficult to amend the Constitution. In more than two hundred years, only four amendments overturned controversial Supreme Court rulings: the Eleventh Amendment (1798), which overturned *Chisolm v. Georgia,*[56] a 1793 decision permitting federal courts to hear suits against a state by citizens of another state; the Fourteenth Amendment (1868), which overturned the 1857 *Dred Scott*[57] holding that a black person could never be a U.S. citizen; the Sixteenth Amendment (1913), which overturned the holding in the 1895 *Income Tax Cases*[58] that a federal income tax was unconstitutional; and the Twenty-sixth Amendment, which effectively overturned the holding in *Oregon v. Mitchell* (1970)[59] that Congress could not set a voting age of eighteen in state elections.

Much more often, attempts to reverse Supreme Court decisions by constitutional amendment have failed. Many of the ten thousand amendments suggested since the 1790s[60] have been aimed at reversing the Court, but only these four have won adoption. Recent unsuccessful attempts to check the Court by amendment include efforts to overturn the rulings on flag burning, school prayer, busing, and abortion.

For several reasons, amending the Constitution is inferior to the ideological review of nominees as a means of democratically checking the Court. First, frequent reversals of the Court—if they were possible—would often target unpopular minorities unable to protect themselves from hostile majorities: "immigrants, prisoners, and the poor—people who don't vote or can't vote."[61] Second, widespread public and elite allegiance to the specialness of the Constitution and its ideals is one of the few ties that bind a nation of incredible diversity and continental scope. That allegiance would be undermined by frequent amendment of the Constitution. Frequent reversals of the Court by amendment would foster a public perception of the Constitution as an ordinary law to be changed like any other, rather than a fundamental compact embodying the nation's most exalted aspirations and principles of government.[62]

One might object here that the political selection of Supreme Court justices itself fosters the perception of the Constitution as a highly malleable political document whose contents are readily shaped by result-oriented presidents and senators and the justices they choose. Paradoxically, however, senatorial review of nominees' ideologies can help to legitimize the justices and their decisions. In democratic nations, all governmental decisions are, or purport to be, "vested with the authority of the society for which the decisions are made."[63] Every Supreme Court decision rests on such a claim of legitimacy—a claim that the justices have been duly empowered to make their decisions by the authority of the whole society.

American Supreme Court justices have a particularly acute need for legitimacy. They must and do issue high-profile decisions that thwart the will of the democratic majority. The justices have no police force of their own to enforce their decisions. They depend on the voluntary compliance of the majority with their antimajoritarian decisions. As former congressman, federal judge, and White House counsel Abner Mikva has written, "The Supreme Court's mandates are usually obeyed not because of soldiers in the street but because of public perceptions of the Court's legitimacy."[64] The justices' need for legitimacy is compounded by the fact that they are not elected. They are nominated by a single individual who may have won election despite losing the popular vote. And that individual, the president, is not usually elected on the basis of his likely judicial nominees.[65]

The democratic ethos of modern America heightens the justices' need for legitimacy. American political history is largely a story of the progressive democratization of the system. Since the early 1800s, the right to vote has been extended to several previously excluded groups. The Seventeenth Amendment provided for the direct election of senators. The Twenty-fourth Amendment outlawed poll taxes in federal elections. In the 1960s, landmark civil rights acts redeemed the promise of equal political rights for African Americans. In the 1970s, congressional reforms dispersed power and democratized Congress,[66] and the power to nominate presidential candidates was taken from party leaders and given to the rank and file, who choose their parties' candidates in primaries and caucuses. The advent of public opinion polling in the 1930s provided an additional means of public influence, one sufficiently powerful to prompt claims that excessive public influence over elected decision makers is actually a major problem for American governance.[67]

In this milieu, a confirmation process in which the people's representatives failed to examine nominees' legal ideologies would be unacceptable for the life-tenured justices who wield so much power over Americans' lives. This is especially true because the nominating power remains in the hands of one person who so often resists the Senate's "Advice" about nominations and is not normally elected on the basis of whom he will nominate for the Court. A justice confirmed by a nonideological process today would lack legitimacy, much like a major party candidate for president who was handed the nomination by a coterie of party leaders in the back rooms of the party convention.

Today's citizens—at least the politically active among them—want to see the nominee for themselves, to hear him or her speak, to know something about what sort of justice he or she will be. Joseph Califano Jr., former secretary of Health, Education, and Welfare under President Jimmy Carter, has vividly expressed this view:

> [S]crutiny of Supreme Court nominees during their testimony before the Senate Judiciary Committee and such scrutiny of the testimony of other witnesses . . . are essential in our society.
>
> Each of the nine members of the Supreme Court has far more power than any [member of Congress]. Each Supreme Court nominee should be subjected to widespread public scrutiny before confirmation. This is of the essence in a free society in which [the judiciary] exercises an enormous amount of power—indeed final power in some matters—with respect to the other two branches and to the people of the country.
>
> As Congress legislates in more detail, it puts more and more

issues into our federal judiciary. . . . [S]cience raises to the level of constitutional dispute a host of issues that involve life and death . . . it puts more and more issues before our federal judiciary. As a citizen, I want to know as much as possible about each of the nine people who are going to decide such issues for me and my country.[68]

A large majority of Americans believes that the Senate should consider the nominee's "beliefs about the Constitution, and his past decisions as a judge" and "how that nominee might vote on major issues the Supreme Court decides."[69] Only such a vetting can lend a new justice the necessary degree of legitimacy. As former Acting Solicitor General Walter Dellinger has pointed out, "In a country otherwise committed to majoritarianism, judicial review is acceptable precisely because of the political nature" of the confirmation process.[70]

Seen in this way, the "political nature" of the process is more than just a necessary majoritarian check on a very powerful and independent Supreme Court. It is a majoritarian check that simultaneously legitimizes the Supreme Court's power to check that same majority. It is the method of democratically checking the Court that most protects the Court's authority and helps to preserve *constitutional* democracy, unlike the impeachment of justices, manipulation of the Court's size, and curtailment of the Court's jurisdiction, all of which subvert the Court's authority, and the frequent reversal of the Court by constitutional amendment, with its similar dangers.

One may ask, however, whether such a political exercise is a double-edged sword that enhances and yet detracts from the Court's legitimacy. Does the process depict the justices as political decision makers like any others, basing their rulings on disguised rationalizations of their policy preferences? And if so, does that not erode the considerable authority the justices derive from their image in the public mind as a Court of "laws and not of men"?[71] As Mikva has explained the problem: "When the Court is perceived to be apolitical, wise, and impartial, the people have evinced a willingness to abide by its decisions. But if the Court is viewed simply as a Congress in black robes, the Court's ability to perform its constitutional function is threatened."[72]

One reason the political confirmation process does not produce this result is that presidents know that a highly ideological, result-oriented nominee may face a stiff fight in the Senate. They will often therefore nominate someone known for political moderation and judicial restraint, such as a John Paul Stevens, a Ruth Bader Ginsburg, or a Stephen Breyer.[73] Both the politically attentive and the wider public will be unlikely to view such a nominee as, in Mikva's terms, a "Congressman in a black robe," because no one will accuse the nominee of being one. But this result obtains largely, if not wholly, because of the prospect that the Senate will evaluate the nominee on ideological grounds. If it were not for this prospect, presidents would be free to nominate highly ideological, result-oriented figures of the very sort who would undermine the Court's legitimacy.

An additional, closely related reason why the ideological evaluation of nominees does not undermine the Court's legitimacy is that if senators who dislike a nominee's apparent views can persuade enough others that the nominee is an ideological activist who will write his or her undesirable personal beliefs into the Constitution, the nominee will be rejected. That is what happened to Robert Bork. After Bork's rejection and the withdrawal of Douglas Ginsburg's nomination, President Reagan chose a compromise nominee, Anthony Kennedy, whom the press correctly portrayed at the time of his nomination as a relatively moderate, nonideological figure.[74]

Nor is Kennedy the only such figure to reach the Court in recent decades. In one of the landmark rulings of the 1990s, the Court's five to four decision to uphold the "essence" of *Roe v. Wade* in *Planned Parenthood v. Casey* (1992), Justice Kennedy and two other moderate nominees-turned-justices, Sandra Day O'Connor and David Souter, seemed almost to go out of their way to protect the Court's integrity as a legal decision maker. In their joint opinion, these three justices based their reaffirmation of *Roe* largely on arguments that the case for overturning *Roe* was not strong enough to overcome the rule of stare decisis, and that the Court must demonstrate that it can uphold an important precedent after political forces hostile to that precedent have won a number of elections and set out to overturn it. The Court and its constitutional interpretations must be resistant to such attempts; otherwise, the Court lacks institutional integrity and the law becomes an object of easy political manipulation.[75] It is, by contrast, virtually certain that the Court would have overturned *Roe* had the Senate not rejected the Bork nomination. Thus did the ideological scrutiny—and rejection—of Robert Bork help protect the Court's stature as a politically impartial body.

Thus far, we have seen how the theory of constitutional democracy and the ideological review of prospective Supreme Court justices reinforce one another. Such review provides a necessary balance between the democratic and antidemocratic elements of a constitutional democracy. It is much preferable to the other balancing tools available to the democratic branches, and consistent with a high degree of judicial independence. It also enhances the legitimacy of the Court and its power of judicial review. The following section explains why the specific institutional structure the Founders designed to effect the purposes of constitutional democracy—a system of separate branches sharing powers—requires that the Senate consider the ideology of nominees.

IDEOLOGICAL REVIEW OF NOMINEES IN A SYSTEM OF SEPARATE BRANCHES SHARING POWERS

The Constitution is commonly described as a "separation of powers" system. This characterization is unfortunate, for as Richard Neustadt and others have pointed out, the system is more accurately described as one of "separated institutions sharing powers."[76] Senatorial review of the legal ideologies of Supreme Court nominees is the only manner of appointment that is consistent with this structure of separate, independent, and coequal branches sharing powers. Such review is necessary to approximate the joint appointment of Supreme Court justices called for by the constitutional language and structure. The Founders' experience with kings and what they viewed as tyrannical state legislatures under the Articles of Confederation had taught them the necessity of a system in which power is shared by separate persons in separate institutions who must normally agree on a course of action before government can act.

A clear example of separate branches sharing powers is the appointment power: "[The president] shall nominate, and by and with the Advice and Consent of the Senate, shall appoint . . . Judges of the supreme Court."[77] This language, although sparse, suggests that the Senate not only has the full power to reject nominees, but suggests also that the president shall seek the Senate's "Advice" when selecting nominees. Certainly, nothing in the constitutional language suggests that the Senate should play a deferential role in the appointment process.

More particularly, nothing in the constitutional structure suggests that presidents may choose nominees on the basis of ideological considerations— as they surely do[78]—while the Senate may not evaluate them on this basis. Indeed, if presidents could nominate ideologically while the Senate limits itself to reviewing nominees' integrity, professional credentials, and judicial temperament, the president could pack the Court with ideological soul mates and influence the future direction of constitutional law subject only to the limits imposed by the number of nominations he is fortunate to make and his ability to discern a prospective nominee's beliefs. (We will see in later chapters that this ability is good but not perfect.) Such presidential dominance of the appointment process and one-sided influence over the Supreme Court, a separate and independent branch of government, is not consistent with a system of separate, independent, and coequal branches sharing powers. As Charles Black has written:

> The judges are *not* the President's people. . . . They are to be as independent of him as they are of the Senate, neither more nor less. . . .
>
> [A nominee] is named by the President . . . because the President believes his worldview will be good for the country. . . . The Constitution certainly permits, if it does not compel, the taking of a separate opinion on this crucial question, from a body just as responsible to the electorate as is the President.[79]

The sharing of the power to appoint Supreme Court justices, complete with a senatorial prerogative to evaluate nominees on ideological grounds— just as presidents select them—therefore serves to prevent either president or Senate from dominating the Court. Insofar as the president and Senate vie for influence over the Court, Madison's dictum in *Federalist* 51 that "Ambition must be made to counteract ambition"[80] is fulfilled.

Several commentators have offered objections to this argument. They see the appointment of justices as a zero-sum or winner-take-all game with three possible outcomes. First, if the Senate rejects the president's initial nominee, the president may nominate someone just as objectionable to the Senate, after which the Senate may capitulate and confirm a nominee no more to its liking than the first one. Richard D. Friedman cites the appointment of Justice Harry Blackmun as an example: "To the extent that the Senate opposed Judges Haynsworth and Carswell on ideological grounds, it abandoned its objective by accepting Judge Blackmun, who was also perceived to be very conservative."[81] Others have cited Justice Anthony Kennedy as evidence that it did Senate Democrats little good to oppose the nomination of Robert Bork.[82]

The second possible outcome is that the president backs down and nominates someone more to the Senate's liking, in which case the "nominee is effectively chosen in large measure by the Senate,"[83] which is contrary to the Constitution. The third alternative is deadlock, which is good neither for the Court nor for the nation.[84]

There are three difficulties in these arguments. First, it is not contrary to the Constitution for the Senate to have substantial input into the president's choice of a nominee. Although the president makes the nomination, the Constitution suggests that the president make that nomination with the Senate's "Advice."

Second, a majority of the Senate did not "abandon" its ideological goals when it accepted Blackmun after rejecting Haynsworth and Carswell. Haynsworth was not rejected solely because of his conservative ideology. Although there was much ideological opposition to him, a majority of the Senate was willing to accept Haynsworth's conservatism. His alleged ethical improprieties, not his ideology, tipped the balance against him. Among the fifty-five senators who voted "no" on Haynsworth were *seventeen* Republicans, including Senate Republican leader Hugh Scott and Republican whip Robert Griffin, the latter of whom helped lead the opposition to Haynsworth.[85] Because Haynsworth had been nominated to replace Justice Abe Fortas, who had been forced from the Court by charges of financial improprieties, Haynsworth's ethical problems made it difficult for these two senators to vote for confirmation, as they and a dozen other senators publicly acknowledged.[86] After a careful statistical analysis of Senate voting on Haynsworth's and three other contentious nominations, George Watson and John Stookey conclude that "This [analysis] conforms with our earlier description of how Robert Griffin and certain other Republicans felt compelled to oppose Haynsworth after having publicly proclaimed their opposition to Fortas on ethical grounds just the previous year. Their votes, then, were not based on ideological or partisan criteria but either on conviction regarding [Haynsworth's alleged] conflict of interest or out of a felt need to remain consistent in their public response to such charges."[87]

Although Republican liberals such as Senators Jacob Javits and Clifford Case might well have voted "no" for ideological reasons, it is virtually certain that at least five or six of Haynsworth's seventeen Republican opponents would have voted to confirm him in the absence of his ethical difficulties, thereby providing sufficient votes for confirmation. As Henry Abraham has written, Haynsworth's conservatism "did play a considerable role" in his rejection, but "the margin of defeat lay elsewhere: in . . . the question of judicial ethics."[88] Friedman therefore overstates the Senate's ideological retreat when it rejected Haynsworth and accepted Blackmun. Because a majority of the Senate was willing to accept Haynsworth's ideology, one cannot conclude that a majority of senators "abandoned" their ideological criteria when they rejected his nomination and accepted Blackmun. Similarly, the Haynsworth-Carswell-Blackmun episode does not support the claim that the Senate will capitulate and approve a second or later nominee it finds as objectionable as the first. Carswell was just as objectionable to the Senate as Haynsworth, and the Senate rejected his nomination.[89]

The third flaw in these arguments is that they understate the possibility of compromise between president and Senate. One example of such a compromise nominee is Blackmun, whom Friedman cites as an example of the futility of ideological opposition to nominations. To Senate liberals, Blackmun was ideologically preferable to either Haynsworth or Carswell. Blackmun's widely acclaimed nomination did not face the opposition from labor and civil rights groups that Haynsworth's did. Nor was there any evidence that Blackmun was a racist, as there was with Carswell.[90] Not a single witness appeared before the Senate Judiciary Committee to oppose Blackmun's nomination. The ideological opposition to Haynsworth and Carswell paid off for Senate liberals when Blackmun went on to become the author of *Roe v. Wade* and, in the words of Henry Abraham, "an almost, albeit not quite, wholly faithful ally of the Court's Brennan-Marshall liberal wing"[91] rather than the "strict constructionist" Nixon had sought to place on the Court.

The appointment of Anthony Kennedy was also a compromise rather than a capitulation by the Senate. After Justice Lewis Powell retired in 1987, President Reagan nominated Robert Bork, a brilliant, ardently conservative figure and passionate proponent of the theory that judges should interpret the Constitution as closely as possible to the original intent of the Founding generation.[92] After the Senate rejected Bork on ideological grounds, a frustrated Reagan vowed to nominate someone that "they'll object to just as much"[93] as Bork. The president tried to make good on his promise by nominating Douglas Ginsburg, a forty-one-year-old federal appeals court judge whose views on issues other than economic regulation, although imprecisely known, were enough to convince Reagan of his conservative credentials and to alarm Senate Democrats.[94]

After Ginsburg's nomination was withdrawn after allegations of relatively recent marijuana use, the president responded more pragmatically by nominating Kennedy, who disavowed Bork's "originalist" philosophy of constitutional interpretation at his confirmation hearings and seemed much more open than Bork to the possibility that Americans have rights not listed in the Constitution.[95] Contrary to claims made after his confirmation,[96] Kennedy has proved to be a much more moderate justice than Bork would have been. Laurence Tribe has said of Kennedy that "He's stuck to his guns, whether they point right or left," and remarked on "how drastically different the constitutional history of the country has been" with Kennedy rather than Bork on the Court, an assessment shared by rueful conservatives.[97]

Kennedy's conservative critics and Tribe can both point to several major decisions on hot-button issues, all decided by a five-to-four margin, in which Kennedy cast a crucial vote for a "liberal" outcome: the flag-burning cases; the 1992 decision upholding the "essence" of *Roe v. Wade*; the decision the

same year extending the ban on public school prayers to graduation ceremonies; the decision striking down state-enacted congressional term limits; a
ruling that Congress may not require cable television systems that do not
scramble their signals to limit sexually explicit programming to late nights,
when children are unlikely to see the programs; and the ruling overturning
Bowers v. Hardwick and decriminalizing homosexual sodomy.[98] Bork has
disparaged all of these rulings except those on term limits (which he has not
discussed) and cable television programming (which he has criticized by
implication).[99] Justice David Souter, who was nominated by President George
Bush largely in order to avoid a Senate confirmation fight,[100] has proved to
be a substantially more liberal figure than Kennedy.[101]

In light of Blackmun, Kennedy, and Souter's performances on the Court,
it is hard to argue that ideological opposition to nominees is futile. Yet
although it is clear that Democratic senators did accomplish something by
resisting conservative nominees, Blackmun, Kennedy, and Souter were still
more conservative or seemingly conservative figures than liberal senators
would have nominated. Thus the Senate did not expropriate the president's
power of nomination in these cases. Likewise, nominees Ruth Bader Ginsburg
in 1993 and Stephen Breyer in 1994 are universally regarded as nominees
whose political qualities were something less—or other—than what President
Clinton had truly hoped for.[102]

NOMINEE TESTIMONY AND THE IMPARTIALITY OF JUSTICE

The final argument against the ideological examination of nominees is that
it compromises the impartiality required of judges by forcing nominees to
reveal in advance to senators, whether explicitly or implicitly, how they will
vote in future cases that come before the Court. Legalist critics of the ideological review of nominees have argued that nominees can tell senators little of their views on contentious legal issues at Senate confirmation hearings
because it would be improper for nominees to state, or even hint at, how
they will decide future Supreme Court cases. Limits on nominees' testimony are said to be necessary for three closely related reasons: (1) to avoid pre-
judging issues and preserve the independence and impartiality required of
judges; (2) to avoid even the appearance of partiality or prejudgment; (3) to
avoid any loss of public confidence in the impartial administration of justice.

Sandra Day O'Connor, one of the least forthcoming of modern nominees, made the classic statement of the first of these concerns when she told

senators that "I do not believe that, as a nominee, I can tell you how I might vote on a particular issue which may come before the Court. . . . To do so would mean that I have prejudged the matter or morally committed myself to a certain position."[103] Antonin Scalia, another conspicuously tight-lipped nominee, likewise expressed the view that commenting on any live controversy risks "prejudicing future litigants."[104] Commentator Max Lerner put it more bluntly when he wrote that senators who ask nominees about their views are trying "to extort commitments on a nominee's doctrinal positions and legal philosophy, which are . . . in a zone of integrity and independence that no nominee should be asked to barter away."[105]

Scalia voiced his concern over the appearance of partiality this way: "[N]obody arguing [a] case before me should think that he is arguing to somebody who has [already] made up his mind either way."[106] Nominees often claim that perceptions of partiality would not only damage public confidence in the impartial administration of justice; they would require justices to recuse themselves from a large number of future cases. As O'Connor put it, "[A] statement by me as to how I might resolve a particular issue or what I might do in a future Court action might make it necessary for me to disqualify myself on the matter."[107] Other nominees have echoed this position.[108] These frequently expressed concerns about judicial impartiality, which we shall refer to collectively as the impartiality argument, have been voiced by every nominee in recent decades. Not surprisingly, Robert Bork—the most candid of modern nominees—has been particularly critical of senators' attempts to force him to make "campaign promises"[109] to decide future cases a certain way as a condition of his confirmation.

The impartiality argument is not without merit. An assurance that a nominee will decide a future case a certain way implies that the nominee has prejudged the matter and that he or she will give short shrift to litigants' briefs, oral arguments, discussion with fellow justices, the particular facts of the case, any doubts the nominee may have now or later, and any other factors that may intervene before the decision is announced. It is also doubtful, as some authors have claimed, that nominees need only refrain from commenting on actual, concrete disputes that have been or soon will be litigated,[110] or that "short of an absolute promise to reach a preordained result, a judicial nominee's discussion of legal issues does not and probably cannot presage" a future opinion.[111]

This position overstates the distinction between cases and issues. Cases do raise issues (that is, after all, why we care so much about Supreme Court appointments), and an opinion on an issue may very well "presage" a future opinion on a case. In 1987, for instance, there was good reason to believe that the Court would someday decide whether to overrule *Roe v. Wade*. Robert Bork's insistence that year that he could find no right to privacy in the Constitution after twenty years of searching was a pointed indicator of how he would rule on abortion, antisodomy laws, the right to die, and probably other privacy-related issues.

As one critic of the impartiality argument has conceded, there are also "borderline" answers that do not involve "an absolute promise to reach a pre-ordained result," but come close enough to pose dangers "almost as grave as those of explicit commitments to the fairness, actual and perceived, of the judicial process."[112] Among such expressions one might number the assurances Ruth Bader Ginsburg and Stephen Breyer gave to Judiciary Committee Democrats that the Constitution includes a right to abortion.[113]

Despite these qualifications,[114] the argument that ideological review of nominees fatally compromises their judicial objectivity falls short for two reasons. First, there are many legitimate questions and answers about judicial philosophy and method that come nowhere near a promise to rule a certain way in future cases. Various nominees have properly given meaningful and diverse answers to senators' questions about the importance of following the Founders' intentions when interpreting the Constitution,[115] the proper methodology for defining the "liberty" protected by the Fifth and Fourteenth Amendments,[116] the use of legislative history in statutory interpretation,[117] the meaning of the Ninth Amendment,[118] the workability of the Court's multitiered approach to equal protection cases,[119] the view that the Constitution's meaning evolves with time,[120] and whether courts must sometimes address social problems neglected by other branches of government (and they do not, even in response to questions from conservative senators, take the easy "out" of downplaying any such role for the courts).[121]

The second difficulty with the impartiality argument is that nominees are simply not required to voice their opinions on contentious issues in order to win confirmation. Although all nominees have answered questions on judicial philosophy and method, nominees have seldom revealed much about their future votes on specific issues that was not already known, or widely believed, before their Senate testimony. Consider, for example, the three most candid testimonies of recent times: the statements of Justices Ginsburg and Breyer on abortion, and the testimony of Robert Bork. There had never been any real doubt about Ginsburg and Breyer's support for a basic right to abortion.[122] Likewise, Bork in his confirmation hearings criticized the reasoning underlying *Roe v. Wade* and the right to privacy on which it rests, as well as "liberal" precedents on free speech and equal protection issues.[123] But his criticisms of these rulings were quite well known long before his nomination to the Supreme Court. Indeed, these views explain why President Reagan nominated him, and why senators focused their questions on these matters. Bork did backpedal from some previously stated views on gender discrimination and free speech, but a majority of the Judiciary Committee discounted these pronouncements,[124] and it was clear from his testimony— as Bork acknowledged—that he held steadfastly to his well-known philosophy of statutory and constitutional interpretation.[125]

Other than Bork, and Ginsburg and Breyer on abortion, nominees have typically held to the line that it would be improper to signal their future votes. They have been conspicuously reticent in response to questions designed to reveal how they might vote on specific issues. Justices O'Connor and Scalia used the impartiality concerns quoted above to avoid questions on abortion,[126] affirmative action,[127] the exclusionary rule,[128] and the power of Congress to curtail the jurisdiction of the federal courts.[129] Justice Ginsburg defended a woman's basic right to abortion, but would not say just how much a state may regulate the exercise of that right, and steadfastly refused to reveal her views on the death penalty or equal rights for gays.[130] Justice Breyer likewise refused to answer questions about the precise scope of abortion rights, the constitutionality of the assault weapons ban, the extent of property rights, and certain questions on the death penalty.[131] Justice Souter similarly deflected several questions on abortion.[132] Justice Kennedy parried senators' questions about abortion, the death penalty, and whether Congress members may sue the executive branch for nonenforcement of a law.[133] Justice Thomas cited impartiality concerns to avoid questions on abortion and recent precedents curtailing the use of habeas corpus petitions by prison inmates.[134] Every nominee—even Bork to a limited extent—has cited the impartiality argument to block questions on some specific issues.[135] All of these nominees except Bork were confirmed (and all but Thomas were confirmed easily). Nominees clearly have no need to overcommit themselves to future outcomes in order to win confirmation.

On the whole, nominees have been so circumspect in their testimony that their circumspection has prompted a long-running chorus of complaints from senators[136] and scholars frustrated by unresponsive nominee testimony, and has produced a raft of proposed reforms to elicit more revealing testimony from nominees. The impartiality argument has proved impervious to all of these suggestions, a reality that is unlikely to change. Grover Rees, for instance, has suggested that senators phrase questions so as to make it clear that they are not seeking a nominee's commitment to vote a certain way in exchange for a favorable confirmation vote.[137] But this tactic has proved unhelpful.[138] And this suggestion overlooks the reality that the desire to win confirmation may be just as important to the nominee as avoiding any appearance of impropriety, and that the nominee will not likely be calmed by such a reassurance. If senators' votes were not contingent to some extent on nominees' answers to questions, senators would likely ask fewer of them.

Albert Melone recommends that senators question nominees who are judges more closely about their written opinions.[139] This approach has shown limited results. Two of the modern justices (O'Connor and Souter) were state court judges[140] whose written opinions involved state law or straightforward applications of federal constitutional precedents, and provided little fertile ground for questioning. Two other nominees, Clarence Thomas and the ill-fated Douglas Ginsburg, had served as federal judges for only sixteen and eleven months, respectively, and had ruled on few controversial issues. Even the record of a highly experienced federal appeals court judge may reveal surprisingly little. In eleven years on the Ninth Circuit Court of Appeals, Anthony Kennedy had authored or joined almost one thousand written opinions.[141] Yet his record revealed little about his views on specific issues.

Stephen Carter has suggested that senators abandon their concern with nominees' judicial philosophies, which he sees senators as incapable of uncovering in any case. He urges them "to get a sense of the whole person, an impression partaking not only of the nominee's public legal arguments, but of her entire moral universe."[142] He holds that "the Senate, which enjoys the political space to reflect on the fundamental values of the nation," because of senators' long, six-year terms, should ask whether the nominee is "a person for whom moral choices occasion deep and sustained reflection . . . an individual . . . possessing the right moral instincts."[143]

This approach faces three major obstacles.[144] First, Carter understates the impact of electoral pressures on senators. After the Senate voted to confirm Clarence Thomas, for instance, press accounts emphasized that political pressures had influenced many senators:

> For many of the members of the . . . Senate, today's vote was heavily influenced by politics. A number of Southern Democrats, for example, including several who are up for reelection next year after narrow victories in 1986, noted privately that black voters in their states backed Judge Thomas. . . .
>
> Many of the Southern Democrats saw their approval ratings plummet when they opposed President [George H. W.] Bush's mili-

tary intervention in the Persian Gulf and felt that they could not afford to take another major stand that was unpopular.[145]

Quantitative analysis confirms that the size of senators' African American constituencies and the proximity of the next election had a positive impact on senatorial support for Thomas.[146] Accounts of the Senate vote on Robert Bork likewise emphasize the powerful impact on southern Democrats of surprising polling data showing that white Southerners were actually less likely to support Bork's confirmation when told of Bork's conservative views on privacy and civil rights.[147]

The second problem with Carter's morality-focused approach is that it runs squarely into the impartiality argument. As Carter recognizes, "The rhetoric of judging requires that judges should put aside their personal beliefs when called upon to decide what the law requires."[148] Justice Souter, to cite one example, used this principle to frustrate Senator Edward Kennedy's repeated attempts to get Souter to state his personal views on the morality of abortion.[149]

The third problem with Carter's approach is that senators are not highly qualified or motivated to judge a nominee's personal moral code. The bitter battle over the fitness for a justiceship of Clarence Thomas, a nominee accused of sexual harassment, demonstrates one or more of three things: how difficult it is to get a nominee's "moral record" straight, how uninterested many senators are in this issue, or how little they can agree on moral standards (a lesson reinforced by the Senate's handling of President Clinton's impeachment trial).

William Ross has recommended that senators ask nominees about the reasoning justices have used in past cases.[150] But such questions have been easily circumvented by nominees taking the position, as Justice O'Connor put it, that a nominee cannot "endorse or criticize specific Supreme Court decisions presenting issues which may well come before the Court again."[151] No nominee who has clung to this position has ever been forcibly dislodged.

These suggestions have failed, in part, because they do not take account of contextual factors—some present in all confirmation settings, some varying from case to case—that inhibit senatorial insistence on highly revealing nominee testimony. One such factor is the great authority of the impartiality argument. An indication of its power is Senator Joseph Biden's elaborate assurance to nominee David Souter that

[W]hile we may ask any questions that we deem proper, you are free to refuse to answer any questions you deem to be improper. No one is going to try to force you to answer any question you think in good conscience you cannot appropriately address. So, Judge Souter, I trust you are fully capable of deciding for yourself which questions you can and cannot speak to. And we or an individual Senator may not agree with your decision, but that decision is yours and will be protected.[152]

A second factor limiting ideological scrutiny is that most senators of the president's party, who will normally comprise a majority or large minority of the Senate, will rely either on their own or the president's judgment that a nominee is ideologically congenial to them. A friendly senator on the Judiciary Committee may not only refrain from quizzing the nominee, but may actively protect the nominee from probing questions, as Senator Strom Thurmond did repeatedly for Robert Bork.[153]

A third factor may be termed the "exhaustion factor." Senators have only a limited willingness to engage one another and the president in political bloodletting over Supreme Court nominations. If the political bloodshed over the previous nomination was particularly heavy, the current nominee is likely to face less intensive review. Nominees Anthony Kennedy (who followed the failed Bork and Douglas Ginsburg nominations) and Antonin Scalia (who followed the battle over William Rehnquist's elevation to chief justice) benefited from this factor. According to one account of the Scalia hearings, "By the time Judge Scalia came before the [Judiciary] Committee, senators seemed worn out and distracted . . . the questioning was perfunctory and the answers were uninformative."[154]

A fourth factor, the perceived effect of a nomination on the ideological balance of the Court, also aided Scalia's nomination. Scalia was nominated to fill the space created by Chief Justice Warren Burger's retirement. Many Democrats viewed Scalia's arrival as merely replacing one conservative with another; hence, his nomination did not induce Democrats to dissect his views. Robert Bork, by contrast, was nominated to replace Justice Lewis Powell, long considered the crucial swing vote on the Burger Court. The belief that Bork would radically alter the Court's ideological balance (in addition to his controversial views) contributed to the painstaking scrutiny he received from Senate Democrats. As one lobbyist quipped at the time, "It's just the most important Supreme Court nomination in fifty years. Lighten up."[155]

A fifth factor that may inhibit Senate questioners is the delicate politics of gender and race. This factor hovered over the testimony of Clarence Thomas: "Several of Judge Thomas's supporters . . . hinted that for the Senate to hold this nominee to a higher standard [of candor than other nominees] might give an appearance of racism."[156] After the debacle of the hearings into Thomas's alleged sexual harassment of Anita Hill, similar considerations also smoothed the Senate passage of the next nominee, Ruth Bader Ginsburg.[157]

Although "realists" may scoff, strong "objective" qualifications for a justiceship may also hinder examination of even very controversial views (but not always, as the example of Robert Bork shows). According to the *New York Times* account of the Scalia nomination, Scalia had

> criticized the Supreme Court's approval of affirmative action plans that include racial preferences, embraced an expansive view of presidential power, questioned the constitutional basis for the independence from the president of the Federal Reserve Board, criticized the Freedom of Information Act and hinted at disagreement with the Court's First Amendment rulings limiting libel suits.
>
> He had also questioned the basis for the Supreme Court's recognition of a constitutional right to sexual privacy, including abortion rights, and has joined a ruling that the Constitution does not protect private homosexual acts between consenting adults.[158]

Despite these well-known views, "lawmakers from both parties said that Judge Scalia's reputation for intellectual brilliance would mute criticism from senators who disagree with his conservative rulings" as a federal Appeals Court judge.[159] Scalia, who had taught law at Stanford, Georgetown, and the Universities of Chicago and Virginia before his four-year federal judgeship, was an unquestionably able figure.

A final factor that may deter senators from insisting on complete disclosure of a nominee's views is the perception by senators not of the president's party that a nominee, although not entirely to their liking, is the best they will likely get from the president. This factor aided the confirmation of Sandra Day O'Connor after Representative Morris Udall, a liberal Democrat from O'Connor's own state of Arizona, told fellow Democrats that "With Ronald Reagan as President . . . the fact that you can get someone as moderate, and as close to the center of the Republican party as she is, is really stunning. It erases the stereotype opposition to Reagan."[160] Senator Orrin Hatch, a conservative Republican, likewise expressed the view of "many Republicans" that nominee Ruth Bader Ginsburg was less "activist" than other Clinton nominees might be, and that Ginsburg was "about as good as you're going to get"[161] from Clinton.

The willingness of Senate Democrats to accept O'Connor, and Republicans to accept Ginsburg, implies a fundamental truth about Senate examination of nominees' ideologies: senators normally can and do learn a great deal from the totality of a nominee's record, including prenomination speeches, judicial opinions, law review articles, and other statements of record. As one critic of the unilluminating testimony of Ruth Bader Ginsburg and Stephen Breyer has conceded, it really was not necessary for senators to insist on more illuminating testimony because the general outlook of these nominees was already so well known.[162] Chapter 6 demonstrates, in response to the claim that senators do not learn enough about nominees' ideologies, that senators can glean enough from a nominee's prenomination record—and nominee testimony about judicial philosophy and method—to predict with a high degree of confidence the nominee's general approach to legal adjudication and approximate future position on the conventional liberal-conservative spectrum (but only less often a nominee's future votes on specific issues). Knowledge of these more general attributes may be more important for projecting a nominee's future position on the Court than the nominee's view on a particular issue because the issues that will come before the Court in the future are multifarious, certain to change, and hard to predict.

In sum, practice has struck a balance that has been acceptable to most actors in the confirmation process most of the time, between too much and too little information about nominee ideologies. Were this not so, there would be a high risk of stalemate, and no nominee might ever win confirmation, either because nominees reveal too much (thereby alienating opposition senators) or too little (thereby alienating frustrated Senate questioners). Because the Supreme Court needs justices and several factors inhibit microscopic examination of nominees' views, ideological scrutiny of nominees will not likely be, nor has it been, excessive. The Senate learns a great deal about most nominees, mostly from their prenomination records, but improperly revealing nominee testimony has seldom occurred.

CONCLUSION

Nothing in the language of the appointments clause requires a passive or non-ideological role for the Senate. Moreover, the battle over that clause at the Federal Convention was highly political in every sense. Although the Founders did not directly address the question of how senators should evaluate Supreme Court nominees, there is no reason to suppose, and good reason to doubt, that they envisioned a confirmation process devoid of ideological considerations.

Nor is there anything in Hamilton's writings in *The Federalist* to indicate that senators should overlook nominees' legal ideologies. Indeed, Hamilton's express concern that judges might be presidential sycophants implies that he would have applauded senators for examining nominees' ideologies (as Hamilton himself did in the battle over the Rutledge nomination).

Political scrutiny of Supreme Court nominees is also a salutary democratic check on the Court. Unlike other means of Court checking, it prevents either elected branch from dominating the Court, preserves a high degree of judicial independence, and legitimizes judicial review. It is implicit in the structure and philosophy of the government the Founders created: a constitutional democracy of separate branches sharing powers. And the modern confirmation process does not, contrary to widely heard concerns, force nominees to make improper promises of future rulings as a condition of their confirmations. The balance struck by practice has served the nation well.

Legalist critics of Senate scrutiny of nominees have charged nonetheless that public examination of nominees and their ideologies has contributed to the overpoliticization and degradation of the confirmation process. To this criticism we now turn.

3

The Politicization of the Confirmation Process

Legalist critics of the modern confirmation process have charged that heavy Senate scrutiny of nominees fosters the overpoliticization of the process by interest groups, the news media, and senators suspicious of nominees' beliefs. The first part of this chapter outlines the complaint that the process has been overpoliticized by interest groups and opposition senators. The next section explains why this complaint is overdrawn. The final part of the chapter analyzes the related claim of overpoliticization by the news media.

This chapter identifies several problems with the claim of overpoliticization. First, as this and later chapters will show, it reflects an unwarranted assumption that conflict over Supreme Court nominations is undesirable. Second, it reflects a related antipolitical perspective that inevitably produces a jaundiced view of the procedures of a constitutional democracy. Third, political gamesmanship has not displaced legitimate discussion of constitutional issues as the essential feature of confirmation debates. Fourth, despite claims to the contrary, senators give considerable weight to nominees' professional qualifications when evaluating nominees. Fifth, the charge, based largely on the Senate's handling of the Bork nomination, that senators and others misunderstand or deliberately distort nominees' views is, at best, exaggerated. The startling implications of Bork's beliefs—and the ardor with which he had propounded them—were well understood and, in the main, accurately represented by his opponents.

Additionally, some commentators have overstated the level of conflict in the confirmation process and misidentified the real source of conflicts when they have occurred. Most Supreme Court nominations since the late 1960s have been noncontroversial; confirmation strategy, tactics, and public appeals counted for little in these cases. In all of the conflictual cases, presidents nominated figures whose ideology the president knew to be unpalatable to a large minority or, in most cases, a majority of senators. All but one of the controversial nominees were also vulnerable to attack on the basis of their ethics. (Robert Bork was the lone exception.) The real source of conflict in the appointment process, when conflict has occurred, has lain in the nomination, not the confirmation, stage.

Finally, complaints about the news media overstate the media's impact on the behavior of participants in the process and on the Senate's decision to confirm or reject nominees. They overstate the media's ability to heighten conflict over nominations and overlook the benefits of heightened media coverage for nominees and the public.

THE OVERPOLITICIZED CONFIRMATION PROCESS

John Anthony Maltese has written that "The confirmation process is now a distinctly public affair, with all of its participants grappling with each other for public support."[1] This description of the process is echoed by others, who describe the active and visible roles played by the nominee, the president and his legislative liaisons, senators and their staffs, the American Bar Association Standing Committee on the Federal Judiciary, interest groups of all stripes, reporters and commentators, and the public itself (as represented by public opinion polls, which especially interest reelection-minded senators).[2] The confirmation process is undeniably more visible since confirmation hearings were first televised in 1981 (in the case of Sandra Day O'Connor).

In addition to the telecast of the hearings, the highly public nature of the contemporary confirmation process is perhaps best exemplified by the participation of a large number of the interest groups that have proliferated in Washington in recent decades. An estimated three hundred groups participated in the bitter struggles over the nominations of Robert Bork in 1987 and Clarence Thomas in 1991. Supporting these nominees were such groups as the Christian Coalition, the National Sheriffs Association, the Center for Judicial Studies, the Heritage Foundation, the Free Congress Research and Education Foundation (a conservative think tank with some forty staffers), the Washington Legal Foundation (which emphasizes economic freedoms of particular interest to the business community), and Coalitions for America (an umbrella organization for a diverse collection of conservative groups). On the opposing side, among others, were the NAACP, the National Abortion

Rights Action League, the National Organization for Women, Ralph Nader's group Public Citizen, the American Civil Liberties Union, the AFL-CIO, the Sierra Club, People for the American Way (a civil liberties group with sixty staffers and over 250,000 members), the Leadership Conference on Civil Rights (a coalition of some two hundred labor, civil rights, religious, and other organizations), and the Alliance for Justice (a smaller but potent liberal umbrella group).[3]

The tactics of these groups in confirmation battles are similar to those in any legislative struggle. They research and investigate nominees and share the results with allied groups. They lobby senators and their staffs and ply them and the mass media with information favorable to their cause. They conduct public opinion polls and focus groups to determine which issues will prove most effective in their campaigns to mobilize public opinion. They send faxes, mass mailings, satellite broadcasts, and electronic mail to their memberships and other segments of the public whom their research has identified as receptive to their message. On a most controversial nomination, such as those of Robert Bork and Clarence Thomas, they may run advertisements on television and radio. And those they mobilize may, on controversial nominations, deluge senators with a million or more letters, postcards, phone calls, and faxes. Presidents, of course, enter the fray with their own considerable resources, such as the White House Offices of Communications and Congressional Liaison. Presidents also use their unrivaled access to the media to lobby the public (a tactic, surprisingly, that was little used until President Reagan nominated Robert Bork in 1987).[4]

Some critics of the confirmation process have asserted that political tactics and public appeals have a great impact on the Senate's decision on the nomination. In his book *The Confirmation Mess*, Stephen Carter laments that "We have built a system in which strategy (especially public relations strategy) is far more important than issues or [the nominees'] qualifications."[5] In a white paper for the National Legal Center, Eugene W. Hickok Jr. concurs:

> [T]he character of the contemporary Senate—an institution more interested in pleasing public opinion than in 'refining and enlarging it'—suggests that it makes some sense to approach each confirmation battle with a campaign strategy. Putting together a strategy aimed at swaying public opinion can produce immediate returns within the Senate. The defeat of Robert Bork demonstrated this, and the narrow victory of Clarence Thomas provides additional evidence of it.
>
> What is missing from contemporary confirmation debate is serious deliberation.[6]

Even scholars who do not argue that the process is overpoliticized have affirmed the importance of political tactics in confirmation struggles. In a study of unsuccessful nominations from that of Abe Fortas (for chief justice in 1968) to that of Douglas Ginsburg just after Bork's rejection in 1987, John Massaro reports that a key part of the confirmation process is "the president's overseeing of the adoption and execution of tactics designed to carry out successfully the strategy for confirmation."[7] Maltese agrees that "the White House must . . . prevent opposition players from dominating its agenda and trashing its nominee."[8]

Of particular importance in descriptive accounts of nominations is the political advantage gained by the side that establishes the "nomination discourse," or the terms of debate for the ensuing struggle. An oft-cited example of seizing the debate in this way is Senator Edward Kennedy's speech on the Senate floor, just minutes after Bork's nomination was announced:

> Robert Bork's America is a land in which women would be forced into back alley abortions, blacks would sit at segregated lunch counters, rogue police could break down citizens' doors in midnight raids, school children could not be taught about evolution, writers and artists could be censored at the whim of the government, and the doors of the federal courts would be shut on the fingers of millions of citizens for whom the judiciary is—and is often the only—protector of the individual rights that are at the heart of our democracy.[9]

The Reagan White House and its conservative allies were unprepared for the speed and ferocity of this attack and the subsequent offensive by groups opposed to Bork, and they never regained their footing in the fight for his confirmation.[10]

Another example of successfully setting the nomination discourse is the carefully conceived public relations strategy of the Bush White House in promoting the nomination of Clarence Thomas. In this skillfully devised scenario, Thomas was a hero in a Horatio Alger tale: an African American born into poverty in tiny, rural Pinpoint, Georgia, in the heart of a segregated society, he had overcome this inauspicious beginning thanks to a strict religious upbringing, the selfless efforts of the nuns who had taught him at his Catholic school, and his own ability and determined efforts. Even senators who opposed Thomas's nomination echoed this line and praised the nominee for his accomplishments. Many actors inside and outside the Senate who almost certainly would have opposed the nomination were persuaded by this partially accurate biography to support it.[11]

Critics of the purportedly too public and politicized confirmation process are also disturbed by evidence that public opinion and the proximity of the next election combine with other political factors to influence senators' votes on nominations. Accounts of the Senate's rejection of Robert Bork credit public opinion polls for the crucial negative votes of moderate Southern Democrats.[12] In the case of nominee Clarence Thomas in 1991, Marvin Overby et al. found that senators with large African American constituencies were more likely to vote to confirm Thomas if they faced reelection in 1992. Such electoral pressure provided Thomas with his 52–48 confirmation when several southern Democrats facing reelection voted to confirm him.[13] This finding was affirmed in a study by Overby and Beth Henschen, who found that senators with a large percentage of women constituents in managerial and professional jobs were slightly less likely to vote for Thomas's confirmation if they faced reelection the next year.[14]

These results suggest that political expediency can spell the difference between a nominee's confirmation and rejection. Senators not facing reelection soon may make a reflective judgment on the merits of a nomination, whereas those facing electoral pressures bow to those pressures and cast the deciding votes, at least in close and controversial cases. In voting on Supreme Court nominations, it seems to be true, as the late Senator Hubert H. Humphrey reportedly said of a senator's six-year term, "The first four years are for God and country. The last two are for the folks back home."[15]

This finding suggests that combatants in a confirmation battle can gain a political advantage by making the contest even more public and political. As Overby et al. have concluded, "[O]ur findings raise the interesting possibility that in an age of televised confirmation hearings and glaring public scrutiny of nominees, 'going public' to raise widespread popular interest and bring constituent pressure to bear on wavering senators might be one of the more productive strategies available to the White House [or to the nominee's opponents] in confirmation struggles with the Senate."[16] It is clear, moreover, that the rhetoric employed in public appeals does not always lend itself to a balanced, dispassionate analysis of a nominee's qualities.[17]

In the bitter aftermath of the titanic struggle over the Bork nomination, which featured most of the participants, political pressures, and tactics just described, members of the legal establishment, including scholars, judges, lawyers, and former and current public office holders, issued urgent calls for the reform of the confirmation process. Those calls only grew more impassioned and indignant after the ugly, superheated fight over the confirmation of Clarence Thomas, which produced an extraordinary televised confrontation about race, sex, the Senate, and the press that transfixed the nation. The general thrust of these proposals was to depoliticize the confirmation process by reducing its visibility, limiting public and interest group participation and influence on the Senate, limiting access to FBI reports on nominees, and concentrating senators' inquiries on nominees' professional qualifications rather than their likely future votes as justices.

Perhaps the most characteristic of these proposals was authored by the Twentieth Century Fund Task Force on Judicial Selection, a group of distinguished scholars, lawyers, judges, and former public officials.[18] The Task Force expressed its dismay at the way the modern confirmation process had come "dangerously close to looking like the electoral process," with the Senate holding a type of "national referendum on the appointment, with media campaigns, polling techniques, and political rhetoric that distract from, and sometimes completely distort, the legal qualifications of the nominee."[19] It criticized participants in the process who used the "televised hearings as a forum for other purposes, ranging from self-promotion to mobilizing special interest groups in order to influence public opinion."[20] The Task Force also complained about the too public and participatory nature of the hearings: "Witnesses are called to testify not principally for their legal expertise, but as advocates for and against the nominees and as representatives of competing interests and constituencies. The confirmation process, in short, has become extremely politicized in a way that denigrates the Court and serves to undermine its prestige as well as public respect for the rule of law."[21]

The Task Force issued four recommendations to correct this distorted process: (1) that the confirmation process be "depoliticized by minimizing the potential for participants to posture and distort the basic purpose of the proceedings"; (2) that "nominees should no longer be expected to appear as witnesses" at the hearings; (3) that if nominees do appear, senators should not seek testimony that would signal nominees' future rulings on specific issues; (4) that senators "base confirmation decisions on a nominee's written record and the testimony of legal experts as to his competence."[22]

Similar criticisms and recommendations, or others in the same spirit, were made by other prominent groups and individuals. Among them were some members of a roundtable of distinguished law professors and a well-known federal judge assembled by the editors of the *ABA Journal*[23]; a panel of distinguished law school deans that testified at the Bork hearings[24]; the late Professor Paul A. Freund of Harvard Law School (himself a potential Supreme Court nominee during the Kennedy-Johnson years), who largely agreed with the Task Force recommendations, although he thought nominees would continue to testify[25]; then–Federal Appeals Court Judge Ruth Bader

Ginsburg (with respect to the third recommendation and to the fourth, as it relates to a nominee's written record)[26]; and law professors David Strauss and Cass Sunstein (who broadly endorsed the first, third, and fourth recommendations).[27]

Of all the recommendations authored by these sources, only one has been adopted. The Senate Judiciary Committee now meets with each nominee in a closed session to discuss sensitive matters that may reflect upon the nominee's character and ethics. All of the other proposals of the sort described above have failed to win adoption[28] because there has been no consensus on their desirability.

We should not regret that failure. The following sections examine the alleged overpoliticization of the confirmation process more critically.

THE POLITICS OF CONFIRMATION AND REJECTION

The first response to the overpoliticization argument is to examine the antipolitical attitude that underlies it. The claim of overpoliticization reflects a widely shared distaste for the give-and-take of contemporary American politics. But critics of overpoliticization tend to idealize law (at least the law made by judges) as the product of a disinterested, contemplative, deliberative process uninformed by normal human prejudices or the judges' policy preferences. The overpoliticization they see in the confirmation process is really just the "constitutional dialogue" among the three branches of government and the public over the Constitution's meaning. Depoliticizing the confirmation process would curtail that dialogue and put in its place a constitutional democracy without the democracy. That is not the American form of government. As Mark Silverstein has written,

> It is in the often unseemly clash of opposing interests that the modern liberal-democratic state seeks to achieve rough consensus on its most pressing and divisive issues. Considering the developments of the last decades, it can scarcely be surprising that a similar struggle now defines the selection of our judges. . . . To those who witnessed the agony of the Thomas [and perhaps Bork] hearings, the value of a return to less visible and contentious proceedings may appear undeniable. Reform, however, is not only unlikely . . . but perhaps ill advised as well. . . . [T]he apparent decorum of the past was achieved at the expense of public participation and accountability. . . . [T]he

fact remains that judges today are important policymakers and that public participation in the process of their selection may be the principal mechanism for ensuring a measure of political accountability.[29]

Long gone is the time when most Supreme Court confirmations, politically charged though some of them were, were handled in a matter of days or a few weeks, with few if any public hearings or open Senate debate on the nominee, and a nonrecorded voice vote on the nomination in a closed session of the Senate.[30] Given that Supreme Court justices are extremely powerful and largely unaccountable policy makers, the participatory ethos in modern American politics, described in the previous chapter, simply will not allow a process that is depoliticized—or more accurately, a process in which only the president is permitted to be political.

Let us now examine the claim that political strategy is more influential than issues in determining the outcome of confirmation processes, and the related claim that senators and interest groups either cannot understand nominees' views or deliberately distort them.

Ideological Evaluations and Senate Confirmation Voting

Studies of Senate confirmation voting leave no doubt that issues, or ideological questions, exert a powerful—probably the most powerful—influence on senators' confirmation voting. This conclusion emerges from historical case studies of individual nominations and from statistical studies that examine senators' votes on one nomination or many nominations simultaneously.[31] (Indeed, if the importance of issues to senators were not so great, we would not see so many claims that senators should not evaluate nominees on the basis of ideology.) Even Overby et al., who point out the advantages presidents or their opponents might gain from behaving more strategically in Supreme Court appointments, also conclude that "In the final analysis, it is unlikely that [strategic maneuvers] will ever replace ideological predispositions and partisan loyalties [which are closely related to ideology] as the principal determinants of Senate confirmation votes."[32]

Some legalist critics of the current confirmation process have asserted that the Senate's procedures for evaluating nominees' beliefs make a fair and principled evaluation of them difficult, if not impossible. Interest groups, they claim, will distort a nominee's views, whether to defeat or to assist the nominee—or even to enlist new members and raise funds (a motivation that has been documented by George Watson and John Stookey).[33] Senators will posture to promote their own causes and impress constituents. They and their interest group allies will attempt to portray a nominee as "out of the mainstream"—or "in the mainstream," as the occasion requires. This distortion is all too easy, the critics contend, because legal issues are complex, and the media, interest groups, and senators oversimplify the issues and focus only on the results of cases, ignoring the reasoning behind those results. Speaking of the Bork hearings, for example, Gerhard Casper, former dean of the University of Chicago Law School, lamented that "Results of Supreme Court cases is the only thing that matters. The integrity of judicial reasoning is viewed as irrelevant to those results. That kind of result orientation which summarizes complex cases in one or two words for the evening headlines on television . . . has been disastrous."[34] Casper also cited the "McCarthyite distortions" of Robert Bork's work.[35] Terrance Sandalow, former dean at the University of Michigan Law School, likewise criticized the "distortions of [Bork's] record in the media, in advertisements, and in these hearings,"[36] a complaint echoed by other legal educators at the Bork hearings and by Stephen Carter.[37]

Moreover, it is said that senators are incapable either of eliciting a nominee's views or understanding them. One commentator has complained that some senators "lack basic cross-examining skills" and "can't resist speechifying rather than focusing pointed questions on the witnesses."[38] Stephen Macedo has cited the "inability of many senators to think with any subtlety about basic constitutional issues."[39] Even Gary Simson, one of the more thoughtful critics of the confirmation process, has written that: "[I]t is vital that the [Judiciary Committee] hearings reveal as fully and clearly as possible information relevant to whether the nominee should be confirmed. Few senators, however, have the substantive expertise and cross-examination skills needed to ensure such informative hearings."[40]

Complaints about distortions of nominees' beliefs and senators' lack of understanding are based largely on a single case: that of Robert Bork. Critics allege that liberal senators were either unable or unwilling to grasp the true meaning of his thought, preferring instead to portray him as a right-wing radical.[41] The first item cited to support this charge is usually Senator Kennedy's floor speech, quoted above. Indeed, any fair observer would have to characterize that speech as inflammatory and hyperbolic.

Because so much commentary has claimed that Democratic senators unfairly maligned Judge Bork and misrepresented his views, any evaluation of the overpoliticization argument requires a careful examination of Bork's beliefs and his opponents' attack on them.

Robert Bork and the Constitutional Mainstream

The evidence does not support the claim that liberal senators and interest groups distorted the thrust of Bork's views. On the basis of newspaper descriptions of nominees' ideologies—from both liberal and conservative papers—Jeffrey Segal et al. have constructed an index of nominees' ideologies covering the twenty-one nominations from Earl Warren in 1953 to Anthony Kennedy in 1987. With a positive 1.0 representing a nominee described exclusively as liberal, and a negative 1.0 a nominee uniformly described as conservative, Bork received a score of −.81, making him the fourth most conservative of these twenty-one nominees. Only Antonin Scalia, G. Harrold Carswell, and William Rehnquist ranked as more conservative.[42] Because there is a very strong correlation (.80) between this measure and the later votes of those nominees who won confirmation, it is likely that Bork would have been a very conservative justice.[43]

On the basis of his extensive prenomination record and his Senate testimony, which he has reaffirmed in subsequent writings, Bork would have been more than just a very conservative justice. He would have been a revolutionary conservative willing to discard several decades—arguably two centuries—of precedent and doctrine whose reversal would anger and astonish most Americans today.

Bork made it clear in his Senate testimony that he saw no basis for a constitutional right to privacy, which the Supreme Court has used as the basis not only of the right to abortion, but the right of married and unmarried couples to practice birth control.[44] In his 1990 book, *The Tempting of America: The Political Seduction of the Law*, Bork made his disbelief in a right to privacy even clearer, calling it "the 'right to privacy' invented by the Warren Court," and strongly implying that the Supreme Court should erase that right.[45] He also made clear in the book that he does not believe that the federal government is constitutionally required, as the states are, to treat all citizens equally, as the Supreme Court has held since 1954.[46] In particular, Bork would at least loosen and probably abandon the requirement, which the Court has adhered to since 1971, that government generally treat men and women equally under the Fourteenth Amendment's guarantee of the "equal protection of the laws."[47] Equally if not more importantly, Bork denounces as "utterly illegitimate" the doctrine of substantive due process, and castigates the Supreme Court for its refusal to abandon the doctrine.[48]

Whatever its intrinsic logical merits (and they are questionable), the Court has used the concept of substantive due process over the last century

for two great purposes. The first has been to require state and local governments to respect the constitutional rights of citizens by locating these rights
within the "liberty" protected against state infringement by the due process
clause of the Fourteenth Amendment. Until the early twentieth century, the
limits on governmental power—as spelled out in the Bill of Rights, for
example—had applied only to the federal government.[49]

The second great use of substantive due process has been to recognize
the existence of unwritten constitutional rights, such as the right to marry and
to have children,[50] the right to live in a house with (only) one's grandchil-
dren,[51] the right to travel,[52] the right to refuse unwanted medical treatment,[53]
and, of course, the right to abortion.[54] Virtually all Americans today would
react with outrage to the suggestion that they do not possess at least the first
five of these rights. Yet Bork is unequivocal about his refusal to recognize the
existence of "judge-invented" rights, such as these, that are not spelled out in
the Constitution. He denounces judicial recognition of these rights as "judicial imperialism," "judicial legislation," "judicial constitution-making," and
"political judging."[55] He has also written that the lack of substantive content
in the due process clauses of the Fifth and Fourteenth Amendments "is more
than enough to condemn the hundreds of cases . . . in which the courts have
given the due process clause[s] substantive content,"[56] such as a right to
marry and have children. Bork does not explicitly call for the overruling of
these cases, but the vehemence of his condemnation of substantive due
process and the decisions based on it certainly cast an ominous shadow over
them.

Americans today also take it for granted that their state and local governments must respect their U.S. constitutional rights, just as the federal government must. Any other rule would provoke shock and outrage. Yet Bork is
ambiguous on the question of whether the due process clause of the
Fourteenth Amendment really "incorporates" these rights and applies them to
the states. Although giving no direct answer to that question,[57] he seems
grudgingly to accept that it does, but mainly because the only alternative
interpretation of the Fourteenth Amendment that the courts are likely to adopt
is even worse: it would permit courts to recognize rights not listed in the
Constitution. In his 1990 book, Bork wrote that

The first [form of substantive due process] consists in applying the
substance of various provisions of the Bill of Rights against state
legislation on the theory that the fourteenth amendment's due
process clause 'incorporates' those provisions. But for that incorpo-

ration, the Bill of Rights would restrain only the federal government. This theory at least has the merit of confining the courts to the enforcement of principles actually in the Constitution.

There is, however, a second form of substantive due process in which the courts create principles of freedom . . . that are nowhere to be found in the Constitution.[58]

But alongside this backhanded endorsement of the Bill of Rights as a set of restraints on state and local governments, Bork implies in two ways that the Bill of Rights really and properly applies only to the federal government. The first argument is based on the language of the Fourteenth Amendment's due process clause: "No State shall . . . deprive any person of life, liberty, or property, without due process of law."[59] This "guarantee of due process," Bork wrote, "is simply a requirement that the substance of any law be applied to a person through fair procedures. . . . [T]he text of the due process clause simply will not support judicial efforts to pour substantive rather than procedural meaning into it."[60] If this is true, however, the due process clause of the Fourteenth Amendment cannot incorporate and apply to the states the written, substantive guarantees of the Bill of Rights or the unwritten rights that Bork objects to.[61]

The inapplicability of the Bill of Rights to state and local governments (as well as the inapplicability of the Fourteenth Amendment's equal protection clause to women) is also implied by Bork's insistence that the only legitimate way for judges to interpret the Constitution is by following the original understanding of those who ratified its provisions: "Only the approach of original understanding meets the criteria that any theory of constitutional adjudication must meet in order to possess democratic legitimacy. Only that approach is consonant with the design of the American Republic."[62]

The Bill of Rights was added to the Constitution immediately after the ratification of the Constitution in order to meet the concerns of those who feared that the new *federal* government would exercise unlimited powers over citizens and strip the states of their traditional functions. Scholars agree that no one believed at the time, or for many years thereafter, that the Bill of Rights limited what the state and local governments could do. Hence if today's judges were to follow the original intentions of the ratifiers of the Bill of Rights, those first ten amendments would not limit the powers of state and local government officials.

As noted above, Bork seems to accept the application of the Bill of Rights to the state and local governments, but only as the least of the available evils.[63] In his half-hearted acceptance of the application of the Bill of Rights to the states and his insistence that Americans possess only those constitutional rights that are explicitly provided or strongly implied by the text of the Constitution, Bork's conception of constitutional freedoms is much more restrictive, and far removed, from the conception held by American jurists over the last century and by the public.

At the time of his nomination, Bork and his defenders denied this conclusion by stressing his purportedly great respect for the Supreme Court's constitutional precedents. In his opening statement to the Senate Judiciary Committee, Bork said that "[A] judge must have great respect for precedent. . . . Respect for precedent is part of the great tradition of our law."[64] He later assured senators repeatedly that he would abide by precedents he did not really agree with concerning freedom of speech, the expansion of federal power under the commerce clause, the requirement that the federal government (and not just the states) treat citizens equally, and the application of the equal protection clause of the Fourteenth Amendment to women.[65] But later in the hearings, Senator Edward Kennedy played a dramatic audiotape of remarks Bork had made to a group of college students less than two years earlier. In response to a question about the importance of adhering to precedent, Bork replied,

> I don't think that in the field of constitutional law precedent is all that important. . . . The [Supreme] Court has never thought constitutional precedent was all that important. . . . Moreover, you will from time to time get willful courts who take an area of law and create precedents that have nothing to do with the name of the Constitution . . . what you have is a ratchet effect, with the Constitution getting further and further and further away from its original meaning because some judges feel free to make up new constitutional law and other judges in the name of judicial restraint follow precedent. I don't think precedent is all that important. I think the importance is what the Framers were driving at, and to go back to that.[66]

Respect for precedent is properly considered a qualification for a seat on the Supreme Court. Yet here is a nominee who professes to respect precedent asserting that the two centuries of precedents in which the Supreme Court has never exclusively followed the founding generation's intentions—and his own favored mode of constitutional interpretation—are "not all that important."

In his 1996 book, *Slouching Towards Gomorrah: Modern Liberalism and American Decline,* Bork renewed his attack on "dozens . . . of decisions"[67] (he also refers to a "list . . . [that] could be extended almost indefinitely"[68]) that constitute the modern Court's "adventures in making and enforcing left-wing policy."[69] The justices of recent decades, Bork claimed, are members of the liberal "intellectual class"[70] and "are responsible in no small measure for the spread of both radical individualism and radical egalitarianism."[71] The embrace of these doctrines has "severely damaged the constitutional structure of the nation."[72] The Court, he wrote, is "despotic" and "responsible in no small measure" for "the declining legitimacy of democratic institutions, the promotion of anarchy and license in the moral order, and advancing tyranny in the social order."[73]

This indictment applies not just to the liberal Warren Court of the 1950s and 1960s, but also to the Rehnquist Court of the years since 1986, a Court of mainly Republican justices that is generally thought of as at least moderately conservative.[74] "Only recently," Bork wrote in 1997, the Supreme Court has "created special rights for homosexuals, protected obscenity on cable television, and, in the grip of radical feminism, ruled, contrary to a century-old understanding, that state-run all-male military colleges violate the Constitution."[75]

To halt the Court's "cultural drive to the left,"[76] Bork has called for "a constitutional amendment making any federal or state court decision subject to being overruled by a majority vote of each House of Congress,"[77] a revolutionary proposal that would place the rights of every unpopular individual and group at the mercy of the barest political majority, an outcome that could not be further from the intentions of the American Founders. (Bork later withdrew this proposal, "but only because Canada has found such a procedure ineffective."[78]) He has even written that because of the "utterly disruptive behavior of left-liberal courts . . . doing away with judicial review altogether . . . would surely be better than our present situation."[79]

The inescapable conclusion of all of this evidence is that the attack on Bork's jurisprudence was correct in its essentials. Bork's beliefs about the Constitution placed him far from the body of law the Supreme Court had established over the previous two hundred years. They also placed him far from the mainstream beliefs of the American people[80] in whose name the Supreme Court interprets the Constitution. His refusal to grant constitutional status to rights not listed in the Constitution, his disregard for precedents and his apparent willingness to overturn "hundreds" of them, combined with his insistence on original intent as the only legitimate guide to constitutional interpretation—a guide the Supreme Court has never exclusively followed in over two hundred years—all make him, in the words of Henry Abraham, "rigid and . . . fair game for being portrayed as beyond the mainstream of contemporary judicial philosophy."[81] In sum, the Senate's experience with Robert Bork does not support the charge that the Senate unfairly maligned him or that senators are incapable of fairly examining a nominee's philosophy.

Nominees' Professional Qualifications

As we have seen, some legalist criticisms of the confirmation process hold that the Senate does not care about the "objective" qualifications of nominees. But there is considerable empirical evidence to the contrary. Scholars of the confirmation process who use the case study method have cited a number of nominations rejected by the Senate as a result of the nominee's poor qualifications, although these scholars cite ideology as the most common cause of rejections.[82]

Two statistical studies of confirmation voting also support a role for qualifications. (This number might be higher, but the authors of most of these studies have not tried to assess the impact of nominees' qualifications on senators' votes.) Jeffrey Segal et al. have found that senators who are ideologically opposed to a nominee will not, in most cases, vote against confirmation unless a good case can be made against a nominee's qualifications, or unless the political setting is unfavorable to the president (as when the other party holds a Senate majority or the president makes the nomination in the last year of his term).[83] These authors have also found that strong qualifications for a justiceship raise the probability of a "yes" vote from a skeptical senator.[84]

At the least, therefore, it seems that poor nominee qualifications may trigger ideological opposition that might otherwise lie dormant, and that strong qualifications might suppress such opposition. There is evidence that strong qualifications may hinder examination of even very controversial views. As noted in Chapter 2, senators of both parties reported that Antonin Scalia's "reputation for intellectual brilliance"[85] and his strong professional credentials served to blunt inquiries into his controversial views on executive power, affirmative action, freedom of the press, and privacy. The importance of strong qualifications is also indicated by the seeming attitude of resignation expressed by the *New York Times* toward the confirmations of both Scalia and Justice William Rehnquist (for chief justice) in 1986: "These able lawyers would not be our choices for the Court. . . . The Senate must carefully weigh the appointments, but given the nominees' qualifications, we assume confirmation."[86]

Of course, the strong qualifications of Rehnquist and Scalia were not the only factors that aided their confirmations. Strong opposition did emerge in Rehnquist's case, and his confirmation would have been much more difficult without the Republican majority in the Senate in 1986. Scalia was also helped by Republican control of the Senate and by the opposition to Rehnquist, whose arduous confirmation hearings took place just before Scalia's and left the participants weary of conflict.[87] At the same time, however, there was nothing in Scalia's unquestionable credentials to energize potential opponents.

A skeptic about the importance of nominees' qualifications might claim that qualifications are important only because, as numerous observers have noted, senators are generally reluctant to oppose a nominee on the basis of the nominee's ideology alone. Senators, it might be said, use allegedly weak professional qualifications as a rationale for what is really ideological opposition. But even if this were the only reason qualifications mattered, they would still be important.

THE NOMINATION MESS

Charles Cameron et al. have concluded from their study of Supreme Court confirmations that

> When a strong president [one whose party holds a Senate majority and who is not in the last year of his term] nominates a highly qualified, ideologically moderate candidate, the nominee passes the Senate in a lopsided, consensual vote. . . . [But] when presidents nominate a less qualified, ideologically extreme candidate, especially when a president is in a weak position [in the last year of his term or facing an opposition Senate], then a conflictual vote is likely. Surprisingly, presidents have nominated quite a few candidates of this description, and conflictual votes occur periodically.[88]

It is important to note that even politically weak presidents are likely to see their nominees win easy confirmation if they choose "highly qualified, ideologically moderate candidates." An example is President Gerald Ford's 1975 nomination of John Paul Stevens to replace the retiring William O. Douglas. Several political factors placed Ford in a weak position. Ford was the only president in American history who had never been elected president or vice president.[89] His public approval rating at the time of the Stevens nomination stood at only 41 percent as a result of his unpopular pardon of former President Nixon and an inflationary recession that placed the unemployment rate at what was then its highest point since the Great Depression. After a

Democratic landslide in the congressional elections of 1974, the president's party held just thirty-eight seats in the Senate. Moreover, as House Republican leader in the early 1970s, Ford had led a quixotic campaign, at the behest of the Nixon Administration, to impeach Justice Douglas, a favorite of liberal Democrats. Senate Democrats were therefore on guard against any attempt by Ford to move the Court substantially to the right by replacing the very liberal Douglas with a solid conservative. And the overwhelmingly Democratic Senate was supporting Ford in Senate votes at a lower rate than any president since Dwight Eisenhower's last two years.[90] The potential for conflict over Ford's nominee to replace Douglas was therefore high.

Ford defused this combustible mixture by deftly nominating the superbly qualified and ideologically moderate Stevens. Henry Abraham reports of Stevens's nomination that politically, "Stevens, a moderate Republican, was considered difficult to characterize, but centrist was the label most often attributed to him; he was professionally perceived as a legal conservative."[91] The nomination was universally acclaimed and confirmed unanimously only sixteen days after Ford sent it to the Senate.

President Bill Clinton followed much the same strategy in choosing his first nominee in 1993. Elected in 1992 with only 43 percent of the vote, beset by the Whitewater inquiry, laboring under a public approval rating of just 37 percent, and pushing a Congress with a recalcitrant Republican minority to approve several major initiatives, Clinton could ill afford an exhausting fight over this nomination. He responded by nominating Judge Ruth Bader Ginsburg, a thirteen-year veteran of the U.S. Court of Appeals for the District of Columbia Circuit. A figure of outstanding credentials, the former Columbia University law professor had successfully argued several major cases before the Supreme Court in the 1970s as part of the movement to win equal rights for women. On the federal bench, however, Ginsburg had acquired a reputation as a "non-ideological moderate who eschews judicial activism."[92] *Congressional Quarterly* typified the political reaction to her nomination by reporting it with the headline, "Clinton's Choice of Ginsburg Signals Moderation."[93] In an instructive act for future presidents, Clinton had paved the way for Ginsburg's confirmation by clearing it with key Republican and Democratic senators.[94]

Clinton behaved similarly in 1994 by nominating Stephen Breyer, Chief Judge of the U.S. Court of Appeals for the First Circuit in Boston. Breyer was one of the best-known nominees in recent times; several Republican and Democratic senators on the Judiciary Committee knew him personally from his earlier stint as chief counsel to the committee. He was universally regarded as well qualified. Politically, Breyer, like Ginsburg, was an accommodating choice. He was believed to be prochoice (as he acknowledged at his con-firmation hearings)[95] but skeptical toward business regulation (about which he had written four books), and moderate if not conservative on crime (he had strongly defended the guidelines of the U.S. Sentencing Commission, which he had helped to write and which some judges and others had criti-cized as harsh and rigid). Among the adjectives most often present in articles about him were "moderate," "centrist," "pragmatic," and "flexible."[96] Again, *Congressional Quarterly*'s headline on his nomination seemed to put it best: "Breyer's Liberal, Conservative Mix Seems To Assure Confirmation."[97] And once again, Clinton had received prior assurances of support for Breyer from the most influential senators of both parties.[98]

There is a lesson of overriding importance here for those who lament the public campaigning and lobbying surrounding some recent confirmation pro-ceedings. This politicking will count for little if presidents nominate well-qualified, ethically clean, and politically moderate nominees whose views are acceptable to a majority of the Senate—even if the president is in a polit-ically weak position. When presidents nominate such persons, interest groups and senators of the opposite party will not oppose the nomination. Confirma-tion strategies and tactics will then be largely irrelevant. Hence the presence or absence of the influences and activities that legalist critics of the confir-mation process find lamentable depends on the president's selection of a nominee. Presidents have often chosen nominees who are politically unpalat-able to the Senate, or of questionable ethics, or not professionally well qual-ified, even when political circumstances indicate that the president should exercise the utmost caution in choosing a nominee.

Consider the six nominations that have been rejected, withdrawn, or approved by very narrow margins since the late 1960s: those of Abe Fortas (for chief justice) in 1968, Clement Haynsworth in 1969, G. Harrold Carswell in 1970, Robert Bork in 1987, Douglas Ginsburg in 1987, and Clarence Thomas in 1991. The political setting was ominous for the Fortas nomination in 1968. President Johnson was a lame duck in the last year of his term. As a result of his failed policies in Vietnam, urban riots at home, and rising rates of crime and inflation, his public approval rating stood at just 43 percent. Republicans had every reason to expect a Republican president to take office the next year. Although the president's party held a large majority in the Senate, the party was badly divided over Vietnam and civil rights.

After Chief Justice Earl Warren's resignation in June (effective upon the confirmation of a successor, which made the appointment of a new chief jus-tice less urgent), Johnson nominated Associate Justice Fortas, a nominee with several major liabilities. Fortas had been a consistently liberal justice on the liberal Warren Court, which was then under attack for being too soft on crime and, in some parts of the country, too hard on civil rights. Although an able lawyer and justice, Fortas was a longtime personal friend and adviser to the president, a well-known fact that exposed the president to charges of crony-ism. Johnson heightened this perception by nominating another old friend—Homer Thornberry, whose legal credentials were modest—to replace Fortas as associate justice. Worse, Justice Fortas had continued to advise the president on political, legal, and even foreign policy questions after he joined the Court in 1965, thereby raising serious questions about the justice's apparent violation of the separation of powers doctrine as well as his own lack of judgment.[99] Fortas generated further doubts about his ethical sensitivities by accepting the then-princely sum of $15,000 for a series of university lectures in the summer of 1968, just as the effort to elevate him to chief justice was beginning.[100] Not surprisingly, considering both the characteristics of the nominee and the political situation, the Fortas nomination was filibustered to death on the Senate floor.

When Justice Fortas later resigned under pressure after revelations of financial dealings with a convicted financier, Republican President Richard Nixon nominated Clement Haynsworth, chief judge of the Court of Appeals for the Fourth Circuit, to take Fortas's seat. An apparently able figure with a Harvard law degree, Haynsworth seemed headed for confirmation in a Democratic Senate despite opposition—of which Nixon received advance warning—by civil rights and labor groups.[101] But previously pent-up ideological resistance among Democrats and liberal Republicans was unleashed when, as Henry Abraham describes it, "the hearings of the Senate Committee on the Judiciary provided clear evidence of the nominee's patent insensitivity to some financial and conflict-of-interest improprieties." (Among other things, Haynsworth was accused of buying stock in a company that had just won a lawsuit in his court—before the decision was announced.)[102] Some seventeen Republicans, including the top two Republican Senate leaders, voted against the nomination, which was defeated 55–45. As we saw in the previous chapter, ideological opposition alone would not have derailed the nomination. But coming so soon after the Fortas scandal, the nominee's ethical lapses combined with ideological opposition and the Senate's Democratic majority to doom the nomination.

Acting out of spite, Nixon then quickly nominated G. Harrold Carswell, a former federal district court judge who had just joined the U.S. Court of Appeals for the Fifth Circuit. With the fight over Haynsworth just concluded, the Senate seemed inclined to confirm Carswell before investigations revealed that while running for the Georgia state legislature in 1948, he had stated his "firm, vigorous belief in the principles of White Supremacy," and promised that "I shall always be so governed."[103] He was also accused of harassment and hostility toward civil rights attorneys, especially black attorneys, in his courtroom.[104] Soon thereafter came evidence that Carswell had participated in the 1956 transformation of a Florida golf course from public to private status in order to circumvent a Supreme Court ruling requiring the desegregation of such facilities. The nominee's hopes of winning confirmation were further damaged by his own misleading testimony on the matter.[105]

Still, Carswell might have won confirmation were it not for abundant evidence of his inferior legal qualifications, which included his ranking as one of the federal trial court judges most frequently reversed by appeals courts. The Dean of the Yale Law School characterized Carswell's credentials as "more slender . . . than any Supreme Court nominee put forth in this century."[106] Even some Carswell supporters could not deny this embarrassing truth. Senator Roman Hruska of Nebraska, the Senate floor manager for the nomination, lamely argued that the nominee's poor qualifications provided an additional reason to confirm him: "Even if he is mediocre, there are a lot of mediocre judges and people and lawyers. They are entitled to a little representation, aren't they, and a little chance? We can't all have Brandeises, Cardozos, and Frankfurters, and stuff like that there."[107] Another Carswell supporter, Senator Russell Long of Louisiana, asked in a similar vein, "Does it not seem . . . that we have had enough of those upside-down corkscrew thinkers? Would it not appear that it might be well to take a B student or a C student who was able to think straight, compared to one of those A students who are capable of the kind of thinking that winds up getting us a one hundred percent increase in crime in this country?"[108] After this almost satirical debate, the nomination went down to a 51–45 defeat.

The next confirmation mess took place in 1987, after President Ronald Reagan nominated Robert Bork to replace the retiring Justice Lewis Powell. (We skip Rehnquist's contentious 1971 and 1986 nominations because he was confirmed by substantial margins both times: 68–26 and 65–33, respectively.) Virtually all observers of the Court had long considered Powell the Burger Court's swing vote on such controversial issues as abortion and affirmative action.[109] Many observers agreed that Powell's resignation gave President Reagan "a historic opportunity to shape the future of the Court."[110]

The resulting high stakes in the appointment of Powell's successor were just one factor adding to a high potential for confrontation. Another was the president's declining political standing. Largely as a result of the Iran-Contra scandal, Reagan's vaunted public approval rating had fallen thirteen points, to 51 percent, since the previous year's successful nomination of Judge

Scalia and promotion of Justice Rehnquist to chief justice.[111] Perhaps more ominously, the president's party had lost the 1986 Senate elections to the Democrats, who now held a 54–46 majority. By 1987, Reagan's influence had also begun to wane as he approached the last year of his term. In the face of these adverse developments, Reagan remained determined to move the Court to the right.

Reagan faced a split between a conservative administration faction led by Attorney General Edwin Meese, who pushed for Bork's nomination, and a group of more pragmatic White House moderates led by White House Counsel A. B. Culvahouse and Chief of Staff (and former Senate Republican leader) Howard Baker, who preferred a more moderate nominee who would avoid a confirmation fight.[112] Despite a clear warning from Senate Judiciary Committee Chairman Joseph Biden and Senate Democratic Majority Leader Robert Byrd that a Bork nomination would ignite a major battle,[113] Reagan chose Bork. The president thereby provoked the long, bitter, and unsuccessful confirmation battle that ensued.

Because the extraordinary implications of Bork's views have been discussed earlier in this chapter, it is not necessary to review them here. It is enough to note that a politically weakened president began a battle royal by nominating as a successor to Justice Powell, the Court's acknowledged swing vote, a candidate of immoderate views while facing a Senate controlled by the opposite party. As Gary Simson has written, President Reagan's nomination of Bork was "exceptionally provocative" and a "solid right to the jaw of the liberals and even the centrists in the Senate. . . . Bork was on record as questioning the validity of a host of Supreme Court precedents that many senators held dear. Moreover, he seemed likely in both the short and the long run to exercise an unusually large influence on the outcome of important cases."[114]

Angered by Bork's rejection, Reagan fulfilled his threat to choose a second nominee that Bork's opponents "would object to just as much as they did" to Bork.[115] The intentionally objectionable nominee was Douglas H. Ginsburg, a forty-one-year-old former Harvard law professor, Reagan White House official, and federal appeals court judge with eleven months' experience on the bench. When President Reagan nominated Ginsburg for the appeals court post a year earlier, the American Bar Association's Standing Committee on the Federal Judiciary, concerned about Ginsburg's lack of experience, gave the nominee its lowest qualified rating.[116] The committee would not have rated him any higher for the Supreme Court.

Ginsburg's views were much harder to discern than Bork's, but they were sufficient to provoke opposition from Senate Democrats and liberal interest groups. Unlike Bork, Ginsburg had only a short paper trail of scholarly writings and had issued no controversial rulings in his eleven months as a judge. The nominee clearly favored the application of free-market analyses to legal problems. A follower of the "law and economics" movement, which evaluates laws and governmental policies by their economic effects, Ginsburg's principal duty in the Reagan White House was to scrutinize proposed regulations to ensure their cost-effectiveness, a task in which he antagonized congressional Democrats, who charged that he was thwarting the intent of the legislation that authorized the regulations.[117] Several longtime acquaintances nonetheless described Ginsburg as libertarian rather than socially conservative, someone who favored a hands-off policy toward personal private behaviors—and possibly abortion—as well as economic activity.[118]

In any case, Reagan clearly thought his nominee was a trustworthy conservative. Ginsburg had been the favorite candidate of the same conservative administration faction that had pushed for Bork's nomination, and Reagan once again sided with them over the opposition of White House moderates, who now favored the nomination of Judge Anthony Kennedy.[119] Reagan chose Ginsburg despite a warning from White House Chief of Staff Howard Baker that Ginsburg would face a confirmation fight especially if, as expected, the ABA gave the nominee another tepid endorsement.[120] Indeed, the *New York Times* reported that Ginsburg's nomination "came after several Democratic senators, citing his relative lack of judicial experience and a strong conservative outlook, advised the White House that he was the most controversial person on the President's list of candidates."[121] The disclosure that this lightly qualified and intentionally provocative nominee had smoked marijuana as a Harvard law professor spared the nation from another likely confirmation fight.

In Clarence Thomas, President George H. W. Bush chose a nominee whose confirmation experience may have topped even that of Robert Bork for the bitterness and division it engendered. It is probable that no one in the White House could have foreseen the controversy that erupted when Thomas was accused of sexual harassment by Professor Anita Hill of the University of Oklahoma Law School,[122] who had worked for Thomas when he served as Assistant Secretary of Education and Chairman of the Equal Employment Opportunity Commission, where he had been excoriated by congressional Democrats for failing to enforce laws against employment discrimination, attempting to cover up his failures, and punishing agency whistle-blowers. At age forty-three, and with sixteen months' experience as a federal appeals court judge, Thomas was one of the youngest and least experienced nominees in a century. He had also made increasingly controversial remarks on the conservative lecture circuit, including caustic denunciations of Congress and praise for Colonel Oliver North, the Reagan White House aide who defied a congressional ban by sending aid to anticommunist rebels in Nicaragua and was later convicted of obstructing Congress's investigation of the scandal. Thomas's background and the Senate's controversial handling of his nomination are analyzed in Chapter 5. For now, it is enough to note that the president dared the opposition Democrats, who held a fourteen-seat Senate majority, to oppose a nominee who was, at best, minimally qualified for a justiceship, ideologically unpalatable to them, a caustic critic of Congress, and—here was the difficulty for Democrats—African American.

In sum, Presidents Johnson, Nixon, Reagan, and the first President Bush ignited every confirmation controversy of the last third of the twentieth century by nominating figures who were of questionable qualifications and/or ethics, or who held views that were known to be objectionable to a majority or a large minority of the Senate.

THE NEWS MEDIA AND THE "DISTORTION" OF THE PROCESS

Among the factors allegedly overpoliticizing the modern confirmation process, few have been cited more frequently than the news media. There are, in general terms, three broad criticisms of the media's role. The first holds that the media dig up and publicize dirt on nominees. The most frequently cited evidence on this point is the behavior of *Newsday*'s Timothy Phelps and National Public Radio's Nina Totenberg, who broke the story of Anita Hill's charges of sexual harassment against Clarence Thomas. These reporters pried enough information from senators or congressional staffers to go with the story despite Hill's attempts to keep the allegations confidential. They thereby exposed this unwilling witness to withering public scrutiny and touched off the public imbroglio that followed.[123] Critics of alleged mud-slinging also cite Totenberg's 1987 story on Douglas Ginsburg's marijuana smoking, which brought down that nomination.

But even a nominee of such integrity as Stephen Breyer was tarred by well-publicized charges that he had failed to pay Social Security taxes for a woman who did housework for his family; had planned to spend more than $200 million on a lavish new courthouse in Boston that included a boat dock, a theater, a restaurant, and an art gallery; that he had decided several cases as a federal appeals court judge in which he had a financial interest; and that he had once flown from Puerto Rico to a family vacation home on St. Kitts at government expense (he promptly reimbursed the government for $215 after the *Washington Post* published the story).[124] After *Newsday* published the conflict-of-interest charges, the *New York Times* editorialized that "[Breyer] will . . . face—if the senators are doing their job—some heavy questioning about his investments and what they reveal about his character and priorities. Hearings that seemed simple until recently now require a searching inquiry into the nominee's wealth [which the *Times* reported at more than $8.5 million] and philosophy."[125] Five of six outside experts on legal ethics who provided information to the Judiciary Committee could find no wrongdoing on Breyer's part,[126] and the American Bar Association's Standing Committee on the Federal Judiciary unanimously found Breyer to be of the "highest standards of integrity."[127]

The second general complaint against the media is that television coverage of confirmation hearings distorts the behavior of participants in the hearings and deflects attention from the truly important issues. The Twentieth Century Fund Task Force found that television coverage has

> invited abuse of the confirmation process. The White House, the Department of Justice, senators, witnesses, and even nominees now seem tempted to use televised hearings as a forum for other purposes, ranging from self-promotion to mobilizing special interest groups in order to influence public opinion. . . .
>
> [I]n light of that extensive media coverage, *the confirmation process needs to be depoliticized by minimizing the potential for participants to posture and distort the basic purpose of the hearings.*[128]

Task Force member and political scientist Walter Berns went on to "suggest further that television cameras be banned from the hearings. This would go some way toward getting senators to attend to the business at hand instead of striking poses to please their favorite constituents."[129]

Stephen Carter agrees that televised hearings have overpoliticized and degraded the process: "Television gave us the Bork hearings. Even without television, there would have been hearings; but the presence of the cameras . . . transformed an inside-the-Beltway ritual into a full-blown national extravaganza."[130] He concludes that "The presence of television cameras probably makes everyone behave worse, but the main damage is done not through televising the hearings but televising the charges and counter-charges."[131] On the capacity of the media to deflect attention from important issues, Carter offers the example of the televised Thomas-Hill drama:

The hearings on Anita Hill's charges of sexual harassment against Clarence Thomas made for riveting television as millions of viewers watched and chose up sides; in fact the spectacle was so riveting that most Americans apparently forgot that there were other issues about the nomination to be debated. Instead, those who believed Thomas's testimony seemed to think he should be confirmed and those who believed Hill's seemed to think he should not.[132]

A number of respected commentators have alleged that the fate of nominees depends significantly, even decisively, on their looks and their ability to perform before the cameras. David Strauss and Cass Sunstein have written that "the hearings sometimes become mired in irrelevant or misleading factors, such as the nominee's telegenic qualities and how the various Senators 'look.' Televised competition between senators and the nominee, or among the Senators, is hardly in the national interest."[133] They add in a footnote that "We note in particular . . . the reliance on general appearance before the cameras in the Bork, Souter, and Thomas hearings."[134]

Michael McConnell has opined that in a televised confirmation hearing, "[T]he principal attribute being judged is television style rather than a whole career," a point seconded by former Acting Solicitor General Walter Dellinger.[135] Even stronger views have been expressed by Judge Alex Kozinski of the U.S. Court of Appeals for the Ninth Circuit, who has voiced his "suspicion" that "[I]n addition to the full-fledged television campaign against him, [Robert] Bork was defeated by the way he looks."[136]

The third general criticism of the media is that their coverage of nominations and confirmation proceedings has too great an impact on the Senate's decision to confirm or reject a nominee. This criticism is implicit in the two criticisms just described, and we have already encountered expressions of this view. One is the lament of the Twentieth Century Fund Task Force that the modern media, especially television, have turned confirmation proceedings into national referendums where the advantage lies with those who can most skillfully exploit the media. A second is the belief of commentators who claim that the nominee's television style and appearance on screen may exert a decisive influence on the Senate's decision on the nomination. A third expression of this view is Carter's contention that all that mattered to many citizens (and some senators) in the case of Clarence Thomas was their view of his innocence or guilt on the sexual harassment charges; because the polls showed that a majority of the public believed Thomas, the nominee was confirmed.

George Watson and John Stookey, who cannot be numbered among the critics of the modern confirmation process, identify the link between media coverage and the Senate's decision more cautiously:

> [T]he public is now more easily aroused to attention as a result of increased media coverage. . . . Supreme Court nominations focus uniquely upon a person and the question of whether that person is fit to be a justice. It is no accident that the *Anita Hill vs. Clarence Thomas* confrontation snared large television audiences. By this personification of issues in single individuals, the media, particularly television, can take a heretofore obscure part of the American political process and elevate it significantly in the public consciousness. A major consequence of such media coverage is to effectively introduce constituency opinion into a senator's decision-making calculus, a factor of considerable importance in controversial nominations.[137]

All of this is true. The following sections analyze the indictment of the media in more detail.

The News Media and the Politicization of Confirmation Hearings

Supreme Court nominations and confirmations receive much more coverage than they did a few decades ago. Various factors account for the increased media attention. One factor is simply the larger number of media, such as National Public Radio and the hundreds of politically oriented talk-radio shows. Especially noteworthy, however, is the advent of television and the proliferation of channels it carries, including all-news networks, C-SPAN, public television, and the creation of group-associated cable channels such as the Christian Broadcasting Network, all of which are likely to devote considerable attention to some Supreme Court confirmation proceedings. A second reason for increased media attention is the more aggressive, investigatory style of contemporary American journalism. A third reason is that the time interval between the announcement of a nomination and the beginning of the confirmation hearings is now much longer than in the past.[138] And a fourth contributor is a greater realization of the importance of a Supreme Court appointment, as the influence of the judiciary extends into more and more areas of public policy and private life.

It is also true, as we have seen, that public opinion, shaped in part by media coverage of nominations and confirmation proceedings, influences senators' votes on at least some nominations. And no one would claim that the impact of public opinion always produces a wiser decision on a nomination. But the strategy of depoliticizing confirmation proceedings by lowering their visibility is neither realistic nor desirable. As we saw in the previous chapter, Americans should have a say over who becomes a Supreme Court justice and hands down decisions of profound importance to their lives. The public should participate in the constitutional dialogue. Input from the public enhances the legitimacy of judicial review and thereby, somewhat paradoxically, protects minority rights. But public input cannot be meaningful if the media do not carry news of the nomination and confirmation proceedings to the public.

Another fundamental difficulty with the antimedia argument is that, as with interest group involvement, the level and impact of media participation in the confirmation process depend crucially on the president's choice of nominee. If the president chooses a well-qualified, ethically clean, and ideologically nonextreme nominee, there will be little dirt for the media to dig up or hurl at the nominee. A carefully chosen and thoroughly vetted nominee will provide little opportunity for hostile fire. This is especially true if the nominee is well known and respected in the legal community. Examples of such nominees are John Paul Stevens, Ruth Bader Ginsburg, and Stephen Breyer, all of whom, as we have seen, won easy confirmation despite the weak political positions of their nominators.

This point is of fundamental importance. If the president does not invite controversy, there will likely be no controversy for the media to distort or otherwise influence, and they will play a marginal role. The media are therefore usually a secondary, not a primary, factor in Supreme Court confirmations. Their importance depends on the basic political factors that have always made a nomination controversial or not. When the political ingredients of a controversial nomination are absent, the media will have little impact. Again, the seeds of controversy in Supreme Court confirmations are found at the nomination stage.

A third problem with the indictment of the media is that it overstates the growth of the media's role over time, especially the significance of television, in the confirmation process. In the pretelevision age, other media played a role not unlike the one they and television play today.

After President Washington nominated John Rutledge for chief justice in 1795, partisan Federalist newspapers throughout the country, upset with Rutledge's vocal opposition to the Jay Treaty with Great Britain, questioned the nominee's sanity and his qualifications for the job. (His credentials were outstanding. Rutledge had served in the First Continental Congress in 1774 and at the Constitutional Convention of 1787, where he chaired the Committee on Detail, which wrote the first draft of the Constitution. He had also been governor and chief justice of South Carolina, and had earlier been confirmed as one of Washington's first nominees for associate justice in 1789, but had resigned before serving.) One open letter to Rutledge that circulated widely in the Federalist press implied that he had failed to repay his personal debts, and suggested that his creditors sue him and that the Senate examine both his public and private affairs. According to the letter, a chief justice of the United States "should be conspicuous for his love of justice in his private dealings, and in his official conduct." But "if anything can be discovered in either, that suggests even a doubt on this point, he must lose the confidence and the respect of the people, [and] his usefulness and his reputation are gone forever."[139] A highly public debate on the nomination ensued as opposition Democratic-Republican newspapers defended the nominee, and charges and countercharges went back and forth. Ultimately, the Senate rejected the nomination by a vote of fourteen to ten. "To use modern parlance," John Anthony Maltese has concluded in his account of this affair, "John Rutledge had been 'Borked.'"[140] There also seems little doubt that, just as the question of whether Clarence Thomas harassed Anita Hill eclipsed other questions about his nomination in the minds of many Americans, other issues in Rutledge's case were eclipsed by his opposition to the Jay Treaty. At least the consuming issue in Thomas's case was directly relevant to his fitness for a justiceship, something one cannot say of Rutledge's opposition to the Jay Treaty.

In 1937, the press reported that Roosevelt nominee Hugo Black, then a senator from Alabama, had once been a member of the Ku Klux Klan, a charge that fueled hostile editorials denouncing Black not only for this transgression but for his allegedly poor legal qualifications and extreme partisanship as a senator.[141] The Senate Judiciary Committee held no public hearings on the nomination. The committee, and later the full Senate, voted not to investigate Black's ties to the Klan, and he won confirmation by a 63–16 vote just five days after his nomination was announced. The *Pittsburgh Post-Gazette* kept the controversy alive by publishing a series of articles alleging that Black was still a Klan member despite denials of the charge by Black's friends and Senate colleagues. Less than a month after Black joined the Court, several senators called for his impeachment. The controversy gradually died down only after Black made a dramatic nationwide radio address—it drew what was then the second largest audience in radio history—some six weeks after his confirmation.[142] If this episode did not constitute a confirmation mess, it is hard to imagine what would. Black then served the Court and the nation for thirty-four years and became a consensus choice as one of the great justices and civil libertarians in American history.[143]

During President Lyndon Johnson's attempt to elevate Justice Abe Fortas to chief justice in 1968, two print sources, *Time* magazine and the *New York Times* magazine, published lengthy articles detailing the continuing close personal and political ties between the two men that helped to kill that nomination.[144] In 1970, a Florida radio station uncovered G. Harrold Carswell's racist speech in his 1948 campaign for the state legislature, as well as his role in privatizing a formerly public, all-white golf club to prevent its integration.[145] The more recent press investigations into the backgrounds of Robert Bork, Clarence Thomas, and other nominees have led Stephen Carter to denounce the media, particularly television, for bringing "gossip" about nominees into Americans' homes.[146] But as the examples of Rutledge, Black, Carswell, and Fortas demonstrate, the public has always been exposed to gossip about nominees.

Indeed, members of the news media showed considerable restraint in pursuing and reporting the story of Thomas's alleged harassment of Anita Hill and interest in pornography. Rumors that Thomas had sexually harassed coworkers had circulated for at least two months before Timothy Phelps and Nina Totenberg broke the story. Totenberg had received a tip about Thomas and sexual harassment several weeks before the Senate Judiciary Committee's vote on the nomination. After her initial investigation produced no solid information, she dropped the matter. Even after her interest in the story was revived by the committee's surprise tie vote on the nomination and committee chairman Joseph Biden's simultaneous and awkward public defense of Thomas's character,[147] Totenberg still did not consider the story a high priority: "If I'd had anything else to do that week, nothing would have happened."[148]

The other reporter who broke the story, *Newsday*'s Timothy Phelps, showed even greater restraint. Two months before the story broke, a Capitol Hill source had given Phelps the story, including Hill's name. As Phelps has described it, he "sat on the story of the year for two months" because he believed Hill was unwilling to come forward and he had promised his source that he would not contact Hill to ask about sexual harassment.[149] In addition, the editors of the *Washington Post*, whose reporters unearthed records of Thomas's X-rated video rentals on the day he was hurriedly sworn in as a justice, declined to publish the records.[150] The behavior of these members of the media clearly does not support an image of scandal-mongering media.

The point here is not that there is nothing different about the present era.

Supreme Court nominations receive much heavier media coverage than they did just a few decades ago. The press is now more aggressive than it was. And undoubtedly, television lends itself to vivid dramas that will attract a large audience in the case, as we shall see, of a very few confirmation proceedings. The point is only that we should be careful not to overstate the changes brought by modern media coverage of confirmations, especially by television.

Television Coverage and the Conduct of Confirmation Hearings

Aside from the studies linking constituents' opinions to senators' votes on the Thomas nomination, there is very little hard, documented evidence on the impact of television coverage of Senate confirmation proceedings. In their book-length description of the nomination and confirmation processes, Watson and Stookey devote only about a page and a half to the effects of television coverage of Senate confirmation hearings. The principal impacts they report are innocuous or even beneficial. Senators are more likely to show up for the hearings and to stay for their entire length. They are more likely to make a formal opening statement. They are likely to ask more questions of the nominee, at least in the first round of questioning. They are more likely to attempt, with the help of their staffs, to appear knowledgeable about the issues. And they are more likely than in the past to talk about legal or constitutional issues of special concern to them, partly in an effort to educate the public about those issues.[151] On the whole, therefore, it seems that television has made senators more likely "to attend to the business at hand,"[152] rather than less.

These changes make the hearings longer, but the hearings are not excessively long. And in the past, they were often excessively short. The Senate Judiciary Committee spent just one day on the hearings for nominees Charles Whittaker (1957), Potter Stewart (1959), Byron White (1962), Abe Fortas (1965), Warren Burger (to be chief justice, in 1969), and Harry Blackmun (1970). The hearings on Burger's nomination for chief justice lasted just one hour and forty minutes. Burger was the only witness, and much of that time was taken up by the exchange of pleasantries between senators and the nominee.[153] The hearings for all nominees since Sandra Day O'Connor's were first televised in 1981 have averaged 5.3 days, including the twelve-day Bork hearings and the total of eleven days in the two-round Thomas hearings.[154] Five days of hearings (fewer for most nominees) are hardly excessive for the appointment of an official who will exercise extraordinary powers, perhaps for decades, with little accountability.

Some other criticisms of television coverage of confirmation hearings may accurately describe events there, but it is not clear that they really point to faults in the process. For instance, by posturing, critics of the confirmation process mean that senators often take the free air time provided by television to advertise their positions on issues and to urge these positions on one another, on the nominee, and on the public. This opportunity may, as at any time a public official appears before the public, provide the opportunity for demagoguery. But demagoguery is by no means the inevitable result. Watson and Stookey, who have provided the most thorough description of senators' behavior at the hearings, report that most of the roles senators play help them make up their minds about the nominee in cases where they are undecided.[155] It is, moreover, hardly bad for Americans to know their senators' positions on the issues. And such posturing reminds the public of the vital role the Supreme Court plays in the everyday lives of Americans. By closely questioning and even arguing with nominees on television, senators educate the interested public about the Court and its work, a benefit of the process conceded by several authors who are otherwise skeptical of the value of these proceedings.[156]

Senators also contribute by this behavior to the "constitutional dialogue" (as do interest group representatives who testify for or against a nominee on the basis of the nominee's beliefs, and not just his or her legal expertise). This contribution is not bad unless one holds the untenable view that only presidents and Supreme Court justices should take part in that dialogue. Some criticisms, as we have seen, hold that television inflames and distorts that dialogue (almost always relying on the Bork confirmation and to a lesser extent that of Thomas, just two of the several televised confirmation hearings since 1981). But as we saw earlier in this chapter, Bork's constitutional vision was accurately depicted in its essentials. And Chapter 6 will show that Thomas's conservatism on the High Court has validated his opponents' stated expectations.

Critics of televised confirmation hearings have cited the evils of televised hearings into purportedly out-of-the-mainstream beliefs or alleged wrongdoing on the part of nominees. They cite the public spectacle into which such hearings degenerate. But this perspective overstates the costs while overlooking the benefits to both the public and the nominee of televising these events.

Television may give skeptical senators a greater incentive to raise questions about a nominee—whether to incite opposition to the nomination, to bring an issue to public consciousness, or to impress constituents with their apparent attention to duty. To the extent this occurs, television may contribute to greater public acrimony and division. Televised coverage of conflictual hearings may also contribute to the common public perception that all that senators do is to bicker and play politics in the lowest sense of the term. And as we have seen, the rhetoric employed in public appeals for or against a nominee does not always lend itself to a fair and rational discourse on the nominee's fitness.

But let us consider some features of the confirmation process that will remain in place with or without television. There will be a longer interval than in the past between the announcement of a nomination and the beginning of Senate hearings, and potential opponents of a nomination will have more time to organize their efforts. Nominees will receive closer scrutiny by Senate investigators, the FBI, interest groups, and the news media. Meanwhile, the courts, including the Supreme Court, will continue to make decisions governing nearly every aspect of American life. For these reasons, there will often be more questions about, and charges against, nominees (especially when presidents and their aides are careless and/or willfully provocative, as they have been in all of the conflictual nominations since the late 1960s).

These factors will remain in place and will contribute to a greater potential for conflictual confirmations, with or without televised hearings. There were, after all, plenty of charges against Supreme Court nominees in the fifteen years before confirmation hearings were first televised in 1981: Justice Fortas was accused in 1968 of financial improprieties, of being too liberal, and of being too close to the chief executive; Judge Haynsworth was charged in 1969 with financial improprieties and harboring hostility to labor and minority rights; Judge Carswell in 1970 was accused of racism and mediocrity; and William Rehnquist was accused in 1971 of being hostile to constitutional rights, of trying to block minorities from voting years earlier in Arizona, and of authoring a memo in 1953 opposing the Supreme Court's forthcoming decision to strike down segregated schools in *Brown v. Board of Education*.[157]

Given that charges and questions will arise with or without televised hearings, several features of the current confirmation process benefit nominees whose fitness for a justiceship has been challenged: nominees have several weeks to prepare their testimony and have the chance to address, with the help of administration personnel and friendly senators on the Judiciary Committee, any distortions of their records and qualifications, or questionable charges of wrongdoing. The highly visible public forum of the confirmation hearing prevents senators from wrongly maligning a nominee behind closed doors and without accountability to the public. Although television may heighten public attention to such charges, it also forces a nominee's accusers to put their credibility on the line very visibly and to risk losing that credibility if the charges do not stick. Live coverage of the hearings also gives the interested public the opportunity to hear the whole unedited exchange between senators and the nominee and thereby blunts the ability of nightly newscasts and newspapers to offer the public sound bites and selective quotations. Moreover, nominees are typically very articulate and intelligent lawyers who are trained to defend against accusations. When serious questions about a nominee arise, would an able and articulate nominee whose adversarial skills and intellect will likely be, at a minimum, on a par with his or her questioners not choose to appear in such a public forum to respond to distortions or false or overblown charges?

The Senate Judiciary Committee has, as previously noted, adopted the practice of meeting with the nominee in a closed session to discuss any questions of wrongdoing or personal fitness for a justiceship. This practice may be useful for disposing of minor matters or charges that are weakly grounded, as apparently happened in 1993, when the committee spent twenty minutes in a closed session with Ruth Bader Ginsburg, reportedly to discuss her failure to list a waiver of her country club fees on her financial disclosure form.[158] But if serious questions about the nominee's fitness arise and/or there is a possibility that the nomination will be rejected, the matters handled in that session will almost certainly leak to the press (as they did in the case of Ginsburg's minor transgression)—assuming the charges are not already known before the session begins. The Judiciary Committee will then probably be forced to conduct its inquiry in public, before the cameras.

For the reasons explained throughout this and the previous chapter, that is as it should be. The filling of a Supreme Court seat is the public's business. The Judiciary Committee should deal publicly with any serious, legitimate doubts about the suitability of a nominee. This is in the best interest of the public, which has the right to know about the matter—and almost certainly will know in any case. For the reasons just described, it is also in the best interests of the nominee, especially if the charges lack merit.

The claim here is not that the televised confirmation hearings of the Senate Judiciary Committee are unassailable. As noted above, they have the potential to promote conflict, public cynicism, and senatorial grandstanding. The point, rather, is that televised hearings are in several ways fairer and more favorable to the nominee than less visible proceedings. They also serve the public's right to know whether those who will exercise great and nearly unaccountable power over their lives are fit for those positions, and whether their senators have investigated this question thoroughly and answered it rightly. Whatever the costs of conducting such an inquiry before the public—and those costs have been inflicted in recent times by the presidents who have selected the nominees—the high public business of appointing a Supreme Court justice should be conducted in the most public forum.

Media Coverage and Confirmation Votes

The final difficulty with the indictment of media coverage of confirmations is that the media, especially television, have less influence on Senate confirmation votes than many observers have claimed. These claims, like some other criticisms of the confirmation process, are based largely on two cases: those of Bork and Thomas. Observers overstate the media's impact because they focus on the Thomas case, the one case in which media coverage clearly influenced the outcome, and on the Bork case, where observers overstate the direct impact of televised coverage of the hearings. The fact is that few people watch most confirmation hearings. The Thomas-Hill collision was the only commercially viable television broadcast of a Supreme Court confirmation hearing. Viewership was low even for the much anticipated Bork hearings (which gave rise to charges that the Senate now judges nominees principally on their telegenic qualities).[159] Because of low ratings, ABC, NBC, and CBS dropped their live coverage of the Bork hearings after just one day and returned to their usual daily programming. Not even those who attribute great importance to television would claim that the televised hearings for Justices Scalia, Kennedy, Souter, Ginsburg, and Breyer, or the 1986 Rehnquist hearings, had any major impact.[160]

In the case of Clarence Thomas, evidence supports Stephen Carter's claim that many citizens focused on the question of whether Thomas or Hill was telling the truth, and based their view of whether he should be confirmed solely on that issue, as if nothing else mattered.[161] And some senators, particularly southern Democrats, cast decisive votes for Thomas's confirmation according to the "verdict" reached by groups of constituents who were important to their reelections.[162] But most senators voting against the nomination were Democrats who were skeptical of Thomas's views and qualifications, and most senators voting for confirmation were Republicans who were receptive to the nominee from the start. So the question of Thomas's culpability on the sexual harassment charges, although playing a decisive role in the context of this singularly close (52–48) vote, did not eclipse other factors in the minds of most of the one hundred citizens who mattered most. And to the extent that Thomas's race inhibited Democrats on the Judiciary Committee from openly questioning his qualifications for a justiceship,[163] that inhibition stemmed mainly from the delicate politics of questioning the qualifications of an African American nominee. Television coverage of the hearings heightened those hazards, but they would have loomed over the hearings with or without television, and no change in the procedures of the Senate Judiciary Committee could alter the reality of racial politics in America. Moreover, the televising of the Thomas-Hill hearings, as maligned as they were, had the salutary effect of catapulting to the forefront of the nation's consciousness the serious and long-neglected problem of the sexual harassment of women.[164]

We must also remember that the Bork and Thomas nominations were conspicuous for the audacity of the president's challenge to a Senate controlled by the other party. There would have been a war over Bork's nomination with or without television. Bork was the sort of nominee the Senate had been contesting and rejecting for two hundred years. There would also have been a tense proceeding over Thomas's nomination, just as there were in the cases of Fortas, Haynsworth, Carswell, and many nominees before them. One can easily imagine the spurious correlation between televised hearings and the level of conflict over nominations that would arise had the telecast of hearings begun in 1968 and included those for Fortas (for chief justice), Haynsworth, Carswell, and the first Rehnquist nomination. Again, media coverage of confirmation proceedings is mainly dependent on the factors that have always governed whether nominations are controversial.

CONCLUSION

The confirmation process has not been overpoliticized. By focusing primarily on the Bork and Thomas cases, legalist critics of the process have overstated the conflict over modern Supreme Court nominations, and the polling, lobbying, and campaigning that have accompanied them. And by focusing on the confirmation stage, they overlook the real source of conflict: the nomination stage. Some commentators have erred in major factual claims about the process. Senators do care about the professional qualifications of nominees. Critics have also wrongly impugned the intelligence and fairness of the Senate for misunderstanding or misrepresenting the constitutional philosophy of Robert Bork. His views were clearly understood. That is precisely why President Reagan nominated him and why the Senate rejected him. Most Americans do not want a justice in a pivotal position who would denigrate the many unwritten rights they enjoy, jeopardize the equal protection of the law for women, and only grudgingly, if at all, accept the requirement that state and local governments respect the federal constitutional rights of citizens.

Many critical commentaries on the confirmation process result from an inappropriately antidemocratic perspective on the process. A more appropriate, constitutionally democratic outlook would see occasional conflict over Supreme Court nominations as part of the nation's constitutional dialogue. The "depoliticizing" of the process sought by some commentators—if it could be had—would also produce at least a partial delegitimization of the Supreme Court and its power of judicial review. That would be a natural and justified response by a public excluded from the constitutional dialogue by a more closed process intentionally sanitized of public involvement.

Many criticisms of the confirmation process overstate the impact of the modern media, especially television, and fail to note how it has made senators more attentive (rather than less) to their duties. An open process also benefits both the public and the nominee even, and perhaps especially, when the qualifications or ethics of the nominee have been questioned.

Legalist critics of the heavy scrutiny directed at nominees have leveled an as yet unexamined charge against the modern confirmation process: the prospect that nominees will undergo glaring scrutiny has prompted recent presidents to nominate quiescent figures of indistinct views and sufficient competence, but less than the exceptional merit we should expect of nominees to the United States Supreme Court. We now examine whether the modern confirmation process has affected the quality of the Court's justices.

4

The Confirmation Process and the Quality of Justices

Among the most serious criticisms of the modern confirmation process is that the process, by subjecting nominees to heavy ideological scrutiny and a heightened risk of opposition, discourages presidents from nominating especially able figures who have thought and written much about legal issues and whose "paper trails" may thereby provide an inviting target for potential opponents of the nomination. The more virulent strain of this thesis holds that "intellectual distinction is a handicap, rather than a hallmark, for appointment to the Supreme Court,"[1] the result of which is a "Court of mediocrity."[2] This charge has been propounded most often by conservatives disappointed over the Senate's rejection of Robert Bork,[3] a candidate of unquestionable professional credentials, whose prolific and provocative paper trail proved a bonanza for his opponents. But similar fears have also been expressed by respected and less ideological (even liberal) figures.[4]

A more nuanced version of this thesis is offered in separate works by David Schultz and Mark Silverstein, who claim that the modern confirmation process does not inevitably produce poor or mediocre justices, but tends to rule out prominent figures whose special qualities make for judicial greatness.[5] According to Silverstein, changes in the confirmation process between the 1950s and 1990s made the appointment of such figures less likely. Largely as a result of the controversial activism of the Warren Court, the resulting heightened realization of the Court's power, and the greater influence of powerful groups of all ideologies who "now consider a sympathetic judiciary essential"[6] to fulfilling their agendas, the politics of Supreme Court confirmations changed in the late 1960s from "the politics of acquiescence to the politics of confrontation."[7] As a result,

> [T]he contemporary confirmation process is not configured to favor nominees to the Court with the stature of a Frankfurter or a Holmes or the legendary experience of a Brandeis or a Marshall.
>
> ... [T]he more eminent and well-known the candidate, the greater the likelihood of divisive and contentious hearings. The present reality is that prominence facilitates the mobilization of opposition.[8]

The upshot is that "Experienced, competent, noncontroversial jurists with a restrained understanding of the role of the federal judiciary in the political system may be the best the modern system can offer."[9] Of course, Silverstein views the appointment of such least common denominator jurists as a second-best solution at most, and regrets the purported unappointability of renowned and legendary figures of the sort he cites.

Some commentators on the appointment process have disagreed with this view. They rank a nominee's acceptability to all major societal interests high among the "qualifications" a nominee should possess in an era of fractured constitutional consensus such as the present. George Watson and John Stookey, for example, have argued that in the constitutional milieu of 1987, the intellectually imposing but divisive Robert Bork was a less "qualified" nominee than the more widely acceptable Anthony Kennedy, an "experienced, competent, noncontroversial jurist" with a more "restrained understanding of the role of the federal judiciary"[10] than Bork.

Whatever the merits of this argument, figures of legendary stature and experience (such as Frankfurter, Holmes, Brandeis, and Marshall) have undoubtedly brought luster, wisdom, and prestige to the Court, as well as enduring constitutional visions and necessary constitutional innovations. Because the confirmation process for Supreme Court nominees will not revert to the closed and (in most cases) speedy, nonconflictual, and relatively low-scrutiny process that characterized the first several decades of the twentieth century, the charge that the modern process disfavors nominees of this caliber is cause for serious concern.

This chapter tests this thesis with data from a survey, distributed to two hundred seventy-five scholars in the field of constitutional law, on the overall quality of the Supreme Court's twentieth-century appointees. The results of the survey provide no indication that the justices appointed since the late 1960s are, as a group, less able than the average justice of the past. Indeed, the results indicate that most of these justices are better than their average twentieth-century predecessor. At the same time, however, the one hundred twenty-eight respondents did not give a mean rating of better than "good"— or above 3.0 on a scale from 0 to 4.0—to any of the justices appointed since the 1960s. One plausible interpretation of these results is confirmation of the Schultz-Silverstein hypothesis that the current process produces competent judicial technicians who do not make truly excellent justices. But the analysis following the presentation of the results underscores the need for caution before reaching this conclusion.

ASSESSING THE QUALITY OF JUSTICES

The most recent survey of the quality of Supreme Court justices, Robert Bradley's 1991 study,[11] is of limited usefulness here, because it asked respondents to list only those justices the respondents considered "great," and it could not provide data on Justices Ruth Bader Ginsburg and Stephen Breyer (appointed in 1993 and 1994). A survey was therefore taken in 1999–2000 of two hundred seventy-five professors of law or political science who held the JD and/or PhD degrees and the rank of assistant professor or above. One hundred thirty-one survey recipients taught in departments of political science; one hundred forty-four taught in law schools (a very few of whom also held an appointment in political science). Faculty at ninety-five colleges and universities and forty-six law schools from all U.S. geographic regions and all levels of notoriety received surveys.

The law faculty members surveyed were chosen in a two-step procedure. First, law schools were identified from randomly selected pages of the American Bar Association's *Official American Bar Association Guide to Approved Law Schools.*[12] Names of faculty in constitutional law were then culled from those schools' printed catalogs or Web sites. At each selected law school, all faculty members identified as professors of constitutional law were surveyed, as a precaution against selection bias. The political scientists surveyed were members of the American Political Science Association (APSA) whose entries in the APSA's *Directory of Members* identified constitutional law and theory or judicial politics among their subfields. APSA members so labeled were chosen at random with one qualification: preference was given to those APSA members who listed constitutional law and theory first among their fields.

As a means to boost the survey's response rate, approximately 90 percent of survey recipients were contacted initially by electronic mail, the rest by surface mail.[13] All survey recipients had the option of receiving and responding to the survey by electronic mail or surface mail; the latter option afforded recipients the opportunity to respond anonymously (as did electronic mail if participants responded to the survey from an unrevealing address). All survey respondents were promised confidentiality and a copy of the results. Survey recipients received reminders to respond to the survey. There was no survey of judges or lawyers, who had low response rates to Bradley's 1991 questionnaire,[14] and many of whom, especially lawyers, do not watch the Supreme Court (much less its individual justices) closely and may not have studied legal history or constitutional theory since law school.

One hundred twenty-eight scholars responded to the survey, for a response rate of 47 percent. Sixty-seven respondents taught political science, forty-one taught law, and twenty respondents were anonymous. As almost all of those requesting paper surveys that could more easily be returned anonymously were law faculty, the approximate response rates were 51 percent for political science faculty and 42 percent for law faculty.

The survey asked respondents to rate the justices appointed in the twentieth century as excellent, good, fair, poor, or failure. These responses were assigned numerical values of 4, 3, 2, 1, and 0, respectively. The survey form instructed respondents to rate the justices "on their overall performance as Supreme Court justices, using such criteria as the quality of their legal reasoning, their 'learnedness' in the law, their ability to communicate their decisions clearly, and their leadership within the Court." These criteria correspond very closely to the criteria most often cited by scholars in response to Bradley's 1991 open-ended question seeking to identify scholars' own criteria of Supreme Court greatness.[15] Respondents were asked to rate the justices "according to these relatively value-neutral criteria, *putting aside, as far as you can, any consideration of whether you usually agree or disagree with their rulings*" (emphasis in the original). The survey also advised recipients that they could refrain from rating any justice of whom they could not offer a confident opinion.

A second question asked respondents to rate the justices on the Court in the year 1999 "in terms of their qualifications for the Supreme Court *as they appeared at the time of their initial selection and confirmation*" (emphasis in the original).

To promote a substantial response rate to the survey, recipients were not asked for personal data such as their own political-legal ideology or party identification. Such questions would have lengthened the survey and provided possible clues to the identities of anonymous respondents, adding to respondents' burdens and anxieties about responding.

Comparisons of the quality of recent justices with earlier ones were performed three ways: (1) by comparing the average quality rating of justices appointed in each of the three 33-year periods of the twentieth century; (2) by comparing the justices appointed since the appointment of Thurgood Marshall in 1967 with the mean of the pre-1967 appointees; (3) by comparing each justice appointed in the twentieth century with the mean of all such justices, with special attention to the ratings of the appointees beginning with Marshall (whom I collectively label the post-1967 justices).

Two methodological issues require comment. The first is the choice of Marshall's appointment in 1967 to divide the recent from the earlier justices. 1967 was chosen because of features of the confirmation process, especially heightened levels of contention and scrutiny, that are best dated to that time.

Stephen Carter,[16] by contrast, traces the beginnings of the modern confirmation process to that great watershed event in modern constitutional law: *Brown v. Board of Education* (1954).[17] And there is reason for this claim. Nominations entered a new era of heightened ideological scrutiny at that time. Every nominee has testified before the Senate Judiciary Committee since the first post-*Brown* nominee, John Marshall Harlan II, in 1955. (Before Harlan, nominees testified intermittently.) Southern senators of the time began to question nominees about their views on desegregation, and a few years later, as the Warren Court issued its controversial rulings on criminal justice, conservative senators began to inquire of nominees' views on this latter issue as well.[18]

As late as the 1960s, most nominees nonetheless testified only briefly and won confirmation quickly. As noted in the previous chapter, the Senate Judiciary Committee spent only one day on the hearings for nominees Charles Whittaker (1957), Potter Stewart (1959), Byron White (1962), Abe Fortas (1965), and Warren Burger (1969). Four of these five nominees were confirmed within three weeks of their nominations.[19] Burger was the only witness at his 1969 confirmation hearing, which lasted only one hour and forty minutes. The transcript of his testimony takes up only twenty-three pages.[20] He was confirmed just nineteen days after his nomination. Such cursory proceedings for the confirmation of a chief justice would be unthinkable today.

Still, the level of scrutiny and of conflict picked up in the late 1960s, with five confirmation battles in five years: those for Thurgood Marshall (confirmed after a protracted proceeding in 1967), Abe Fortas (rejected for chief justice in 1968), Clement Haynsworth (rejected in 1969), G. Harrold Carswell (rejected in 1970), and William H. Rehnquist (confirmed as associate justice by a vote of 68–26 in 1971). It seems most appropriate, therefore, to consider the "recent" justices as those beginning with Marshall in 1967.

As we shall see later in this chapter, the conclusion that the "recent" justices do not compare unfavorably with their predecessors does not change whether one labels as recent the justices beginning with Marshall in 1967, Burger in 1969, Harry Blackmun in 1970, or even—following Carter's suggestion—John Marshall Harlan II in 1955.

The second methodological issue is: Against whom do we compare the post-1967 appointees? Intuitively, it would seem that the most direct and valid test would compare them to the mean of the pre-1967 appointees rather than to the mean of *all* twentieth-century appointees. Because the recent justices are also twentieth-century appointees, comparing them against the mean for the whole century entails comparing them against a mean of which they are a part. And to that extent, we are comparing them against themselves, which reduces the probability of finding any statistically significant distinction the recent justices may show, because individuals cannot stand out in comparison with themselves.

Against this, our survey may understate the quality of the pre-1967 group and thereby enhance the apparent stature of the post-1967 appointees. The survey respondents may have given unduly low marks to the lesser known of the early twentieth-century justices, such as William Day, William Moody, and Horace Lurton (appointed in 1903, 1906, and 1909, respectively). It may be tempting for contemporary scholars who know little about these justices to dismiss them as historical nonentities and consign them to the lower tiers of justices when, perhaps, most of these now-obscure figures should be considered as good as today's average justice, who may not be well remembered a century from now. On the other hand, our respondents may have underestimated some recent justices who will someday be—but are not yet—recognized as great or near great. As we shall see below, studies identifying great justices tend to exclude current and other recent justices from the ranks of the great. Because it is impossible to resolve these dilemmas a priori, the post-1967 appointees are compared against the mean of the earlier group as well as the mean of all twentieth-century appointees.

The Results

Table 4.1 summarizes the ratings for the fifty-two justices from Holmes (appointed 1902) to Breyer (appointed 1994). They range from a high of 3.79 for Louis Brandeis to a low of 1.11 for Charles Whittaker. The mean for all twentieth-century appointees is 2.46, with a standard deviation of 0.72.

A few preliminary observations are in order. First, the survey clearly identifies the justices commonly regarded as great by students of the Court

Table 4.1. Individual Ratings: All Twentieth-Century
Justices

Justice	Mean	SD	n
Holmes	3.78	0.47	128
Day	1.97	0.69	60
Moody	1.85	0.68	54
Lurton	1.58	0.73	50
Hughes	3.44	0.62	118
Ed. White	2.52	0.76	82
VanDevanter	1.74	1.06	106
Lamar	1.74	0.71	54
Pitney	1.70	0.71	50
McReynolds	1.16	1.12	105
Brandeis	3.79	0.48	125
Clarke	2.00	0.90	67
Taft	2.89	0.73	114
Sutherland	2.60	0.94	107
Butler	1.68	0.81	93
Sanford	1.77	0.68	70
Stone	3.37	0.68	118
Roberts	2.23	0.68	105
Cardozo	3.52	0.67	122
Black	3.50	0.64	125
Reed	1.98	0.69	97
Frankfurter	3.27	0.78	127
Douglas	2.90	1.08	127
Murphy	2.63	0.86	100
Byrnes	1.23	0.86	83
Jackson	3.35	0.61	117
Rutledge	2.43	0.72	96
Burton	1.81	0.65	90
Vinson	1.69	0.72	107
Clark	2.10	0.71	112
Minton	1.43	0.72	89
Warren	3.47	0.85	126
Harlan	3.55	0.65	121
Brennan	3.56	0.90	126
Whittaker	1.11	0.90	89
Stewart	2.55	0.60	125
B. White	2.45	0.67	125
Goldberg	2.21	0.86	118
Fortas	2.25	1.04	114
Marshall	2.74	0.99	127
Burger	1.84	0.74	126
Blackmun	2.66	1.01	125
Powell	2.78	0.76	126
Rehnquist	2.71	0.88	126
Stevens	2.78	0.80	125
O'Connor	2.60	0.71	126
Scalia	2.80	1.07	126
Kennedy	2.43	0.75	124
Souter	2.79	0.89	125
Thomas	1.57	1.10	124
Ginsburg	2.79	0.66	121
Breyer	2.76	0.66	120
All justices	2.46	0.72	52

and ranked as such by compilers of previous lists[21]: the ratings for Holmes, Hughes, Brandeis, Stone, Cardozo, Black, Frankfurter, Jackson, Warren, Harlan, and Brennan all easily top 3.0, placing them well above the next highest scoring justice, William O. Douglas, whose score is 2.90. All justices with scores of 3.0 or higher had been rated "great" or "near great" in at least one of the four previous surveys of Supreme Court greatness administered to scholars, judges, and lawyers.[22] The congruence between the criteria of judicial ability respondents were asked to employ in this study and those most frequently cited by scholars themselves, and the congruence between these results and those of earlier studies testify to the validity and reliability of our measure of individual performance on the Court.

A second observation provides further confidence in the survey results: the high standard deviations for both the conspicuously liberal and conspicuously conservative justices, such as Douglas, Brennan, Marshall, Scalia, and Thomas. These indicate that some respondents did not separate ideological criteria from their evaluations of the justices (although it would be unrealistic to expect them to do so completely). But the wide range of assessments of both the most liberal and most conservative justices indicates that the survey respondents were an ideologically balanced group—neither lopsidedly liberal nor conservative. Were the respondents predominantly liberal (conservative) and their responses correspondingly so, one might expect small standard deviations for the most liberal (conservative) justices, reflecting the biased sample's positive consensus view of them. One might also expect a biased liberal (conservative) sample to produce small standard deviations for the most conservative (liberal) justices, reflecting the sample's consensus view of them as well. But the high standard deviations reflect a wide range of opinion concerning both the most liberal and the most conservative justices and indicate that the sample was not systematically distorted in either ideological direction. This interpretation of the results is supported by inspection of individual cases in the data set, which quickly identified highly liberal and highly conservative survey respondents (that is, respondents who consistently favored highly liberal over highly conservative justices, and vice versa).

A third striking result is that only three of the thirteen justices appointed since 1967 rank below the mean for all twentieth-century appointees (2.46): Anthony Kennedy—just barely below at 2.43, Warren Burger at 1.84, and Clarence Thomas, whose score of 1.57 places him fifth from the bottom of the whole list, above only Justices Whittaker, McReynolds, Byrnes, and Minton. Fourth is the narrow variation among rankings of the post-1967 appointees: nine of thirteen score between 2.60 (O'Connor) and 2.80

(Scalia). Last is the observation, alluded to above, that none of the recent justices would seem to rank among the greats.

Comparison of Eras

A preliminary analysis of the average scores of the justices appointed in the five 20-year periods of the twentieth century revealed no statistically discernible differences among them.[23] A redivision of the twentieth century into three periods of equal length was then undertaken on the probability that the larger number of justices in these longer periods would increase the likelihood of finding statistically significant differences among them. This tripartite division also has the advantage of allowing comparisons of the justices appointed in the first two-thirds of the century with those appointed beginning with Thurgood Marshall's appointment in 1967, when conflictual confirmation proceedings became more frequent. Table 4.2 shows the average quality rating and standard deviation of the ratings for each of these three periods.

The most striking difference among the periods is in their standard deviations, which are much larger for the two earlier periods. This result is likely because the survey respondents were less knowledgeable about the earlier justices than the later ones, as shown by the smaller n values for many of the earlier justices in Table 4.1. The respondents were given to rating the earlier justices as either very good (such as Holmes, Brandeis, Hughes, Stone, and Cardozo) or rather poor (such as Day, Moody, and Lurton).

The period means were compared by t-tests. Table 4.3 shows no statistically discernible difference among these periods; the probability values are far above the customary .05 level of significance. Although the respondents as a group gave no outstanding ratings to any recent justice, it would seem the recent appointees are at least as good, on average, as those of earlier periods.

Comparisons of Pre- and Post-1967 Justices

Table 4.4 compares the individual post-1967 appointees with the mean score of those appointed earlier (2.43). A positive (negative) t-statistic indicates a

Table 4.2. Summary Data for Thirty-three-Year Periods

Period	Mean	SD	No. of Justices
1901–33	2.39	0.84	19
1934–66	2.47	0.80	20
1967–99	2.56	0.39	13
All	2.46	0.72	52

Table 4.3. Comparison of Thirty-three-Year Periods

Period	1901–33		1934–66		1967–99	
	t	pr	t	pr	t	pr
1901–33	0.00	1.00	...	...	...	...
1934–66	0.33	0.74	0.00	1.00	...	...
1967–99	0.77	0.45	0.40	0.69	0.00	1.00

NOTE. A t-test normally assumes that the variances of the two variables being compared are equal. Since the standard deviation (and hence variance) of the last period was much less than the earlier two, the t-statistics reported in line 3 were computed under the assumption of unequal variances. The t-statistics were little different, however, under the contrary assumption of equal variances.

justice who scored above (below) that mean. The two-tailed probability values in the last column represent the probability that the mean for a justice is not significantly different from the mean of the earlier group. As shown in the right-hand column, six of the thirteen recent justices (Powell, Stevens, Scalia, Souter, Ginsburg, and Breyer) score above the mean of the earlier justices at the .05 level of significance, and Justice Marshall and Chief Justice Rehnquist do so at the .10 level. Two of the post-1967 appointees, Chief

Table 4.4. Post-1967 Justices Versus Pre-1967 Justices

Justice	Mean	t-statistic[a]	pr > [t]
Marshall	2.74	1.78	.0762
Burger	1.84	−4.23	.0001
Blackmun	2.66	1.28	.2008
Powell	2.78	2.48	.0143
Rehnquist	2.71	1.76	.0802
Stevens	2.78	2.36	.0195
O'Connor	2.60	1.31	.1937
Scalia	2.80	2.32	.0227
Kennedy	2.43	−0.01	.9932
Souter	2.79	2.27	.0244
Thomas	1.57	−4.50	.0001
Ginsburg	2.79	2.77	.0062
Breyer	2.76	2.56	.0114
Post-1967 justices	2.56	0.76	.4533
Justices in 1999	2.58	0.82	.4196

[a] For those comparisons where an F' test for equal variances indicated less than a .10 probability of equal variances, the t-statistics were computed under the assumption of unequal variances. A t-test also assumes the variables being compared are normally distributed. Tests for skewness and kurtosis indicate that the justices' scores are approximately normally distributed except for those justices scoring far above or below the mean justice, for whom a mean substantially different from the norm can safely be presumed.

Justice Burger and Justice Thomas, score below the mean for the pre-1967 period at the .0001 level.

The last two lines of Table 4.4 show the group comparisons. As a group, the thirteen post-1967 appointees (and the nine justices sitting in 1999) cannot be statistically distinguished from the pre-Marshall justices, although their mean ratings are slightly higher than that of the earlier group (2.56 and 2.58 versus 2.43 for the earlier era).

The conclusion that the recent justices are of comparable average quality to the nonrecent does not appear to depend on where we draw the line between the two groups. The recent appointees as a whole are statistically indistinguishable from the earlier appointees if, following Stephen Carter, we define as recent those justices beginning with the first justice appointed after *Brown v. Board of Education* (John Marshall Harlan II), when scrutiny of nominees' views on civil rights became prevalent. The mean scores are 2.41 for the pre-*Brown* appointees, 2.55 for the post-*Brown*. The *t*-test for different means yields a *t*-statistic of 0.67 and a probability value of .5082, clearly implying no statistically distinguishable difference in the means. The same is true if we regard Burger's very quick and easy confirmation as placing his appointment in an earlier era, and compare the appointees starting with the first post-Burger justice (Harry Blackmun) with their predecessors. The post-Burger group has a mean of 2.61, their predecessors a mean of 2.42; the *t*-statistic equals 1.11, and the probability value equals .2730. The difference in the means would be smaller, and the difference between them even less significant if, for some reason, one chose to consider as recent those appointees beginning with and including Burger, whose low score lowers the mean of the recent group.[24]

Clearly, the evaluations for Burger and Thomas, which lie far below those of any other recent justice, are a major drag on the recent justices in group comparisons. Without them, the recent justices as a group compare favorably, though not spectacularly, against their average twentieth-century predecessor. If we remove Chief Justice Burger and Justice Thomas from these comparisons, the post-1967 appointees are statistically distinguishable from the mean of the earlier group at the .04 confidence level (*t*-statistic = 2.12; pr = .0401), whereas the justices sitting in 1999—minus Thomas—score above the mean of the pre-1967 group at the .05 level (*t* = 2.03; pr = .0489). Even with Burger and Thomas, however, there is no support here for any claim that the modern confirmation process has contributed to an overall less capable Court than in the past. The discussion section comprising the last part of this chapter addresses the question of whether characteristics of the confirmation process could be faulted—assuming there is any fault—for the confirmation of Burger, and leads to a detailed examination of the same question for the almost universally condemned confirmation process for Thomas.

It bears repeating that one must approach these results with caution. Our respondents may have underrated the lesser known justices of the first half of the century, thereby pulling down the mean for the earlier group. Or they may have underrated those recent justices who will someday be recognized as great or nearly so. It is also worth noting that on the basis of these results, we cannot rule out the subtler Schultz-Silverstein hypothesis that the modern confirmation process impedes the appointment not of able figures, but of nominees with special qualities that make for judicial greatness, a hypothesis examined in greater detail in the final section of this chapter.

Comparisons Against the Mean of All Justices

Table 4.5 compares the rating for each appointee of the twentieth century with the mean of all such appointees (which is 2.46). Once again, a positive (negative) t-statistic indicates a justice who scored above (below) the mean. The two-tailed probability values in the last column give the probability that the mean score for a justice is not significantly different from the mean of the whole century.

Most of the post-1967 appointees fare well in this comparison. Seven of the thirteen (Marshall, Powell, Stevens, Scalia, Souter, Ginsburg, and Breyer) score above the mean for all justices at the .05 level, and Rehnquist does so at the .10 level (pr = .0761). Burger and Thomas are again notable for their low evaluations.

Group comparisons are in the last two lines of Table 4.5. The means for all the post-1967 appointees (2.56) and for those sitting in 1999 (2.58) are not statistically distinguishable from the mean of the whole century (2.46). Minus Burger and Thomas, the post-1967 appointees and those sitting in 1999 score above the mean for the century at the .03 level (.0213 and .0302, respectively). Again, there is no evidence here that the recent justices are not as good overall as those of earlier eras, nor any evidence that any of them possesses judicial greatness.

Rating Recent Nominations

Finally, the survey asked respondents to rate the qualifications of the justices sitting in 1999 as they appeared at the time of their nominations. Possible responses of excellent, good, fair, poor, and unacceptable were assigned val-

Table 4.5. Individual Ratings Against the Mean of All Justices

Justice	Mean	t-statistic[a]	pr > [t]
Holmes	3.78	12.16	.0001
Day	1.97	−3.70	.0003
Moody	1.85	−4.45	.0001
Lurton	1.58	−6.11	.0001
Hughes	3.44	9.01	.0001
Ed. White	2.52	0.48	.6298
VanDevanter	1.74	−5.03	.0001
Lamar	1.74	−5.19	.0001
Pitney	1.70	−5.37	.0001
McReynolds	1.16	−8.76	.0001
Brandeis	3.79	12.20	.0001
Clarke	2.00	−3.09	.0025
Taft	2.89	3.55	.0005
Sutherland	2.60	1.02	.3118
Butler	1.68	−5.80	.0001
Sanford	1.77	−5.37	.0001
Stone	3.37	7.93	.0001
Roberts	2.29	−1.96	.0513
Cardozo	3.52	9.28	.0001
Black	3.50	9.47	.0001
Reed	1.98	−3.98	.0002
Frankfurter	3.27	6.41	.0001
Douglas	2.90	3.16	.0020
Murphy	2.63	1.21	.2270
Byrnes	1.23	−8.59	.0001
Jackson	3.35	8.29	.0001
Rutledge	2.43	−0.27	.7878
Burton	1.81	−5.49	.0001
Vinson	1.69	−6.31	.0001
Clark	2.10	−3.02	.0029
Minton	1.43	−8.20	.0001
Warren	3.47	7.53	.0001
Harlan	3.55	9.77	.0001
Brennan	3.56	8.53	.0001
Whittaker	1.11	−9.75	.0001
Stewart	2.55	0.87	.3880
B. White	2.45	−0.11	.9109
Goldberg	2.21	−1.83	.0695
Fortas	2.25	−1.48	.1421
Marshall	2.74	2.09	.0384
Burger	1.84	−5.10	.0001
Blackmun	2.66	1.45	.1501
Powell	2.78	2.57	.0109
Rehnquist	2.71	1.78	.0761
Stevens	2.78	2.45	.0152
O'Connor	2.60	1.22	.2252
Scalia	2.80	2.46	.0151
Kennedy	2.43	−0.27	.7859
Souter	2.79	2.59	.0110
Thomas	1.57	−6.31	.0001
Ginsburg	2.79	2.88	.0045
Breyer	2.76	2.64	.0092
All	2.46	…	…
Post-1967 Justices	2.56	0.65	.5220
Justices in 1999	2.58	0.72	.4802

[a] For those comparisons where an F' test for equal variances indicated less than a .10 probability of equal variances, the t-tests assume unequal variances.

Table 4.6. Ratings of Nominations of Justices Sitting in 1999

Justice	Mean	SD	n
Rehnquist (1971)	2.31	0.93	121
Rehnquist (1986)	2.74	1.07	125
Stevens	2.97	0.70	115
O'Connor	2.41	0.65	124
Scalia	3.14	0.92	124
Kennedy	2.66	0.76	124
Souter	2.28	0.77	127
Thomas	1.14	0.93	127
Ginsburg	3.29	0.71	126
Breyer	3.14	0.77	124
All nominations	2.61	0.63	10

ues of 4, 3, 2, 1, and 0, respectively. The results appear in Table 4.6. The nominations of all of these justices average 2.61.

For the justices in 1999, there is considerably more variation in their ratings as nominees than as justices. Thomas's rating as a nominee, 1.14, is substantially below his 1.57 rating as a justice. Three of the ten nominations (the two Rehnquist nominations count separately) rate above 3.0 and thereby qualify as somewhat better than good: those for Scalia, Ginsburg, and Breyer.

Evaluation of these results depends on the answer to a difficult question: How good, according to a sample of scholars, should a Supreme Court nominee be? The most one can say is that the overall rating of 2.61 places the average nominee a little closer to good than to fair; without Justice Thomas, the average of the justices sitting in 1999 is 2.77, which is much closer to good than to fair. Because scholars likely hold up high standards for nominees to the U.S. Supreme Court, these ratings (minus Thomas), like those presented above, can fairly be labeled solid, though not spectacular.

DISCUSSION

The preceding analyses provide no evidence that the justices appointed since 1967 are any less capable on the whole than those appointed earlier in the twentieth century. The data lean toward the opposite conclusion: six of the thirteen justices appointed since 1967 rate higher than their average twentieth-century predecessor at the .05 confidence level and two do so at the .10 level, while two others rank far below the mean of the pre-1967 period.

Nor is there evidence of judicial greatness among recent appointees. The highest-rated post-1967 appointee, Antonin Scalia, received a mean rating of 2.80 (with a very high standard deviation, indicating a wide divergence of scholarly—and probably political—opinions about him). This score places him far below the ranks of the eleven twentieth-century justices ranked as great or near great in other surveys. (Felix Frankfurter, the lowest rated among these eleven, received a score of 3.27.)

The low ratings of Burger and Thomas in our survey raise the question of whether the Senate deserves reproach for their confirmations. Burger ranks thirty-ninth among the fifty-two justices in the survey, placing him just above the bottom quartile—a rather low but not abysmal rating. In a number of respects, Burger was a strong nominee. He was an experienced and dedicated jurist with a keen interest in administrative reform of the courts. After practicing law privately for twenty-two years, during which he argued nearly a dozen cases before the Supreme Court and taught law part-time at the night law school from which he had graduated magna cum laude, Burger served for three years as assistant attorney general in the Eisenhower Administration. He spent the next thirteen years on the Court of Appeals for the District of Columbia Circuit, where he established a reputation for hard work, interest in judicial reform, conservatism on criminal justice issues, and general moderation in other areas (a pattern he would repeat as chief justice).[25]

Burger's poor showing in the survey may result in part from his lackluster performance of the tasks required of a chief justice, which are more extensive and more difficult than those of an associate justice. Had he been an associate justice, his rating would likely have been higher. But he was not an associate justice, and it is fair to evaluate the confirmation process based on its capacity to produce chief justices with the special qualities required in that post. High among these is the ability to lead and elicit respect from a collection of intelligent and strong-minded colleagues of varying jurisprudential persuasions and, if not to unify and marshal the Court, at least to contain to some degree the Court's inevitable internecine struggles.

Burger's mediocre performance—some would say failure—at these tasks was foreseeable. Although the *New York Times* reported that nominee Burger was "invariably characterized as 'competent' rather than 'brilliant,'" some of his colleagues on the Court of Appeals—most if not all of them his liberal adversaries—reportedly thought him "unsuited by talent" for the chief justiceship.[26] Burger also had experienced—and to some extent engendered—poor personal relationships and a reported "mutual disrespect" between him and some colleagues.[27]

The Senate's almost cursory review of Burger might be faulted for not examining these matters. Liberal senators were not, however, about to fault him for being a law-and-order nominee or for lacking the intellectual or personal skills needed to marshal the Court in a conservative direction. Those senators do not deserve blame for failing to insist on a nominee who would lead the Court to what they considered the wrong outcomes. And any senators inclined to question Burger's legal competence and interpersonal skills would have faced an ugly, uphill struggle. Readily available witnesses supporting Burger's fitness on these criteria (including at least eight past presidents of the American Bar Association) would have undercut any opposition to the nomination.[28] Liberal interest groups met the Burger nomination with quiescence. The American Bar Association Standing Committee on the Federal Judiciary unanimously gave the nominee its highest rating: "highly acceptable from the viewpoint of professional qualifications" (without addressing any broader criteria).[29] And most of the criticisms of Burger came from his longtime ideological adversaries on the Court of Appeals, whose views were suspect. Considering the substantial evidence that Burger would be at least a competent justice of only moderate conservatism—President Richard Nixon was not going to nominate a liberal—there was little reason or opportunity for potential opponents of the nomination to mobilize. The only route to the appointment of a more illustrious chief justice would have been the nomination of one by the president.

The extraordinary confirmation battle over Clarence Thomas cannot be analyzed in detail in this space. One conclusion is clear, however: Thomas's nomination does not support the claim that the glaring scrutiny directed at modern Supreme Court nominees discourages presidents from nominating high-profile, politically controversial figures. Thomas was not nominated because nominations receive glaring scrutiny. Indeed, as the many chronicles of his nomination by the first President Bush amply demonstrate, Thomas was nominated despite that reality, as a result of his controversial record as a civil rights enforcer in the Reagan Administration, his record of extreme conservatism, and his questionable personal ethics (even before anyone had heard of Anita Hill).[30]

There is, moreover, empirical evidence that strong "objective" qualifications for a justiceship raise the probability of a favorable vote from senators skeptical of a nominee.[31] Thomas's nomination could only have been helped had he demonstrated a level of professional distinction more like that of President Bill Clinton's two widely acclaimed and easily confirmed nominees, Ruth Bader Ginsburg and Stephen Breyer.

On the basis of the survey results reported here, we cannot rule out the Schultz-Silverstein claim that the modern confirmation process, while not favoring incompetence, screens out especially prominent figures whose special vision and abilities make for judicial greatness.[32] The generally solid but not outstanding ratings of most recent justices might be seen to confirm that hypothesis. Common sense suggests that the ideological polarization and divided government prevalent since the late 1960s may often necessitate, in Silverstein's words, the appointment of "experienced, competent, noncontroversial jurists with a restrained understanding of the role of the federal judiciary"[33] rather than prominent, innovative legal thinkers with a talent for selling their constitutional visions to Court and country.

To the extent this is true, it is not necessarily cause for despair. Although disputes over federalism and civil rights and liberties are almost certainly perpetual, these divisions need not always be as deep as they have been from the late 1960s to the early twenty-first century. Excepting the momentous battle over de jure segregation, the nation was not so deeply fractured between the late 1930s and the 1960s. Periods of relative constitutional unity may recur. It is also possible, as noted in the introduction to this chapter, that "experienced, competent noncontroversial jurists with a restrained understanding of the role of the federal judiciary"—even if they are less keenly intellectual than other potential nominees with more divisive worldviews—are desirable at a time of ideological polarization, or at any time.

In any case, the Schultz-Silverstein hypothesis is as yet unproved. Not surprisingly, given the incomplete careers of sitting justices and the lack of historical perspective inherent in evaluating all recent justices, lists of great justices tend to exclude current and other recent justices from the ranks of the great. Nine of thirteen such lists that have appeared since 1928 listed no current justices among the greats—studies that appeared during the tenures of such figures as Oliver Wendell Holmes Jr., Louis Brandeis, Harlan Fiske Stone, Felix Frankfurter, Hugo Black, Robert Jackson, Earl Warren, John Marshall Harlan II, and William Brennan.[34] Two of the thirteen lists include two incumbents: Hugo Black and William O. Douglas, both identified as great in two 1970 and 1971 studies, after they had both served on the Court more than thirty years.[35] And two other lists identify only one incumbent as great. One of them was William H. Rehnquist, rated by a sample of attorneys in 1991.[36] The ultimate test of whether modern confirmation politics discourages the appointment of great justices can only take place when students of the Court can evaluate the full careers of the late twentieth-century justices, and the constitutional doctrines they fashioned, within a complete historical context.

In the interim, there are other reasons to doubt the Schultz-Silverstein hypothesis. Consider the three appointees of the 1950s who now, according to this survey, rank among the greatest justices of the twentieth century: Earl Warren, John Marshall Harlan II, and William Brennan. A cautious judicial conservative such as Harlan could be nominated and easily confirmed today. Harlan is the sort of safe figure the modern process would favor under that hypothesis. Likewise, the jurisprudential vision and special qualities of Warren and Brennan were unknown and probably unknowable at the time of their nominations. Although Warren's progressivism was no secret, he had also compiled a record as a tough district attorney and had supported the internment of Japanese Americans during World War II.[37] Brennan's views were largely unknown; his nomination was based on President Dwight Eisenhower's election-year desire to nominate a relatively young Catholic judge with bipartisan appeal and state-court experience (Brennan was a fifty-year-old Catholic Democrat on the New Jersey Supreme Court).[38] Similarly hidden qualities probably could not be detected and used to block the appointment of similar figures today. At a minimum, no one could have confidently predicted Warren and Brennan's future contributions. Their nominator, President Eisenhower, certainly did not predict them. These justices are evidence for Paul Freund's observation that "historical happenstance and unpredictable senatorial reaction have led to some of our finest Justices."[39]

Nor are the conditions for the appointment of great justices invariably absent in the modern context. In 1986, the Senate unanimously confirmed a nominee who seemed to possess all the requirements for judicial greatness. Antonin Scalia possessed a distinctive—and controversial—constitutional vision, a widespread "reputation for intellectual brilliance,"[40] and, in the words of one Democratic senator, a seemingly "congenial personality" and persuasive ability that might "assist the other judges on the Court . . . in arriving at a consensus."[41]

By most accounts, Scalia has lived up to his reputation for a first-rate intellect, as reflected by his relatively high rating in this survey. But his often acerbic written opinions and propensity to alienate his colleagues have left him unable to lead anyone on the Court, with the possible exception of Justice Thomas.[42] Whatever history's ultimate verdict on him, Scalia was a genuine prospect for judicial greatness when the Senate confirmed his nomination.

Similarly, Justice Ruth Bader Ginsburg, whose 1993 nomination received the highest rating in the survey (3.29), arrived at the Court after a career so remarkable as an advocate of legal equality for women that some observers had dubbed her "the Thurgood Marshall of gender discrimination law."[43] In her testimony before the Senate Judiciary Committee, she passionately defended a woman's right to abortion, the hot-button constitutional issue of the late twentieth century, and still won confirmation overwhelmingly. She was certainly one of the most illustrious nominees President Clinton could have put forward, quite possibly the closest he could have come to a nominee, as Silverstein has put it, "with the legendary experience of a Brandeis or a Marshall."[44]

Scholars who regard possession of a new paradigmatic vision as a necessary characteristic of a great justice might point out that Ginsburg was nonetheless a safe choice because Ginsburg—who had graduated tied for first in her class at Columbia Law School and later taught there—had earned a reputation for judicial restraint in her thirteen years on the federal Court of Appeals for the District of Columbia. But if a progressive conservative such as John Marshall Harlan II could earn a place among the Court's great justices, so could a gifted, judicially conservative progressive such as Ginsburg. However history may judge her, she also was a candidate for judicial greatness at the time of her appointment.

And as the examples of Warren and Brennan illustrate, it is hard to predict from where greatness will emanate. Justice David Souter, whose nomination received the second-lowest rating in Table 4.6 and gave rise to the sobriquet "stealth nominee," is virtually tied with Justice Scalia as the top-rated sitting justice in our survey, with a mean score of 2.792, versus Scalia's 2.802. Souter's reputation as an unusually thoughtful, scholarly figure has clearly risen since his nomination; the relatively high standard deviation of his ratings by our respondents (0.89 in Table 4.1) may result in part from ideological sentiments arising from his acknowledged status as an intellectual leader of the Court's current "liberal" bloc.[45]

It bears repeating that conclusions derived from this survey must be qualified by caveats arising from the inherent difficulties of asking contemporary observers to rate the justices of a century ago and those of the present. But those difficulties can cut two ways, as discussed above. The respondents may have underrated some of the lesser known earlier justices, dragging down the mean for that group. Or they may have underrated recent justices who will someday, but do not yet, rank among the Court's greats or near greats. For now, we can safely conclude that the data presented in this survey do not support the more far-reaching claims of "a Court of mediocrity."[46] The verdict is still out on the more qualified claim that the modern confirmation process will produce fewer great justices than in the past.

Any analysis of the confirmation process and the quality of contemporary justices would be incomplete, however, without further discussion of the tumultuous confirmation of the one recent justice whose rating in the survey places him among the worst justices of the last century: Clarence Thomas.

5
The Confirmation of Clarence Thomas

Whether Justice Thomas truly deserves his poor ranking, his confirmation warrants close scrutiny in any evaluation of the confirmation process. Thomas's professional qualifications were slim, his politics were increasingly extreme during his years as chairman of the Equal Employment Opportunity Commission (EEOC) from 1982 to 1990, and his judicial temperament and personal character were questionable. His confirmation proceedings left everyone—supporters, opponents, and the general public—dismayed. In a Gallup poll taken immediately after the Senate hearings on Anita Hill's charges of sexual harassment against Thomas, 48 percent of respondents reported having "less confidence" in Congress as a result of the hearings; only 21 percent reported having "more confidence." Respondents replied similarly to a question about confidence in "the nomination process for the Supreme Court."[1] The percentage of Americans expressing "a great deal" or "quite a lot" of confidence in the Supreme Court itself fell from 48 percent before the Thomas nomination to 39 percent during the Hill hearings (its lowest level since Gallup first asked the question in 1973), but rebounded to its pre-Thomas levels by 1997.[2]

This chapter examines the roles played in Justice Thomas's appointment by the principals in the process: President George H. W. Bush; Senator Joseph Biden, the Democratic chairman of the Senate Judiciary Committee; other Democrats on the committee; Thomas himself; Senator John Danforth, Republican of Missouri (Thomas's principal political patron); Republicans on the Judiciary Committee; and Professor Anita Hill, who brought charges of sexual harassment against Thomas.

A brief preview of the conclusions reached in this chapter is appropriate as a guide to what follows. First, some aspects of Thomas's confirmation appear to validate frequent criticisms of the confirmation process. But most of these features of his confirmation were unique to his case. Second, any examination of sexual harassment charges against a nominee who denies them will inevitably prove ugly. Third, several seemingly regrettable senatorial decisions and behaviors, especially in the hearings on Hill's charges, were, upon closer inspection, at least justifiable under the circumstances. Fourth, those decisions and behaviors that were not defensible were failures of character and judgment by the persons in the process much more than failures of the process per se. Last, and unlike any appointment since Thurgood Marshall's in 1967, the politics of race pervaded every stage of Thomas's appointment to the Supreme Court and ultimately overwhelmed all other factors.

PRESIDENT GEORGE H. W. BUSH

When Justice Marshall retired in 1991, President Bush faced heavy pressure to nominate a Republican conservative. He chose Thomas despite warnings from Senate Democrats, going back to Thomas's confirmation as a federal Appeals Court judge the year before, that Thomas would face heavy going if nominated for the Supreme Court.[3] The White House reckoned that civil rights groups and their liberal allies would balk at opposing a conservative black nominee. Yet the president publicly denied that Thomas's race was a factor in his nomination.[4] As the following pages show, the president had chosen a nominee with enormous liabilities.

The Nominee's Qualifications

At age forty-three, and with only five years of law practice and sixteen months as a federal judge, Thomas was one of the youngest and least experienced nominees in a century. The president's claim that he had selected Thomas solely on merit was universally disbelieved.[5] Twelve members of the American Bar Association Standing Committee on the Federal Judiciary found Thomas "qualified" for a justiceship, two found him "unqualified," and one abstained; none found him "well qualified," the committee's highest rating. The committee had never rated a Supreme Court nominee this low.[6] The majority of twelve praised Thomas's eighteen Appeals Court opinions, in which he had demonstrated legal acumen and writing skills "well within the zone of competence" for the Supreme Court.[7] But they criticized Thomas's several law review articles for displaying "little analysis . . . and, in part, rely[ing] upon an undefined reference to 'natural law,'" a philosophical construct Thomas had often defended. ABA "Reading Committees" found these articles "disappointing in presentation, content and scholarship."[8] The majority of twelve concluded that Thomas's performance on the Court of Appeals outweighed concerns about his scholarship and inexperience.[9]

A Political History

The president could hardly have chosen a more provocative nominee. Thomas had a ten-year history of increasingly controversial political remarks and bitter conflicts with Congress, civil rights groups, and senior citizens groups over his alleged failures to enforce civil rights laws during his one year as Assistant Secretary of Education for Civil Rights (1981–82) and eight years as chairman of the EEOC (1982–90).

At the Department of Education and the EEOC, Thomas had:

- Raised the ire of a federal judge who openly doubted that Thomas's office was making a "good-faith effort to comply" with a court order requiring faster processing of civil rights claims (Thomas later portrayed the judge's position very differently).[10]
- Moved civil rights enforcement away from broad-based remedies such as class-action lawsuits and affirmative action (from which he himself had benefited),[11] although early in his tenure at the EEOC, Thomas had in some cases endorsed race-conscious policies such as affirmative action.[12]
- Publicly "hoped" that Justice Antonin Scalia's dissent to a pro–affirmative action ruling would "provide guidance for lower courts."[13]
- Misinformed Congress (deliberately, said Democrats) about the EEOC's failure to investigate thousands of complaints of age discrimination (Congress twice had to extend the statute of limitations on the complaints to keep them from lapsing).[14]
- Offered "no excuses" for the lapsed age discrimination claims while placing the blame entirely on EEOC district managers and cuts in his agency's budget.[15]
- Failed to repeal an admittedly erroneous rule allowing discrimination against older workers in pension plans, a failure that one federal judge called "at best slothful" and "at worst deceptive to the public" because

of the EEOC's "repeated false assurances" that it would fix the problem.[16]

- Issued rules limiting the right of workers pressed into early retirement to sue for age discrimination—rules Congress quickly suspended and later repealed permanently.[17]
- Resisted congressional oversight of his agency and questioned the legitimacy of the congressional oversight function.[18]
- Attempted to punish one or more EEOC managers who criticized him publicly (a federal judge who blocked Thomas's attempted transfer of one such employee compared Thomas's vindictiveness to that of J. Edgar Hoover).[19]
- Repeatedly blamed Congress for his agency's problems, in one instance calling Congress "an enormous obstacle to the positive enforcement of civil rights laws."[20]
- Suggested that there was no need for several cabinet departments or the EEOC, whose mission is to investigate complaints of job discrimination.[21]
- Criticized the pending Family and Medical Leave Act.[22]
- Signed a Reagan Administration report advocating the reversal of *Roe v. Wade* (Thomas later claimed that he had not read the relevant section of the report).[23]

Thomas's actions as EEOC head so angered congressional Democrats that when Thomas was mentioned as a possible nominee for the federal Court of Appeals in Washington in 1989, fourteen House Democrats, most with oversight responsibilities for the EEOC, wrote President George H. W. Bush to accuse Thomas of "undermining" the civil rights laws while simultaneously misleading Congress and the public. They accused Thomas of "an overall disdain for the rule of law," a charge eleven of them repeated after Bush sent Thomas's nomination to the Senate.[24] At his Supreme Court hearings, members of the Congressional Black Caucus likewise called Thomas "a lawless administrator" who displayed "great contempt for the law."[25]

On the conservative lecture circuit and in articles and interviews in his second term at EEOC (1986–1990), Thomas had provided abundant evidence of increasingly extreme political views and his seemingly injudicious temperament. Thomas had:

- Called for "an activist Supreme Court, which would strike down laws restricting property rights,"[26] such as environmental regulations and, in particular, the minimum wage, which he labeled an "outright denial of economic liberty."[27]

- Stated that "economic rights are protected as much as any other rights,"[28] a proposition rejected by the Supreme Court since the New Deal.
- Called for a constitutional jurisprudence based on a vague "natural law," which for Thomas meant "the liberation of commerce"[29] from government regulation and, Democrats feared, a right to life for the unborn and other conservative beliefs.[30]
- Praised an antiabortion article as a "splendid example"[31] of applying natural law.
- Championed executive over legislative power.[32]
- Applauded Colonel Oliver North, who had funneled money illegally from Iranian arms sales to Nicaraguan anticommunist rebels, and was later convicted of obstructing the investigation of the scandal (Thomas told one conservative audience that *"Ollie North made perfectly clear . . . it is Congress* [and not North] *that is out of control!*).["]33
- Attacked congressional Democrats in a series of caustic speeches, accusing them of public posturing and hypocrisy.[34]
- Suggested that women and minorities disproportionately hold low-wage jobs because they choose to.[35]
- Wrote that "random chance" helps explain disparities in hiring and income between racial groups and discrimination does not.[36]
- Attacked the leaders of the major civil rights groups, whom he called "childish" and "our enemies."[37]
- Likened affirmative action to apartheid.[38]
- Alluded to the Ninth Amendment, which states that Americans may have rights not listed in the Constitution, as a judicial "invention" that "plays into the hands of those who advocate a total state."[39]
- Expressed his admiration for the controversial Nation of Islam leader Louis Farrakhan.[40]
- Declared that unnamed "demagogues . . . hope to harness the anger of the so-called under class" to advance "a political agenda that resembles the crude totalitarianism of contemporary socialist states" (which at the time included the Soviet Union).[41]
- Claimed that "the leftist exploitation of poor black people . . . is simply a means to advance the principle that the rights and freedoms of *all* should be cast aside."[42]
- Charged that those who favor redistribution of wealth—which he called "the very definition of slavery"[43]—are really attacking "hard work, intelligence, and purposefulness."[44]

- Charged that "critics of 'the rich' really do mean to destroy people like my grandfather [who had worked hard to build a successful small business in segregated Georgia], and declare his manliness to be foolishness and wasted effort."[45]
- Told an audience at the libertarian Cato Institute that he "agree[d] wholeheartedly" with former Treasury Secretary William Simon's statement that America was "careening with frightening speed toward collectivism and away from free individual sovereignty, toward coercive, centralized planning and away from free individual choices, toward a statist, dictatorial system and away from a nation in which individual liberty is sacred."[46]

Thomas had also served for eleven years on the editorial board of the *Lincoln Review,* an ultraconservative African American journal edited by an acknowledged friend of Thomas who lobbied for the white supremacist government of South Africa.[47] Many of the *Review*'s articles merely celebrated capitalism and emphasized black self-help. Others were undeniably extreme. A 1990 *Review* article suggested that blacks would have more jobs if employers could pay them less than whites.[48] A 1983 article described abortion as an "attempt to judicially slaughter the poverty class"—particularly blacks— and compared Justices William Brennan and Thurgood Marshall, supporters of abortion rights, to "the 'Kapos' recruited among the Jewish prisoners in the death camps to carry out exterminations."[49] In 1986, the *Review* gave a favorable review to a book that characterized atheists as forerunners of the Antichrist.[50]

When the press reported Thomas's continued association with the *Review* after his nomination to the Supreme Court, the White House portrayed his involvement as divorced from the *Review*'s content. A spokeswoman said the *Review*'s editor had failed to remove Thomas's name from its masthead, as Thomas had requested when he became a federal judge the year before.[51] One cannot assume that Thomas agreed with all of the *Review*'s content. But he was undoubtedly sympathetic to much of it, given his membership on its board, his own writings in it,[52] his conservatism, his emphasis on black self-help, and his friendship with the *Review*'s editor, Jay Parker.[53]

Questions of Ethics

Thomas's actions as a federal Appeals Court judge raised questions about his judicial ethics. Thomas had written the opinion for a unanimous court that overturned a $10 million damage award against the Ralston-Purina compa-

ny, the source of a multimillion-dollar fortune held by Thomas's chief political patron, Senator John Danforth of Missouri. Legal ethicists disagreed
about whether Thomas had committed a violation.[54] Thomas had also voted
with the majority of the Appeals Court to deny the Iran-Contra special prosecutor's motion for a rehearing of an earlier ruling overturning the criminal
convictions of Oliver North, whose defiance of Congress Thomas had
praised.[55] Finally, Thomas's continued service on the editorial board of the
Lincoln Review after becoming a federal judge in 1990 may have violated
strictures that require judges to avoid activities suggesting a lack of impartiality or judicial temperament.[56]

The Pin Point Strategy

Together with conservative groups and the nominee, the Bush Administration
implemented the "Pin Point strategy," a confirmation strategy that emphasized Thomas's climb up from poverty and segregation in his birthplace of
Pin Point, Georgia, and portrayed him as sympathetic to the disadvantaged.
The strategy aimed to paralyze or split the civil rights community and its
white allies, and divert attention from Thomas's record, beliefs, and qualifications.[57]

The extensive and sophisticated plan involved radio ads, talk shows, ads
in black publications, staged events such as the busing of people from Pin
Point to Washington to appear with Thomas, published photos of the nominee with the nuns who had taught him at his Catholic elementary school, and
calls or visits with prominent blacks such as Vernon Jordan, the former head
of the Urban League and an influential Democrat, who offered Thomas
advice on winning confirmation, and John Johnson, publisher of *Ebony* and
Jet magazines, who placed a flattering cover story emphasizing Thomas's
rise from poverty on the cover of *Jet*.[58] Thomas's record as an antidiscrimination enforcer and his extraordinary political pronouncements were glossed
over in the process.

The White House and the Sexual Harassment Charges

When Anita Hill's charges of sexual harassment reached the White House,
officials sought to suppress the news. After the story broke, White House
aides told reporters that they had "determined that the allegation was
unfounded" on the basis of the FBI report on Hill's charges—although the
report, which refrained from drawing any conclusions, contained a partial
corroboration of Hill's charges from Susan Hoerchner, a California adminis-

trative law judge and law school classmate and confidante of Hill's.[59] Privately, administration officials argued over whether Thomas should deny all the charges or issue a partial admission, an argument that reflected concern for the nominee's confirmation rather than for the truth.[60]

President Bush told the press that he was "not in the least" concerned about the charges, which the White House labeled a "smear."[61] But there was great concern in the office of the White House Counsel, which undertook immediately to find information to discredit Hill.[62] A few days later, when another former female employee of Thomas's, Angela Wright, made her own claim of improper sexual attentions against Thomas, the White House immediately dismissed Wright, whom Thomas had fired at the EEOC, as "the classic disgruntled employee."[63]

After Thomas's 52–48 confirmation on October 15, the White House sought an expedited swearing-in ceremony, fearing that more charges or evidence of Thomas's personal misbehavior might surface. But the death of Chief Justice Rehnquist's wife intervened. On October 23, the day after Mrs. Rehnquist's funeral, Thomas asked Rehnquist to swear him in that day. Rehnquist did so in a private ceremony. A Court spokeswoman said that Thomas sought the early investiture mainly to get his staff on the Court's payroll, although most of them were Thomas's Appeals Court aides and already on the payroll of that court.[64]

CLARENCE THOMAS

At his confirmation hearings, Thomas, as he later acknowledged,[65] ran from his record. He repeatedly professed his candor while he downplayed or disavowed his previous statements on property rights, natural law, affirmative action, congressional oversight, the Ninth Amendment, civil rights leaders, Oliver North, the right to privacy, the need for entitlement programs, the underrepresentation of women and minorities in the professions, the Supreme Court's rulings on voting rights, the constitutionality of the special prosecutor law, his caustic denunciations of Congress, and the purported proliferation of rights he had criticized, including children's rights.[66]

Several times, Thomas explained that he did not mean what he had said.[67] More than a dozen times, he assured senators that he had made his many controversial pronouncements as a policy "advocate" in the executive branch; when he joined the judiciary in 1990, he had "stripped" himself of his ardent beliefs and adopted a judicial neutrality that precluded him from making policy.[68] In a famous exchange with Democratic Senator Patrick

Leahy, Thomas denied ever having or expressing an opinion on *Roe v. Wade*. He also implied that he had not thought much about the case, although he agreed it was "one of the most important" and controversial cases in decades.[69] Thomas also denied knowing that his admittedly good friend, Jay Parker, was a lobbyist for South Africa. Parker, however, claimed he had shared this information with Thomas in 1981. And one or more anonymous EEOC staffers told the press that Thomas had discussed Parker's South African lobbying at the EEOC in the mid-1980s.[70]

After his confirmation, Thomas acknowledged that despite his repeated professions of candor, he had hidden his beliefs under oath to win confirmation: the confirmation process, he claimed, "forces you to dilute the edges you've had on prior statements. . . . [T]he country had never seen the real person. . . . I had pretended in the first hearing."[71] Thomas did more than "dilute the edges" of his beliefs, and his obfuscations were not as successful as some accounts of his confirmation suggest.[72] Senators loath to question his professional competence openly questioned the honesty of his testimony, citing to his face the "complete repudiation of your past record" and "the vanishing views of Judge Thomas." Senator Howell Heflin publicly questioned whether Thomas's apparent "confirmation conversion" reflected a lack of "integrity." Even Republican Arlen Specter told the nominee that his testimony was irreconcilable with his previous statements.[73] Nor did senators believe that this previously opinionated nominee would eschew policy making as a justice.[74]

In the hearings on Anita Hill's charges of sexual harassment, Thomas subtly undermined Hill's character and insinuated ignoble motives for her testimony, while seeming high-minded by simultaneously expressing his disbelief in these motives and his unconcern with her purported character flaws. Thomas described Hill as "aggressive, strong, and forceful" in advancing her policy views at the EEOC. She was also a "somewhat distant and perhaps aloof" figure who, because she was "young," occasionally caused "problems" by "taking a firm position and being unyielding . . . and then storming off or throwing a temper tantrum." But, he claimed, "I didn't see that as a character flaw or vindictiveness."[75]

Thomas also suggested that Hill was professionally frustrated and jealous of coworkers at the EEOC, where "she was no longer my top assistant [as she had been at the Department of Education] . . . and certainly not the most senior and not the one who received the better assignments." He described Hill as disappointed when he passed her over for promotion. But, he said, "that doesn't seem to be too much of a basis for her being angry with me," thereby suggesting that she was petty and he was unsuspecting.[76]

Thomas also testified that a former aide at the EEOC had once told him that Hill was his "enemy." He told senators that "loyalty" had been "very important" to him, but he had nonetheless dismissed this warning,[77] thereby portraying himself as a guileless and betrayed figure.

Like his supporters on the Judiciary Committee, Thomas referred to Hill's charges as "uncorroborated," although the news media had reported the existence of witnesses who would testify that Hill told them of the alleged harassment years earlier. He also characterized Hill as his only accuser, although the media had similarly reported on Angela Wright's claims and her expected testimony.[78] In a line of questioning planned in advance with Senator Orrin Hatch, Thomas characterized Hill's charges as resting on racial stereotypes. He thereby sought to discredit the accusations and present himself as the archetypal black victim, as he did with his repeated claim that the Judiciary Committee was "lynching" him.[79]

SENATOR JOSEPH BIDEN

By all accounts, Senator Joseph Biden, chairman of the Judiciary Committee, labored to be fair to the Republicans and their nominees.[80] In contrast to the White House, which worked with conservative groups to promote Thomas's nomination, Biden, a liberal Democrat, had refused to work with liberal groups since he was criticized for doing so in opposition to the Bork nomination in 1987.[81]

In the first round of hearings, Biden aided Thomas in several ways. Before the hearings opened, Biden ruled out any investigation of reports that Thomas, as EEOC head, used public funds for more than twenty trips that appeared to be largely personal in nature. These trips included thirteen trips to St. Louis, where Thomas lived before moving to Washington, five trips to his hometown of Savannah, several trips on which he gave some of his most controversial speeches, and three trips that included visits to a California child welfare agency chaired by Nancy Reagan. The head of the EEOC's Boston office was willing, if subpoenaed, to testify that Thomas conducted no agency business on a trip there, but Biden refused to issue the subpoena.[82] When several witnesses at the hearings—mostly African Americans—questioned Thomas's qualifications for a justiceship, Biden suggested that they were holding Thomas to a higher standard than other recent nominees.[83] Biden also suggested that Thomas did not intend to endorse an antiabortion article when he called it "a splendid example of applying natural law."[84]

The Sexual Harassment Charges

Biden's staff told him of Hill's charges on Thursday, September 12—the third day of the first round of Thomas's hearings. Citing Hill's request for confidentiality, Biden took no action. He did nothing to assess Hill's credibility, sent no one to interview her, issued staffers no directive to inquire cautiously of Thomas's other female colleagues about sexual harassment, and did not speak to Hill.[85]

On Monday, September 23, Hill agreed to Biden's requirement for an investigation of her charges: that she submit to questioning by the FBI. The FBI followed standard procedure and informed the White House of the investigation, as Biden knew it would. There is no evidence that anyone warned Thomas about the pending inquiry, but White House personnel had nearly two days to do so before the FBI questioned Thomas.[86] Biden briefed the Senate majority and minority leaders, George Mitchell and Bob Dole, and briefed Judiciary Committee Democrats on Wednesday and Thursday, September 25 and 26. His staff had briefed aides to Senator Strom Thurmond, the committee's ranking Republican, a few days earlier, on Monday, September 23.

In an anguished Senate speech on September 27, the morning of the committee vote on the nomination, Biden announced his reluctant opposition to the nomination: "Every instinct in me wanted to support Clarence Thomas for sound as well as unsound reasons." Biden called his decision "a very close call" and asserted that someone of his liberal views could reasonably support Thomas.[87] He repeatedly praised Thomas's "high character, competence, and . . . legal credentials and credibility."[88] He cited the sincerity of Thomas's testimony before the Judiciary Committee. Biden also promised to oppose any delay in the final Senate vote or any revived "campaign" against the nomination.[89] Biden received a call that morning from Professor Laurence Tribe of Harvard Law School, a sometime adviser to Biden who had got wind of Hill's allegations. Tribe urged Biden to distribute a copy of Hill's statement of her charges to all Judiciary Committee Democrats. Biden's staff did so less than one hour before the committee vote.[90]

When the committee voted 7–7 on the nomination, Biden could have killed the nomination by holding it in committee. But that would have been a daring act for any Judiciary Committee chairman, and Biden had assured Senator Danforth that he would not do so.[91] Before the committee voted 13–1 to send the nomination to the full Senate without recommendation, Biden again vouched for Thomas's character and said he had promised Thomas that he would be Thomas's "advocate" if anyone "personaliz[ed] this battle."[92]

After Hill's charges became public on Sunday, October 6, Biden opposed any delay in the final Senate vote set for October 8. He said that Judiciary Committee members saw no need for delay when they voted on the nomination in committee—a statement Republicans would repeat often in an attempt to discredit both the committee's reopened investigation and Hill's charges.[93] Biden maintained that publication of Hill's charges had changed nothing. This defensiveness was perhaps unsurprising. But someone more astute—or more concerned by the charges—might have taken the position that the committee had proceeded as it did because of Hill's request for confidentiality, and that events now required another course of action.[94]

After a growing number of senators called for a delay, the Republicans, fearing Thomas's rejection by the full Senate, agreed to put the vote off. In closed-door negotiations, Biden and the majority leader, Senator Mitchell, agreed to begin the reopened hearings in three days, on Friday, October 11, and delay the final Senate vote one week, until October 15, a schedule that would make a thorough investigation of Hill's charges impossible. Biden agreed to several other Republican requests: Thomas could testify before or after Hill; there would be no questions on "extraneous matters" such as Thomas's publicly funded travel as EEOC chairman; and the committee would take no second vote on the nomination. Most importantly, Thomas's personal life was off limits, including any consumption of pornography.

Under the Senate's unanimous consent procedures, every senator had to agree on the date of the rescheduled vote. Biden could therefore have insisted on a longer delay. But he sought to be fair to Thomas and his supporters. In Danforth's memoir of the episode, he agreed with Senator Hatch that Biden and Mitchell were "bending over"[95] to be fair. To Senator Howard Metzenbaum, a liberal Ohio Democrat, it appeared that "[Biden] bent over too far to accommodate the Republicans, who were going to get Thomas on the Court come hell or high water."[96] When the hearings resumed, Biden allowed Thomas to testify both before and after Hill. At least six times, Thomas claimed that the Judiciary Committee was "lynching"[97] him. Biden had no response to this assault on him and his committee. Nor did he point out that Thomas, who had so often admonished his fellow African Americans not to blame their problems on their race, was now doing just that.

Biden's questioning of Thomas was ineffectual. When Thomas alleged that Hill and others unknown had "concocted" her allegations, Biden vouched for Thomas's sincerity and said he could not "refute that."[98] Biden did not ask Thomas how this conspiracy theory could be true when, as Biden knew, four corroborating witnesses were waiting to testify that Hill had told them of the alleged harassment years earlier, three of them while she worked at the EEOC. Instead, he allowed Thomas and Republican senators to refer to Hill's charges as "uncorroborated."[99] And despite the allegations of Angela Wright and Sukari Hardnett, two other former female employees alleging improper personal attentions by Thomas, Biden defended Thomas by pointing to the absence of a pattern of sexual harassment.[100] Biden also failed to speak up, or did so belatedly, when Republicans questioned Hill's morals, her mental health, and her romantic, political, and financial motives. Several months later, Biden said his one regret was not having stood up more frequently to Hill's "attackers."[101]

Biden's allocation of the little time available for the reopened hearings maximized the time and exposure available to Thomas and his defenders. Hill testified during the day on Friday, October 11, and Thomas appeared three times: before Hill's testimony, again during prime time on Friday evening, and all day Saturday. Biden recessed the hearings at 6:30 on Saturday evening, pushing the next scheduled witnesses, Hill's corroborators, out of prime time on Saturday night and back to Sunday afternoon.

After Republicans asked why Hill had endured the alleged harassment and followed Thomas from a job at the Department of Education to another at the EEOC, Biden canceled the scheduled testimony of an expert on sexual harassment who might have explained why many victims of sexual harassment behave as Hill had. Biden both affirmed and dismissed the relevance of such knowledge in a confusing statement:

> I don't know why we have so much trouble understanding the [behavior] of the victimized person, but that is not the issue here today. The issue here today is whether or not . . . there was harassment. Although this is relevant, I want to keep bringing it back.
> . . . [T]hose who are making, as they should, Judge Thomas's case keep coming forward and saying, "why would you stay?". . . .
> [The question] is not the overall pattern of harassment in America, but whether or not Anita Hill was harassed. This will only continue to be brought up as long as we continue to ask the question "why would she stay?" These are both legitimate questions.[102]

After Hill's corroborators testified, all three remaining panels testified for Thomas. Most of these witnesses were women who had worked with Thomas. Some had been hired or promoted by him. They monopolized the broadcast testimony in prime time on Sunday evening.

Biden assisted Thomas's cause in yet other ways. He gave Republican senators additional time to pursue lines of questioning that were not probative.[103] But when Republican Senator Hank Brown probed for a political motive on Hill's part by asking her whether she and Thomas disagreed on abortion, Biden cut off the question because it did not concern sexual harassment. Had Hill attributed to Thomas any view on abortion, she would have countered his claim that he had never expressed an opinion on the issue.[104] Biden also defended Thomas by suggesting that if Thomas had harbored the political ambitions others claimed he did, he would have been stupid to sexually harass his employees.[105] When Thomas's personal secretary testified that Hill had not, contrary to another witness's testimony, been condescending to her, Biden suggested an ulterior motive on Hill's part: that she had treated the secretary well in order to gain greater access to Thomas's office, where she could advance her political views.[106]

Biden repeatedly agreed with Republicans that Thomas deserved the benefit of any doubt about the charges, as though he were facing life in prison rather than life on the Supreme Court.[107] By joining Republican denunciations of the leaking of Hill's charges, Biden abetted the strategy of diverting attention from Thomas's culpability.[108] Even eight months after the hearings, Biden equated the behavior of Senate Democrats, who had sought to be fair to both Thomas and Hill, with that of the Republicans who, as described below, did not.[109]

The Decision Not to Call Other Witnesses

Biden's most controversial move was his decision not to call other female employees of Thomas who had accused him of improper sexual attentions. The day before the hearings reopened, a second former employee, Angela Wright, told Judiciary Committee lawyers that Thomas repeatedly suggested she date him, asked about her breast size, commented on the "anatomy" of other women in his office, and showed up uninvited one night at her apartment. She claimed that other women at the agency had told her that Thomas sought to date them, and that when Thomas fired her from her job at the EEOC, he cited her failure to wait for him outside his office at day's end as one reason for her dismissal. Major elements of Wright's story were confirmed by Wright's friend and coworker, Rose Jourdain, in a telephone interview with Senate staffers three days later, on the last day of the reopened hearings.[110]

Biden's staff also received a call from Kaye Savage, a former EEOC employee who was willing to testify that while visiting Thomas's apartment in 1982 she had found the walls covered with photos of naked women.[111] Another former Thomas employee, Sukari Hardnett, told the committee in a letter dated Sunday, October 13 (the last day of the hearings), and in a sworn affidavit the next day that Thomas had discussed other "females in his office" with her; that he "inspected and auditioned as a female" every attractive young black woman in his office, and that she had "told all of this" to Biden's staff "in the weeks following the nomination."[112] Biden's staff also learned that a Washington attorney, Fred Cooke, had allegedly seen Thomas renting a sexually explicit videotape in 1989. The attorney would not testify unless Biden subpoenaed him. Biden did not do so.[113] Finally, Lovida Coleman, a law school friend of Thomas's, told the press that Thomas, while in law school, had occasionally given friends humorous descriptions of X-rated films he had seen, much as Hill alleged he had done with her, although Coleman claimed that no one had found these stories offensive.[114] None of these potential witnesses ever testified. Democrats and Republicans on the Judiciary Committee agreed that Wright and Jourdain's interviews with staffers, and Hardnett's last-minute letter, would be published "without rebuttal" in the record of the hearings. The information from Savage, Coleman, and Cooke was never used.

Biden's decision not to call Angela Wright was especially controversial. The principals in the process have offered conflicting, self-defensive explanations for her nonappearance. Biden has claimed that he was the only senator who wanted Wright to testify, a claim three other senators have disputed.[115] Biden has also said that Hill and her advisers did not want Wright to testify because they feared that Wright's self-acknowledged quick temper and assailable motives (Thomas had fired her) would undermine Hill's testimony. Hill's legal counsel at the hearings has labeled this claim "unequivocally, categorically and positively false," a position affirmed by Hill and her other advisers.[116] Wright and her attorney rejected Biden's assertion that it was Wright's decision not to testify. On this question, the evidence strongly suggests that several factors—including the preferences of senators from both parties and Wright's own ambivalence—kept her from testifying. Although Wright was willing to testify, her feelings were understandably mixed. She had watched the questioning of Hill and, given her poor employment record and history of interpersonal conflicts,[117] expected a heavy assault on her own testimony. Wright's friend and corroborating witness, Rose Jourdain, had also been fired by Thomas and was similarly assailable. And Jourdain was ill: on Sunday afternoon, Jourdain was released from a Washington hospital and was still in considerable pain. Wright became upset when she learned that Judiciary Committee lawyers had interviewed Jourdain in her hospital bed; her reluctance to involve Jourdain in the process grew after Wright and Jourdain learned they might not testify until the early hours of

Monday morning. Biden later claimed that Wright could have testified in prime time on Sunday evening if she had wished, a claim that Wright's lawyer "absolutely" denied.[118] But Wright's lawyer also relayed Wright's ambivalence to the committee. He made it clear that Wright was willing to testify, but did not truly want to.[119]

In conversations on Sunday evening, Biden's staff gave Wright's attorney the impression that the committee did not want Wright to testify. After negotiations between the attorney and Biden's staff, Wright accepted their proposal to place her and Jourdain's interviews in the record of the hearings in lieu of their live testimony.[120] After her "second woman" story had received extensive press coverage, the senators could not have kept Wright from testifying had she insisted on doing so. By deferring to the committee, Wright accepted a consensus reached by Republican and Democratic senators that she should not testify. Republicans did not want Wright to bolster Hill's claims. Democrats feared that Wright would make a weak witness because of her poor job history, her assailable motives, and her fiery temperament, all of which Republicans promised to highlight.[121]

The Judiciary Committee's Democratic lawyers wrongly thought they had won a "tremendous victory" when Republicans agreed to place Wright and Jourdain's interviews in the record "unrebutted." But the transcripts had little impact; only a few media outlets published even brief excerpts of them.[122] Thus the critical question of a pattern in Thomas's behavior went unanswered.

OTHER DEMOCRATS

In the first round of hearings, no one asked Thomas about his qualifications for a justiceship, although many Democrats later questioned his qualifications in Senate speeches. Nor did they ask Thomas about his attendance at a 1987 dinner with the often-shunned South African ambassador to Washington, a dinner arranged by Thomas's friend Jay Parker, the South African lobbyist and *Lincoln Review* publisher.[123]

Democrats declined to press Thomas on his caustic critiques of Congress. Senator Herbert Kohl quoted portions of these, but allowed Thomas to escape by pleading a poor memory of his prior statements and affirming his belief in the importance of Congress.[124] Senator Paul Simon briefly quoted Thomas's celebration of Oliver North's victory over an "out of control" Congress, but asked no follow-up questions when Thomas claimed that he had merely noted North's political dexterity.[125] No one asked Thomas whether his caustic speeches betrayed a lack of judicial temperament. Nor did anyone ask Thomas why, as he acknowledged, he had never considered recusing himself from hearing, or voting to deny, the Iran-Contra prosecutor's motion for a hearing to reinstate North's criminal convictions.

After Biden told Judiciary Committee Democrats of Hill's charges, each of them had the opportunity to read Hill's statement to the committee and the FBI report of its interviews with Hill, Thomas, Hill's partial corroborator Susan Hoerchner, and a few others. Only two of seven Democrats—Dennis DeConcini and Simon—did so.[126] Senate rules allowed any committee member to request a one-week delay in the committee vote, set for September 27, or to insist on moving back the final Senate vote. But none did. When the press published Hill's charges, Majority Leader George Mitchell joined Biden in opposing any delay in the full Senate vote on the nomination, and called demands for a delay "pure politics."[127]

Like Biden, other Democrats questioned Thomas ineffectively at the second hearings. None of them answered Thomas's accusations of "lynching" until he had left the witness table.[128] On Friday evening, faced with the nominee's furious denials, his unanswered charges of "lynching," and his claim that he had not listened to Hill's testimony, Senator Howell Heflin, one of the Democrats' designated questioners, responded ineffectually: "Judge, I don't want to go over this stuff but, of course, there are many instances in which she has stated, but—and, in effect, since you didn't see her testify I think it is somewhat unfair to ask you specifically about it."[129] The following day, immediately after Thomas again denounced the process and propounded his unlikely conspiracy theory, Biden offered Senators Kennedy and Metzenbaum the opportunity to question the nominee. Neither senator asked a question or had any substantive comment.[130]

When Democrats questioned witnesses effectively, they typically did so quietly. On Sunday, a day after Thomas left the room, Senators Kennedy, Kohl, and Leahy pointed out how the testimony of Hill's corroborating witnesses belied Republican claims of a last-minute conspiracy to derail the nomination. Kohl and Leahy did so belatedly, nearly five hours into the testimony of these witnesses, and without drama or repetition.[131] When Leahy asked Thomas whether he had ever discussed pornographic movies with women other than Hill, Leahy apologetically accepted Thomas's refusal to answer a personal question.[132] No one asked Thomas about Lovida Coleman's claim that he had told his friends stories about pornographic films in law school. No one mentioned Coleman's name until nearly midnight on Sunday, after which the matter quickly died.[133]

Like Chairman Biden, committee Democrats countered the Republican assault on Hill belatedly or not at all. Former Democratic party chairman John C. White echoed the views of many observers when he called the conduct of Judiciary Committee members "outrageous on both sides, the character assassination of a person coming forward to testify and the Democrats' sitting there and letting that occur."[134] Finally, Democratic senators undermined their investigation of Hill's charges by joining Republican attacks on the hearings and publicly debating which one of themselves had been hurt the most by leaks of embarrassing information in the past.[135]

ANITA HILL

Anita Hill kept her claims of sexual harassment to herself and a small circle of friends for nearly ten years. She bypassed opportunities to present these claims in 1986, when Thomas was renominated as EEOC chairman, and again in 1990, when Thomas was nominated for the federal Court of Appeals. Her emergence at these earlier times would have permitted a thorough investigation of her claims, and perhaps those of Angela Wright, Sukari Hardnett, and possibly others.

Hill's silence is understandable. She had no wish to relive the painful and, to her, embarrassing events she was alleging. She rightly feared that media attention would forever alter her quiet and apparently happy life as a law professor in her home state of Oklahoma. She also feared that no one would believe a single accuser. (She had no knowledge of other possible complainants.) Hill likewise knew that accusations of sexual misbehavior are often turned against the women who bring them.[136] Nonetheless, Hill's silence over several years, her reluctance to state her claims even after Senate investigators asked her about sexual harassment, her request for confidentiality when she finally responded to these inquiries, and her refusal to cooperate with the press undeniably delayed investigation of her claims and helped result in their publication just two days before Thomas's expected confirmation. The ostensible timing of her allegations produced understandable suspicions about her motives in the minds of independent observers.

After Thomas's nomination on July 1, 1991, Hill had agonized over whether to come forward. Despite her growing conviction that she should do so, she "decided to wait until the investigators came to me."[137] She thereby shifted the need to decide, and control over events, to others. This posture allowed her to have it both ways and to blame senators and staffers for her lengthy silence and its consequences. Hill said, for example, that she remained silent when Thomas was nominated for the federal Appeals Court in 1990 because "they [the Senate] never approached me."[138] Of the imbroglio that followed the last-minute publication of her charges the next year, she said, "If I hadn't been asked, none of this would have happened."[139]

Hill did, however, tell an old law school friend about the alleged harassment a few weeks after July 1. The friend, whom Hill did not swear to secrecy, told the story to others who told the Alliance for Justice, who passed the tip to Metzenbaum's staff in late July. When a Metzenbaum staffer first called Hill on September 5—six weeks later—Hill made no claim of harassment and said only that reports of sexual harassment by Thomas merited investigation.

In two later calls from a Kennedy aide, Hill expressed a qualified willingness to go forward. But she did not give a full account of her charges until she was called by another Metzenbaum staffer, a law school friend named James Brudney, on September 10, the opening day of Thomas's hearings.[140] When Brudney later told her that Metzenbaum had handed the matter to Biden's staff, who refused to contact her, Hill called Biden's staff on September 12. She related her charges in a general way, expressed her fear of being the lone complainant, and agreed to speak to a possible corroborating witness. Hill also made a crucial, controversial request for confidentiality. Biden and his staff claimed that Hill would not allow them to confront Thomas with her charges and name her as the source, a step that Biden (but not all committee chairmen) required before investigating such allegations. Hill later recalled a much greater willingness to attach her name to the charges.[141]

The evidence favors the staffers' version of events. Hill has acknowledged balking upon learning that Thomas must be told of the charges and their source. More tellingly, perhaps, Hill's later request to Senator Simon that he inform all one hundred senators of her charges without using her name bordered on, if it did not constitute, a request that senators act on an anonymous accusation. Among chroniclers of these events, even Hill's sympathizers have criticized her for naivete surprising in someone with her legal training and Washington experience.[142]

In any case, Hill moved slowly. Apprised on September 13 and 15 that Judiciary Committee aides may have misinterpreted her request for confidentiality, she did not call back to clear up any misunderstanding until September 19. Hill also waited four days, from September 12 to 16, to call her corroborator—her law school friend Susan Hoerchner—who called staffers on September 17 to confirm portions of Hill's story. On September 20, Biden's staff asked Hill if she would agree to an FBI interview. She refused. On September 23, three days after Thomas's scheduled hearings had ended, Hill changed her mind and agreed to the FBI interview. That same day, she faxed Senate staffers a detailed statement of her allegations.[143]

The accusations remained confidential from September 23 to October 6—a surprisingly long silence in which knowledge of the charges spread through the Washington political community.[144] The story would have broken sooner, but Hill refused to cooperate with the two reporters pursuing the story—*Newsday*'s Timothy Phelps and National Public Radio's Nina Totenberg—until Saturday, October 5, when they both called her with sufficient information to go with the story with or without her help.[145] By the time the story surfaced, a solid majority of senators had announced their support for Thomas, a development that effectively increased the burden of proof on Hill if her charges were to affect the Senate's decision.[146]

At a press conference on October 7, the day before the scheduled final vote on the nomination, Hill made several statements that damaged the credibility of the Judiciary Committee and its future exploration of her charges. She overstated her willingness to cooperate with the committee over the preceding month and her willingness to testify, accused the committee of violating its "understandings" with her, and denied that her ambivalence had delayed the investigation of her charges, though it clearly had.[147]

REPUBLICAN SENATORS

Thomas's supporters on the Judiciary Committee contributed to the imbroglio principally through their unconcern with the possible truth of Hill's charges and a series of attacks on her veracity, character, and mental health. After Biden informed Thurmond's staff of Hill's charges, they withheld the information from Republican senators.[148] After Senator Specter learned of the matter from the Democrats, he asked Thomas about the accusations, and accepted Thomas's denial at face value, shortly before voting to confirm Thomas in committee. When Hill's charges surfaced, Specter was the only Republican senator to publicly support a delay in the final vote on the nomination.[149] Nearly all the Republicans who spoke in the Senate denounced the accusations as a smear—before the Senate had investigated them—or affirmed their belief in Thomas's good character.[150]

Some Republican senators misrepresented the FBI report on the allegations. Echoing the White House, Senator Thurmond called this hasty collection of interviews a "complete and thorough" investigation. Although the FBI interview of Susan Hoerchner partially corroborated Hill's account, Republicans claimed that the report found no basis for Hill's allegations, or that the FBI considered the charges unfounded.[151] In reality, the FBI had offered no opinion on the truth or falsity of the charges. Republicans also adopted a strategy of diverting attention from Hill's charges and onto the process. As Senator Danforth later explained, "The issue was not Anita Hill and whatever she might say. The issue was the confirmation process: the groups, the lies, the leaks, what that process had done to Clarence Thomas . . . [and] to America."[152]

Senators Thurmond and Hatch impugned Hill's integrity on the Senate floor by reading a letter from Armstrong Williams, a personal friend and public relations aide to Thomas at the EEOC. Williams, who later became a conservative talk show host, claimed that Hill had once admired Thomas, but later became "untrustworthy, selfish, and extremely bitter" when Thomas passed her over for promotion. "These [charges]," Williams wrote, and senators repeated in language suggesting Hill was mentally unstable, "are the rantings of a disgruntled employee" who "always had to have the final word and the last laugh."[153] When Democrat John Kerry of Massachusetts called this a "countersmear," Senator Alan Simpson portrayed Hill as a politically savvy Washington insider who should expect such attacks.[154]

In the reopened hearings, Simpson hurled innuendo at Hill: "I really am getting stuff over the transom about Professor Hill. I have got letters hanging out of my pockets . . . faxes . . . statements from her former law professors . . . from people that know her, statements . . . saying, watch out for this woman." He repeated these remarks on NBC's *Meet the Press,* where he said he would not use such materials, and then agreed that he was doing precisely that.[155]

At the reopened hearings, Senator Specter distorted Hill's testimony to create seeming inconsistencies in it, and then accused her of lying. On Friday morning, Specter asked Hill about a *USA Today* report that Senate staffers had told her that her anonymous accusations would "quietly and behind the scenes" cause Thomas to withdraw his nomination. Hill denied that report six times.[156] When Specter renewed these questions in the afternoon, Hill acknowledged that James Brudney had discussed with her, among other possibilities, the possibility that her charges might, after "intermediate steps" such as "a full hearing" or "questioning by the FBI" or "questioning by some [senators]," eventuate in Thomas's withdrawal. But Hill again denied any talk of Thomas withdrawing quickly or quietly in response to anonymous charges.[157] Specter reduced her testimony to "Brudney told you that if you came forward, Judge Thomas might withdraw."[158] The next day, Specter selectively quoted her testimony about the newspaper report and accused her of "flat-out perjury."[159] Specter also misrepresented Hill's statement that it was "garbage" to infer from records of her phone calls to Thomas after she left Washington that she had any romantic interest in him. Specter implied that Hill, who accepted the records' accuracy, had labeled the records themselves, as opposed to their significance, as "garbage."[160]

SENATOR JOHN DANFORTH

Thomas's patron, Senator Danforth, was particularly active and, by his own admission, unprincipled, in Thomas's defense. In his memoir, *Resurrection: The Confirmation of Clarence Thomas,* Danforth recalled advising Thomas before the reopened hearings to seize on the popular "contempt for Congress"[161] by attacking the Judiciary Committee and its processes. He believed that his advice fed the nation's "toxic cynicism" about politics and "ran counter to what I believe": "the Senate is a great institution that serves our nation well." Danforth urged Thomas, who repeatedly called the process a "lynching," to attack the Senate "more so by far than he actually did."[162]

Danforth also related his "obsession" with obtaining affidavits from Hill's former law students who, he claimed, told Republican staffers that Hill was "a left-wing radical feminist . . . who had made certain racist statements," sprinkled her pubic hairs on students' papers, and spoken of Long Dong Silver (the pornographic movie star Hill accused Thomas of describing to her). "Getting the dirt on Anita Hill," Danforth wrote, "did not bother me."[163]

After Senator Biden ruled out any statements from former students or testimony about Hill's mental health by psychiatrists who had never met her, Danforth was eager to give these materials to the press, so that skeptical senators could not cross-examine their sources.[164] He helped to do this by appearing on television to claim that Hill was "fantasizing."[165] "I was," he later acknowledged, "accusing a perfect stranger of having a psychiatric condition."[166]

Danforth's staff admonished him for these activities and sabotaged some of them. His legislative director considered resigning over the "dirt-digging and purposeful character assassination" of Hill. When he complained to Danforth about his "end justifies the means approach," Danforth replied that "We just disagree on that."[167] Another staffer called Danforth's actions "wild and erratic." Kenneth Duberstein, the administration's chief lobbyist for the nomination, told Danforth that using the affidavits he sought would be "below you."[168] Danforth's staff destroyed copies of an affidavit from a psychiatrist speculating on Hill's mental health and canceled a press conference with the psychiatrist. When Danforth insisted on holding it, they arranged it so that it drew little press coverage. They also stopped the senator from releasing an affidavit impugning Hill's job history that other Republicans had refused to release.[169]

Danforth's efforts continued beyond the hearings: "Unfortunately, for months thereafter, I was intent on peddling my theories about Anita Hill to whoever would listen." This behavior continued in Danforth's memoir, where he repeated the disparaging descriptions of Hill heard at the hearings.[170]

Danforth's book also offered new material. Thomas and his personal secretary, Diane Holt, allegedly told Danforth that Hill had complained that Thomas "liked" or "dated" only women with complexions lighter than her own.[171] At the hearings, Holt and Thomas had many opportunities to attribute Hill's charges to such personal jealousy, but neither did; Holt repeatedly expressed bewilderment when asked about Hill's motives.[172] Danforth also states in two places that Thomas had twice told a friend upon first hearing Hill's accusations that Hill "wasn't attractive . . . and she had bad breath."[173]

Danforth's memoir bespeaks a striking moral ambivalence. His confessions of shame are tinged with ambiguity. He does not apologize or foreswear similar future actions. His closest approach to a moral resolution is his belief that his behavior was justified because Hill's charges were "scurrilous"[174] and threatened Thomas with a grave wrong. Near the book's end, Danforth, an ordained minister, cites Saint Paul's injunction that Christians not "be overcome by evil but . . . overcome evil with good." "[It] is a doctrine I readily set aside. . . . [The hearings were] a time for war, and we had to win that war or a terrible injustice would be done."[175]

THE WEIGHT OF RACE

Senator Biden acknowledged after Thomas's confirmation that "Had Thomas been white, he never would have been nominated. The only reason he is on the [Supreme] Court is because he is black."[176] Thomas's conservatism was also necessary to his appointment, but it is inconceivable that any president would have nominated a white person with Thomas's questionable qualifications and ethics, his fraternization with representatives of apartheid, his record on race and age discrimination and his intolerance of dissent at the EEOC, his embrace of conservative judicial activism, his association with the *Lincoln Review,* his celebration of Oliver North, his warfare and lack of credibility with congressional Democrats, his insults to civil rights leaders and to Congress, and his record of growing political extremism across the board. It is equally clear that no white nominee with Thomas's record and his patently obfuscatory testimony in the first round of hearings—putting the second aside—would have won confirmation in a Senate of fifty-seven Democrats.

A white analog to Thomas would have received no help from prominent blacks such as Vernon Jordan and Benjamin Hooks, the executive director of the NAACP, who spoke favorably of Thomas in public while working covertly with the White House to keep his organization undecided on the nomination for a month after it was announced.[177] (The NAACP had opposed Thomas's nomination for a second term at the EEOC in 1986 and later sought his resignation from that post. It took no position on his 1990 nomination to the Court of Appeals for the District of Columbia because it did not want to oppose a black nominee for such a prestigious position.)[178]

The NAACP's month-long neutrality paralyzed several of its liberal allies, who waited for the NAACP to act before announcing their own opposition. These groups included the AFL-CIO, the Alliance for Justice, and the Leadership Conference on Civil Rights, all of which had contributed mightily to the Senate's rejection of Robert Bork.[179] Stymied until the end of July, these groups did not even begin to raise grassroots opposition to Thomas before senators went home to gauge public opinion during the August recess.

As the White House had hoped, the nomination split the rest of the civil rights community. After the National Urban League remained neutral on the nomination, its president allowed that President Bush had "checkmated" African American groups by nominating a black conservative.[180] The venerable Southern Christian Leadership Conference endorsed Thomas, an action unthinkable for a nonblack nominee with Thomas's record.[181]

Elite and mass black sympathy toward a black nominee sapped the opposition of its intensity[182] and gave southern Democratic senators highly dependent on black votes, who had opposed Bork, a powerful reason to support Thomas, whose approval rating among blacks rose from 41 percent to 61 percent in the month after the nomination.[183] Quicker action by a unified, black-led anti-Thomas coalition may have swayed black public opinion against Thomas. If not, that failure would have provided all the more evidence of the power of race in the confirmation of Clarence Thomas.

Elites and ordinary citizens who would have opposed a nonblack nominee with Thomas's record would neither have heard nor accepted, as many did, the claim that the nominee would recall his roots in poverty and segregation and "grow" to sympathize with the downtrodden after joining the Supreme Court.[184] Blacks supportive of Thomas would not likely have argued that a nonblack nominee who embraced Thomas's self-help doctrine stood in the proud tradition of black nationalists such as Malcolm X and Marcus Garvey.[185] No one would have claimed, long before Anita Hill emerged, that the nominee was being "lynched."[186] Nor would any black intellectual have explained the behaviors Anita Hill described as a part of the nominee's native culture that conflicted with white "neo-Puritan feminism [and] its reactionary sacralization of women's bodies."[187] Thomas also benefited from arguments that "We won't get another black" if the Senate rejected him[188]; that Thomas, as a black, must be preferable to any white alternative[189]; and that his accuser, Anita Hill, was a "traitor"[190] to her race. By contrast, a nonblack nominee to replace Thurgood Marshall would have faced certain opposition on racial grounds.

Fear of the racial dimensions of the nomination helps explain why nearly all of those who challenged Thomas's qualifications, and all who cast doubt on his Horatio Alger–like biography, were African American.[191] In both rounds of hearings, the race-related timidity of Judiciary Committee Democrats was cited by figures as diverse as Jesse Jackson, the black historian John Hope Franklin, and Senator Robert Byrd of West Virginia, a conservative Democrat and one-time Klan member who told the Senate that Thomas's attack on the confirmation process and charges of racism in the second round of hearings were "blatant intimidation and . . . it worked."[192]

The quantitative studies and many qualitative accounts of the Senate's 52–48 vote to confirm Thomas, including the assertions of crucial southern Democrats, provide the final evidence that race was the decisive factor in his confirmation.[193]

EVENTS RECONSIDERED

Although Thomas's confirmation proceedings provide abundant grounds for legitimate criticism, any evaluation of the confirmation process must consider its uniqueness. Similarly, some of the seemingly censurable features and behaviors were justifiable upon a close examination of the circumstances in which the actors, who lacked the benefit of hindsight, found themselves.

In addition to the overbearing power of racial politics, the Thomas confirmation was unique in several respects. First, the campaign to "sell" a deceptive image of the nominee was uniquely extensive, sophisticated, and successful. A similar strategy failed miserably in Robert Bork's case, and would have failed in Thomas's case but for the nominee's race.[194]

The Thomas nomination was unique in another, spectacular way: no other nominee faced last-minute charges of a highly salacious nature. The lateness of the charges added time pressures to the inherent difficulties they presented. Critics of Senate Democrats have claimed that these senators were partly responsible for this lateness. They allege that staffers were slow to investigate the sexual harassment charges because they believed, for a variety of reasons, that their senators did not want to hear them: a number of Judiciary Committee Democrats, especially Biden, Kennedy, and DeConcini, had been damaged by allegations of personal or professional wrongdoing they did not want to resurrect; these allegations led them to sympathize with Thomas; they had a visceral distaste for investigating personal charges against nominees; they misunderstood the seriousness of sexual harassment—or, alternatively, they recognized the explosive nature of the charges and shrank from them.[195] Whatever the case, the clear if not easy solution is the election of senators who will investigate charges of serious, disqualifying wrongdoing by a nominee. Potential accusers must also decide whether to come forward in a timely fashion, as difficult as that decision may be.

The Thomas confirmation was also unique in the decisive role of public opinion and vast public attention. Hill's daytime testimony drew more than 50 percent of a larger-than-normal national audience. More than 50 million Americans watched Thomas's testimony on Friday night. On Sunday night, when the three major commercial networks broadcast other fare, CNN's broadcast of the hearings increased its normal audience nearly sevenfold.[196] By contrast, no other Supreme Court confirmation hearings proved commercially viable, even those for Robert Bork. The quantitative and qualitative accounts of the Senate's vote to confirm Thomas demonstrate that the public's (especially the black public's) two-to-one verdict in favor of Thomas sealed his confirmation.[197]

Defensible Actions

Several of the Senate's seeming missteps were at least defensible, if not more than that. Compared with other nominees, Thomas's qualifications for a justiceship were thin. But it was not a plain empirical fact that he was unqualified. Twelve of fifteen members of the ABA Committee on the Federal Judiciary found him "qualified," as did some others who admittedly opposed his nomination on ideological grounds.[198]

Claims that Thomas might prove a moderate figure on the High Court, while highly dubious, had some foundation in his ideological wanderings over a lifetime, his early support for some race-conscious policies, his criticisms of the Reagan Administration for marginalizing black appointees and defending the tax-exempt status of colleges that practice discrimination, his occasional statements about the inescapability of American racism, and the autonomy he would possess once on the Supreme Court.[199]

The pivotal figure in the Senate was, of course, Chairman Biden, whose solicitude toward Thomas and many questionable judgments this chapter has detailed. Any evaluation of Biden's role must note that Anita Hill's request for confidentiality placed him in a difficult position. Had senators used Hill's information to reject the nomination, following any conceivable course of action, no matter how discreet or indirect, the eventual disclosure of Hill's story and name was inevitable. Political reality requires senators to explain a decision to reject a president's Supreme Court nominee. Senators may place the burden of proof on the nominee and the president to prove the nominee's fitness, but senators opposing the nomination must still explain how the nominee falls short. Given the virtual certainty that Thomas would have won confirmation with at least fifty-five votes absent Anita Hill,[200] the explanation for his otherwise inexplicable rejection would have begun with the disclosure of Hill's accusations.

Biden's chief legal counsel later recalled that "the pressure to maintain Hill's confidentiality was driving a lot of what was, in retrospect, bad decision-making. . . . [T]he better decision would have been to call Hill and tell her that her accusations were 'just too charged, too visible, and someone's going to leak this. . . . You have to go public.'"[201] Hill and especially Biden should have recognized this from the outset. Their hope that Hill could avoid publicity was wishful thinking. But Biden found himself, mainly because of Hill's years of silence and her request for confidentiality, in an extremely high-stakes and difficult situation in which wishful thinking is at least understandable.

Biden's stated desire to honor Hill's request for confidentiality reflected a very legitimate concern (whether it truly or wisely formed the basis for his inactions). Biden had involved himself in legislative efforts to protect women victims of sexual violence and was aware of the trauma Hill could suffer if her claims became the nation's top news item.[202] At the reopened hearings, he defended his committee on this ground: "Some have asked how we could [let] the U.S. Senate vote on Judge Thomas's nomination and leave senators in the dark about Professor Hill's charges. To this, I answer, how could we have forced Professor Hill against her will into the blinding light where you see her today."[203]

Hill might have been urged gently, rather than "forced," to come forward. Her earlier emergence would have provided more time to evaluate her charges. There would have been less need for rush judgments. Pressure to hear from Angela Wright and her corroborating witness, and perhaps others, would likely have resulted in their testimony. But there is no guarantee that persuasion would have convinced Hill to state her claims publicly. Her dogged resistance against the reporters working the story demonstrates her determination to avoid publicity. And any Democratic attempts to urge Hill forward would have produced even more charges that Thomas's opponents pushed or manipulated her to testify. Biden had this concern in mind when he sent the FBI, rather than Democratic staffers, to interview Hill in Oklahoma (an action that tipped off the Bush Administration to the budding scandal).[204]

Biden also had good reasons not to call other witnesses. Angela Wright was a belated, reluctant witness with assailable motives. So was her corroborator, Rose Jourdain (who, like Wright, had been fired by Thomas). Wright's self-acknowledged incendiary temperament posed another problem. Had she seemed credible and responded effectively to the certain assault on her testimony, she could have doomed the Thomas nomination. But had she seemed volatile or vindictive, her testimony could have aided Thomas. The allegations from Sukari Hardnett were much less specific and less serious than Hill and Wright's; their presentation might have seemed a desperate attempt to stop the nomination after all else had failed. And Hardnett, who had political differences with Thomas before leaving his employ under disputed circumstances, was another assailable witness.[205]

Democrats also had a legitimate fear of provoking a public backlash if they produced evidence of Thomas's private consumption of pornography years earlier. This danger increased in tandem with the growing public disgust at the hearings (although Democrats had accommodated the growing revulsion by allowing Thomas to indict them and their process and by attacking it themselves).

Unavoidable Unpleasantries

A credible accuser, combined with an categorical denial of charges of disgraceful personal conduct, guarantees an ugly confrontation.[206] Despite suggestions that a private hearing would have been preferable, that confrontation had to be public. As one Biden aide explained, "closed hearings would have [had] no credibility." They "would have been reconstructed in the newspaper. . . . The story would have been inaccurate, and there would have been tremendous pressure on both sides to leak."[207] Closed hearings would also have magnified the importance of the adversaries' spin control.

The reopened hearings might have been held in public but not televised. But a decision not to televise them would have been difficult for senators to justify. Every confirmation hearing of the previous ten years had been televised, and senators were already facing charges of a cover-up. Without television, the public would still have depended largely on other media's recon-struction of the hearings and the adversaries' spin.

Less visible hearings would also have had fewer positive collateral effects. Despite their shortcomings, the televised hearings educated the pub-lic about sexual harassment; contributed to an immediate, dramatic, sus-tained increase in the number of sexual harassment complaints; and led many employers to establish or reinforce sexual harassment policies.[208] Leaders of women's groups credited the televised hearings for these developments, some of which were replicated in other nations.[209] Television also helped force senators who had so visibly attacked Hill's credibility or failed to defend her to apologize for their behaviors.[210] Some women's anger at the perceived mistreatment of Hill contributed to a record number of women congressional candidates in 1992. After that election, the number of women House members rose from twenty-eight to forty-seven; the number of women senators rose from two to six.[211] Two new female senators, Carole Moseley Braun and Dianne Feinstein, joined the previously all-male Judiciary Com-mittee.

CONCLUSION

Justice Thomas was placed on the Supreme Court by a coalition of forces. First was a president content to nominate a lightly qualified, politically extreme, and temperamentally injudicious black man while banking on the nominee's color to ensure his confirmation, all the while denying that color played any role in his nomination. Second were conservatives who cared about little but the nominee's ideology and who displayed a near-perfect lack of ethics during the hearings on Hill's charges of sexual harassment. Third were Senate moderates—mostly southern—who gave the nominee every benefit of every doubt and acquiesced in the judgment of their electoral con-stituencies. Although senators may rightly consider constituency opinion while assessing Supreme Court nominees, the correlation between Demo-cratic votes and the proximity of the next election[212] suggests that senators' concern for their political futures played an important role as well. For sev-eral key senators, these factors, in the evaluation of a figure who would like-ly serve longer and exercise far greater power than any senator, overcame a panoply of competing concerns: the nominee's slender qualifications; his seemingly injudicious temperament as evidenced by vindictive and petulant behavior toward his many "enemies" and a record of growing political extremism over the previous decade, including an expressed profound contempt for Congress; his readiness to trade on his race while advocating color blindness for others; the disregard for law displayed by the manner in which he attempted to change, or did not enforce, lawful civil rights policies; and the lack of integrity evidenced by his palpably unbelievable testimony at congressional hearings.

A fourth group was made up of African American elites, liberal senators and interest groups, and the news media, who had all the resources they needed to analyze and open to public view Thomas's qualifications, temperament, public record, integrity, and beliefs. That they failed to do so despite an expanded confirmation process designed to perform precisely this function—excessively so, according to the legalist school of thought—is the final testament not to flaws in the confirmation process, but to the political fecklessness and overwhelming power of race in Thomas's confirmation.

6

Unrevealing Inquiries: Are Nominees All That Stealthy?

This and the following chapter examine concerns about the confirmation process flowing from the "political" perspective on the process. Rather than holding that nominees are scrutinized excessively, this critique maintains that they are not scrutinized enough. The most frequent complaint is that senators do not learn enough about nominees' legal ideologies to give meaningful, informed consent to Supreme Court nominations. A consequent concern raised by the Senate's alleged inability to discern the beliefs of nominees, or to get nominees to divulge their beliefs openly, is that presidents may pack the Supreme Court by slipping their ideological kin through the Senate. Laurence Tribe, for instance, has expressed the fear that "A President with any skill and luck . . . can, with fair success, build the Court of his dreams."[1] Although it is "entirely understandable"[2] that presidents nominate figures who they think share their views, the Senate's limited ability to air or debate upon nominees' ideologies may allow presidents excessive influence over the Court's ideological makeup and its decisions on vital matters concerning the fundamental rights of citizens and powers of government. It may even allow a president to put on the Court a nominee whose values are "abhorrent,"[3] or at least seriously at odds with those of the people whom the Senate represents.[4] These are the greatest dangers posed by senatorial consent to nominees of opaque views.

Though the frustration and alarm felt by stymied senators and worried commentators of the political school are thus quite understandable, this chapter demonstrates that the Senate has considerable ability to identify the relevant beliefs of Supreme Court nominees. With only one exception (David

Souter), modern nominees' general approaches to legal adjudication and approximate positions on the conventional left-right spectrum have been highly predictable. Moreover, although nominees' future votes on specific issues are not as highly predictable (nor entirely *un*predictable), more detailed information about nominees' current views on specific issues, even if such knowledge could be had, would likely prove dysfunctional to the operation of the constitutional system and an unreliable guide to their future votes on the Court.

The next section presents the political school's characterization of the Senate's inability to identify nominees' beliefs. The following section demonstrates that in almost all cases the general character of nominees' views is clearly discernible even if their views on specific issues are not. The final part of this chapter identifies the dubious consequences of a more revealing confirmation process. The next chapter evaluates the related concern that presidents may be able to pack the Court, possibly with nominees of worrisome beliefs.

THE CHARGE

Claims about the Senate's seeming inability to examine nominees' ideologies are legion. Most of these perceptions arise from observation of Senate confirmation hearings. They date back at least to the 1950s, when a young lawyer named William H. Rehnquist observed sardonically in the *Harvard Law Record* that Senate debate on the nomination of Charles Whittaker

> succeeded in adducing only the following facts: (a) proceeds from skunk trapping in rural Kansas assisted him in obtaining his early education; (b) he was both fair and able in his decisions as a judge of the lower federal courts; (c) he was the first Missourian ever appointed to the Supreme Court; (d) since he was born in Kansas but now resided in Missouri, his nomination honored two states.[5]

In the 1970s, L. A. Powe observed that "Senate questioning [of nominees] has proved astonishingly ineffective in eliciting the desired information."[6] In the 1980s, Grover Rees complained that

> Supreme Court confirmation hearings seem designed to create the illusion that important things are being discovered when in fact

> Senators learn little about the nominee's judicial philosophy.
> . . . [N]ominees can be expected more or less uniformly to endorse
> liberty but not license, speech but not obscenity, adherence to prece-
> dent except where the precedents are wrong. Above all, nominees
> will oppose 'judicial activism' and favor 'judicial restraint.'[7]

In 1995, after the confirmations of Justices Ruth Bader Ginsburg and
Stephen Breyer, Elena Kagan complained,

> their confirmation hearings became official lovefests. . . . [B]oth
> nominees felt free to decline to disclose their views on controversial
> issues and cases. They stonewalled the Judiciary Committee to great
> effect. . . . [T]he discussion of a nominee's views on legal issues had
> almost completely lapsed. Justices Kennedy, Souter, and Thomas, no
> less than Justices Ginsburg and Breyer, rebuffed all attempts to
> explore their opinions of important principles and cases. . . .
>
> If recent hearings lacked acrimony, they also lacked seriousness
> and substance. The problem was . . . not that the Senate focused too
> much on a nominee's legal views, but that it did so far too little. . . .
> [T]he current 'confirmation mess' derives not from the role the
> Senate assumed in evaluating [nominees' beliefs], but from the
> Senate's subsequent abandonment of that role and function. When
> the Senate ceases to engage nominees in meaningful discussion of
> legal issues, the confirmation process takes on an air of vacuity and
> farce, and the Senate becomes incapable of either properly evaluat-
> ing nominees or appropriately educating the public.[8]

Senators have likewise complained that every nominee except Robert Bork
has refused to engage them in serious discussions of constitutional philosophy.[9]

It is not hard to see why senators and scholars complain. Bork responded willingly to almost all questions at his lengthy confirmation hearings, but
his testimony was exceptional in that regard. Most nominees have deflected
probing questions by resorting to a variety of defenses or dodges. Nominees
sometimes claim, for instance, that controversial statements they made in the
past reflected not their own views, but those of persons they worked for at
the time. The best known example of this defense is William Rehnquist's
claim that he was merely expressing Justice Robert Jackson's views when, as
Jackson's law clerk, he authored a memorandum supporting the constitutionality of racial segregation.[10] David Souter also used this defense to attribute

to his governor controversial positions he had advocated as New Hampshire's attorney general.[11]

In another common maneuver, nominees disavow their previously stated views by asserting that they did not really mean what they said. Thus Clarence Thomas could assert that his controversial statements concerning property rights were uttered not as a jurist, but only as a "part-time political theorist," and that his praise for an antiabortion article was merely a "throwaway line" directed at a conservative audience.[12] Robert Bork similarly tried to establish the irrelevance of his "professor's writings" on the ground that "A professor is absolutely free to speculate, to think, to try out arguments. . . . [A]ll writing is an experiment," just an attempt to "start a debate."[13]

Nominees who can make no plausible claim that they did not mean what they had earlier said or wrote can claim that they nonetheless forswear any reliance on their previously stated views when they ascend to the High Court. Clarence Thomas made the classic statement of this claim: "[W]hen one becomes a member of the judiciary . . . one ceases to accumulate strong viewpoints, and rather begins to, as I noted earlier, to strip down as a runner and to maintain and secure that level of impartiality and objectivity necessary for judging cases."[14] Robert Bork made the same point more concisely: "As a judge, you are responsible to the law, not to some speculative theory you once developed."[15]

The most common and effective maneuver to avoid senators' questions is the claim, examined in Chapter 2, that judges must not make up their minds in advance of hearing a case; to reveal to senators how they would rule, or be likely to rule, on any question likely to come before the Court would compromise the impartiality required of judges. Every recent nominee has made this claim, and no nominee has ever been dislodged from it.[16]

In addition to these devices, several contextual factors discussed in Chapter 2 inhibit intense Senate scrutiny of nominees' ideologies. First, senators of the president's party are likely to rely on the president's judgment that a nominee of unclear views is an acceptable nominee, and are not likely to insist on a thorough airing of the nominee's views. Second, senators have only a limited willingness to engage in political bloodletting over nominations: if the previous nomination was highly conflictual, senators are less likely to press the present nominee on ideological issues, a factor that aided Anthony Kennedy after the storm over Robert Bork and the withdrawn nomination of Douglas Ginsburg, and aided Antonin Scalia after the battle over William Rehnquist's elevation to chief justice. Third, ideological scrutiny of a nominee will be relatively light if senators believe that a nomination will probably not cause a major shift in the Court's overall ideology, another factor that aided Antonin Scalia. Fourth, a nominee possessing strong professional credentials will likely face smoother waters in the Senate. Fifth, the race or gender of a nominee may restrain even senators highly suspicious of a nominee from publicly grilling the nominee.

Clarence Thomas utilized several of these devices and factors to avoid meaningful discussion of his constitutional beliefs,[17] as he freely confessed after his confirmation: "In the [first] hearing, I played by the rules. And playing by those rules, the country has never seen the real person. There is an inherent dishonesty in the system. It says, don't be yourself. If you are yourself, like Bob Bork, you're dead."[18] Despite these limitations, the next section will demonstrate that senators have, in fact, succeeded in eliciting useful testimony from modern nominees, and that the prenomination records of every modern nominee but David Souter have supplied abundant evidence of their ideological orientations.

QUESTIONS, ANSWERS, AND NOMINEES' TRACK RECORDS

As described in Chapter 2, nominees have given useful (and varying) testimony before the Senate Judiciary Committee about the importance of following the Founders' intentions when interpreting the Constitution,[19] the proper methodology for defining the "liberty" protected by the Fifth and Fourteenth Amendments,[20] the use of legislative history in statutory interpretation,[21] the meaning of the Ninth Amendment,[22] the workability of the Court's multitiered approach to equal protection cases,[23] the free exercise of religion,[24] and the view that the Constitution is a "living document" whose meaning may change over time.[25] Some nominees have also been surprisingly candid in endorsing the view, often disparaged by conservatives, that the courts must sometimes address social problems that the other branches of government have neglected.[26] Because a nominee may sit on the Court for decades to come and decide many issues that can scarcely be imagined, this sort of information about a nominee's general approach to adjudication may be much more valuable than the often sought but seldom gained information about the nominee's current view on a particular contemporary issue.

Critics of the Senate's alleged inability to discover nominees' ideologies also sometimes forget that the confirmation hearings are only the last step in the Senate's information-gathering process. Before the hearings, senators receive information from letters, opinions, speeches, and articles written by and about the nominee. They also receive information from media reports, phone calls to and from senators' offices and committee staff, FBI reports, the majority and minority counsels, the questionnaire filled out by the nominee, and the private meeting between the nominee and each senator on the Judiciary Committee.[27] These sources normally illuminate a nominee's beliefs very well. As discussed in Chapter 3, Jeffrey Segal et al., using newspaper descriptions of nominees' views at the time of their nominations, have constructed an index of nominees' ideologies that correlates very strongly (.80 of a possible 1.0) with their future votes as justices.[28] This result was later affirmed and expanded upon by Segal and Harold Spaeth.[29]

This finding is borne out by an individual-level analysis of the nominees who became justices in the 1980s and 1990s. Consider first the three most conservative of the Reagan-Bush appointees: William Rehnquist, Antonin Scalia, and Clarence Thomas.[30] Rehnquist's conservatism was thoroughly documented at the time of his 1971 nomination for associate justice, as was his belief that judges' political preferences inevitably influence their rulings.[31] Over the next fifteen years, he established a well-deserved reputation as the Court's most conservative justice. At the time of his nomination for chief justice in 1986, Rehnquist "made resolutely clear during his confirmation hearings . . . that his questioners could not, and should not, expect any change in his jurisprudence; that his years as associate justice were on the record."[32] Rehnquist's record as chief justice has been consistent with that testimony. In civil rights and liberties cases, Rehnquist was the most conservative of the fourteen justices who served on the Court between 1986 and 2000.[33] He has also spearheaded the movement to revise the Court's jurisprudence on federalism and curb federal legislative and (in some respects, such as limiting habeas corpus) judicial power.[34]

When Antonin Scalia was nominated in 1986, he was already a well-known spokesman for conservative jurisprudence. As we saw in previous chapters, the *New York Times* reported at the time of Scalia's nomination that he had: "criticized the Supreme Court's approval of affirmative action plans . . . embraced an expansive view of presidential power . . . criticized the Freedom of Information Act and hinted at disagreement with the Court's First Amendment rulings limiting libel suits . . . [and] questioned the basis for the Supreme Court's recognition of a constitutional right to sexual privacy, including abortion rights," among other things.[35] Predictably, Scalia ranks as one of the Rehnquist Court's three most conservative members (along with Rehnquist and Thomas).[36]

As for Clarence Thomas's views, there was only a shadow of a doubt, occasioned mainly by his flirtation with black nationalism while he was a Yale law student.[37] In the twenty years between that time and his nomination, he had become a prominent black conservative who used his status as chairman of the Equal Employment Opportunity Commission during the Reagan Administration to publicly praise an antiabortion article,[38] make controversial statements about the revival of constitutionally protected economic rights,[39] champion executive over legislative power,[40] applaud the actions of Colonel Oliver North,[41] disparage the role of discrimination in producing disparities in hiring and income,[42] attack the policies and leaders of the mainstream civil rights movement,[43] speak of some vague higher law behind the Constitution,[44] and repeatedly express his opposition to racial preferences.[45] In line with the heavy preponderance of the evidence at the time of his nomination, he quickly took his place with Justice Scalia and Chief Justice Rehnquist at the Court's conservative end, where he regularly votes with Scalia and Rehnquist between 80 and 100 percent of the time in civil rights and liberties cases (measured on a term-by-term basis).[46]

Even the lesser-known Reagan-Bush nominees clearly displayed the more moderate postures they would later assume on the Court. Within days of her nomination, media reports described Sandra Day O'Connor as a "sometime conservative with a moderate, even progressive streak,"[47] a record compiled largely on issues with constitutional overtones. As an Arizona state senator, she had voted to restore the death penalty, to ban compulsory busing to integrate schools, and to oppose gun control. She had also suggested that Congress limit the scope of the Civil Rights Act of 1871, which authorizes civil rights suits against state and local officials. She displayed her "progressive streak," however, by voting to oppose public aid to private and parochial schools, to oppose an antipornography bill that she considered overly broad, and to revise laws that discriminated against women in areas such as employment and child custody.[48] On abortion, she had on four occasions cast votes that might be termed prochoice, including votes against a right-to-life amendment and a measure to ban abortions in state hospitals.[49] O'Connor's prenomination record was clearly one of moderate conservatism.

That is precisely the record she has compiled as a justice. Between 1986 and 2000, O'Connor voted in favor of civil rights and liberties claims 40 percent of the time, a score that places her significantly below that of the next most liberal justice (David Souter at 61 percent) and virtually identical to Justices Kennedy and Lewis Powell.[50] O'Connor has joined conservatives in narrowing the procedural rights of criminal suspects,[51] usually—but not always—championing a color-blind Constitution over race-conscious remedies[52] and restricting the scope of federal (as opposed to state) power.[53] But she has also cast crucial fifth votes to preserve the "essence" of Roe v. Wade[54] and to extend the ban on public school prayers to graduation ceremonies,[55] and joined the Court's 1996 opinion that for the first time applied the Fourteenth Amendment's Equal Protection Clause to gays, striking down an antigay amendment to the Colorado constitution.[56] She later concurred on narrower grounds with the five-justice majority that struck down Texas's antisodomy law that applied only to gays.[57] Justice O'Connor's record is clearly that of a moderate conservative.

Even before the announcement of Anthony Kennedy's nomination, press accounts described him as a judge with a tough-on-crime approach who had nonetheless earned the mistrust of some conservatives who doubted whether he would overrule *Roe v. Wade*.[58] Shortly after his nomination, *Congressional Quarterly* described Kennedy as a conventional, orthodox conservative who avoided "broad theoretical declarations" in favor of a case-by-case approach.[59] One activist conservative lawyer told the *New York Times* that although "Judge Kennedy would probably side with conservatives most of the time, . . . they couldn't count on him in the tough ones."[60]

This preconfirmation portrait describes Justice Kennedy's later record accurately. According to Henry Abraham, Kennedy may have no "overarching theory of constitutional interpretation," but rather follows a "case-by-case approach" that is "normally guided by deference to precedent and legislative intent" and normally leads to conservative results.[61] Although a regular member of the Court's conservative majority on criminal justice and federalism[62] and a regular opponent of race-conscious remedies,[63] Kennedy has disappointed conservatives in such "tough ones" as the cases protecting flag burning as an act of speech, the Court's refusal to permit prayers at public school graduations and sporting events, its refusal to overrule *Roe v. Wade,* its rejection of state-imposed term limits for members of Congress, its decisions striking down the Colorado antigay law and overturning *Bowers v. Hardwick,* a decision invalidating a restriction of sexually explicit cable television programming to late night hours, and a ruling striking down a ban on "virtual" child pornography.[64] Kennedy is sufficiently nonideological to inspire popular and scholarly articles entitled "The Agonizer" (over his reported indecision in difficult cases), "The Limitations of Labeling," and "Is Anthony Kennedy a Conservative?"[65]

David Souter was the only nominee in recent times who deserved the label "stealth nominee." His opinions as a New Hampshire Supreme Court justice revealed little of his views on major issues. Although his record provided little guidance as to his judicial leanings, news reports described Souter as a highly intelligent, deeply thoughtful, moderate conservative whose opinions were carefully reasoned.[66] According to *Congressional Quarterly,*

Souter's Senate testimony revealed a "detachment and propensity for the middle of the road."[67]

Justice Souter is the only Reagan-Bush appointee to deviate from the performance that the best evidence at the time of his nomination would have predicted. On the one hand, Souter's record validates his initial depiction as an intelligent and unusually thoughtful jurist.[68] Likewise, his record displays the "detachment and propensity for the middle of the road" he voiced at his hearings. Of the fourteen justices who served between 1986 and 2000, Souter ranked seventh in his support for "liberal outcomes" in civil rights and liberties cases.[69]

Souter has surprised Court observers, however, by a leftward drift that has made him an identifiable member of the Court's relatively liberal wing since his second term on the Court (1991–92).[70] Since then, he has, among other rulings, joined the five-justice majority upholding the "essence" of *Roe v. Wade*,[71] joined the opinion overturning *Bowers v. Hardwick*,[72] dissented from major rulings favoring states' rights over federal power,[73] supported race-conscious civil rights policies,[74] opposed greater governmental accommodation of religion,[75] and voted against conservative interests in cases involving the Fifth Amendment's takings clause, which business and conservative organizations hoped to use to block economic and environmental regulations.[76] One should not, however, overstate Souter's liberalism: he leans to the left only on what is generally a moderately conservative Court and is not a liberal in the mold of a William Brennan or a Thurgood Marshall.[77] Souter cast liberal votes in 63 percent of civil rights and liberties cases from his second term on the Court (1991–92) through the 2000 term. Brennan and Marshall cast liberal votes over 80 percent of the time during the early years of the Rehnquist Court (1986 through 1990 terms), although the issues may have been different in those years just before Souter joined the Court.[78]

Based on her thirteen-year record on the federal Court of Appeals for the District of Columbia, Ruth Bader Ginsburg was widely described upon her nomination as a moderate liberal with a preference for judicial caution.[79] As a justice, she has amply fulfilled the widespread expectation that she would continue in that mold. In federalism and commerce cases, Ginsburg has resisted the Rehnquist Court's reversal of the historical trend toward greater federal power.[80] She has opposed its move toward greater governmental accommodation of religion.[81] On civil rights and liberties, she quickly aligned herself with Justice Souter, who by then had moved to a moderately liberal position (where they were later joined by Justice Breyer).[82] Like Souter, Ginsburg is clearly not a Brennan- or Marshall-style liberal. In her first eight years on the Court, her liberal voting rate of 63 percent in civil rights and liberties cases made her the fifth most liberal of the fourteen justices who served on the moderately conservative Rehnquist Court between 1986 and 2000.[83] She has not been notably liberal in criminal justice cases.[84] Jeffrey Rosen has described her juridical approach as

> in most cases, a paragon of judicial restraint. . . .[S]he has shown as a justice precisely the same qualities that guided her for 13 years on the Court of Appeals: an affinity for resolving cases on narrow procedural grounds rather than appealing to broad principles of social justice; a preference for small steps over sweeping gestures, and an aversion to bold assertions of judicial power. . . .
>
> As an avatar, in most cases, of judicial minimalism, Justice Ginsburg is the antithesis of Justice William Brennan, the liberal lion of the Warren Court.[85]

In an overview of Ginsburg's first ten years on the High Court, Judith A. Baer notes that Ginsburg "is not an innovator; even . . . in gender cases,"[86] which had earlier gained her fame as an advocate for greater legal equality for women. Baer writes that "as a judge, Ginsburg has shown a respect for precedent and a cautious approach to doctrinal change,"[87] exactly the qualities she had displayed over thirteen years on the federal Court of Appeals in Washington.[88]

Stephen Breyer was perhaps the best known nominee of modern times. As described in Chapter 3, several members of the Senate Judiciary Committee knew him from his earlier stint as chief counsel to the committee. Although his views on some issues were unknown, he was widely described by his acquaintances and the many members of the legal community familiar with his work as prochoice (as he acknowledged at his confirmation hearings),[89] skeptical toward business regulation (the subject of his four books), moderate to conservative on crime (he had defended the guidelines of the U.S. Sentencing Commission, which he helped to write and which some judges and others see as too rigid), and a defender of the use of legislative history to interpret statutes.[90] Among the words most often used to describe him in articles about his nomination were "moderate," "centrist," "pragmatic," and "flexible,"[91] characteristics he had displayed as an appeals court judge.

Justice Breyer is very much the moderate liberal he was expected to be. In federalism and commerce cases, he opposes the Rehnquist Court's diminutions of federal power.[92] On governmental accommodation of religion, Breyer has displayed his pragmatism by occasionally, but not usually, siding with his

conservative colleagues.[93] On civil rights and liberties more generally, however, Breyer quickly formed an identifiable voting bloc with Justices
Ginsburg and Souter, where he has remained since.[94] When ranked with all
of the justices who served on the Rehnquist Court from 1986 to 2000,
Breyer's record of liberal voting in civil rights and liberties cases (62 percent) places him significantly below Justices Blackmun and Stevens (at 71
and 72 percent) and about midway between the very liberal Brennan-
Marshall pairing (87 and 88 percent) and the moderately conservative
Kennedy-Powell-O'Connor group (38 to 40 percent).[95] The close correspon-
dence between Justices Breyer and Ginsburg's prenomination records and
their later performances on the Court validates Elena Kagan's admission that
although senators learned little new about their views at their confirmation
hearings, it was hardly necessary for senators to question them.[96]

In sum, seven of the last eight appointees (counting Rehnquist's appointment to chief justice) have been very much what they appeared to be at the
time of their nominations. This individual analysis of the eight appointees
from Presidents Reagan through Clinton is consistent with the statistical
finding of a strong relationship between justices' votes and newspaper
descriptions of their beliefs at the time of their nominations.[97] It is therefore
doubtful that more forthcoming Senate testimony or other additional material is needed to uncover the general tone of nominees' legal, political, and
philosophical values. With the lone exception of David Souter, the Senate of
recent years has had sufficient data to accurately gauge the ideological orientation of the nominees before it.

It is also doubtful whether the Senate needs more information on nominees' views on specific issues. As we saw in Chapter 2, judges in our constitutional system are to be equally independent of both president and Senate.
Every recent nominee has sworn that the president and his aides did not ask
the nominee how he or she would vote on any particular issue,[98] and there is
no evidence to contradict these claims. If presidents and their aides do not get
this kind of information from nominees, there is no need for the Senate to do
so. And the nominee's judicial philosophy and view as to whether there is,
for example, a right to privacy in the Constitution are as accessible to the
Senate as to the president.

One might object here that senators' inability to get nominees to actually say what they think nonetheless prevents senators from acting on what
they believe a nominee's beliefs to be. We consider this argument in the next
section, where we examine the harmful consequences that would follow from
more revealing information on nominees' beliefs.

THE DUBIOUS CONSEQUENCES OF GREATER INFORMATION

The previous section demonstrated that even if nominees are unresponsive to Senate questioning, senators can normally identify the ideologies of potential justices. This fact, however, does not imply that a nominee's silence or evasion is without consequence. Without a nominee's clearly stated endorsement of a controversial view, a suspicious senator may feel that there is no practical recourse but to respect the president's choice and vote to confirm a nominee that he or she would rather vote against.[99] Candor on the part of the nominee might bring about a contrary result. The Senate's rejection of Robert Bork may be one example of this, although Bork may very well have been rejected even without his candid testimony, given his widely known controversial views and the Democratic Senate he faced. Antonin Scalia and Clarence Thomas might also have been rejected had Democratic senators been able to force them to voice their true thoughts on a variety of issues. This is especially true of Thomas, who faced a Democratic Senate and considerable opposition from a wide array of liberal groups even before Anita Hill's charges of sexual harassment surfaced.[100] Thus, although the general posture of a nominee is normally foreseeable, it does not follow that a nominee's silence or evasive testimony is inconsequential.

More candid testimony could even have endangered the nominations of Justices O'Connor, Kennedy, and Souter (the latter two of whom faced Democratic Senates). Although we cannot know for certain their thoughts at the time of their nominations on *Roe v. Wade* (the hot-button issue at the time of their confirmation hearings), it is likely that all three harbored serious reservations about the decision. Justice O'Connor and Kennedy's subsequent opinions were critical of *Roe,*[101] and the joint opinion of all three justices in *Planned Parenthood v. Casey* (1992), while upholding the "essence" of *Roe,* deemphasized *Roe*'s intrinsic merits and rested more on other arguments for retaining the essence of *Roe.*[102] As their rulings suggest, Justices O'Connor and Kennedy also likely harbored serious doubts about the types of affirmative action programs Congress had long favored.[103] Thus, it is true that the silence or evasive testimony of their nominees facilitated President Reagan and George H. W. Bush's installation of conservative—in some cases *very* conservative—justices.

The next chapter examines the possibility that these presidents were thereby able to pack the Court, or even to move the Court so far to the right as to place it at odds with the mainstream beliefs of the American people. The remainder of this chapter examines the likely consequences of the more revealing information and candid nominee testimony some authors in the political school seek. The consequences of greater knowledge of nominees' views—if such knowledge could be had—would be very different from the favorable outcomes the critics hope for.

The Likely Consequences of More Candid Testimony

Even assuming the validity of the widespread belief that nominees must not tell senators how they would vote in any case likely to come before the Court, nominees might still provide senators with more revealing testimony than they typically do on important issues they will address on the Court. They might, for example, identify and explain their present inclination on these issues while explicitly reserving the right to reach a different conclusion in an actual case. Or nominees who are genuinely uncertain as to their leanings on a particular issue could elaborate candidly on the source of their uncertainty and recount their present thinking without resolving the matter.

Five possible consequences of such testimony present themselves. All of them, contrary to the hopes of those who favor more candid testimony, suggest that such testimony would be impractical and/or harmful. First, if nominees stated more specific views than they usually do on current constitutional issues, they may feel constrained to adhere to the opinions they stated at their confirmation hearings, at least during their early years on the Court. They will thereby compromise their independence and perhaps their impartiality as well.[104] And if such adherence to the approaches voiced at the hearings endured for more than a few years, it would also rob the nation of the benefits to be had from the justices' experience and evolving wisdom. The less illuminating testimony of the present process may preserve these benefits as well as the justices' independence. The clearly evolving views of Justice Souter in his early terms on the Court represent such a process of jurisprudential evolution.[105] A senator may, of course, vote against a nominee for any reason, including a nominee's refusal to signal a future vote on a single issue—even one the nominee has not had occasion to think deeply about. But if senators insist on knowing with a high degree of specificity how a nominee will vote on the issues, they will confirm only those nominees who swear not to profit from experience.

A second problem with statements of opinion on contentious issues is that a justice might be ethically bound to recuse him- or herself, or explain why recusal is not necessary, in what may be a large number of future cases raising those issues.[106] It does little good, and threatens substantial harm on a court whose decisions are as vital as the Supreme Court's, to appoint a justice who cannot decide cases. Those who minimize this possibility should recall that then-Justice Rehnquist was asked to recuse himself from a matter about which he had expressed an opinion at his 1971 confirmation hearings, and felt obliged to issue a lengthy opinion defending his decision to participate in the case, a decision for which he was later called to task.[107] Critics who deny the need for frequent recusals do not, for some reason, deny the need for justices to issue frequent explanations of why they have denied a motion for recusal on matters they have testified about, motions that are sure to come from one litigant or the other.[108] Perhaps the critics have not thought about this ramification of more specific testimony, or how a substantial number of defensive, self-justifying opinions from the justices could impair the perceived, if not real, fairness of the Court's proceedings.

Another example of such impairment is Justice Scalia's long and, to some, unpersuasive explanation of his refusal to recuse himself from a case involving his friend, Vice President Dick Cheney, in 2004. The justice had taken a hunting trip with Cheney early that year, shortly after the Supreme Court had decided to hear Cheney's appeal of an unfavorable lower court ruling regarding his chairmanship of the second Bush Administration's task force on energy policy. Justice Scalia's twenty-one-page opinion denying a motion for recusal acknowledged that his involvement in the case had brought him "a good deal of embarrassing criticism and adverse publicity" from "newspaper editorials" and "late-night comedians." Legal ethicists disagreed over Scalia's refusal to recuse himself.[109]

A third possible consequence of more revealing testimony is the rejection of what are, from a long-run systemic point of view, "acceptable nominees." As noted above, candid testimony might well have endangered and even killed the nominations of Justices Souter, O'Connor, and Kennedy. These justices are "acceptable" on the basis of the following criteria: None of them is or was ideologically rigid or extreme, and they are all competent justices of good character and fair temperament. Given these characteristics and the widespread authority of the norm of judicial independence, it is not likely that Democratic senators in the years after these justices' confirmations would have voted to remove them, even if the opportunity to do so had somehow presented itself. Yet their confirmations might well have been blocked by more candid testimony on abortion and, in the cases of O'Connor and Kennedy, affirmative action and federalism. Hence, the unrevealing testimony of the current process may be just as functional, if not more so, than a more revealing process that is likely to reject nominees who fulfill the criteria just described.

This third consequence of more candid testimony points to a fourth: deadlock over appointments. As we have seen, even the nominations of the more moderate Reagan-Bush nominees may well have been jeopardized or rejected as a result of such testimony. Hence the current, relatively unilluminating nominee testimony is functional for the purpose of moderating conflict over nominations and filling vacant Supreme Court seats.

The fifth possible consequence of more illuminating testimony by nominees is that the Senate may actually be misled by such testimony, no matter how sincere the testimony may be. If the Senate does confirm more candid nominees whose views evolve on the Court and who do not feel obliged to adhere to the approaches or likely results they outline at their hearings, these justices will issue opinions at odds with their Senate testimony, leaving senators to feel that the nominees misled them. Had, for example, Anthony Kennedy been somehow made to share his innermost thoughts on abortion with the Senate at the time of his nomination, he most likely would have said that he did not believe strongly in *Roe v. Wade* and was not highly disposed to defend it. Yet five years later, in *Planned Parenthood v. Casey,* he cast a crucial vote to uphold a basic right to abortion. (Of course, such candor might have resulted in Kennedy's rejection, in which case the Senate would have acted on the basis of misleading information, Kennedy would have been the third nominee—after Robert Bork and Douglas Ginsburg—to fail to win confirmation, and the agony of filling Justice Lewis Powell's seat would have continued.) The current brand of nominee testimony may offer few insights into a nominee's views on specific issues, and may even at times be disingenuous, but the more revealing testimony many commentators seek would be unreliable for a different reason: however sincere such testimony may be, it would be an untrustworthy guide to the nominee's future votes as a justice.

CONCLUSION

The charge that contemporary Senates have confirmed nominees without adequate information on their judicial philosophies has little support. With the lone exception of David Souter, the prenomination records of modern nominees and their testimony at Senate hearings have allowed senators to identify the nominees' legal ideologies and to predict their future positions on the liberal-conservative spectrum with a high degree of confidence.

The more revealing, issue-specific information sought by critics of the confirmation process in the political school could very well result in frequent recusals or else threaten the public's perception of a fair Court. It could heighten and prolong bitter and wearisome conflicts over vacancies, and result in the rejection of nominees who would serve the nation well. It could also produce less independent and flexible justices who fail to express the fruits of their growth on the Court, or, alternatively, yield testimony that the Senate cannot trust. Seen in this light, the consequences of the present mode of proceeding are positive.

To explore this possibility further, the next chapter examines, primarily through an analysis of the rulings of the Rehnquist Court, two of the concerns most often expressed or reflected by political school critics of the current confirmation process: that presidents can use the allegedly inadequate confirmation process to pack the Court, and that the process may help produce a Court at odds with the nation's values.

7

Court Packing and an Aberrant Court

The political school's concern over the Senate's ability to conduct informed ideological review of nominees (or to act on the results of that review) contributes to a fear that presidents can place their ideological allies on the Court and acquire excessive influence over the evolution of constitutional law. Laurence Tribe is not alone in his fear that a president with "any skill and luck" can "build the Court of his dreams."[1] Gary Simson has likewise expressed concern that "Presidents are so able to put people to their ideological liking on the Court that the line separating the executive and judicial branches can become dangerously blurred."[2] Of even greater concern is the possibility that presidents may surreptitiously slip onto the Court justices whose values are "abhorrent"[3] to the nation or, as Bruce Ackerman has framed the problem, insufficiently in accord with the values of the nation to legitimize the transformations of constitutional law their decisions bring about.[4]

This chapter evaluates these concerns by examining presidents' ability to move the Supreme Court in their own ideological direction and, in particular, how successful President Ronald Reagan and the first President Bush were at making the Court more conservative. It also examines the relationship between the Supreme Court's rulings and public attitudes toward the Court, with special attention to this relationship in the era of the Rehnquist Court. The analysis concludes that presidents can and do move the Court in their direction, but they will very likely achieve only mixed success at influencing the Court's doctrines. There is even less danger that presidents may create a Court of immoderate views.

CAN PRESIDENTS PACK THE SUPREME COURT?

Fears of presidential Court packing such as those expressed above exaggerate the realities because presidents face several obstacles to packing the Court. First is the limited number of appointments most presidents make. From 1869 (when the Court's size was set at nine) through the spring of 2004, twenty-six presidents served an average of 5.2 years and "appointed" ("nominated" is more accurate) sixty-nine justices, an average of 2.7 per president.[5] Supreme Court vacancies occurred at an average rate of .51 per year over this period. Because Supreme Court vacancies follow what statisticians call a Poisson distribution, we can use the .51 figure to calculate the probability that a president serving any given number of years will fill any given number of seats.[6] A president has only about a 37 percent probability of filling more than two seats in one term. Hence a president will quite likely need to win a second term—and retain the support of the Senate—to fill a majority of five or more seats with persons truly to the president's liking. But even after eight years in office, a president has only a 43 percent chance of filling five or more seats. Since 1869, only three of twenty-six presidents have been this fortunate: William Howard Taft, who named six justices; Franklin Roosevelt, who named eight (one of whom served only one year) in his now-impossible twelve-year presidency; and Dwight Eisenhower, who named five.[7]

By themselves, these probabilities provide an incomplete picture of the president's ability to change the Court's ideological balance. On the one hand, they may overstate the president's ability to effect ideological change on the Court because a large number of successful nominees are not the president's first choice on ideological grounds (such as Justice Anthony Kennedy, to cite just the clearest case in recent decades).[8] And some nominees will not perform as the president had hoped. Examples here are Justices Harry Blackmun, John Paul Stevens, and David Souter, all of whom turned out to be substantially more liberal than their nominators had hoped (and perhaps Justices O'Connor and Kennedy who, as we have seen, have contributed to several 5–4 or 6–3 "liberal" victories on major issues or, in O'Connor's case, tempered conservative rulings by writing concurring opinions). On the other hand, a president may not need a large number of vacancies to tip the balance on a closely divided Court. The point, however, is that most presidents will fill a significant proportion of the Court's seats, but quite likely less than a majority, and they have an even smaller chance of naming five justices whose views are close to their own.

Another barrier to presidential Court packing is the contemporary Senate. In comparison with that of the first two-thirds of the twentieth century, the modern Senate is increasingly able and willing to reject presidents' first choices. Between 1894 and 1968, the Senate rejected just one of some forty-six nominees.[9] Since 1968, the Senate has rejected four nominees— Abe Fortas (for chief justice), Clement Haynsworth, G. Harrold Carswell, and Robert Bork. It also forced the withdrawal of Douglas Ginsburg and confirmed another nominee, Clarence Thomas, by a margin of only four votes (although the Senate's treatment of Thomas was hardly an example of senatorial assertiveness).

This enhanced activism is due in part to the Senate's increased capacity and proclivity to investigate nominees' backgrounds. Judge Carswell, for instance, was rejected partly on the basis of embarrassing evidence that he had helped privatize a publicly owned golf course to prevent its desegregation, and then dissembled in his Senate testimony on the matter.[10] This experience contrasts sharply with the 1937 confirmation of Hugo Black, whose past membership in the Ku Klux Klan the Senate chose not to investigate before voting to confirm him, just five days after he was nominated.[11]

In recent decades, the Senate has been transformed into "a more open and effective forum for the expression of diverse interests,"[12] the very characteristic that distresses legalist critics of the modern confirmation process as too open and democratic. These changes have made the Senate a more effective and independent evaluator of presidential proposals.[13] From the administration of Warren G. Harding through that of John F. Kennedy, an average of just twenty-three days elapsed between the announcement of a Supreme Court nomination and the Senate's confirmation vote. Setting aside the long-delayed confirmations of four Eisenhower nominees, the Senate spent an average of only fifteen days reviewing the nominations of that period.[14] By contrast, President Clinton's highly acclaimed, "consensual" nominations of Ruth Bader Ginsburg and Stephen Breyer took seven and eleven weeks, respectively, to pass through the Senate. During that time, congressional staffers, senators, the FBI, and numerous interest groups and reporters sifted through volumes of material on the nominees. This transformation of the Senate, along with the proliferation of interest groups and expanded media reporting, ensures that the heightened scrutiny today's nominees face, compared to most of those from the 1890s to the 1960s, will continue.

A third obstacle to Court packing is that presidents must balance the ideology of potential nominees against other criteria: their age, partisan affiliation, geographical origins, and confirmability. In recent decades, the heightened scrutiny of nominees has made concerns over confirmability more prominent. Race, ethnicity, and gender have also joined the list of factors competing with ideology. President Reagan's choice of Sandra Day O'Connor, for instance, was influenced greatly by his 1980 campaign promise to put a woman on the Court.[15] Justice O'Connor is assuredly a woman, but as we have seen, not so assuredly conservative.

A fourth problem for would-be presidential Court packers is that a "stealth nominee" may evade the president's radar as much as the Senate's. Sometimes the best that presidents can do is to nominate someone who seems reasonably close to them ideologically, but whose views on specific issues are unknown. The selection of such a nominee is most often a reflection of one or more limits on the president's discretion: the inability to win confirmation for a figure more clearly to the president's liking, the need to placate rival wings of the president's party, and/or the president's wish for a non-controversial confirmation proceeding. The first of these considerations produced the nomination of Harry Blackmun after the Senate's rejection of Haynsworth and Carswell, and Anthony Kennedy after the Senate's rejection of Robert Bork. The third factor was a principal reason for President Ford's nomination of John Paul Stevens, President George H. W. Bush's nomination of David Souter, and President Clinton's nominations of Ruth Bader Ginsburg and Stephen Breyer.[16] Such nominees may disappoint the president after reaching the Court, as did Blackmun, Stevens, and Souter. Although presidents have usually judged the ideologies of their nominees accurately (70 percent or more of the time, apparently), history offers many examples to the contrary.[17]

A fifth problem for presidential Court packers is their limited ability to predict the crucial constitutional issues of the future. President Eisenhower, for example, apparently failed to foresee the upcoming importance of desegregation in choosing Earl Warren for chief justice in 1953.[18] (The same limitation applies to the Senate. Senators did not ask any of President Nixon's six nominees, two of whom the Senate rejected, a single question about abortion just a few years before *Roe v. Wade*.)[19]

A related problem is that justices may employ the doctrines of their appointers in ways that undercut their appointers' own positions. The judicial restraint favored by New Deal liberals did not serve the liberal cause after the Democratic party embraced the principles of civil rights and expansive civil liberties.[20] Likewise, the attachment of most Reagan-Bush appointees to color-blind civil rights policies has hindered the creation of congressional districts in which a majority of voters are racial minorities, a practice that produces larger numbers of Republican representatives elected from adjacent districts shorn of minority voters.[21] And the Rehnquist Court's notable insistence that the Supreme Court is the definitive interpreter of the Constitution can aid conservative causes or it can thwart them, as it did when the Court cited its interpretive supremacy to strike down congressional attempts to expand religious freedoms and overturn *Miranda v. Arizona,* efforts supported by conservatives.[22]

President Nixon's public crusade to reverse the direction of the Warren Court and the mixed results he achieved despite his appointment of four justices illustrate the difficulties presidents face in trying to pack the Court.[23] As a further measure of a president's ability to bring about constitutional change through the appointment of ideological allies, the next section examines the success of two more recent presidents who made equal or greater, and reputedly more successful, efforts to build a Court in sympathy with their views: Ronald Reagan and the first President Bush.

THE REHNQUIST COURT AND THE CONSERVATIVE AGENDA

David O'Brien echoed many observers of the Supreme Court when he wrote that the Reagan Administration's "ambitious agenda for judicial reform was part of its plan to have the federal judiciary carry . . . [its] conservative social agenda and a free-market economic philosophy into the next century."[24] The first President Bush was not as socially conservative as Reagan, and he placed more weight than Reagan on a potential nominee's confirmability. His administration nonetheless faced unrelenting pressure to choose solidly conservative nominees.[25] He was assured that in nominating David Souter he had done so,[26] and in nominating Clarence Thomas, he clearly did so.

Several obstacles necessarily limit the following assessment of the jurisprudence of the Rehnquist Court that Presidents Nixon, Reagan, and the first President Bush brought about. First, there have been several Rehnquist Courts, with the elevation of Rehnquist to chief justice and the appointments of Scalia (in 1986), Kennedy (1988), Souter (1990), Thomas (1991), Ginsburg (1993), and Breyer (1994). But because the Court went ten years without change of personnel after Breyer's appointment and no justice changed ideologically during that time, it makes considerable sense to speak of a Rehnquist Court, at least during that decade.

Second, *liberal* and *conservative* are relative terms. As of early 2004, the Court contains no liberal giants such as William Brennan and Thurgood Marshall. And the five relative conservatives on the Rehnquist Court are not equally conservative. Nonetheless, for the sake of convenience and saving space, I will often speak of the five "conservatives" (Rehnquist, O'Connor, Scalia, Kennedy, and Thomas) and the four "liberals" (Stevens, Souter, Ginsburg, and Breyer). More nuanced language will appear as needed.

Third, I follow Hensley, Smith, and Baugh in defining a conservative decision as one "rejecting individuals' claims of improper government interference with constitutionally protected rights" or, in civil rights cases, rejecting the position of the litigant that is trying to promote greater equality for racial minorities or women, or accepting the claim of a litigant attempting to widen the definition of economic or property rights or curtail the scope of governmental, especially federal, regulatory powers.[27]

Fourth, the spatial limits of a portion of a chapter prohibit detailed analysis of the Rehnquist Court's decisions. I have tried to include enough nuance (such as citing concurring opinions in ostensibly 5–4 rulings) to avoid misunderstandings. Fifth, spatial limits preclude examination of the claim that the Rehnquist Court has ruled by proxy—by accepting fewer appeals of the conservative rulings of the federal Courts of Appeals.[28] Finally, only with the passage of time can we separate the Rehnquist Court's lasting contributions to constitutional doctrine from its evolutionary dead ends. Many if not most generalizations about the Rehnquist Court—or any Court—can be contravened, either by pointing to existing rulings or by waiting for time to cast one's conclusions into doubt.[29] Unpredictable turns in the Rehnquist Court's jurisprudence and the diverse ideological perspectives of observers help to explain why the Rehnquist Court has been characterized as everything from left-wing activist[30] to incrementalist[31] to right-wing revolutionary.[32]

Despite these hurdles, we must attempt an assessment of the Rehnquist Court's jurisprudence between the advent of Rehnquist's chief justiceship in 1986 and the early twenty-first century in order to evaluate the claim that the modern confirmation process, for all its increased senatorial assertiveness, permits presidential domination of the overall appointments process. We move roughly from those issues where conservative appointees have had the greatest impact to those where they have had the least.

Federalism

Conservatives seeking to reduce the power of the federal government have won several major victories in the Rehnquist Court. In the 1990s, the Court fashioned an "anticommandeering" principle that limits Congress's power to use state or local governments to enforce congressional policies. The most noted of these cases struck down the requirement that state and local police conduct background checks on gun buyers,[33] and barred state employees from suing their employers for violating federal labor laws in state as well as federal courts.[34]

In another series of decisions, the five conservatives expanded the states' sovereign immunity from lawsuits by ruling that the Eleventh Amendment bars citizens from suing their states for money damages for violating citizens' rights under federal labor, patent, copyright, age, and handicapped discrimination laws.[35] These rulings rested partly on the Tenth Amendment and the purported "dual sovereignty"[36] of the federal and state governments. Citizens may also be barred from bringing complaints about state conduct to federal executive branch agencies.[37] Justices O'Connor and Rehnquist surprisingly broke with this line of cases in a 6–3 decision in 2003 permitting state employees to sue states for violating the Family and Medical Leave Act. The majority opinion viewed the law as a protection against sex discrimination, which the Court views as less justifiable than discrimination against the aged and handicapped.[38]

In 2001, the five conservatives rejected on statutory grounds the federal government's asserted authority to regulate isolated, nonnavigable ponds and wetlands under the Clean Water Act (which explicitly authorizes regulation only of "navigable waters") despite the presence of migratory birds in those waters. The majority in the case expressed its wider concern for the states' "traditional and primary" powers.[39]

One must be cautious, however, in assessing the Rehnquist Court's record on federalism. It has handed down many decisions favoring federal authority. The 1995 *Term Limits* ruling[40] rejected a Tenth Amendment argument that states may set qualifications for members of Congress beyond those stated in the Constitution, a position embraced by conservatives at the time. In preemption cases alleging conflicts between state regulatory powers and federal legislation, the Rehnquist Court has followed the Warren and Burger Courts by favoring federal legislation in a large majority of cases,[41] although some observers have charged that the conservative justices uphold federal authority when doing so produces conservative or probusiness results.[42]

Even some of the Rehnquist Court's harshest critics have allowed, however, that no true revolution on federalism will occur unless the Court revises its preemption doctrines, which allow federal laws to override state laws even when they do not directly conflict and Congress has expressed no intent to override state laws; and unless the Court curtails Congress's ability to impose its will on the states by conditional spending. The Court has shown little inclination to do these things.[43] This reluctance may serve conservative goals such as promoting a national and global economy for business, and the ability of Congress to place conditions on federal benefits for individuals as well as states. But the result in any case is inimical to enhanced state autonomy.[44]

The rulings expanding state immunity did not leave citizens entirely without legal recourse against alleged violations by states of their rights under federal statutes. The federal government may sue states for monetary damages on citizens' behalf, and citizens may sue for injunctive relief, although such constricted alternatives will likely allow states considerable freedom in many instances to ignore federal law. The decisions on state immunity are also far from settled law. The Court's four more liberal justices have repeatedly promised their continued opposition to these 5–4 rulings.[45]

Church and State

In several controversial free exercise cases in the late 1980s and early 1990s, five- and six-justice majorities jettisoned long-standing doctrine applying strict scrutiny to government acts that seriously but unintentionally impair traditional religious practices.[46] Strict scrutiny still applies when government intentionally burdens a particular religion, or free exercise is not the only right at stake.[47]

On separation of church and state, the Court's decisions have shifted with changes in its personnel. "The Warren Court," David O'Brien has written, "moved constitutional law in the direction of a high wall of separation, and then the Burger and Rehnquist Courts swung back."[48] The Rehnquist Court has allowed the use of public funds for premarital counseling by both religious and secular agencies; required public schools to allow student religious groups the same opportunity as other groups to meet on school grounds after hours; allowed public funds to subsidize remedial classes and personal assistants for disabled students in parochial schools; barred state universities from refusing to fund student religious publications while funding others; and overturned two precedents to permit greater public provision of instructional materials to religious schools.[49] The capstone of this line of cases was undoubtedly the Cleveland school vouchers case, where the five conservatives upheld the use of taxpayer-funded vouchers to send children to religious as well as public and secular private schools.[50] In *Locke v. Davey* (2004), however, the Court permitted states to exclude students preparing for the ministry from state-funded college scholarship programs, thereby refusing to create a broad "neutrality principle" that would require governments that subsidize secular activities to extend like funding to analogous religious activities.[51]

In other cases, however, the Rehnquist Court has struck down laws giving tax-exempt status to religious magazines, requiring public schools to teach creationism, and creating a special school district for a village of Hasidic Jews. It extended the ban on public school prayers to graduations and sporting events.[52] It barred cities from displaying a nativity scene but allowed the display of Christmas trees and menorahs because of their "secular" meanings.[53]

The justices are divided over government accommodation of religion and disagree on the appropriate test for these cases. Where a constitutional violation is relatively clear, a substantial majority will strike down a practice—such as mandating creationism classes in public schools (struck 7–2) or creating a school district for a particular sect (struck 6–3). But in less clear-cut cases, the decision is likely to be 5–4, with the result more likely than not to favor accommodation.[54] Seven of the thirteen decisions described above were 5–4, with five of the seven permitting accommodation.

Criminal Justice

The Reagan-Bush justices have had a major conservative impact on criminal justice. From 1986 to 2003, the Court limited protections against self-incrimination in several cases,[55] rejected claims of inadequate jury instructions in capital cases,[56] restricted habeas corpus in at least eight cases,[57] restricted the right to counsel for indigents,[58] rejected claims of ineffective counsel,[59] narrowed the protection against double jeopardy,[60] upheld "three-strikes" laws that mete out long prison terms for minor offenses,[61] permitted the eviction of innocent public housing tenants for drug offenses committed by others,[62] issued mixed rulings on prosecutors' authority to seize property,[63] and limited Fourth Amendment protections in two dozen cases (including one that allows schools to perform drug tests on all students participating in extracurricular activities).[64] The Court overturned two precedents to allow prosecutors in capital cases to introduce evidence about a murder victim's good character and the murder's impact on the victim's family.[65] It ruled that "sexually violent predators" may be confined to mental hospitals after their prison terms, upheld a federal law restricting judges' power to supervise state and local prisons, and upheld the death penalty for sixteen-year-olds.[66]

The Rehnquist Court's retrenchment on criminal justice issues is a notable turnaround from the Warren era. But the Court has not been uniformly hostile to claims of criminal rights. Since 1991, when the very conservative Justice Thomas replaced the very liberal Justice Marshall, the Court has ruled in favor of such claims in at least one case involving police entrapment,[67] three cases on assistance of counsel,[68] two cases on self-incrimination (including one explicitly declining to overturn *Miranda* partly because it has "become part of our national culture"[69]), four Eighth Amendment cases,[70] one case on double jeopardy,[71] one on excessive police discretion,[72] one ex post facto case,[73] two cases on the right of prisoners to sue their jailers,[74] eight cases on due process,[75] and nine cases on searches and seizures.[76] Although the Court has restricted habeas corpus, it has upheld or expanded habeas review in thirteen cases (including two involving criminal aliens facing deportation).[77] The Court has disallowed, absent special circumstances, the indefinite detention of deportees whom no foreign country will take.[78] And in 2002 the Court banned executions of the mentally retarded, overturning its own 1989 decision.[79] This record shows that blanket statements about the Rehnquist Court's record on criminal justice are dubious.

The Commerce Power

In *U.S. v. Lopez* (1995),[80] a majority of the Supreme Court, for the first time since the 1930s, struck down a federal law because it exceeded Congress's commerce power: the Gun-Free School Zones Act of 1990. In *U.S. v. Morrison* (2000), the five conservatives struck down on the same ground a part of the federal Violence Against Women Act that allowed women victims of "gender-motivated" crimes to sue their assailants in federal court.[81] That same year, in *Jones v. U.S.,*[82] a unanimous Court ruled on statutory grounds, but in language echoing *Lopez*'s insistence that the commerce power must be limited, that the federal antiarson law does not protect structures that are not used for some commercial purpose.

The ramifications of these decisions are uncertain but likely to prove limited. The majority's distinctions between "what is truly national and what is truly local," and between economic activities Congress may regulate and noneconomic activities it may not,[83] echo pre–New Deal distinctions but leave untouched vast swaths of congressional power. Justices Kennedy and O'Connor recognized this in their concurring opinion in *Lopez,* which stressed the "immense stake" in adhering generally to the Court's post–New Deal Commerce jurisprudence.[84]

Moreover, as the majority argued in both *Lopez* and *Morrison,* if measures like the Gun-Free School Zones Act fall within the commerce power because education affects commerce, it is hard to imagine what does not.[85]

The defenders of these challenged regulations have arguably conceded this point. When the justices asked Solicitor General Drew S. Days, who defended the Gun-Free Schools law in *Lopez,* whether his interpretation placed any limits at all on the commerce power, he could offer none and suggested that Congress could define its regulatory powers for itself.[86] The principal dissenting opinion in the case repeated this suggestion.[87]

This posture might convert the commerce power, in the words of the liberal scholar Laurence Tribe, into a "plenary national power over all spheres of life not otherwise protected from congressional intrusion by external limits like those of the Bill of Rights."[88] Some scholarly critics of *Lopez* and *Morrison* have suggested fashioning Congress's commerce and civil rights enforcement powers into much the same thing: "the effective equivalent of a general [federal] police power" that would exclude "very few things."[89] It is hardly radical for a majority of the Court to maintain that there is some very broad limit to the commerce power. Recent Republican presidents have not packed the Court with commerce clause extremists. Only Justice Thomas has suggested replacing the Court's post–New Deal jurisprudence on commerce with something much stricter.[90]

Equal Protection for Minorities

This section covers the Rehnquist Court's decisions on civil rights for groups other than women and gays who, as discussed below, have fared better during the Rehnquist era than most other traditionally disadvantaged groups. The Rehnquist Court has a bifurcated record on affirmative action. The five conservatives have ruled that in the awarding of public contracts, affirmative action programs sponsored by all levels of government must undergo strict scrutiny and be narrowly tailored to remedy actual instances of discrimination (and not just statistical disparities).[91]

The debate among the justices in these cases resembled the debate over affirmative action in American society. The majority argued that government affirmative action plans may both reflect and promote the perception that minorities cannot succeed on their merits[92]; that a preference for minorities "assures that race will always be relevant in American life"[93]; and that low minority representation in many spheres of life is not proof of actual discrimination.[94] The dissenters have responded that remedial race-conscious policies are different from the invidious discrimination of the past; racial discrimination is still widespread; color-blind policies perpetuate the vestiges of discrimination; and that low minority representation in many spheres does prove discrimination.[95]

But in higher education, the four liberals and Justice O'Connor have affirmed the 1978 *Bakke*[96] holding that permits race-conscious admissions policies that consider applicants individually and avoid a mechanical or quota-like approach. O'Connor's majority opinion in *Grutter v. Bollinger* (2003)[97] even buttressed the justification for affirmative action by going beyond the need for diversity in the classroom as described in *Bakke* to include the cultivation of a diverse set of national leaders for a diverse nation.[98] The majority did, however, express its expectation that affirmative action would no longer be needed in twenty-five years.[99]

As in the public contracting cases, the Court has rejected arguments that statistical evidence from drug prosecutions and capital sentencing could demonstrate racial bias in the criminal justice system.[100] The five conservatives also have applied strict scrutiny to curtail drawing the boundaries of congressional and other legislative districts to create "majority-minority" districts.[101] The four more liberal justices issued dissents echoing their position on affirmative action.[102] But in three cases, the majority has upheld majority-minority districts drawn with race in mind as long as race was not the "predominant factor" in the redistricting (if it was, strict scrutiny applies).[103] And in 2003, the five conservatives rejected the Republican party's position that a state must retain its majority-minority districts (that reduce Democratic representation by concentrating black voters in a few districts) to comply with the Voting Rights Act.[104]

The five conservatives departed from their usual adherence to color-blindness by holding that an intentionally discriminatory redistricting plan is consistent with the Voting Rights Act of 1965 as long as neither the purpose nor the effect of the plan is to leave a disfavored minority worse off than it was before the redistricting.[105] The decision overturned the Justice Department's decades-long interpretation of the act. The majority allowed the possible perpetuation of discrimination because a proposed plan, although discriminatory, might be less discriminatory than the status quo, and the plan could still be challenged under section 2 of the act (although section 2 suits are harder for plaintiffs to win). This ruling seems a cramped interpretation of the act's broad language and intent, which requires historically discriminatory jurisdictions to show that any change in a "voting qualification, prerequisite, standard, practice, or procedure" has neither the intent nor effect of "denying or abridging the right to vote on account of race."[106]

On private employment discrimination, several decisions, most dating from the late 1980s, restricted the rights of women and minorities to sue. The major effects of these decisions were reversed in the Civil Rights Act of 1991.[107] The five conservatives later interpreted the act, which authorized punitive damages for intentional discrimination, to prohibit punitive damages unless company policy allows such discrimination.[108] But in two cases the Court has ruled unanimously that a plaintiff can win a job discrimination suit with only circumstantial evidence of discrimination in "mixed motive" cases alleging race or sex was one factor among others in an adverse job action,[109] and when the plaintiff can show the employer lied when explaining its behavior.[110] And six justices have allowed the Equal Employment Opportunity Commission to sue on behalf of employees whose arbitration agreement bars private suits.[111] The Court also effectively extended the deadline for filing job discrimination complaints to cover the earlier episodes in a long series of related discriminatory incidents.[112]

In 2001, the five conservatives ruled that Title VI of the Civil Rights Act of 1964 does not permit private lawsuits challenging state policies that discriminate unintentionally.[113] No federal Appeals Court had ever barred such suits, which constituted the largest category of Title VI cases.[114] This ruling was part of a trend in which the Court has barred suits by individuals seeking enforcement of federal statutory rights because the law does not authorize such suits in "clear and unambiguous terms" or because the defendant is a state shielded by sovereign immunity.[115]

Civil rights advocates won victories when the Court unanimously upheld tougher sentences for "hate crimes" and overturned new rules that would have required plaintiffs alleging intentional discrimination by public officials to produce "convincing" *pretrial* evidence of discriminatory intent.[116] A unanimous Court also endorsed an intermediate level of scrutiny for discrimination claims by "illegitimate" children rather than the more lenient rational basis test.[117] But the Rehnquist Court has followed the Burger Court in applying minimal scrutiny to discrimination claims based on age, indigence, and mental retardation.[118]

The Rehnquist Court has a mixed record on Americans with Disabilities Act (ADA) cases. A unanimous Court ruled that beneficiaries must have a disability that impairs their functioning in daily life and not just on the job, a requirement echoing the statute's language.[119] The Court has denied protection to people with easily corrected impairments.[120] It has also ruled that employers usually need not violate seniority rules to accommodate disabled workers.[121] The Court's ruling in a federalism case, *Alabama v. Garrett* (2001), barred state employees from suing their employers for damages under the ADA.[122] And the Court has barred punitive damages under two sections of the ADA and the 1973 Rehabilitation Act.[123] Yet the Court has also extended ADA protection to asymptomatic people with the AIDS virus, to a professional golfer who must use a golf cart, to state prison inmates, to patients in state-run institutions, and persons on social security disability.[124] Seven justices interpreted a federal law that exempts school districts from paying for disabled students' "medical services" to require schools to provide such students with often expensive medical monitoring in school.[125] Because the Court is deeply divided on the permissibility of race-conscious policies, and the majority is willing to allow some consideration of race in legislative districting and higher education, future decisions on race-conscious policies will depend crucially on changes in the Court's personnel and on the Court's strictness in applying existing doctrines.

On school desegregation, the Rehnquist Court has moved toward ending court-ordered desegregation plans, including those involving busing.[126] In particular, districts could end busing and reinstitute neighborhood schools that produce substantial de facto segregation. As David O'Brien has written, these decisions "chart a new course, not a dramatic reversal . . . in which lower courts gradually . . . relinquish" control of public schools.[127]

Finally, a series of decisions from 1985 to 1992 effectively barred attorneys in civil and criminal cases from excluding potential jurors because of their race.[128] The majority in these cases expressed the same adherence to color-blindness that has underlain most, but not all, of the Rehnquist Court's decisions on race.

Economic and Property Rights

As noted above, the Reagan Administration in particular sought to win judicial recognition of free market economic and property rights, partly by restricting Congress's power to regulate interstate commerce and partly by expanding the concept of "takings" of private property for which government must compensate property owners under the Fifth Amendment. In 1988 and 1992, the Court decisively (6–2 and 9–0) rejected claims that economic regulations such as rent controls and restrictions on evicting tenants constitute takings.[129] In *Nollan v. California Coastal Commission* (1987) and *Dolan v. Tigard* (1994),[130] the Court toughened its scrutiny of land use restrictions. The majority in *Dolan* declared that the takings clause should no longer be "relegated to the status of a poor relation"[131] in the Bill of Rights. The Court also ruled in *Lucas v. South Carolina Coastal Commission* (1992)[132] that a taking occurs whenever a land use regulation reduces a property's value to zero—unless the prohibited use constituted a nuisance. In *Palazzolo v. Rhode Island* (2001),[133] the five conservatives allowed property owners to make a takings claim even if they bought their property years after restrictions on development were imposed.

Another ruling declined to expand the takings concept, but still advanced the cause of property rights. The Court denied that a law requiring coal companies to pay their past employees' health care costs imposed a taking. But the law was struck down 5–4 with the vote of Justice Kennedy, who ruled it violated the companies' due process rights.[134] The Court has also rejected some takings claims. In a 1998 case, the Court seemed poised to rule that a taking occurs when the (normally negligible) interest from lawyers trust accounts is taken to fund legal services for the poor.[135] But the Court, 5–4, explicitly rejected that claim in 2003.[136] In 2002, six justices rejected a claim that a thirty-two-month moratorium on development around Lake Tahoe was a per se taking. The Court also reaffirmed the distinction between a physical taking of property and a regulation limiting its use, and affirmed that a regulation does not necessarily constitute a taking if it destroys the value of only a *portion* of a property.[137]

These cases underscore the qualified nature of the Rehnquist Court's rulings on takings. *Lucas*'s holding that a taking occurs whenever regulations extinguish a property's value has little force because few property regulations destroy all of a property's value. The Court in the Lake Tahoe case ruled that the ability of property buyers to challenge preexisting land use restrictions is likewise limited because courts must consider all "relevant circumstances," including how long the restrictions had been in place before the property's purchase and whether a buyer who knew of the restrictions could have reasonably expected to develop the property.[138]

In 1995, six justices bolstered enforcement of the Endangered Species Act by broadly interpreting the "harm" to a species that triggers the act's protections.[139] But several decisions may impair enforcement of federal environmental laws by extending the right to bring citizen suits to property owners *fighting* enforcement of the Endangered Species Act and restricting citizens' ability to sue for enforcement of these laws. This latter trend was arrested at least temporarily in *Friends of the Earth v. Laidlaw* (2000), which rejected arguments that only government agencies may enforce these laws and that citizen suits should be dismissed if the pollution has stopped.[140]

In a 2000 regulatory powers case, the five conservatives ruled that the U.S. Food and Drug Administration lacks the power to regulate tobacco products.[141] All nine justices agreed on the long-standing principle that an agency may regulate if Congress has clearly authorized it; the familiar 5–4 split likely reflected an ideological division over how strictly to apply the standard. In *Whitman v. American Trucking* (2001), eight justices affirmed that Congress need only provide a rather broad "intelligible principle" to guide rule making, and that the Clean Air Act forbade the Environmental Protection Agency from considering the cost its regulations impose on industry.[142]

The Rehnquist Court has a mixed record on product-liability issues. In decisions unfavorable to business, it unanimously rejected manufacturers' claims that their compliance with federal regulations bars product liability suits,[143] rejected settlements of class-action suits against asbestos manufacturers that bar future suits by people exposed to asbestos who are not yet sick,[144] ruled that some workers with noncancerous asbestos-related diseases may recover damages for their fear of developing cancer,[145] required closer judicial scrutiny of class settlements to ensure that plaintiffs are fairly represented and compensated while also impeding the spread of "mandatory" settlements binding on all members of the class,[146] and granted persons not named as plaintiffs greater ability to challenge settlements.[147]

In five other cases, the Court has used the due process clauses to build greater protections for businesses against "irrational and arbitrary" punitive damage awards, suggesting in a 2003 case that when compensatory damages are already "substantial" and the harm to the plaintiff is economic and not physical, a punitive damage award greater than the compensatory damages might be unconstitutional.[148] In two decisions regarded as generally harmful to plaintiffs' interests, the Court expanded judges' authority to exclude testimony from allegedly "expert" witnesses.[149] Two unanimous decisions seemingly favorable to consumer interests allowed manufacturers to set maximum retail markups on their products, and refused to allow American manufacturers to use copyright laws to prevent foreign wholesalers from reselling goods in the United States for less than the price manufacturers normally charge Americans.[150] But critics have charged that the Court has approved companies' predatory low-price strategies designed to destroy competitors.[151]

In sum, a bare majority of the Rehnquist Court is willing to interpret the commerce and perhaps due process clauses to place some modest limit on Congress's regulatory powers, to use the takings clause to scrutinize land-use regulations more carefully, and to lessen companies' exposure to punitive damages. But the majority is unwilling to adopt pre–New Deal conceptions of economic rights or limitations on government. The Court has issued several decisions clearly inimical to business interests, especially concerning class-action settlements, and compiled a mixed record on other economic issues.

Separation of Powers

The Rehnquist Court has dealt three significant setbacks to conservatives under the heading of the separation of powers. In 1988, the Court voted 7–1 to uphold the now-defunct Independent Counsel Act.[152] Conservatives saw the law as an intrusion on executive power and hoped to use a favorable ruling to promote presidential control over independent regulatory agencies.[153] Another setback came in *Whitman v. American Trucking* (2001), when eight justices rejected an attempt to resurrect the "nondelegation doctrine" the Court had used until the 1930s to thwart agency-authored regulations.[154] Conservatives suffered a third defeat when the Court struck down the line-item veto, enacted in an attempt to hold down federal spending, in *Clinton v. City of New York* (1998).[155] On habeas corpus, the Rehnquist Court has accepted some restrictions enacted by Congress (including some provisions codifying earlier Rehnquist Court rulings).[156] But it has also cast doubt on Congress's ability to eliminate habeas review of petitions from aliens challenging deportation and detention policies.[157]

One of the most debated features of the Rehnquist Court's separation-of-powers jurisprudence is its assertion of judicial supremacy—the doctrine that the Supreme Court is the definitive Constitutional interpreter. The Rehnquist Court has made this claim explicitly in rulings limiting Congress's commerce power, denying Congress power to define rights under the Fourteenth Amendment more broadly than the Court has, and refusing President Clinton's request that a sexual harassment suit against him be delayed until he left office.[158] But the Court has also asserted judicial supremacy in "liberal" rulings striking down congressional restrictions on the arguments federally funded legal aid lawyers can make, and rejecting Congress's attempt to effectively reverse the *Miranda* ruling. The Court also asserted its interpretive supremacy when it struck down the Religious Freedom Restoration Act, a law passed overwhelmingly by liberals and conservatives alike.[159] It is arguable whether the Rehnquist Court is more judicially supreme than the Warren Court, whose assertions of judicial supremacy the Rehnquist Court has thrice cited,[160] or the Burger Court, which asserted judicial supremacy in *U.S. v. Nixon*.[161] The Rehnquist Court's claims of judicial supremacy have nonetheless provoked much scholarship disparaging, and some scholarship defending, judicial supremacy.[162]

A benign interpretation of the Rehnquist Court's doctrine is that "the Court will not tolerate tampering by other actors with what [it] views as constitutional bedrock."[163] A second interpretation is that the Court's conservatives are confident that they can decide issues more competently than the other branches.[164] Evidence for this view would be the conservatives' handling of *Bush v. Gore,*[165] in which they overrode the Florida Supreme Court's interpretation of its own state's law and precluded congressional resolution of the disputed election. Additional evidence would be the sovereign immunity decisions blocking Congress from using its Fourteenth Amendment remedial powers to breach the states' Eleventh Amendment immunity against federal suits for allegedly violating citizens' constitutional rights. These rulings rest on the conservative justices' determination that the remedy Congress has fashioned—for example, allowing citizens to bring federal lawsuits against their states for violating federal laws against age and disability discrimination—is not, in the conservative majority's view, "congruent and proportional" to any actual state violation of constitutional rights.[166]

A brief search in an electronic database of Supreme Court opinions will reveal assertions of judicial supremacy by justices of all ideological stripes during the Warren, Burger, and Rehnquist eras. These pronouncements demonstrate that justices across the ideological spectrum will embrace judicial supremacy in some form. The question is how emphatically and readily they will invoke it. In any case, if the second, more muscular form of judicial supremacy accurately characterizes a majority of the Rehnquist Court, that posture is surely not a product of the modern confirmation process. By subjecting nominees to careful ideological scrutiny by skeptical senators, the process reduces the probability of the confirmation (and as we have seen, nomination) of ideologically zealous figures for whom the more virulent form of judicial supremacy facilitates the accomplishment of an ideological agenda. The modern process has also enhanced the role of senators who by the very nature of their positions have an institutional interest in keeping virulent judicial supremacists off the Court in order to promote, to the extent possible, judicial respect for Congress's views on constitutional issues. If anything, the modern confirmation process is therefore a prophylactic measure against judicial supremacy in its more grasping form.

Civil Rights for Women

The Rehnquist Court has compiled a generally proplaintiff record on sexual harassment and sex discrimination. In 1986, all nine justices agreed that the Civil Rights Act of 1964 forbids sexual harassment on the job.[167] In 1991, a unanimous Court ruled that federal law forbids employers from barring fertile women from jobs deemed hazardous to them; a majority applied this rule even to pregnant women.[168] In 1993 and 1998, unanimous Courts lessened the burden of proof for sexual harassment claims and authorized suits for same-sex harassment.[169]

In two 7–2 decisions that won praise from women's groups and most employer (but not some conservative) groups, the Court ruled in 1998 that an employee may sue for sexual harassment by her supervisors even if the employer had no knowledge of the behavior and the employee suffered no adverse job action from resisting harassers' demands, but that employers could defend themselves by showing that they had an effective antiharass-ment policy that the employee had unreasonably failed to use.[170] In 1992, a unanimous Court allowed students who are sexually harassed by teachers in schools receiving federal funds to sue for damages, but a five-justice major-ity later made recovery of damages difficult.[171] In 1999, the four liberals and Justice O'Connor made school districts liable under the same difficult stan-dard for student-on-student harassment. The dissenters objected that the rul-ing expanded federal authority over education.[172]

The Rehnquist Court has heard only two cases alleging sex discrim-ination under the equal protection clause. In 1994, six justices barred trial courts from excluding potential jurors because of their sex.[173] And in 1996 the Court struck down, 7–1, male-only admissions policies at state-run mili-tary academies in the Virginia Military Institute case.[174]

Privacy

This section covers the Rehnquist Court's decisions on privacy issues unre-lated to gays, who are discussed below. In 1992, a five-justice majority includ-ing three Reagan-Bush appointees—O'Connor, Kennedy, and Souter—dis-appointed conservatives' fondest hopes by refusing to overturn *Roe v. Wade* in *Planned Parenthood v. Casey.*[175] In 2000, five justices struck down a Nebraska law banning so-called partial-birth abortions. (But Justice O'Connor clearly indicated her willingness to uphold a more narrowly drawn statute.)[176] The Court's other abortion cases since *Casey* concerned restric-tions on antiabortion protests. In 1994, the Court unanimously approved the application of a federal antiracketeering law to some antiabortion protest groups.[177] But in 2003, eight justices ruled that protesters may not normally be sued under the Hobbs Act, which outlaws extortion.[178] In other cases, the majority has applied the principle that courts may enjoin protesters from harassing patients and clinic personnel or disrupting a clinic's operations, but may not limit protests unnecessarily.[179]

In other decisions protecting privacy, the Court ruled that the attorney-client privilege survives the client's death, that the patient records of psychotherapists are protected from compelled disclosure in court, and that patients may refuse life-saving treatment if they clearly indicate their preferences.[180] In 1997, the Court rejected what it interpreted as a claim that the terminally ill have a right to assisted suicide as part of a general right to suicide.[181] But a majority of the Court left open the question of whether the terminally ill but not others may have some such right.[182] The Court, voting 6–3, affirmed parental rights by striking down a Washington state law that allowed judges to grant visitation rights to grandparents and others seeking to visit children over the objections of a parent.[183] A defeat for privacy rights was *Gonzaga v. Doe* (2002), where seven justices ruled that a federal law prohibiting the release of students' records without their consent does not authorize student lawsuits against offending schools.[184]

Freedom of Speech and Press

The Rehnquist Court has upheld free speech claims in several decisions disappointing to conservatives. A majority of the Court—including Kennedy and Scalia—twice upheld the right to burn the American flag as a form of speech.[185] In 1989 and 1991, unanimous Courts struck down a federal law banning "dial-a-porn" services and state laws confiscating the royalties of criminals who publish accounts of their crimes.[186] In several decisions, the Rehnquist Court expanded the freedom of commercial speech. But only Justice Thomas has favored applying to commercial speech the same strict scrutiny that applies to political speech.[187] On press freedoms, the Court ruled 6–3 in 2001 that the media may not be sued for printing the contents of a cell phone conversation intercepted illegally by others if the contents are of "public importance."[188]

A major disappointment to cultural conservatives was *Reno v. ACLU* (1997),[189] in which a unanimous Court struck down a part of a 1996 law that made it a crime to display "indecent" material accessible to children on the Internet. Seven justices struck another provision making it a crime to *knowingly* provide "obscene or indecent" materials to minors.[190] In 2002, six justices struck down a federal law criminalizing the possession of "virtual" child pornography; seven justices struck a similar provision banning sexually explicit films that use youthful-looking adult actors.[191]

In 1996, the Court upheld a federal law permitting cable television companies to refuse to carry "patently offensive" programming, but struck down a provision requiring them to scramble the signals of such programs they do carry and to make them available only to subscribers who request them in writing.[192] In 2000, five justices struck down a federal law restricting sexually explicit programs to late-night hours.[193] In 1992, a unanimous Court struck down an anti–hate speech ordinance.[194] In 2003, a fractured Court allowed states to prosecute cross burners, but required prosecutors to prove that the defendant intended the act as a threat.[195] Between 1999 and 2002, the Court struck down on free speech grounds a state law restricting the activities of people trying to place initiatives on the ballot, an ordinance requiring religious proselytizers to get a permit, a federal law barring federally financed lawyers from attacking the legality of welfare regulations, and a state code of judicial ethics prohibiting candidates for elective judgeships from speaking on legal and political issues.[196]

On campaign finance, the Rehnquist Court began by reaffirming the Burger Court's holdings that limits on donations do not restrict protected speech, but limits on "independent expenditures" do.[197] It also held that Congress may limit spending by political parties that is coordinated with campaigns—to prevent large donors from circumventing limits on contributions to campaigns by routing the money through the parties.[198] In its most important campaign finance case—*McConnell v. FEC*[199]—the four liberals and Justice O'Connor upheld the "McCain-Feingold" law's ban on unlimited contributions to political parties (known as "soft money" donations) and a limitation on the financing of "issue ads" (thinly disguised campaign advertisements) by corporations and labor unions in the weeks just before an election. The majority broke new ground by upholding this restriction on spending by nonparty groups, but it did so on behalf of a conception of free speech championed by some civil libertarians.[200]

The Rehnquist Court has rejected some other claims of free speech. In *National Endowment for the Arts v. Finley* (1998),[201] eight justices upheld a federal law instructing the NEA to consider "general standards of decency" when awarding grants. But six justices upheld the provision only after interpreting it as "advisory."[202] In 1999, the Court ruled that aliens who had spoken or raised funds for an organization on the federal government's terrorist list may not claim selective enforcement based on their political views as a defense against deportation.[203] Two additional defeats for free speech were *Rust v. Sullivan* (1991),[204] in which five justices upheld the Reagan Administration's ban on abortion counseling at publicly funded birth control clinics, and *U.S. v. American Library Ass'n* (2003),[205] which upheld, 6–3, a congressional requirement that libraries receiving federal funds to access the Internet must install antipornography filters on all of their online machines.

On the whole, however, the Rehnquist Court has strongly supported free speech claims. Burt Neuborne, former legal director of the American Civil

Liberties Union, has written that despite fault lines among the justices on campaign finance and subsidized speech, "a First Amendment Era of Good Feelings unites all factions on the Rehnquist Supreme Court behind vigorous judicial protection of free speech."[206]

The Rights of Gays

In 1996, Justices Kennedy and O'Connor and the four liberals applied the equal protection clause to antigay legislation for the first time,[207] striking down an amendment to the Colorado constitution prohibiting the state and its cities from guaranteeing equal rights to gays. In *Lawrence v. Texas* (2003),[208] Kennedy and the four liberals ruled that the constitutional right to privacy invalidated the sodomy laws that criminalized private, consensual, homosexual acts between adults, overturning *Bowers v. Hardwick* (1986).[209] Kennedy's majority opinion was notable for its passionate denunciation of *Bowers*. It was also notable for its activism; the majority could have joined Justice O'Connor in striking the Texas law at issue on equal protection grounds.[210]

The Rehnquist Court has twice ruled against gays on free speech grounds. In 1995, a unanimous Court cited the free speech rights of parade organizers to exclude Irish American homosexual groups from a privately organized St. Patrick's Day parade.[211] The five conservatives later used this rationale to allow the Boy Scouts to exclude gays.[212] The newness of *Lawrence v. Texas,* its reversal of *Bowers* by a single vote, and uncertainties about changes in the Court's personnel make future rulings on gay rights unpredictable. But if *Lawrence* marks the start of a judicial revolution, it will not unfold as conservatives had planned.

Summary

Table 7.1 summarizes the major doctrinal developments from the advent of the Rehnquist Court in 1986 until early 2004. Subjects are arrayed approximately from those where conservatives have made the least gains (at the top of the table) to the most gains (at bottom). Presidents Reagan and George H. W. Bush (and Nixon, by appointing Rehnquist) clearly left their conservative stamp on the Court. Justice Stevens, whose voting record on civil rights and liberties places him well to the right of William Brennan and Thurgood Marshall, is now the Court's most liberal justice.[213] The absence of a commanding voice on the left has narrowed the range of discourse on the Court. Not a single justice took the opportunity to extend the right of privacy to

Table 7.1. Major Doctrinal Developments of the Rehnquist Court, 1986–2004*

Subject	Developments
Freedom of speech and press	Flag-burning, dial-a-porn, virtual child pornography, profits from criminals' writings, judicial candidates' speech protected; censorship of internet, anti–hate speech law, most restrictions on adult cable TV programming struck; greater protection for commercial speech; limits on publicly funded lawyers' arguments struck; media may publish "publicly important" cell phone conversations illegally intercepted by others; NEA "decency test" upheld but diluted. Prohibition of publicly funded abortion counseling upheld (overturned by presidential order in 1993); limits affirmed on campaign contributions, parties' coordinated expenditures with campaigns, "soft money" donations and some independent expenditures; requirement of antipornography filters on publicly subsidized library computers upheld; cross burners subject to prosecution if act was a threat.
Gays	Equal protection clause invoked, *Bowers v. Hardwick* overturned; private groups may exclude gays on free speech grounds.
Sex discrimination	Sexual harassment, including same-sex, made actionable; employee need not prove employer knew or employee was punished for resisting; recovery of damages permitted but difficult for student victims. All-male public military colleges, women's exclusion from juries, job bans on fertile/pregnant women struck.
Privacy	"Essence" of *Roe* upheld, but greater regulation allowed; partial-birth abortions protected (provisionally). General right to suicide rejected; decision on narrower right for terminally ill deferred; right to refuse medical treatment recognized; psychotherapists' patient records, hospital patients' drug tests privileged; attorney-client privilege survives death of client; parental primacy in child visitation affirmed. Suspicionless drug testing of students upheld; privacy of student records not privately enforceable.
Separation of powers	Line-item veto struck; independent counsel statute upheld; revival of nondelegation doctrine rejected. Congressional attempts to widen constitutional rights rejected. Judicial supremacy affirmed.

include assisted suicide for the terminally ill (although the majority left open that possibility).[214] When the Court struck down the Religious Freedom Restoration Act, no justice defended the proposition that Congress can define a civil liberty more expansively than the Court.[215] And no justice dissented from the ruling permitting public housing authorities to evict unknowing tenants for illegal drug use by others.[216]

Table 7.1. Continued

Subject	Developments
Economic rights	Takings expanded incrementally; "arbitrary" punitive damages disallowed; due process may limit statutory financial exactions; standing to sue against environmental enforcement expanded. Maximum retail prices upheld; some probusiness class-action settlements barred; mixed record on product liability suits.
Minority rights	Burden of proof raised for some job discrimination claims (overturned by Congress); private disparate-impact suits disallowed under 1964 Civil Rights Act; redistricting plans may perpetuate but not aggravate discrimination; racial disparities in criminal justice disregarded. Affirmative action upheld in higher education, curbed in public contracting; race-conscious redistricting, court-supervised school desegregation curbed. Hate-crime laws upheld; greater protection for illegitimate children; race-based exclusion of jurors barred; plaintiff's showing that employer lied may prove discrimination. ADA eligibility cases mixed; easily correctable disabilities not protected.
Criminal justice	Habeas corpus restricted; *Miranda* and exclusionary rule upheld but weakened; "victim-impact" statements allowed in capital sentencing; death penalty upheld for sixteen-year-olds; postsentence confinement of sexual predators upheld; three-strikes laws that count minor offenses upheld; right to counsel limited; innocent public housing tenants may be evicted for others' drug use. Mixed rulings on prosecutors' property seizures; indefinite detainment of deportees curbed; habeas review preserved for criminal aliens; death penalty for mentally retarded struck.
Religion	Unintentional burdens on free exercise receive lesser scrutiny. Greater governmental accommodation of religious organizations, including school vouchers, but broad neutrality principle rejected. Mandatory creationism classes, special school districts for religious groups struck; school prayer ban extended. "Secular" public displays regarding religious holidays upheld.
Federalism and the commerce power	Limit on commerce power enforced; state immunity from lawsuits and complaints before federal agencies expanded; "anticommandeering" principle limits federal direction of states; federal regulation of nonnavigable waters curtailed. State-enacted congressional term limits struck; preemption and conditional spending doctrines stand.

* Through February 2004.

But if President Nixon, President Reagan, and the first President Bush packed the Court on the hot-button issues of the late twentieth century, they did so by the narrowest possible margin. As of 2003, the Court is best thought of as divided into a relatively liberal bloc of four justices (Stevens, Souter, Ginsburg, and Breyer) and a conservative bloc of five justices (Rehnquist,

O'Connor, Scalia, Kennedy, and Thomas), with Souter, Ginsburg and Breyer more moderately liberal than Stevens, and O'Connor and Kennedy more moderately conservative than Rehnquist, Scalia, and Thomas.[217] The Rehnquist Court has been a major disappointment to cultural conservatives on abortion, school prayer, gay rights, and most free speech issues. The principal victories of the cultural right have come in 5–4 rulings on the establishment clause (culminating in the school vouchers case)[218] and, with some important qualifications, rollbacks of liberal precedents in criminal justice (although "conservative" rulings on criminal justice are often broadly popular).

The Rehnquist Court has been more satisfactory to mainstream conservatives seeking to bolster federalism (most notably, states' sovereign immunity) and curtail federal regulatory powers. But even here there have been setbacks in cases involving the separation of powers and class-action suits against business, and limited progress in 5–4 rulings on the takings clause and federalism. Two commerce clause decisions in 1995 and 2000 (*U.S. v. Lopez* and *U.S. v. Morrison*) contain the language of a counterrevolution that only the three most conservative justices appear willing to undertake. And those decisions have had very little impact at the lower court level.[219] The thrust of the Rehnquist Court's civil rights jurisprudence has been favorable to women, most favorable to gays, and largely unfavorable to racial minorities, although affirmative action in higher education received a (possibly temporary) boost in the Michigan Law School case of 2003.[220] Justices Kennedy and O'Connor have clearly been the balance wheels on the Rehnquist Court. Thomas Hensley, Christopher Smith, and Joyce Baugh conclude from their quantitative study of voting patterns on the Rehnquist Court from 1986 to 2001 that

> Most of the justices show relatively stable voting patterns over the years. Justices O'Connor and Kennedy, however, have shown far greater fluctuation in their liberal/conservative voting patterns, they have had a strong tendency to fluctuate together . . . and the Court's liberalism/conservatism changes have been closely associated with the changes in Kennedy's and O'Connor's voting patterns. . . . Kennedy and O'Connor appear to have had an extraordinary influence on the decisional patterns of the Rehnquist Court.[221]

This finding confirms the conclusion of more qualitative assessments,[222] as well as other quantitative indicators of influence on the Court. One such is bloc analysis of the justices' voting patterns.[223] Another is the frequency with which a justice is on the winning side (that is, in the majority). From 1992 to 2003, Kennedy and O'Connor were in the majority more often than their colleagues, most notably in 5–4 cases, and have dissented less often than any other justice.[224] For the most part, Rehnquist, Scalia, and Thomas have substantially advanced conservative doctrine only when they have won O'Connor and Kennedy's votes. Key issues on which the liberals have successfully wooed one or both of these justices and defeated conservative hopes include abortion, school prayer, free speech, gender discrimination, gay rights, affirmative action in higher education, and the term limits, special prosecutor, and line-item veto cases.

Still, several caveats must temper this analysis. First, it is always true that the center (whoever may be there) rules.[225] And the center has moved to the right on criminal justice, federalism, civil rights policies, the establishment clause, and, with clearly delimited consequences thus far, the commerce and takings clauses. Second, we cannot rule out or even examine, in a portion of one chapter, the claim that the Rehnquist Court has ruled by proxy—by accepting fewer appeals of the conservative rulings of the federal Courts of Appeals.[226] It is certain, for reasons partly unclear but partly institutional, that the Court greatly reduced the number of cases it hears during Chief Justice Rehnquist's tenure.[227]

Additionally, the Court, especially with the possible arrival of additional conservative justices, could advance conservative causes including, among others, extending the Eleventh Amendment's sovereign immunity to local governments[228]; further curtailing Congress's power over "noneconomic" matters that could, for example, include protecting endangered species[229]; revising its conditional spending and preemption doctrines, putting real teeth into what has been a counterinsurgency rather than a true counterrevolution on federalism[230]; and permitting additional regulations on abortion, including a ban on partial-birth abortions.[231]

It is clear, however, from the Rehnquist Court's varied record across the issue areas surveyed above that although President Nixon, President Reagan, and the first President Bush ended the Court's Warren-style liberal judicial activism, they rolled back its doctrines substantially only on selected issues. It is noteworthy that recent presidents have not been more successful in moving the Court further in their own direction. After the Warren era formally ended in 1969, Republican presidents seeking to blunt or reverse its jurisprudence placed the next ten newcomers on the Court.[232] President Nixon was assisted in his attempt to move the Court rightward by his opportunity to replace three liberal justices: Warren, Fortas, and Black (although Black's literalism was not always liberal in its results). Presidents Reagan and George H. W. Bush were aided by their ability to name successors for Lewis Powell and Potter Stewart, the oft-acknowledged swing votes on the Burger Court, and William Brennan and Thurgood Marshall, the Court's longtime liberal lions.[233] After the appointment of five justices in twelve years by President Reagan and the first President Bush, and Rehnquist's elevation to chief justice, the Court had exactly five conservatives, a net gain of two or three (because Rehnquist, Warren Burger, and Byron White, who was sometimes labeled a conservative, were serving when Reagan took office). Two of these additions (Kennedy and O'Connor) are moderate conservatives, and another Republican appointee, David Souter, is moderately liberal. If ideology were the president's only criterion for new justices, O'Connor would have been an unlikely choice. If the president truly dominated the appointment process, Robert Bork would sit in Kennedy's seat. A possibly much more conservative justice would occupy Souter's. President Bill Clinton might also have made the Court more liberal than he did by nominating strong rather than moderate liberals, but he nominated Ginsburg and Breyer largely to avoid confirmation battles.[234] An assertive Senate confirmation process, aided by divided government during Reagan's last two years and all of George H. W. Bush's four, constrained these presidents and forestalled these alternative outcomes.

The conclusion is that presidents exert substantial influence over the ideological makeup of the Court, but they do not dominate the appointment process or the Court itself. The real but partial successes of recent presidents in moving the Court their way are consistent with Chief Justice Rehnquist's own observation that "Those [presidents] who have tried [to pack the Court] have been at least partially successful, but . . . a number of factors militate against a President having anything more than partial success."[235] If presidents can only partially pack the Court, it is unlikely that they can take the Court in a direction sharply at odds with deeply held public sentiments. We now consider how the decisions and dominant values of the Rehnquist Court comport with the sentiments of the American people, and the trend of public support for the Court during the Rehnquist years.

THE REHNQUIST COURT AND THE AMERICAN MAINSTREAM

Observers of the confirmation process who seek more revealing scrutiny of nominees have sometimes expressed concern that presidents will slip through the Senate nominees whose constitutional values are substantially at odds with the values of the nation. The feared result of such an outcome is the delegitimation of the Court, its consequent inability to legitimize its more controversial decisions, and a loss of general support for the Court's role in the constitutional system.[236]

Empirical evidence on public reaction to Supreme Court rulings and subsequent public confidence in the Court provides tepid support for the fear that unpopular rulings may produce any long-lasting erosion of the Court's public support. Numerous empirical studies have shown that several factors produce overall public support for the Court that is higher and more stable than for Congress or the presidency. First, most Americans are unaware of most High Court rulings and therefore have little reason to disapprove of the Court. Second, the occasional salient controversial rulings sometimes produce as many new Court supporters as detractors, producing no net change in the Court's measured approval rating. Third, occasional declines in the Court's public standing in response to salient, unpopular rulings are typically followed by increased public support flowing from a deeply held public belief in the Court's essential legitimacy.[237] A fourth factor is that the Court's salient decisions more often comport with public opinion than diverge from it.[238]

These quantitative studies support the conclusion of historical scholars such as Alexander Bickel and Robert McCloskey that on most issues the Supreme Court will not stray too far for too long from dominant public values.[239] It is noteworthy that these studies cover nearly two centuries during which the Supreme Court confirmation process took various forms. The Court has been far from extremist, abhorrent, or even consistently countermajoritarian, despite the silence or absence of nominees at Senate confirmation hearings, or even the absence of hearings themselves. Although the Court is not ordinarily in danger of powerful hair-trigger reactions to unpopular decisions, it is not fully insulated from public backlash against such rulings. Even scholars who find a public "reservoir of goodwill and commitment" undergirding the Court's legitimacy allow that a "wholesale shift in style" toward judicial activism, or results-oriented jurisprudence, may undermine the Court's legitimacy.[240]

Clearly, however, no long-term decline in the Court's public standing has occurred since regular polling on the Court began in the 1970s, a fact that should relieve concerns that the modern confirmation process might produce an aberrant Court whose rulings alienate the nation. The percentage of the public expressing "a great deal" or "quite a lot" of confidence in the Court rose from the mid-40 percent range in the 1970s to the mid-50 percent range in the mid-1980s, slipped to the high 40s by 1990, fell to about 40 percent after the Thomas confirmation in 1991, rebounded to the 50 percent range by the late 1990s, and stood at 47 percent in 2003 (identical to its June 2000, pre–*Bush v. Gore* level).[241] In the late 1990s and early 2000s, only two major public or private institutions (of seven included in Gallup surveys) engendered as much public confidence as they did in the 1970s: the Supreme Court and the military.[242]

The evidence indicates that the Supreme Court's contentious opinion in *Bush v. Gore* had very little long-term impact on the public's confidence in the Court. Public opinion polls on the Court's standing before and after that decision vary somewhat according to whether respondents are asked if they "approve of the way the Supreme Court is handling its job" or if they have "confidence" in the Court. Polls taken shortly after the decision found a large increase in Republicans approving of the Court's performance, and a large drop in the percentage of Democrats approving, producing no net change in the Court's overall approval rating.[243]

The percentage of poll respondents expressing "a great deal" or "quite a lot" of confidence in the Supreme Court rose very slightly, from 47 percent to 50 percent, between June 2000, six months before *Bush v. Gore,* and June 2001, six months after it.[244] Most importantly, Democrats' "confidence" in the Court fell only slightly between June 2000 and June 2001, from 48 percent to 44 percent.[245] And the significance of *Bush v. Gore* declined further after two additional developments: a protracted recount by news organizations suggested that Bush would likely have won the recount the Court aborted, and the terrorist attacks of September 11, 2001, that produced the subsequent extraordinary public approval of President George W. Bush's leadership. All of these factors warrant optimism that *Bush v. Gore* did not inflict any lasting damage to the Court's legitimacy.

The Court's increased public support in the decade after the early 1990s is consistent with the congruence between public opinion and Rehnquist Court rulings on highly salient issues such as abortion, criminal justice, and the rights of gays. On abortion, the *Casey* decision upheld the basic right to abortion but permitted certain state regulations. The controlling opinion of Justices Souter, O'Connor, and Kennedy specifically cited widespread public acceptance of *Roe v. Wade* as a major justification for the decision.[246] Sixty-four percent of respondents in a Gallup poll shortly after *Casey* agreed with the decision not to overturn *Roe.* Seventy to 80 percent supported the three abortion regulations the Court upheld: a twenty-four-hour waiting period, a parental consent requirement for minors, and mandatory counseling about alternatives to abortion. (A large majority also supported the spousal notification requirement the Court struck down.[247])

As noted above, the Rehnquist Court has limited several of the Warren Court's liberal criminal justice precedents. Many of those precedents were unpopular.[248] The percentage of Americans saying that the courts are too lenient with criminals rose from 48 percent in 1965 to more than 80 percent by the late 1980s.[249] By 1993, the public cited crime as the nation's most important problem in most public opinion polls.[250] Given the great concern over violent crime in recent decades, there can be little doubt that the Rehnquist Court's generally tough stance on criminal justice accords with the public mood. At the same time, the Court's 2002 opinion barring execution of the mentally retarded specifically cited growing public opposition to that practice.[251]

Regarding gays, the public appears to endorse the Supreme Court's view, expressed in *Lawrence v. Texas,* that private, consensual, homosexual relations between adults are no proper concern of government. In a Pew Research Center poll conducted four months after *Lawrence,* 61 percent of respondents "completely agree[d]" and 19 percent of respondents "somewhat agree[d]" that "society should not put any restrictions on sex between consenting adults in the privacy of their own home."[252]

On racial issues, the Rehnquist Court, as we have seen, has moved to ease the release of school districts from desegregation plans, to heighten scrutiny of affirmative action programs that involve racial preferences, and to curtail race-based congressional districting. These decisions are consistent with the expressed opposition of every American racial group to race-based districting.[253] And they are consistent with the opposition of some 80 percent of all Americans (and a plurality of African Americans) toward school busing for purposes of integration.[254]

The Rehnquist Court's heightened scrutiny of affirmative action, especially in public contracting, is consistent with the public's opposition to racial preferences. But polls show that the Court's rulings on preferences in university admissions, including *Bakke* (1978) and the University of Michigan Law School case (2003),[255] contravene public opinion. A majority of poll respondents will say that "affirmative action programs designed to increase the number of black and minority students on college campuses" are "a good thing"; a plurality will say that such programs are "fair."[256] But such approval extends only to "programs that give . . . assistance—but not preference—getting into college, getting a job or getting a promotion."[257] In a Gallup poll conducted just before the Court issued the Michigan Law School decision, over two-thirds of all respondents (and 44 percent of blacks) agreed that "applicants should be admitted solely on the basis of merit, even if that results in few minority students being admitted."[258] The public rejects the argument, endorsed by the Court since *Bakke,* that the need for diversity justifies racial preferences in admissions. If the Court has violated the public consensus by approving race-conscious admissions policies designed to foster diversity, it has at least consistently withheld its approval from the cruder forms of these policies, such as quotas[259] and automatic bonus point plans for minority applicants.[260] It has also curtailed affirmative action in public contracting. In any case, if the Court has been more liberal than the public on this issue, that is certainly not the result of Court-packing by recent conservative presidents.

The values that underlie the Rehnquist Court's generally conservative positions on racial issues are controversial but hardly extreme. Although some may see the Court's holdings on civil rights (other than university admissions) as a threat to the achievement of the venerable American ideal of equal opportunity, the Court's rulings reflect other equally fundamental American ideals such as the color-blind application of the law, legal (but not necessarily social) equality, redress for the proven (not presumed) victim of discrimination, and fairness to the accused (not presumed) perpetrator of discrimination. The Court's faith in these principles may be "wooden" and even "naive,"[261] but they are worthy and widely held principles nonetheless.

Aside from allowing race-conscious university admissions, the Rehnquist Court has been markedly out of step with a clearly expressed public view only on the issues of school prayer, congressional term limits, and some issues involving free speech.[262] But if the Court has acted contrary to dominant public values in these cases, it has done so by issuing what are considered liberal rulings, which is hardly the result of the Court having been packed with conservative justices.

Finally, it is worth noting that the Court has decisively rejected the view, held only by Justices Scalia and Thomas, that the due process clauses of the Fifth and Fourteenth Amendments guarantee only that government treat citizens with procedural fairness and do not provide them with substantive rights such as familial privacy.[263] The Court has also eschewed the view, held by Justice Scalia and Chief Justice Rehnquist (and likely held by Thomas, but explicitly rejected by O'Connor and Kennedy) that the Court should recognize unwritten constitutional rights only at the "most specific [that is, narrowest] level at which a relevant tradition protecting, or denying protection to, the asserted right can be identified."[264]

In sum, when judged by the totality of its record and prevailing public norms, the Rehnquist Court is not abhorrent, out of the mainstream, consistently countermajoritarian, or unduly conservative.

CONCLUSION

The unresponsiveness of Supreme Court nominees at their Senate hearings helps presidents, including relatively ideological ones, to move the Court in their direction. Yet several major obstacles remain in the way of a president who wants to pack the Court. These include the limited number of nominations a president can make, the president's need to consider factors other than ideology when choosing nominees, the irreducible level of uncertainty about a nominee's future performance, the president's inability to foresee the major constitutional issues of the future, and the sometime inability of the president to gain confirmation for his ideologically favorite nominee, in large part because of the increased propensity of the Senate since the 1960s to evaluate very carefully, and to reject, nominees.

The Rehnquist Court, which the unresponsive testimony of various nominees has helped to bring about, is substantially more conservative than its predecessors on the issues of crime, civil rights, the separation of church and state, some aspects of federalism, and, to a lesser extent, property rights, but not on issues of free speech, gender discrimination, school prayer, equal treatment of gays, and privacy (including abortion). It has also disappointed conservatives in some major separation of powers cases. The present Court is neither incapable of protecting individual and minority rights nor so protective of them—or some subset of them—that it jeopardizes its legitimacy, as the Court did in the 1930s. Its behavior is largely consistent with the conclusion of the statistical and historical studies that presidents can only partially pack the Court, and that the Court will usually not long offend widely and deeply held public values.

8

Conclusion: Reforming a Machine That Would Run of Itself

This book has contrasted two competing critiques of the process for confirming U.S. Supreme Court nominees: the legalist and the political. This chapter summarizes how the analysis of these two schools has highlighted the strengths of the confirmation process (some already identified by others), discusses the relatively few valid concerns about the process, and examines four reform proposals identified by the foregoing analysis as among the more worthy proposals for consideration.

THE LEGALIST MODEL

This book has rejected the legalist model almost entirely, primarily as a result of its exaggeration of conflict in the confirmation process, its mischaracterization of the innocuous and beneficial consequences of conflict as harmful, and its futile and misplaced hope of removing politics from the process. George Watson and John Stookey have cited three reasons why conflictual nominations attract attention. First, observers are "drawn by the confrontation that controversy brings."[1] Second, controversy allows us to analyze conflicting points of view (and to vent our sometimes passionate feelings on these controversies). Third, social scientists need variations in behaviors in order to explain those behaviors (we cannot tell, for example, whether party membership affects senators' votes for or against nominees if all senators of both parties vote the same way). Hence social scientists need a contested nomination, which produces a divided Senate, in order to answer questions such as this one.[2]

Yet most modern confirmation proceedings have been nonconflictual. Six of the fourteen vacancies from Justice Tom Clark's retirement in 1967 to Justice Harry Blackmun's retirement in 1994 produced nominations opposed by fifteen or more senators on the final roll-call vote.[3] Although this level of conflict was much higher than in the 1894–1967 period, fewer than half of the vacancies in the last third of the twentieth century eventuated in serious conflict. The legalist school's more serious misstep is its misinterpretation of political combat in the confirmation process, which it views as an inappropriate intrusion of politics into the process. As D. Grier Stephenson Jr. has explained, the Supreme Court has always been a "political" body in the larger, Aristotelian sense of the term. The Supreme Court

> is not only a legal body. . . . but a "political" body, too. That is, as it resolves conflicts between litigants who disagree over the correct meaning of a clause in the Constitution or a provision in an act of Congress, the Court affects the allocation of power and shapes public policy. In this sense, the Court has been political from practically the beginning. After all, the Court has consisted mainly of politicians who have been nominated and confirmed by politicians to perform what, at heart, are largely political tasks.[4]

As Chapter 2 demonstrated, nothing in the Constitution, the drafting of the appointments clause, the *Federalist Papers,* or indeed in American history suggests anything to the contrary. The legalist school devalues the democratic half of the constitutional democracy the Founders created. In the context of Supreme Court appointments, it advocates to a large degree the suspension of the system of separate branches sharing powers by arguing for a diminished senatorial role at the confirmation stage.

As Watson and Stookey have written, any circumscription of that system in the Supreme Court appointment process would be harmful:

> In periods of considerable consensus in the country, the executive and legislative branches tend to reflect that consensus by being controlled by the same political party and ideological view. . . . Presidential nominees are more readily accepted by the Senate, and nominations are least likely to generate controversy.
>
> Conversely, . . . in the midst of fundamental disagreements over the direction the nation should go, this democratic system struggles to find a compromise that can permit the nation to move forward in

a way that is at least tolerable to most if not exactly desirable. Public debate becomes relatively more critical in order to find the most acceptable solution for the situation at hand.[5]

The period following the 1960s surely qualifies as one of broken constitutional consensus over civil rights policies, criminal justice issues, privacy rights, governmental accommodation of religion, and federalism. Conflict over agenda-driven Supreme Court nominations at such times—especially when they come overwhelmingly from presidents of one party—is then a positive good. It is a critical part of the constitutional dialogue and tends to produce justices who are more widely acceptable to the polity, less activist, more likely to afford the democratic branches the space to work out their differences, and less likely to perpetuate the Court itself as an issue.

Of the two potential threats posed by political combat over the Court's composition, the evidence permits us to dismiss one and requires us to allow at least the possibility of the second. The first threat, that conflictual confirmation proceedings will diminish the Court's public stature, has not come to pass, at least at the level of conflict that has prevailed since the late 1960s. Indeed, despite a temporary drop following the confirmation of Clarence Thomas, the Court is one of the few American institutions that has retained a relatively high public standing over recent decades. Fortunately, the Thomas episode will almost certainly prove aberrational, having resulted largely from extraordinary circumstances (a uniquely flawed nominee with the protective armor of racial politics in his favor and a dramatic confrontation, guaranteed both to snare a large audience and to turn ugly, between an accuser and a nominee charged with sexual misconduct). We cannot, however, rule out the second danger: that the current confirmation process makes the appointment of great justices less probable. It is likely that a figure of controversial views such as Louis Brandeis would have a very hard time winning confirmation today (as he did in his time). But for reasons discussed in Chapter 4, it is also likely that great justices will continue to grace the Court.

Several writers have suggested that perceived problems in the confirmation process are not the fault of the process itself, but of the attitudes and resulting behaviors of the people in the process.[6] On at least one occasion, the people in the process were indeed a problem. That, of course, was the confirmation of Clarence Thomas, where Republicans displayed a deplorable lack of ethics and Democrats displayed an equally deplorable absence of political backbone and mental agility. But unethical behavior was not, as is sometimes alleged, a significant problem in the case of Robert Bork, whose politicolegal philosophy was correctly portrayed by his opponents. Bork's supporters, unable to win his nomination on the merits, reacted to his defeat by attacking the process, just as supporters of Clarence Thomas would do with greater short-term success (by winning Thomas's confirmation) four years later.

To the extent that the behaviors resulting in Thomas's appointment arose from overweening concern with the nominee's ideology, concomitant unconcern with his ability and temperament, and a win-at-all-costs attitude on the part of his supporters, one clear if not easy response is the election of more presidents and senators who will place a greater emphasis on nominee quality (whatever the nominee's other characteristics), and senators who will fairly and effectively combat inappropriate behaviors of those on the other side, as could have been done in Thomas's case. Another, more practical solution is to make the Supreme Court less of an issue by keeping ideological activists off of it, a course of action that requires the sort of ideological review advocated by the political school.

THE POLITICAL SCHOOL

The political school correctly advocates an active role for the Senate. Its analysis of the Senate's specific procedures and their consequences is more accurate than the legalist school's, but some of its fears are overdrawn and some of its recommended changes are either needless or, although worthy of consideration, of marginal value. Some writers in the political school have exaggerated the power of presidents to pack the Supreme Court with their ideological kin. Whatever the power of any president (or group of presidents of similar views) to pack the Court, the American form of representative democracy demands a "second opinion"[7] from the Senate on a nominee's ideology. In the early twenty-first century, America lacks a constitutional consensus on several vital issues. The Supreme Court very often decides these issues for the nation. And in recent decades the Court has proclaimed its supremacy over the other branches as the Constitution's authoritative interpreter. As a factual matter, it often does have the last word on deeply divisive issues such as abortion and school prayer. And it is largely unaccountable to anyone. Although precedent, the norm of judicial restraint, and other factors limit the justices' discretion, there is abundant evidence that justices' personal preferences exert a powerful influence over their rulings.[8] The justices' values reflect the values of their presidential nominators some 70 to 90 percent of the time.[9] Those percentages would be higher were it not for the willingness of some senators, or most senators at some times, to oppose nominees on the basis of ideology. No one person, including the president, should have a unilateral power to determine what values predominate among the nine people who effectively determine the Constitution's meaning with so few effective checks on their power.

For two reasons, however, the Senate is very unlikely to achieve full parity with the president in the High Court appointment process, as some writers have urged.[10] First, as nominator, the president gets to choose one individual from among a large number of qualified candidates. Second, by making the nomination, the president sets the agenda, which provides him with an inherent advantage in determining the outcome. Writers in the political school have nonetheless advocated several changes in the confirmation process to reduce or eliminate the president's advantage. Although the president's advantage may well diminish the longer the nation remains divided over constitutional fundamentals, the president's advantage will persist as a result of the two dominating realities just cited. And it is more likely to diminish because of attitudinal changes by senators than by formal procedural changes. To see why this is so, it is helpful to review some of the major reforms advocated by the political school.

Greater Interbranch Consultation on Nominations

Many observers of the confirmation process have suggested that presidents consult more closely and genuinely with the Senate when selecting nominees.[11] Not surprisingly, this suggestion has often been made by senators not of the president's party.[12] The suggestion has taken various forms. Some writers have suggested that the Senate submit a list of recommended nominees to the president.[13] Others have suggested that the president draw up a list of potential nominees and submit it to senators for their review.[14] A third group has suggested that senators and presidents collaborate to narrow the field of potential nominees, but in a manner less structured than the two preceding proposals.[15] One goal of these proposals is to reduce conflict in the confirmation process. As we have seen, however, recent levels of conflict in the process have not proved harmful, excepting the aberrational Thomas episode. And in that one case, the nature rather than the level of conflict drew the public attention and condemnation that temporarily lowered the Court's public standing.

As William Ross has pointed out, attempts to select a nominee through closer consultations between the branches could actually increase interbranch conflict if, for example, the president nominated someone senators had not previously suggested, or nominated someone whom influential senators had earlier disapproved.[16] Given the president's need to satisfy his political base, he must often risk alienating the opposite party by rejecting their advice. And given the diversity of views within the Senate, presidents who consult widely will inevitably disappoint many senators. Attempts at closer consultations could also simply displace conflict to an earlier stage of the appointment process, where it is less visible and less instructive to the public.

In any event, presidents are likely to oppose any agreed-upon change of procedure that requires closer consultations on nominations. The first President Bush, for example, rejected a recommendation of informal interbranch consultations authored by a Task Force of Senate Democratic Committee chairmen after the Thomas confirmation.[17] Given the need to please their own political base, and with the stakes so high in making Supreme Court appointments, presidents are likely to continue to consult with senators of the other party only as they need to in order to win confirmation for their nominees or to conserve scarce political capital for other issues.

We should not, however, understate the extent to which interbranch consultations on nominations have taken place. Presidents have at least occasionally consulted senators informally, whether directly or by floating trial balloons (that is, releasing potential nominees' names in order to gauge senatorial as well as wider reactions). And most presidents have engaged in a kind of silent consultation by considering the confirmability of potential nominees even if they solicited no explicit feedback from senators or others.[18]

Questioning of Nominees by Special Counsel

Several observers of the confirmation process have suggested that senators employ expert special counsel to question High Court nominees because senators lack a deep understanding of constitutional issues and/or the ability to ask penetrating follow-up questions.[19] The likelihood of this reform's adoption, and its probable results if adopted, may well depend on the nature of the Judiciary Committee's inquiry. For inquiries into nominees' ideologies, employment of counsel is unlikely to occur, possibly unproductive, and largely unneeded. For the elucidation of facts concerning possible wrongdoing by a nominee, skilled questioners might play a useful role.

For examining nominees' ideologies, senators have shown no interest in hiring skilled interrogators. Even after the confirmation hearings for Clarence Thomas, whose refusal to answer questions and frequent repudiations of his past statements genuinely angered some senators,[20] the Senate Democratic Task Force on the confirmation process declined to advocate more questioning by special counsels, noting merely that current rules allow for it if a committee so desires.[21]

Senators have two incentives against using counsel, and few incentives in favor of doing so. The first reason not to use counsel is that a decision to do so would be tantamount to an admission that senators are incapable of discovering and exploring the consequences of nominees' ideologies by themselves. The second drawback to using counsel is that senators would lose much of the free television exposure they now receive.

Although senators have something to lose by employing counsel, they have little to gain by doing so. For compromise nominees, there is no incentive to grill the nominee, and the process goes smoothly for all involved. The same is true for nominees such as Sandra Day O'Connor, Ruth Bader Ginsburg, and Stephen Breyer (the last two arguably compromise nominees themselves), who are regarded by opposition senators as "the best we are likely to get" from the president. For a nomination that comes soon after a major battle over the previous nomination (such as that of Antonin Scalia, who followed immediately on the nomination of William Rehnquist for chief justice), potential opponents may lack the stomach for a second consecutive confirmation fight. Senators seem also not to suffer for giving the second nominee a free pass, as Democrats did in Scalia's case. In the case of a contentious nominee such as Clarence Thomas, senators may vigorously question the nominee, whether out of conviction or a desire to impress their political bases. Or they may choose to avoid alienating the nominee's supporters by modulating the severity of their questioning or asking about arcane matters such as the use of natural law in constitutional interpretation, as Senator Joseph Biden did with Thomas.[22] Although a nominee's willingness to give controversial answers to controversial questions may facilitate a vote against confirmation, a nominee's refusal to answer such questions may also justify a senator in voting "no"—and without the senator having to take a stand on any controversy. Senators therefore have reasons not to use counsel to probe nominees' ideologies, and few reasons for doing so or for questioning nominees harder themselves.

Questioning by special counsels could also prove unhelpful in uncovering nominees' ideologies. Most nominees are highly intelligent lawyers skilled in avoiding direct answers when they choose to withhold them. They hone their skills at sidestepping questions by watching tapes of earlier nominees doing so and by parrying the questions of "senators" played by administration personnel at mock hearings called "murder boards."[23] With the well-entrenched impartiality norm at their disposal, their refusals to answer questions, even those from professional counsels, could well prove impossible to counter. Senators supportive of the nomination may also interject to protect nominees from probing questions, as they have in the past, and will almost certainly hire their own partisan counsel to blunt the efforts of the opposition's interrogator. Under these circumstances, even highly skilled questioners may fail to shed much additional light on nominees' beliefs.

Questioning by special counsel is also of limited value because senators normally know the general nature of a nominee's views before the confirmation hearings begin. As we have seen, there is a strong but not perfect correlation between the positions nominees express before their nominations and those they later take as justices.[24] And as Chapter 6 has shown, more revealing nominee testimony may have several harmful effects.

For all these reasons, the use of counsel to probe nominees' ideologies is both unlikely and of questionable value. A healthy substitute for the improbable questioning by expert counsel would be a greater willingness by senators to base their confirmation votes on the normally considerable amount they already know about nominees' ideologies and to withhold their approval from nominees whose beliefs are suspect and who fail to answer legitimate questions (as well as those few nominees whose beliefs are largely unknown). In the American constitutional democracy, such a posture would help to provide the necessary check on both the president and the judicial figures who will be largely uncheckable once confirmed. The Senate cannot assume a truly equal role in making High Court appointments, but as Watson and Stookey have argued,[25] a check of some sort is especially important in times such as the late twentieth and early twenty-first centuries, when constitutional consensus has broken down and presidents of one party have made a large majority of Supreme Court nominations.

There are signs that senators in this era are increasingly willing to evaluate nominees ideologically and increasingly unwilling to give their uninformed consent or the benefit of the doubt to presidents and their nominees for all levels of the federal bench.[26] It is virtually certain that the longer the nation lacks consensus on basic constitutional values and the Senate remains divided along partisan ideological lines, senators' willingness to defer to presidents in filling Supreme Court seats, so prevalent at mid-twentieth century, will erode.

A Two-Thirds Vote for Confirmation

Some analysts in the political school have advocated a rule change to require a two-thirds vote of the Senate to confirm Supreme Court nominees.[27] This proposal has attracted no significant support in the past and would likely fail in the future as a result of opposition by members of the president's party in Congress as well as some opponents of the measure in the other party. In 2003, Republican supporters of President George W. Bush sought to abolish the filibuster on presidential nominations and thereby lower the number of votes required for confirmation from sixty to fifty-one.[28] They are hardly likely to agree to increase the required number to two-thirds of the Senate, or sixty-seven.

The proposal for a two-thirds confirmation vote nonetheless has more to commend it than most other proposed procedural reforms. The proposal's purpose is to force presidents to nominate well-qualified, relatively moderate, judicially restrained figures more acceptable to potential opponents. The proposal would shift more power over appointments to the Senate, especially in times of ideological schism and/or divided government, such as the late twentieth and early twenty-first centuries.

The two modern Supreme Court nominees most affected by this proposal would have been two of the most conservative justices of that period— William H. Rehnquist and Clarence Thomas. Rehnquist's 1971 confirmation as associate justice came by a vote of 68–26, his 1986 elevation to chief justice by a vote of 65–33. Under a two-thirds rule, he would not have become chief justice, as he won the support of neither two-thirds of the whole Senate nor of those voting. Rehnquist's initial appointment as associate justice would have faced some jeopardy as well. Two votes switched from "yes" to "no" would have put him at 66–28, below two-thirds of the entire Senate; six switched votes would have placed him at 62–32, below two-thirds of those voting.

These vote switches may have occurred under a two-thirds rule. With only a majority required for confirmation, many senators may have seen a "no" vote as a futile gesture and concluded that the easier political course was to vote for confirmation. But under a two-thirds rule, Rehnquist's confirmation would not have been so clearly a fait accompli, and six of sixty-eight senators might conceivably have been persuaded to vote "no," killing the nomination. And had a two-thirds rule been in place and the Nixon—and later Reagan—White House correctly gauged the level of opposition to a potential Rehnquist nomination, it is possible that neither president would have nominated him (although no one can say confidently that either president's decision would have been different, given their combativeness on High Court nominations).

The Thomas nomination, approved 52–48, would have fallen far short of a two-thirds vote. Even before the emergence of Anita Hill, Thomas had the support of roughly fifty-five or sixty senators, and his nomination may well have failed. Without the fait accompli reasoning the bare majority requirement encouraged, his nomination would have faced extreme jeopardy (even assuming that President George H. W. Bush had nominated him in the face of a two-thirds rule). Without Rehnquist and/or Thomas, the Court's rightward turn in the late twentieth century may have been significantly moderated.

Whatever one thinks of these justices and the Court's rightward turn, a two-thirds requirement for confirmation would almost certainly force presidents to nominate more moderate, widely acceptable, and judicially restrained figures of the sort least likely to rule on the basis of their personal values and to perpetuate the Court as a major issue in American politics—precisely the sort of justices the nation needs, according to some authorities.[29]

But a two-thirds rule for confirmation has drawbacks. It would raise the barrier against confirmation for innovative and controversial figures of potential excellence. It could also heighten conflict over nominations if presidents do not sufficiently accommodate the Senate. This development could, in turn, damage the Court's or Congress's prestige. (The conflict levels of the late twentieth century did not have this result, but we cannot say that higher levels of conflict would not do so.) Given the infrequency with which the justices persist in defying the fundamental values of the American people whose Constitution they interpret, one may also question whether a required two-thirds vote for confirmation would serve a useful purpose in the long run. And there is the ever-present rule of unintended consequences, always a cautionary voice against altering existing procedures.

Because the benefits of a two-thirds rule do not clearly outweigh the costs, the improbability of the proposal's adoption may well be for the better. There are, in addition, other ways to bring about greater power sharing between president and Senate in the appointment process and to produce more restrained justices: greater acceptance of senators' overtly ideological evaluation of nominees, and a greater willingness by senators to shift the burden of proof onto the nominee and the president to prove the nominee's suitability for a justiceship. The seeming trend in these directions lessens the need for a two-thirds requirement.

Placing the Burden of Proof on the Executive Branch

Several analysts of the confirmation process have suggested abolishing the presumption in favor of a nominee's confirmation, still espoused by many senators, and shifting the burden of proof to the nominee and the president to prove the nominee's suitability for a justiceship.[30] This proposal is related to the argument that senators should examine nominees' ideologies, but differs from it by including broader criteria and, more importantly, addressing the question of who must meet what burden of proof for a nominee to win confirmation. Even universal agreement on which factors the Senate should consider would leave "much room for questions about . . . the extent to which the Senate ought to defer to the president's choice."[31] Such deference undoubtedly exists. Scholars have described it and explained its origin.[32] The cursory confirmation proceedings for most nominees from the 1890s to the late 1960s are evidence of it. Senators of both parties expressed their belief in it as late as the 1990s.[33]

Perhaps the clearest modern example of senatorial deference to the president was the 1990 confirmation of David Souter, who won confirmation by a vote of ninety to nine.[34] Souter was an undistinguished nominee. His career on the New Hampshire Supreme Court included very few cases involving the federal statutory and constitutional questions that preoccupy the Supreme Court. His views on those questions were unknown. Although often described as "scholarly," his lone published article consisted only of a tribute to a fellow New Hampshire Supreme Court justice.[35] In Souter's manner and temperate Senate testimony, some senators found reassurance (or disappointment) that Souter was no right-wing conservative. But he was still viewed largely as a "stealth nominee" after his confirmation hearings. He later proved to be a surprisingly liberal and, according to the survey results in Chapter 4, surprisingly able, justice. But guessing at nominees' beliefs and hoping for unexpected ability are hardly sound strategies for voting on U.S. Supreme Court nominees.

For at least three reasons, senators owe the president no deference in appointing justices. First, as Chapter 2 implied, presidents get no entitlement to deference from the text, structure, or spirit of the Constitution, nor from the intentions of the Framers. Second, most presidents have no popular mandate to place a particular type of justice on the Court. In most presidential elections, the Supreme Court is not a major issue.[36] Third, the nation requires the president to prove the worth of his significant legislative proposals. Why should he not do so for his equally if not much more important Supreme Court nominations?[37]

If a senator harbors any reasonable doubt about a nominee's character, temperament, professional ability, or commitment to core constitutional values, the senator should vote against confirmation. One can argue that a senator would be justified in voting to confirm a nominee, despite such doubts, because the president may then nominate someone even worse. But the nomination will not fail unless a majority of all senators entertains such doubts. And if a majority of the whole Senate has reasonable doubts about a nominee's character, temperament, ability, or philosophy, the nomination should fail. The Senate will thereby send the president a message to nominate someone better, and most presidents will respond accordingly. The Carswell nomination is the only modern instance of a president (in this case, an unusually spiteful president) reacting to a rejected nomination by naming a second figure who was clearly inferior to the first.[38] And Carswell was rejected. There is, moreover, a large pool of qualified candidates from whom the president can choose a second nominee.

The proposal that senators place the burden of proof on the president is often made in terms suggesting that the Senate should be an "equal partner"[39] with the president in naming new justices. The Senate will never be the president's equal in this process because the president can act with one mind, choose a nominee from a large number of qualified candidates, place his inevitably formidable imprimatur on the nominee, and set the agenda for the confirmation process. Senators ideologically allied with the president will seldom question much about the nominee, and those who are not his allies will often vote for his nominees because they know he could have nominated someone worse. And even if the burden of proving the nominee's fitness shifts to the president and the nominee, senators opposed to confirmation must still offer a plausible explanation of how the president and nominee failed to meet their burden. Moreover, a senator with reasonable doubts about the nominee might vote against confirmation only if the senator's concerns about the nominee outweigh any political dangers from voting "no," such as alienating the senator's party or a key constituency.

For all these reasons, shifting the burden of proof onto the president and the nominee will not bring about an equal role for the Senate. But greater willingness by senators to place a heavier burden on the executive branch will move the process closer to that state. The longer the nation and its representatives remain polarized over constitutional fundamentals, the more likely senators are to adopt such a stance.[40]

CONCLUSION: THE ROBUST CONFIRMATION PROCESS

Periods of constitutional schism, such as the late twentieth and early twenty-first century, call for an especially robust constitutional dialogue over who should receive life tenure on the nation's Supreme Court and issue nearly uncheckable rulings on the fundamental constitutional questions that divide the American people. It is therefore well that greater power sharing by president and Senate in the Supreme Court appointment process has come about, and is likely to grow, by placing more clearly on the shoulders of the president and his nominee the need to prove the nominee's suitability for a seat on the Court. This development is the most salutary—perhaps the only salutary—reform of the normally well-functioning High Court confirmation process that Americans could hope for.

An intelligent citizenry worthy of that designation can—or can be made to—understand that people who are unqualified, unethical, or politically extreme should not sit with life tenure on America's nine-member, nearly unaccountable Supreme Court, and that conflict over nominees who at least arguably fit these descriptions is predictable and healthy. Indeed, most Americans almost certainly understand that weakly qualified or questionably ethical people do not belong on their Supreme Court. The public's approval of senators' ideological scrutiny of nominees[41] is evidence that Americans also understand both the undesirability of political extremity on the Court, and the desirability of democratic opposition to nominees about whom there are legitimate concerns about extremity. Perhaps in this instance those who are deeply interested by processes of American government should listen to the usually good sense of the American people.

List of Cases

AARP v. EEOC, 655 F. Supp. 228 (1987)
Abrams v. Johnson, 521 U.S. 74 (1997)
Adarand Constructors v. Pena, 515 U.S. 200 (1995)
Agostini v. Felton, 521 U.S. 203 (1997)
Aguilar v. Felton, 473 U.S. 402 (1985)
Alabama v. Garrett, 531 U.S. 356 (2001)
Alabama v. Shelton, 535 U.S. 654 (2002)
Albertson's v. Kirkingburg, 527 U.S. 555 (1999)
Alden v. Maine, 527 U.S. 706 (1999)
Alexander v. Sandoval, 532 U.S. 275 (2001)
Alexander v. United States, 509 U.S. 544 (1993)
ALPO Petfoods v. Ralston Purina, 286 U.S. App. D.C. 192; 913 F.2d 958 (1990)
Amchem Products v. Windsor, 521 U.S. 591 (1997)
Amtrak v. Morgan, 536 U.S. 101 (2002)
Apprendi v. New Jersey, 530 U.S. 466 (2000)
Aptheker v. Secretary of State, 378 U.S. 500 (1964)
Arizona v. Evans, 514 U.S. 1 (1995)
Arizona v. Hicks, 480 U.S. 321 (1987)
Arizona v. Mauro, 481 U.S. 520 (1987)
Ashcroft v. Free Speech Coalition, 535 U.S. 234 (2002)
Atkins v. Virginia, 536 U.S. 304 (2002)
Atwater v. Lago Vista, 532 U.S. 318 (2001)
Austin v. United States, 509 U.S. 602 (1993)
Babbitt v. Sweet Home Chapter of Communities for a Great Oregon, 515 U.S. 687
    (1995)
Baker v. Carr, 369 U.S. 186 (1962)
Barnes v. Gorman, 536 U.S. 181 (2002)
Barron v. Baltimore, 32 U.S. (7 Pet.) 243 (1833)
Bartnicki v. Vopper, 532 U.S. 514 (2001)
Batson v. Kentucky, 476 U.S. 79 (1986)

Morgan v. Illinois, 504 U.S. 719 (1992)
Morrison v. Olson, 487 U.S. 654 (1988)
Murphy v. United Parcel Service, 527 U.S. 516 (1999)
Murray v. Giarratano, 492 U.S. 1 (1989)
National Endowment for the Arts v. Finley, 524 U.S. 569 (1998)
National Organization for Women v. Scheidler, 510 U.S. 249
Nevada Department of Human Resources v. Hibbs, 123 S. Ct. 1972 (2003)
New York v. Burger, 482 U.S. 691 (1987)
New York v. United States, 505 U.S. 144 (1992)
Nixon v. Shrink Missouri Government PAC, 528 U.S. 377 (2000)
Nixon v. United States, 506 U.S. 224 (1993)
Nollan v. California Coastal Commission, 483 U.S. 825 (1987)
Norfolk & Western Ry. v. Ayers, 538 U.S. 135 (2003)
O'Connor v. Ortega, 480 U.S. 709 (1987)
O'Dell v. Netherland, 521 U.S. 151 (1997)
Ohio v. Reiner, 532 U.S. 17 (2001)
Ohio v. Robinette, 519 U.S. 33 (1996)
Olmstead v. L.C., 527 U.S. 581 (1999)
O'Lone v. Shabazz, 478 U.S. 342 (1987)
Oncale v. Sundowner Offshore Services, 523 U.S. 75 (1998)
Oregon v. Mitchell, 400 U.S. 112 (1970)
Ortiz v. Fibreboard Corp., 527 U.S. 815 (1999)
Pacific Mutual v. Haslip, 499 U.S. 1 (1991)
Palazzolo v. Rhode Island, 533 U.S. 606 (2001)
Patterson v. McLean Credit Union, 491 U.S. 164 (1989)
Payne v. Tennessee, 501 U.S. 808 (1991)
Pennell v. San Jose, 485 U.S. 1 (1988)
Pennsylvania v. Bruder, 488 U.S. 9 (1988)
Pennsylvania v. Finley, 481 U.S. 551 (1987)
Pennsylvania v. Yeskey, 524 U.S. 206 (1998)
Pennsylvania Board of Probation v. Scott, 524 U.S. 357 (1998)
Penry v. Johnson, 532 U.S. 782 (2001)
Penry v. Lynaugh, 492 U.S. 302 (1989)
PGA Tour v. Martin, 532 U.S. 661 (2001)
Phillips v. Washington Legal Foundation, 524 U.S. 156 (1998)
Planned Parenthood v. Ashcroft, 462 U.S. 476 (1983)
Planned Parenthood v. Casey, 505 U.S. 833 (1992)
Powell v. McCormack, 395 U.S. 486 (1969)
Powers v. Ohio, 499 U.S. 400 (1991)
Printz v. United States, 521 U.S. 898 (1997)
Proceedings before the Supreme Court of the United States: U.S. v. Lopez. Case
    No. 93-1260, 8 November 1994. Washington, D.C.: Alderson Publishing
Quality King Distributors v. L'Anza Research International, 523 U.S. 135 (1998)
R.A.V. v. City of St. Paul, 505 U.S. 377 (1992)

Reeves v. Sanderson Plumbing, 530 U.S. 133 (2000)
Regents of the University of California v. Bakke, 438 U.S. 265 (1978)
Reno v. American-Arab Anti-Discrimination Committee, 525 U.S. 471 (1999)
Reno v. American Civil Liberties Union, 521 U.S. 844 (1997)
Reno v. Bossier Parish, 528 U.S. 320 (2000)
Republican Party of Minnesota v. White, 536 U.S. 765 (2002)
Richardson v. McKnight, 521 U.S. 399 (1997)
Richmond v. Croson, 488 U.S. 469 (1989)
Roe v. Wade, 410 U.S. 113 (1973)
Romer v. Evans, 517 U.S. 620 (1996)
Rosenberger v. University of Virginia, 515 U.S. 819 (1995)
Rust v. Sullivan, 500 U.S. 173 (1991)
Sable Communications v. FCC, 492 U.S. 115 (1989)
Santa Fe Independent School District v. Doe, 530 U.S. 290 (2000)
Scheidler v. National Organization for Women, 537 U.S. 393 (2003)
Schenck v. Pro-Choice Network of Western New York, 519 U.S. 357 (1997)
Seminole Tribe v. Florida, 517 U.S. 44 (1996)
Shaw v. Hunt, 517 U.S. 899 (1996)
Shaw v. Reno, 509 U.S. 630 (1993)
Shelley v. Kraemer, 334 U.S. 1 (1948)
Simmons v. South Carolina, 512 U.S. 154 (1994)
Simon & Schuster v. New York Crime Victims Board, 502 U.S. 105 (1991)
Skinner v. Oklahoma, 316 U.S. 535 (1942)
Skinner v. Railway Labor Executives' Association, 489 U.S. 602 (1989)
Slack v. McDaniel, 529 U.S. 473 (2000)
Solid Waste Agency v. U.S. Army Corps of Engineers, 531 U.S. 159 (2001)
South Carolina v. Gathers, 490 U.S. 805 (1989)
Stanford v. Kentucky, 492 U.S. 361 (1989)
State Farm v. Campbell, 538 U.S. 408 (2003)
State Oil v. Khan, 522 U.S. 3 (1997)
Steel Co. v. Citizens for a Better Environment, 523 U.S. 83 (1998)
Stenberg v. Carhart, 530 U.S. 914 (2000)
Stewart v. Martinez-Villareal, 523 U.S. 637 (1998)
Stogner v. California, 123 S. Ct. 2446 (2003)
Stringer v. Black, 505 U.S. 222 (1992)
Sullivan v. Louisiana, 508 U.S. 275 (1993)
Sutton v. United Airlines, 527 U.S. 471 (1999)
Swann v. Charlotte-Mecklenburg Board of Education, 402 U.S. 1 (1971)
Swidler & Berlin v. United States, 524 U.S. 399 (1998)
Tahoe-Sierra Preservation Council v. Tahoe Regional Planning Agency, 535 U.S.
    302 (2002)
Texas v. Cobb, 532 U.S. 162 (2001)
Texas v. Johnson, 491 U.S. 397 (1989)
Texas Monthly v. Bullock, 489 U.S. 1 (1989)

Thompson v. Western States Medical Center, 535 U.S. 357 (2002)
Thornburgh v. American College of Obstetricians and Gynecologists, 476 U.S. 747 (1986)
Toyota v. Williams, 534 U.S. 184 (2002)
Treasury Employees v. Von Raab, 489 U.S. 656 (1989)
Troxel v. Granville, 530 U.S. 57 (2000)
United States v. A Parcel of Land, 507 U.S. 111 (1993)
United States v. American Library Association, 539 U.S. 194 (2003)
United States v. Armstrong, 517 U.S. 456 (1996)
United States v. Arvizu, 534 U.S. 266 (2002)
United States v. Bajakajian, 524 U.S. 321 (1998)
United States v. Dixon, 509 U.S. 688 (1993)
United States v. Drayton, 536 U.S. 194 (2002)
United States v. Dunn, 480 U.S. 294 (1987)
United States v. Eichman, 496 U.S. 310 (1990)
United States v. Good, 510 U.S. 43 (1993)
United States v. Knights, 534 U.S. 112 (2001)
United States v. Lopez, 514 U.S. 549 (1995)
United States v. Monsanto, 491 U.S. 600 (1989)
United States v. Morrison, 529 U.S. 598 (2000)
United States v. Nixon, 418 U.S. 683 (1974)
United States v. North, 287 U.S. App. D.C. 146; 920 F.2d 940 (1990)
United States v. Paradise, 480 U.S. 149 (1987)
United States v. Playboy Entertainment Group, 529 U.S. 803 (2000)
United States v. Sokolow, 490 U.S. 1 (1989)
United States v. Ursery, 518 U.S. 267 (1996)
United States v. Virginia, 518 U.S. 515 (1996)
United Steel Workers v. Weber, 443 U.S. 193 (1979)
US Airways v. Barnett, 535 U.S. 391 (2002)
U.S. Term Limits v. Thornton, 514 U.S. 779 (1995)
Vacco v. Quill, 521 U.S. 793 (1997)
Vernonia School District 47J v. Acton, 515 U.S. 646 (1995)
Virginia v. Black, 538 U.S. 343 (2003)
Wards Cove Packing v. Atonio, 490 U.S. 692 (1989)
Washington v. Glucksburg, 521 U.S. 702 (1997)
Watchtower Bible Society v. Stratton, 536 U.S. 150 (2002)
Webster v. Reproductive Health Services, 492 U.S. 490 (1989)
Westside Community Schools v. Mergens, 496 U.S. 226 (1990)
Whitman v. American Trucking, 531 U.S. 457 (2001)
Whren v. United States, 517 U.S. 806 (1996)
Wiggins v. Smith, 123 S. Ct. 2527 (2003)
Williams v. Taylor, 529 U.S. 362 (2000)
Williams v. Taylor, 529 U.S. 420 (2000)
Wilson v. Layne, 526 U.S. 603 (1999)
Wisconsin v. Mitchell, 508 U.S. 476 (1993)

Notes

1. INTRODUCTION: CONTRASTING PERSPECTIVES ON THE CONFIRMATION PROCESS

1. David M. O'Brien, "Background Paper," 99. Reagan's second Attorney General, Edwin Meese III, affirmed that the Reagan Administration sought to use judicial appointments "to institutionalize the Reagan revolution so it can't be set aside no matter what happens in future presidential elections." In David M. O'Brien, *Storm Center,* 70.

2. Steven V. Roberts, "Reagan Vows New Appointment as Upsetting to His Foes as Bork's," *New York Times,* October 14, 1987, A1.

3. At the time Bush nominated him, Souter, who had spent seven years on New Hampshire's Supreme Court, had just joined the federal Court of Appeals for the First Circuit but had yet to hear a case on it.

4. See Chapter 6 for a review of Souter's record on the Supreme Court.

5. Chapter 5 tells the story of Thomas's leadership of the EEOC, and his nomination and confirmation for the Supreme Court.

6. Some examples of this literature are Twentieth Century Fund, *Judicial Roulette;* Richard D. Friedman, "Tribal Myths"; Max Lerner, "Has the Senate Gone Too Far?"; Norman Vieira and Leonard E. Gross, "Appointments Clause"; Eugene W. Hickok Jr., "Senate"; Bruce Fein, "Court of Mediocrity"; and the remarks of Michael McConnell in Stephanie B. Goldberg, "What's the Alternative?"

7. Some examples of these writings are Elena Kagan, "Confirmation Messes"; David Strauss and Cass R. Sunstein, "The Senate, the Constitution"; Laurence H. Tribe, *God Save This Honorable Court;* Nina Totenberg, "Confirmation Process"; Grover Rees III, "Questions for Supreme Court Nominees"; Stuart Taylor Jr., "Senate Should Claim Full Parity"; Ginsburg Report, 40; and, with respect to some issues, Gary J. Simson, "Thomas's Supreme Unfitness."

8. E.g., George L. Watson and John A. Stookey, *Shaping America;* Jeffrey A. Segal, Albert D. Cover, and Charles M. Cameron, "Senate Confirmation"; John D.

Felice and Herbert F. Weisberg, "Changing Importance of Ideology"; Gregory Caldeira, Marie Hojnacki, and John R. Wright, "Lobbying Activities."

9. John Anthony Maltese, *Selling;* Mark Silverstein, *Judicious Choices.*

10. Maltese, *Selling;* Silverstein, *Judicious Choices.*

11. Maltese, *Selling;* Silverstein, *Judicious Choices.*

12. John Massaro, *Supremely Political.*

13. Maltese, *Selling.*

14. See, e.g., Neil A. Lewis, "Hatch Defends Senate Action on Judgeships," *New York Times,* January 2, 1998, A1.

15. William H. Rehnquist, "The 1997 Year-End Report on the Federal Judiciary," available at: http://www.uscourts.gov/ttb/jan98ttb/january.htm.

16. See, e.g., Bill Keller, "Reagan's Son."

17. After the elections of 2000, the Senate held 50 Democrats and 50 Republicans. In May 2001, Republican Senator James Jeffords of Vermont became an Independent, giving Democrats a 50–49-seat edge over the Republicans. After the elections of 2002, the Republicans held 51 seats and the Democrats 48, with one Independent (Jeffords, who caucused with the Democrats).

18. David L. Greene, "Partisanship Reigns in Battle over Courts; Judgeships: President Bush and Senate Democrats Are Fighting over Several Nominees, with Abortion Rights and the Supreme Court Ultimately at Stake," *Baltimore Sun,* June 15, 2003, 1C.

19. Elisabeth Bumiller, "Bush Vows to Seek Conservative Judges," *New York Times,* March 29, 2002, 24.

20. When George W. Bush took office in 2001, Justice John Paul Stevens was 80, Chief Justice Rehnquist 76, Justice Sandra Day O'Connor was 70.

21. Neil A. Lewis, "Expecting a Vacancy, Bush Aides Weigh Supreme Court Contenders," *New York Times,* December 27, 2002, A1.

22. E.g., Maltese, *Selling;* Silverstein, *Judicious Choices.*

23. Kagan, "Confirmation Messes," 935. For arguments that ideological review of nominees is improper or entails grave dangers, see Richard D. Friedman, "Transformation in Senate Response," 87, n. 558; Richard D. Friedman, "Tribal Myths"; Bruce Fein, "Commentary"; Orrin G. Hatch, "Politics of Picking Judges"; Max Lerner, "Has the Senate Gone Too Far?"; and Norman Vieira and Leonard E. Gross, "Appointments Clause."

24. Historical studies documenting this point are Henry J. Abraham, *Justices, Presidents, and Senators;* and Tribe, *God Save This Honorable Court.* As Overby et al. summarize the quantitative literature, "[M]ost recent work has concluded that ideology consistently has a larger effect [than other factors] on senators' voting behavior on controversial nominations." L. Marvin Overby et al., "Courting Constituents?", 997.

25. Richard D. Friedman, "Transformation in Senate Response," 4.

26. Ibid., 31–32.

27. For evidence of regionalism, see Friedman, "Transformation in Senate Response," 30–35; and Abraham, *Justices, Presidents, and Senators,* 96; on patronage and partisanship, see Friedman, "Transformation in Senate Response," 26–30;

and Abraham, *Justices, Presidents, and Senators,* 96, 108. On personal rivalry, see Abraham, *Justices, Presidents, and Senators,* 108–10.

28. Friedman, "Transformation in Senate Response," 4.

29. Ibid.

30. Ibid., 49. In addition to Friedman, see Felix Frankfurter and James M. Landis, *Business of the Supreme Court,* esp. chaps. 1 and 2.

31. Friedman, "Transformation in Senate Response," 42–48.

32. Ibid.

33. Ibid., 5.

34. The rejected nominee was Hoover nominee John. J. Parker in 1930. Lee Epstein et al., *Supreme Court Compendium,* table 4-13, 322–28, at 326.

35. Maltese, *Selling,* 109–10; Stephen L. Carter, *Confirmation Mess,* 65–68.

36. D. Grier Stephenson Jr., *Campaigns and the Court,* 172.

37. Silverstein, *Judicious Choices,* 25–26.

38. Examples of such attacks are at U.S. Senate Committee on the Judiciary, *Nominations of Abe Fortas and Homer Thornberry: Hearings Before the Committee on the Judiciary,* 153–59, 160–63, 181, 214–15, 218–23, 234–36, and 239–47.

39. Stephenson, *Campaigns and the Court,* chap. 7.

40. Ibid., 182.

41. Qualitative and quantitative analyses of the Senate votes in these two cases agree that the opposition to the nominees was primarily ideological. For a representative qualitative analysis, see Abraham, *Justices, Presidents, and Senators,* 9–13, 31. A representative quantitative analysis is Watson and Stookey, *Shaping America,* 183–87.

42. See Abraham, *Justices, Presidents, and Senators,* 15–16, 267–70, 291–93; and Watson and Stookey, *Shaping America,* 188–91.

43. *Swann v. Charlotte-Mecklenburg Board of Education,* 402 U.S. 1 (1971).

44. See, respectively, *Regents of the University of California v. Bakke,* 438 U.S. 265 (1978); *United Steel Workers v. Weber,* 443 U.S. 193 (1979); *Fullilove v. Klutznick,* 448 U.S. 448 (1980).

45. *Roe v. Wade,* 410 U.S. 113 (1973).

46. Herman Schwartz, *Packing the Courts,* 7, 39–40, 196–98.

47. For various reasons described in Chapter 6, there was no opposition to the nomination of Scalia.

48. Epstein et al., *Supreme Court Compendium,* 322–28.

49. Ibid.

50. Ibid., at 326.

51. Alexander Hamilton, James Madison, and John Jay, *The Federalist* (No. 76), 430.

52. Ibid.

53. See the remarks of Republican Senator Arlen Specter in Stuart Taylor Jr., "Supreme Disappointment"; Democratic Senator Dennis DeConcini of Arizona in Thomas Hearings, 95; remarks of (Democratic) Senator Wyche Fowler of Georgia on the Supreme Court of the United States, 102nd Cong., 1st sess., *Congressional Record* (October 3, 1991), 137: S14297 (before the Anita Hill controversy erupted);

remarks of (Democratic) Senator Bob Graham of Florida, ibid., S14662; remarks of (Republican) Senator William Cohen of Maine, ibid., S14624.

54. Ruth Marcus, "Conservative Mindset, Careful Jurist; Nominee's Legal Opinions Offer No Insight into His Views on Abortion, Civil Rights," *Washington Post,* July 25, 1990, A6.

55. Souter also benefited from the ardent campaign on his behalf by his friend and former colleague in New Hampshire, the much respected Senator Warren Rudman.

56. Remarks of Senator Robert Byrd, 102nd Cong., 1st sess., *Congressional Record* (October 15, 1991), 137: S14633–34; remarks of Senator Paul Simon, ibid., S14641; remarks of Senator Edward Kennedy, ibid., S14642–43.

57. Abraham, *Justices, Presidents, and Senators,* 329.

58. Massaro, *Supremely Political,* 141; Segal, Cover, and Cameron, "Senate Confirmation," 485, 506–7.

59. For arguments that recognition of the Court's power has produced a "sea change in the Supreme Court appointments process," including the changes discussed in this chapter, see Stephen M. Griffin, "Has the Hour of Democracy Come Round at Last?", 696; and Silverstein, *Judicious Choices,* introduction, esp. 6–8. For powerful evidence that nominees' substantive beliefs affect their rulings as justices, see Jeffrey A. Segal and Harold J. Spaeth, *Attitudinal Model.*

60. Segal and Spaeth, *Attitudinal Model,* 300.

61. See, e.g., Segal and Spaeth, *Attitudinal Model.*

62. Maltese, *Selling,* 89, 90–91, 101, 104, 107.

63. The four were Harlan F. Stone in 1925, Felix Frankfurter in 1939, Frank Murphy in 1940, and Robert H. Jackson in 1941. Ibid., 104, 107.

64. Burger Hearings.

65. Abraham, *Justices, Presidents, and Senators,* 11–14.

66. Bork Hearings.

67. For questions on natural law, economic rights and originalism, see Thomas Hearings, 110–29, 236–43; on criticisms of civil rights, leaders, 449–52; on praise of Oliver North, 382–83, 464–65; on abortion 127–29, 146–48, 218–24; on equal employment opportunities, 140–41, 144–46, 227–36, 354–61.

68. Thomas Hearings, pts. 2–4.

69. Maltese, *Selling,* 90–91.

70. Ibid.

71. For a sample of an ABA report on a nominee, see Thomas Hearings, pt. 1, 522–33.

72. On interest groups generally, see Watson and Stookey, *Shaping America,* 104–12; for law firm work in Clarence Thomas's case, see Jane Mayer and Jill Abramson, *Strange Justice,* 183–84.

73. "Chief Confidant to Chief Justice," *Time,* July 5, 1968, 12–17; Fred P. Graham, "Many-Sided Justice Fortas."

74. Timothy Phelps and Helen Winternitz, *Capitol Games,* 227–36; Mayer and Abramson, *Strange Justice,* 250–57.

75. See Jeffrey M. Berry, *Interest Group Society,* chap. 2.

76. Maltese, *Selling,* 86–87.

77. Ibid., 107.

78. Paul A. Freund, "Appointment of Justices."

79. Epstein et al., *Supreme Court Compendium,* table 4-13, 322–28.

80. Maltese, *Selling,* 115.

81. On White House involvement in the process, see ibid., chaps. 6, 7.

82. For these benefits in the case of nominee Clarence Thomas, see Overby et al., "Courting Constituents?"; L. Marvin Overby and Beth M. Henschen, "Race Trumps Gender?" For evidence that unfavorable opinion polls helped defeat the Bork nomination, see Ethan Bronner, *Battle for Justice,* 151–59, 288–90; Mark Gitenstein, *Matters of Principle,* 112–17, 178, 247, 255–56, 267–68, 271, 287–88.

83. For such effort on behalf of Robert Bork, see Gitenstein, *Matters of Principle,* 188–92, and Maltese, *Selling,* 110; for Clarence Thomas, Mayer and Abramson, *Strange Justice,* 178–79, 185–86, 201–2; and Phelps and Winternitz, *Capitol Games,* 78.

84. A description of Thomas's confirmation strategy is in Mayer and Abramson, *Strange Justice,* 169–201, 205–9.

85. On "murder boards," see Maltese, *Selling,* 112, and Mayer and Abramson, *Strange Justice,* 19, 211; on tape watching, see Ruth Marcus, "Souter Shows Senate a Case Study on Confirmation," *Washington Post,* September 16, 1990, A10; on the refresher course for Clarence Thomas, see Mayer and Abramson, *Strange Justice,* 210–11. For a criticism of this Justice Department function, see the comments of Michael McConnell in Goldberg, "What's the Alternative?", 41.

86. See, e.g., Mayer and Abramson, *Strange Justice,* 173.

87. Ibid., 217–18.

88. Maltese, *Selling,* 112–15.

89. "Senate and Executive Branch Appointments" (quotation at 35).

90. Barbara Sinclair, *Transformation of the U.S. Senate,* chap. 5.

91. Watson and Stookey, *Shaping America,* 181.

92. Ibid.

93. Daniel J. Parks, "Partisan Voting Holds Steady." The datum on 1995 comes from Karen O'Connor and Larry J. Sabato, *American Government,* 249.

94. O'Connor and Sabato, *American Government,* 441.

95. Epstein et al., *Supreme Court Compendium,* table 4-13, 322–28.

96. Segal, Cover, and Cameron, "Senate Confirmation"; Watson and Stookey, *Shaping America,* 92, 177–91; Robert G. Scigliano, *The Supreme Court and the Presidency,* 97–98.

97. Thomas's nomination and confirmation are also the subject of Chapter 5.

2. THE SENATE'S CONSTITUTIONAL ROLE IN THE CONFIRMATION PROCESS

1. Elena Kagan, "Confirmation Messes" (quotation at 935). For arguments that ideological review of nominees is improper or entails serious dangers, see Richard D.

Friedman, "Transformation in Senate Response," 87, n. 558; Richard D. Friedman, "Tribal Myths"; Bruce Fein, "Commentary"; Orrin G. Hatch, "Politics of Picking Judges"; Max Lerner, "Has the Senate Gone Too Far?"; and Norman Vieira and Leonard E. Gross, "Appointments Clause."

2. U.S. Constitution, art. 2, sec. 2, cl. 2.

3. Henry J. Abraham, "Can the President Really Pack the Supreme Court?", 39–40.

4. Max Farrand, *Records of the Federal Convention of 1787,* 1:128 (June 5).

5. Farrand, *Records of the Federal Convention of 1787,* Edmund Randolph at 2:81 (July 21); Morris and Wilson at 2:389 (August 23).

6. Ibid., Nathaniel Gorham at 2:42 and 2:43 (July 18); Morris at 2:82 (July 21).

7. Ibid., Gorham at 2:42 (July 18); Randolph at 2:81 (July 21).

8. Ibid. On the relative corruptibility of the president and Senate, see Roger Sherman at 2:43 (July 18); Ellsworth at 2:81 (July 21). On their relative knowledge of suitable appointees, see Sherman at 2:41 and 2:43 (July 18); and Ellsworth at 2:81 (July 21).

9. The remainder of this section owes much to James E. Gauch, "Intended Role."

10. Ibid., 347–49.

11. Farrand, *Records of the Federal Convention of 1787,* 2:44.

12. Ibid., at 2:83.

13. Ibid.

14. Ibid., at 2:80–81 (July 21). See also the remarks of Gunning Bedford, 2:43 (July 18); Roger Sherman, 2:41 (July 18); George Mason, 2:41–42 (July 18); and Nathaniel Gorham, 2:42 (July 18).

15. Ibid. (quotations at 2:82–83) (July 21).

16. Joseph P. Harris, *Advice and Consent* (quotation at 26).

17. See below, n. 19, and the accompanying material.

18. An analysis of Hamilton's writings on this subject in *The Federalist* appears in the next section. Rutledge's nomination was defeated by Federalists rankled by his opposition to the Jay Treaty with Great Britain, which attempted to settle disputes left over from the Revolution. For an excellent account of the battle over Rutledge's nomination, see John Anthony Maltese, *Selling,* chap. 2.

19. The Rutledge quotation is at Farrand, *Records of the Federal Convention of 1787,* 1:119 (June 5); Ellsworth's concurrence is at 2:81 (July 21).

20. One author who equates his interpretation of Hamilton with the views of "the Framers" is Fein, "Commentary," 672–73.

21. Harris, *Advice and Consent,* 27–28.

22. Alexander Hamilton, James Madison, and John Jay, *Federalist,* 430.

23. Ibid. The emphasis is Hamilton's.

24. Ibid.

25. On the compromise nature of several recent nominations, see Chapters 6 and 7.

26. Charles L. Black Jr., "Note on Senatorial Consideration," 662.

27. Hamilton, Madison, and Jay, *Federalist,* 430–31 (emphasis mine).

28. Ibid., 434.

29. If Hamilton did take that view when he coauthored *The Federalist,* he must have changed his mind by 1795, when he led the opposition to Washington's nomination of John Rutledge to be chief justice. See above, n. 18.

30. For an excellent exposition on constitutional democracy, see Walter F. Murphy, James E. Fleming, and Sotirios A. Barber, *American Constitutional Interpretation,* chap. 3.

31. Ruth Bader Ginsburg, "Confirming Supreme Court Justices," 112.

32. Robert Bork, *Tempting of America,* 347.

33. For an excellent exposition on constitutional interpretation as a dialogue, see Louis Fisher, *Constitutional Dialogues.* Some writers, particularly liberal scholars unhappy with conservative rulings by the Rehnquist Court and that Court's assertions of judicial supremacy (i.e., the claim that the Supreme Court is the final and ultimate interpreter of the Constitution) have suggested the need for a wider dialogue or greater sharing of constitutional interpretation than that which prevailed in roughly the first fifteen years of the Rehnquist Court (1986–2000). See, e.g., Mark Tushnet, *Taking the Constitution away from the Courts.* This position is discussed in Chapter 7, which reviews the doctrinal developments of the Rehnquist Court.

34. "Too Much Talk."

35. Stephanie B. Goldberg, "What's the Alternative?", 43.

36. Survey data show that Americans elect presidents primarily on the basis of economic performance, issues of war and peace, and general competence. For the determinants of presidential election outcomes, see Herbert B. Asher, *Presidential Elections.* In a careful study, D. Grier Stephenson Jr. has found the Supreme Court a significant issue in about one-fifth of all presidential elections; *Campaigns and the Court,* esp. chaps. 1 and 9.

37. Stephen L. Carter, *Confirmation Mess,* 149.

38. *U.S. v. Eichman,* 496 U.S. 310 (1990), affirming *Texas v. Johnson,* 491 U.S. 397 (1989). The 1990 decision struck down a federal statute, the Flag Protection Act of 1989, which was enacted in response to the decision in *Johnson.* In a *Newsweek* poll taken after the 1989 decision, 71 percent of those polled said they would favor a constitutional amendment to overturn that decision. Tamar Jacoby, Ann McDaniel, and Peter McKillup, "Fight for Old Glory."

39. *U.S. Term Limits, Inc. v. Thornton,* 514 U.S. 779 (1995).

40. *U.S. v. Lopez,* 514 U.S. 549 (1995).

41. *Lee v. Weisman,* 505 U.S. 577 (1992); *Santa Fe Independent School District v. Doe,* 530 U.S. 290 (2000).

42. *Reno v. American Civil Liberties Union,* 521 U.S. 844 (1997).

43. *Ashcroft v. Free Speech Coalition,* 535 U.S. 234 (2002).

44. Goldberg, "What's the Alternative?" (quotation at 42).

45. Until 1891, Supreme Court justices "rode circuit" and presided over criminal proceedings in trial courts.

46. For an account of the Chase episode, see Walter F. Murphy, *Congress and the Court,* chap. 2. Impeachment proceedings were a possibility in the case of Justice Abe Fortas, who was forced to resign from the Court in 1969. Though his support for

"liberal" outcomes on the Warren Court made him a welcome target for conservatives, his principal transgressions were financial in nature. See "Congress, Showing
Relief, Drops Fortas Inquiry Plan," *New York Times,* May 16, 1969, 20.

47. Roosevelt's failed "Court-packing" scheme is well chronicled in James
McGregor Burns, *Roosevelt,* chap. 15. Only twenty senators supported the plan.

48. After defining the original jurisdiction of the Supreme Court, the Constitution
provides that "In all the other Cases before mentioned, the supreme Court shall have
appellate Jurisdiction, both as to Law and Fact, with such Exceptions, and under such
Regulations as the Congress shall make." Art. 3, sec. 2, cl. 2.

49. The rejected provision was aimed at negating decisions such as *Miranda v.
Arizona,* 384 U.S. 436 (1966).

50. For a discussion of Congress's authority to curtail the Supreme Court's jurisdiction and its reluctance to do so in modern times, see Louis Fisher and Neal Devins,
Political Dynamics, 44–54.

51. Quoted in ibid., 52.

52. Linda Greenhouse, "How Congress Curtailed the Courts' Jurisdiction," *New
York Times,* October 27, 1996, sec. 4, p. 5.

53. Fisher and Devins, *Political Dynamics,* 52.

54. Greenhouse, "How Congress Curtailed," sec. 4, p. 5.

55. Friedman, "Transformation in Senate Response," sections 2–4.

56. 2 Dall. (2 U.S.) 419 (1793).

57. 60 U.S. 393 (1857).

58. 157 U.S. 429 (1895).

59. 400 U.S. 112 (1970).

60. The ten thousand figure comes from John R. Vile, *Rewriting the United
States Constitution,* 5. The figure includes redundant proposals.

61. David Cole, quoted in Greenhouse, "How Congress Curtailed," sec. 4, p. 5.

62. This second argument is taken from Kathleen M. Sullivan, who offers other
powerful arguments that increasing the frequency of constitutional amendments
would subvert the integrity of the Court and the constitutional system. Kathleen M.
Sullivan, "Constitutional Amendmentitis."

63. From Jack C. Plano, Robert E. Riggs, and Helenan Robin, *Dictionary of
Political Analysis,* 109.

64. Abner Mikva, "How Should We Select Our Judges?", 555. For a sophisticated discussion of how justices aiming to make public policy according to their own
preferences—which allegedly includes most justices most of the time—must consider public opinion, see Lee Epstein and Jack Knight, *Choices Justices Make,* 46–48,
157–77.

65. See above, n. 36.

66. For a good account and analysis of congressional reforms in the 1970s and
1980s, see Leroy N. Rieselbach, *Congressional Reform.*

67. See, e.g., Carl M. Cannon, "Hooked on Polls."

68. Twentieth Century Fund Task Force on Judicial Selection, *Judicial Roulette,*
8–9.

69. George L. Watson and John A. Stookey, *Shaping America,* 120–21.

70. Goldberg, "What's the Alternative?" (quotation at 42–43).

71. This concern has been raised by Vieira and Gross, "Appointments Clause," 332–33.

72. Mikva, "How Should We Select Our Judges?", 555.

73. The selection of these consensus nominees by Presidents Ford and Clinton is discussed in Chapter 3.

74. Chapter 6 describes in greater detail the press's depiction of Kennedy as a nominee, and the moderately conservative justice, with a definite independent streak, he has become.

75. *Planned Parenthood v. Casey,* 505 U.S. 833. The three justices' defense of *Roe* on its own merits takes up three pages (850–53), the argument for adhering to *stare decisis* ten pages (854–64), and the argument for upholding the Court's institutional integrity five pages (864–69).

76. Richard E. Neustadt, *Presidential Power,* 26. For a masterful exposition on the system of separate branches sharing powers, see Murphy, Fleming, and Barber, *American Constitutional Interpretation,* 71–77.

77. U.S. Constitution, sec. 2, cl. 2.

78. David A. Yalof, *Pursuit of Justices;* Abraham, *Justices, Presidents, and Senators.*

79. Black, "Note on Senatorial Consideration," 660 (emphasis in original).

80. Hamilton, Madison, and Jay, *Federalist,* 319.

81. Friedman, "Transformation," 88, n. 559.

82. Vieira and Gross, "Appointments Clause," 333.

83. Friedman, "Transformation," 88.

84. Ibid.

85. For a good contemporary account of Senate voting on Haynsworth, see E. W. Kenworthy, "All but One of Eleven Senators Regarded as Undecided Vote Against Haynsworth: Williams and Griffin Held Most Persuasive," *New York Times,* November 22, 1969, 20.

86. Kenworthy, "All but One," 20; John Massaro, *Supremely Political,* 80.

87. Watson and Stookey, *Shaping America,* 188. The other three confirmation votes were those for Abe Fortas (to be chief justice) in 1968, G. Harrold Carswell in 1970, and William H. Rehnquist (for associate justice) in 1971.

88. Henry J. Abraham, *Justices, Presidents, and Senators,* 31.

89. Some might argue that the Senate found Carswell even more objectionable than Haynsworth because of Carswell's poor qualifications and alleged racism. See Abraham, *Justices, Presidents, and Senators,* 11–12. But Carswell received as many "yes" votes as Haynsworth: 45.

90. For a description of Carswell's segregationist past, and lingering allegations of racism against him, see ibid.

91. Ibid., 260–61.

92. Bork's beliefs are analyzed in detail in Chapter 3.

93. Steven V. Roberts, "Reagan Vows New Appointment as Upsetting to His Foes as Bork's," *New York Times,* October 14, 1987, A1.

94. Ginsburg, who had served only eleven months as a federal judge after work-

ing in the Reagan White House, was best known for his conservative views on economic regulation and antitrust issues. See Stuart Taylor Jr., "Youthful Conservative Judge," *New York Times,* October 30, 1987, D23. The extent of his conservatism at the time, as opposed to his bent toward free-market libertarianism, is debatable. For a more thorough description of his views and Democratic opposition to his nomination, see Chapter 3.

95. Kennedy told Democratic senators at his confirmation hearings that the intentions of the Constitution's Framers and ratifiers—which Bork took as a nearly exclusive guide to interpreting the Constitution's vaguer clauses—was "one of the things that we want to know," but "The doctrine of original intent does not tell us how to decide a case. . . . I just did not think that original intent was very helpful as a methodology." Kennedy Hearings, 140. His testimony on unlisted rights is in Kennedy Hearings, 87–88.

96. Vieira and Gross, "Appointments Clause," 333. A similar sentiment is expressed by Michael McConnell in Goldberg, "What's the Alternative?", 43.

97. Quoted in Linda Greenhouse, "Speaking for the Majority," *New York Times,* May 26, 1996, sec. 4, p. 4. Examples of stinging conservative criticisms of Kennedy are in Jeffrey Rosen, "Agonizer." For Kennedy's relative centrism, see Chapter 6. For his well-justified reputation as a swing vote on the Rehnquist Court, see Chapter 7.

98. *Texas v. Johnson,* 491 U.S. 397 (1989); and *U.S. v. Eichman,* 496 U.S. 310 (1990); *Planned Parenthood v. Casey,* 505 U.S. 833 (1992); *Lee v. Weisman,* 505 U.S. 577 (1992); *U.S. Term Limits v. Thornton,* 514 U.S. 779 (1995); *U.S. v. Playboy Entertainment Group,* 529 U.S. 803 (2000); and *Lawrence v. Texas,* 123 S. Ct. 2472 (2003).

99. Robert H. Bork, *Slouching Towards Gomorrah.* On flag burning, see 99–101; on abortion, 103; on school prayer, 102–3; on the rights of gays, 112–14; on cable television programming, Bork has denied that even adults have the right to see pornographic materials (135–39, 145–53; also Robert H. Bork, "The Sanctity of Smut," *Wall Street Journal,* April 23, 2002, A22).

100. For a discussion of Bush's motives in nominating Souter, see Abraham, *Justices, Presidents, and Senators,* 304–5.

101. For a review of Souter's migration to a moderately liberal position on the Court, see Chapter 6.

102. On the compromise nature of these nominees, see Mark Silverstein and William Haltom, "You Can't Always Get What You Want"; Maltese, *Selling,* 149–57.

103. O'Connor Hearings, 57–58.

104. Scalia Hearings, 87.

105. Lerner, "Has the Senate Gone Too Far?", 18.

106. Scalia Hearings, 38.

107. O'Connor Hearings, 58.

108. See, e.g., Kennedy Hearings, 164; Scalia Hearings, 33; U.S. Senate Committee on the Judiciary, *Nomination of Thurgood Marshall,* 9.

109. Bork, *Tempting of America,* 346.

110. For expressions of this view, see Steven Lubet, "Confirmation Ethics"; Albert P. Melone, "Senate's Confirmation Role."

111. Lubet, "Confirmation Ethics," 252–53.

112. Kagan, "Confirmation Messes," 939.

113. Ginsburg Hearings, 207–8; Breyer Hearings, 269.

114. Melone and Lubet (and Kagan, perhaps somewhat inconsistently) have separately rejected these concessions to the impartiality argument on the grounds that the impartiality required of judicial nominees cannot mean that nominees must be utterly devoid of opinions on controversial issues, even opinions they have strongly expressed. Melone, "Senate's Confirmation Role," 76–77; Lubet, "Confirmation Ethics," 237–45, 253–59; Kagan, "Confirmation Messes," 937–38. In a 1972 case, Justice Rehnquist made a similar argument when denying a motion that he recuse himself in a matter about which he had expressed an opinion at his 1971 confirmation hearings for associate justice. *Laird v. Tatum,* 490 U.S. 824 (1972). I do not delve further into this issue because for my purposes in this chapter, it is enough to show that nominees may properly reveal their general judicial ideologies to senators and that nominees are not, as a factual matter, forced to violate ethical standards to win confirmation, even when those standards are strictly applied.

115. Bork Hearings, 103–4, 131–32; Souter Hearings, 130–32; Kennedy Hearings, 140; Scalia Hearings, 48–49.

116. Bork Hearings, 103–4; Breyer Hearings, 166–67, 222–23; Kennedy Hearings, 121–22; Souter Hearings, 200–202; Scalia Hearings, 88–90.

117. Breyer Hearings, 267, 296; Ginsburg Hearings, 223–25; Souter Hearings, 130–32; Thomas Hearings, 231–33; Scalia Hearings, 65–68, 106–7 (indicating skepticism about the value of congressional pronouncements in committee documents as opposed to the actual legislative text).

118. Bork Hearings, 248–49; Breyer Hearings, 166–67, 222; Kennedy Hearings, 87–88, 121–22; Thomas Hearings, 224–26; Ginsburg Hearings, 209.

119. Bork Hearings, 119, 256, 317, 330, 396; Thomas Hearings, 202–4; Kennedy Hearings, 118–20; Souter Hearings, 127–30.

120. Antonin Scalia told the Judiciary Committee that "[T]he Constitution is obviously not meant to be evolvable so easily that [the Supreme Court] can . . . fill it up with whatever content the current times seem to require. . . . So I would never use the phrase, living Constitution." Scalia Hearings, 48–49. Ruth Bader Ginsburg, by contrast, spoke eloquently of the Constitution as an evolving document. Ginsburg Hearings, 118–19, 126–27.

121. David Souter told Republican Senator Charles Grassley that "courts must accept their own responsibility for making a just society. . . . [T]he Supreme Court is left to act alone when the political branches do not act beforehand." Souter Hearings, 142. Ruth Bader Ginsburg similarly told a moderately conservative Democrat, Senator Dennis DeConcini of Arizona, that "when political avenues become dead-end streets judicial intervention in the politics of the people may be essential," citing *Baker v. Carr,* 369 U.S. 186 (1962), as an example, and that a court "must serve as a surrogate legislature" when elected officials fail to remedy a constitutional violation. Ginsburg Hearings, 168, 171.

122. Breyer's thin record of judicial opinions on abortion before his nomination was unrevealing, but he was generally believed to support the right to abortion.

Ginsburg had argued that the Court in *Roe v. Wade* might more firmly have anchored the abortion right in the Fourteenth Amendment's Equal Protection clause rather than, as it did, in the Amendment's Due Process clause. She had also stated that a more incrementalist approach would not have provoked the backlash that *Roe* did. But the implication of these remarks is that a better (in Ginsburg's view) approach would have strengthened rather than weakened the abortion right.

123. For his criticisms of the constitutional right to privacy, see Bork Hearings, 114–20, 149–51; for his rejection of *Bolling v. Sharpe,* 347 U.S. 497 (1954), which struck down racially segregated schools in the District of Columbia, 286–87; for his criticisms of *Shelley v. Kraemer,* 334 U.S. 1 (1948), which forbade judicial enforcement of restrictive covenants in the sale of real estate, 113–14; for his criticisms of the Supreme Court's "one-man–one-vote rulings," 156–59; for his rejection of the ruling striking down state poll taxes as discriminatory, 154–55; for his rejection of "liberal" opinions upholding speech claims, 428–34.

124. Bork Report, 93–96.

125. Bork Hearings, 855.

126. O'Connor Hearings, 107–8, 198–99; Scalia Hearings, 102.

127. O'Connor Hearings, 84; Scalia Hearings, 45.

128. O'Connor Hearings, 80.

129. Scalia Hearings, 84–85.

130. On abortion, Ginsburg Hearings, 149–50; on the rights of gays, 341; on the death penalty, 263–67.

131. On abortion, Breyer Hearings, 138; on gun control, 262–63; on property rights, 113–14; on the death penalty, 137, 192–93.

132. On abortion, Souter Hearings, 58–60, 192–97.

133. On abortion, Kennedy Hearings, 88, 164; on the death penalty, 136; on standing, 137–38.

134. On abortion, Thomas Hearings, 183, 220, 224, 262; on habeas corpus, 352–53.

135. Bork Hearings, 261 (on affirmative action), 266 (on federalism), and 292 (on abortion).

136. A classic expression of senatorial frustration is Senator John East's anguished protest to nominee Sandra Day O'Connor: "If you are arguing that a Supreme Court nominee cannot indicate particular values or sentiments on prominent issues of the time, it seems to me the confirmation process becomes almost meaningless. . . . I query as one lowly freshman Senator whether we are able really to get our teeth into anything." O'Connor Hearings, 199–200. Another is Senator Biden's 1992 pledge to the Senate that "As a senator I cannot make a nominee answer questions that I deem appropriate or important. But I need not vote for one who refused to do so either, and I will not." *Congressional Record,* June 25, 1992, S8866. See also Biden's statement to Justice Ginsburg that "I doubt whether any nominee would ever satisfy me in terms of being as expansive about their views as I would like." Ginsburg Hearings, 259.

137. Grover Rees III, "Questions for Supreme Court Nominees," 967.

138. See, e.g., Thomas Hearings, 179–83.

139. Melone, "Senate's Confirmation Role," 79.

140. At the time of his nomination to the Supreme Court, David Souter, who had served seven years on the New Hampshire Supreme Court, had sat for two months on the federal appeals court in Boston but had not yet participated in any of its cases.

141. Kennedy Hearings, 23.

142. Stephen L. Carter, "Confirmation Mess," 1198. Carter repeats this suggestion in his 1992 book, *Confirmation Mess,* 150–55.

143. Carter, "Confirmation Mess," 1199.

144. In fairness to Carter, he notes that senators are reluctant to undertake such inquiry—although he thinks their reluctance "mysterious"—and suggests that his approach may be more an "aspiration" than a practical proposal. "Confirmation Mess," 1198.

145. R. W. Apple, "Senate Confirms Thomas 52–48, Ending Week of Bitter Battle," *New York Times,* October 16, 1991, A1.

146. L. Martin Overby et al., "Courting Constituents?"

147. See, e.g., Ethan Bronner, *Battle for Justice,* 151–52, 158–60, 288–91.

148. Carter, "Confirmation Mess," 1198.

149. Souter Hearings, 211–14.

150. William G. Ross, "Questioning of Supreme Court Nominees," 164.

151. O'Connor Hearings, 57.

152. Souter Hearings, 52.

153. Bork Hearings, 292, 340, 343.

154. Linda Greenhouse, "The Court, the Congress and the White House," *New York Times,* August 10, 1986, sec. 4, p. 1.

155. Linda Greenhouse, "The Bork Nomination: In No Time at All, Both Proponents and Opponents Are Ready for Battle," *New York Times,* July 9, 1987, A24.

156. Linda Greenhouse, "Sticking to the Script," *New York Times,* September 12, 1991, A21.

157. Michael Comiskey, "Usefulness of Senate Confirmation Hearings." Thomas's confirmation, including the hearings into Anita Hill's allegations of sexual harassment, is detailed in Chapter 5.

158. Stuart Taylor Jr., "More Vigor for the Right," *New York Times,* June 18, 1986, A1.

159. Stephen Roberts, "Selection Praised by GOP Senators," *New York Times,* June 18, 1986, A32.

160. Hedrick Smith, "Reagan's Court Choice: A Deft Maneuver," *New York Times,* July 9, 1981, A17.

161. Holly Idelson, "Quiet Confirmation Expected."

162. Kagan, "Confirmation Messes," 937.

3. THE POLITICIZATION OF THE CONFIRMATION PROCESS

1. John Anthony Maltese, *Selling,* 115.

2. See also Stephen L. Carter, *Confirmation Mess;* George L. Watson and John A. Stookey, *Shaping America;* Mark Silverstein, *Judicious Choices;* Terri Jennings

Peretti, *In Defense of a Political Court.* These authors are generally not critical of the public nature of the modern confirmation process, with the exception of Carter, who is critical but ultimately ambivalent toward the process.

3. The names of many of these groups, along with their numbers of staff and membership, and the overview of their activities, come largely from Watson and Stookey, *Shaping America,* 96–108.

4. For a description of presidential efforts, see Maltese, *Selling,* 112–15.

5. Carter, *Confirmation Mess,* 14. Note that Carter implies here that "issues" aside from the nominee's professional qualifications are a legitimate consideration for the Senate, a point on which he equivocates throughout his book.

6. Eugene W. Hickok Jr., "Senate," 49.

7. John Massaro, *Supremely Political,* 142. Massaro also emphasizes the importance of the president choosing a strong nominee in the first instance.

8. Maltese, *Selling,* 142.

9. Quoted in Watson and Stookey, *Shaping America,* 1. The concept of the nomination discourse is central in these authors' framework for analyzing Supreme Court confirmations; *Shaping America,* 17.

10. For an account of the slow and ineffectual response to the liberal offensive against Bork, see Ethan Bronner, *Battle for Justice,* chaps. 7 and 8; Maltese, *Selling,* 133.

11. For a detailed case study of the Thomas nomination, see Chapter 5.

12. Bronner, *Battle for Justice,* 151–59, 288–90; Mark Gitenstein, *Matters of Principle,* 112–17, 178, 247, 255–56, 267–68, 271, 287–88.

13. L. Marvin Overby et al., "Courting Constituents?"

14. L. Marvin Overby and Beth M. Henschen, "Race Trumps Gender?"

15. Richard C. Elling, "Ideological Change" (quotation at 75).

16. Overby et al., "Courting Constituents?" (quotation at 1002).

17. For an analysis of the claims in the celebrated anti-Bork commercial made by People for the American Way and featuring the actor Gregory Peck as spokesperson, see Stuart Taylor Jr., "Ads Against Bork Still Hotly Disputed," *New York Times,* October 21, 1987, A23.

18. Twentieth Century Fund Task Force on Judicial Selection, *Judicial Roulette.*

19. Ibid., 9.

20. Ibid.

21. Ibid.

22. Quotations at ibid., 9–11.

23. Stephanie B. Goldberg, "What's the Alternative?" The law professors on the panel were Michael W. McConnell of the University of Chicago, R. Lea Brilmayer of New York University, Walter Dellinger of Duke, and Martin H. Redish of Northwestern, who served as moderator. The federal judge was Alex Kozinski of the U.S. Court of Appeals for the Ninth Circuit. Those most supportive of "depoliticizing" the confirmation process in the spirit of the Twentieth Century Fund Task Force Report were McConnell and Kozinski and, to a much lesser extent, Dellinger.

24. The members of the panel were Terrance Sandalow, professor and former dean of the University of Michigan Law School; Gerhard Casper, professor and for-

mer dean of the University of Chicago Law School; Steven Frankino, dean of the Villanova Law School; Eugene Rostow, former professor and dean of the Yale Law School; Thomas Morgan, professor and former dean of the Emory University Law School; Maurice Holland, professor and dean at the University of Oregon Law School; and Ronald Davenport, former professor and dean of the Duquesne University Law School. Bork Hearings, 3240–312.

25. Paul A. Freund, "Appointment of Justices."

26. Ruth Bader Ginsburg, "Confirming Supreme Court Justices."

27. David Strauss and Cass R. Sunstein, "The Senate, the Constitution." See also, in agreement with the third recommendation, Norman Vieira and Leonard E. Gross, "Appointments Clause," 330–36.

28. One other minor "reform" was adopted. After the first Bush Administration denied senators access to FBI reports on judicial nominees in the wake of the Clarence Thomas imbroglio, dissatisfied senators from both parties reached an agreement with the administration over these files that largely restored the status quo ante. Helen Dewar, "Deal Gives Senate Access to FBI Data on Court Nominees," *Chicago Sun-Times,* February 9, 1992, 26.

29. Silverstein, *Judicious Choices,* 164–65.

30. Maltese, *Selling,* preface, xii.

31. Historical studies concluding that ideological differences are the principal cause of rejected nominations are Henry J. Abraham, *Justices, Presidents, and Senators;* Daniel McHargue, "Appointments to the Supreme Court"; Laurence Tribe, *God Save This Honorable Court,* 92; Charles Warren, *Supreme Court;* and, focusing on unsuccessful nominations since that of Abe Fortas for chief justice in 1968, Massaro, *Supremely Political,* 135, 159. As Overby et al. summarize the quantitative literature, "[M]ost recent work has concluded that ideology consistently has a larger effect on senators' voting behavior on controversial nominations." "Courting Constituents?" (quotation at 997). Donald R. Songer reports that in the fourteen most controversial Supreme Court nominations in the twentieth century, "Senate opposition to Supreme Court nominees [was] due primarily to a predictable dissatisfaction with the policy-relevant voting of the nominee after confirmation." "Relevance of Policy Values," 927. David Rohde and Harold Spaeth found a similar result in a study of the Haynsworth, Carswell, second Fortas, and first Rehnquist nominations: *Supreme Court Decision Making,* 105–6. John D. Felice and Herbert F. Weisberg studied Senate voting on eight nominations in which more than 10 percent of senators voted against confirmation between 1953 and 1988. They found that "Ideology is most determinative of voting on these nominations." "Changing Importance of Ideology," 526. Jeffrey A. Segal, Albert D. Cover, and Charles M. Cameron ("Senate Confirmation") report that senators will cast ideologically motivated votes against a nominee, but only if the nominee can be portrayed as unqualified or if the political environment is unfavorable to the president (i.e., the president's party is in the minority in the Senate or the president is in the last year of his term). These authors find in another study that "Confirmation voting is decisively affected by the ideological distance between senators and nominees." Cameron, Cover, and Segal, "Senate Voting," 530. See also Overby et al., "Courting Constituents?", 999–1003. Overby and

Henschen, "Race Trumps Gender?", 62–73, find that both a senator's ideology and the ideology of the senator's constituents have a significant impact on a senator's vote. Watson and Stookey find that "partisanship and ideology" are the most important factors in voting on nominations (*Shaping America,* 177–89, quotation at 186).

32. Overby et al., "Courting Constituents?" (quotation at 1002).

33. Watson and Stookey, *Shaping America,* 102–3.

34. Bork Hearings, 3306. See also Carter, *Confirmation Mess,* 15.

35. Bork Hearings, 3306.

36. Ibid., 3291.

37. For a partial list of those witnesses, see above, n. 24; Carter, *Confirmation Mess,* 45–49.

38. John P. MacKenzie, "The Trouble with Hearings," *New York Times,* September 24, 1991, A30. Similar behavior was also noted by Yale Kamisar in David Margolick, "Questions to Thomas Fall Short of the Mark," *New York Times,* September 15, 1991, A15.

39. Stephen Macedo, "Stricter Senate Review," *New York Times,* October 23, 1991, A23.

40. Gary J. Simson, "Better Way to Choose Supremes," *National Law Journal,* March 21, 1994, A19–20 (quotation at A20).

41. For alleged distortions of Robert Bork's record, see Carter, *Confirmation Mess,* 44–53. For Bork's own retelling of the misconstrual of his views, see Robert H. Bork, *Tempting of America,* chaps. 14–16.

42. If Rehnquist's 1971 and 1986 nominations are counted separately, Bork was the fifth most conservative of twenty-two.

43. Segal, Cover, and Cameron, "Role of Ideology," 497–98.

44. The Supreme Court first held that a right to privacy inhering in the marital relationship protected the right of married couples to use birth control in *Griswold v. Connecticut,* 381 U.S. 479 (1965). The Court ruled that unmarried couples have the same right in *Eisenstadt v. Baird,* 405 U.S. 438 (1972). The Court's holding in *Eisenstadt* was, at least technically, based on equal protection grounds. But the Court's language seemed to place the constitutional right of unmarried couples to use birth control under the category of privacy: "It is true that in *Griswold* the right to privacy in question inhered in the marital relationship. Yet . . . [i]f the right of privacy means anything, it is the right of the *individual,* married or single, to be free from unwarranted governmental intrusion into matters so fundamentally affecting a person as the decision whether to bear or beget a child" (453, emphasis in the original).

45. Bork, *Tempting of America,* 110. The suggestion that the right to privacy be abolished is at 116.

46. Ibid., 83–84. The Court's ruling on this question was *Bolling v. Sharpe,* 347 U.S. 497 (1954).

47. Bork, *Tempting of America,* 328–30. The Supreme Court has interpreted this requirement flexibly. See David M. O'Brien, *Constitutional Law and Politics: Civil Rights and Civil Liberties,* 2:1475–507.

48. Bork, *Tempting of America,* 31–32; also 180.

49. The Supreme Court ruled that the Bill of Rights did not limit what state and

local governments could do in *Barron v. Baltimore,* 32 U.S. (7 Pet.) 243 (1833).

50. The Court recognized the right to marry in *Zablocki v. Redhail,* 434 U.S. 374 (1978); the right to have children in *Skinner v. Oklahoma,* 316 U.S. 535 (1942). The holding in Zablocki was based ostensibly on equal protection grounds. But Professor Gunther has written, "The case . . . ultimately rests on a substantive due process analysis despite its equal protection form." *Individual Rights,* 229. *Skinner* was also decided at least partly on equal protection grounds, but Professor Gunther again writes that *Skinner* was "an equal protection case in part [that] rested ultimately on a view akin to substantive due process" (163).

51. *Moore v. East Cleveland,* 431 U.S. 494 (1977).

52. *Aptheker v. Secretary of State,* 378 U.S. 500 (1964).

53. *Cruzan v. Director, Missouri Department of Health,* 497 U.S. 261 (1990).

54. *Griswold v. Connecticut,* 381 U.S. 479 (1965); *Roe v. Wade,* 410 U.S. 113 (1973).

55. Bork, *Tempting of America* (quotations at 37, 60, 94, 180, 351).

56. Ibid., 180.

57. Bork avoids the question when he writes, "There is no occasion here to attempt to resolve the controversy concerning the application of the Bill of Rights to the states." Ibid., 93.

58. Ibid., 60.

59. U.S. Constitution, Amendment XIV, sec. 1.

60. Bork, *Tempting of America,* 31–32.

61. Because Bork agrees that the Due Process clause requires states to observe due process when *administering* laws, he could still allow that the Supreme Court, by construing "due process" to include the written *procedural* guarantees the Constitution imposes on the federal courts (such as the right to counsel), could require state courts to afford their citizens these same protections.

62. Bork, *Tempting of America,* 143. Bork insists that what counts is the understanding of the ratifiers of a constitutional provision, not its framers, "since they [the ratifiers] enacted it and made it law." See 144.

63. Bork's unenthusiastic acceptance of the application of the Bill of Rights to the states, as expressed in his 1990 book, *Tempting of America,* contrasts with his testimony at his 1987 confirmation hearings, in which he claimed to have "no quarrel" with using the Due Process clause to achieve this result. Bork Hearings, 320–21.

64. Ibid., 104.

65. On the Commerce Clause, see Bork Hearings, 112–13; on the equal protection obligations of the federal government, 288; on the equal protection of women, 436; on freedom of speech, 428.

66. Ibid., 663. The question was: "Now, the relationship between the judge, the text, and precedent, what do you do about precedent?" Nor did Bork respond to the question by citing the customary criteria the Court employs in deciding whether to overrule a precedent, such as whether the ruling in the earlier case has proved unworkable, whether the public's reliance on the previous ruling necessitates continued adherence to that rule, or whether events since the ruling necessitate a change in the earlier holding.

67. Bork, *Slouching Towards Gomorrah,* 114.

68. Ibid., 107.

69. Ibid., 109.

70. Ibid., 97.

71. Ibid., 96.

72. Ibid., 115.

73. Ibid., 119.

74. Among the Rehnquist Court decisions that Bork condemned are *Lee v. Weisman,* 505 U.S. 577 (1992), prohibiting prayers at public school graduations; *Texas v. Johnson,* 491 U.S. 397 (1989), upholding the burning of the American flag as an act of speech; *Planned Parenthood v. Casey,* 505 U.S. 833 (1992), upholding the "essence" of *Roe v. Wade;* and *Romer v. Evans,* 517 U.S. 620 (1996), which struck down, on equal protection grounds, an amendment to the Colorado state constitution that forbade localities in the state from passing equal rights ordinances for gays. These decisions are, respectively, in *Slouching Towards Gomorrah,* 102, 99–101, 103, 112–14.

75. Robert H. Bork, "The Conservative Case for Amending the Constitution," *Weekly Standard,* March 3, 1997, 21–24 (quotation at 22). The decisions Bork refers to are *Romer v. Evans* (1996); *Denver Area Educational Telecommunications Consortium v. F.C.C.,* 518 U.S. 727 (1996), in which a divided Court issued a decision that, in part, struck down a federal law permitting cable operators to ban indecent materials from public access channels, and another provision requiring cable operators to scramble the transmission of indecent channels to any customer who did not request that the signal be unscrambled; and *U.S. v. Virginia,* 518 U.S. 515 (1996), which held that state-funded military colleges cannot refuse admission to women.

76. Robert H. Bork, *Slouching Towards Gomorrah,* 117.

77. Ibid.

78. Robert H. Bork, "Robert Bork Replies," *Washington Post National Weekly Edition,* July 20–27, 1998 (quotation at 26).

79. Bork, "Conservative Case," 24.

80. In a Harris poll taken during the Bork Hearings, 68 percent of respondents "agreed" that they were "worried" about Bork's refusal to recognize a right to privacy for married couples. This poll and a similar Roper poll, both of which found a majority of Americans opposed to Bork's confirmation, have been criticized with some justice for "leading" respondents to express opposition to Bork (Bronner, *Battle for Justice,* 151–53). Still, the finding that two-thirds of the public were troubled by Bork's views on privacy cannot be gainsaid. And polls by CBS/*New York Times* and ABC/*Washington Post* both found a majority of the public unknowledgeable about Bork or his nomination several weeks after Bork's nomination, suggesting that the anti-Bork campaign had little effect on the public. These latter polls, which did not "lead" respondents in any way, also found public opinion becoming more knowledgeable and turning against Bork by a modest plurality during and immediately after his Senate testimony, suggesting that the public airing of Bork's views at those hearings hurt the nominee. See Opinion Research Service, *American Public Opinion Index.*

81. Abraham, *Justices, Presidents, and Senators,* 298.

82. Ibid.; Daniel McHargue, "Appointments to the Supreme Court"; Warren, *Supreme Court.*

83. Segal, Cover, and Cameron, "Senate Confirmation," 506–7.

84. Cameron, Cover, and Segal, "Senate Voting."

85. Scalia's prenomination pronouncements are in Stuart Taylor Jr., "More Vigor for the Right," *New York Times,* June 18, 1986, A1; quotation in Stephen Roberts, "Selection Praised by GOP Senators," *New York Times,* June 18, 1986, A32.

86. *New York Times,* "Toward a Rehnquist Court," June 18, 1986, A34.

87. Linda Greenhouse, "The Court, the Congress, and the White House," *New York Times,* August 10, 1986, sec. 4, p. 1.

88. Cameron, Cover, and Segal, "Senate Voting," 532.

89. Upon Vice President Spiro Agnew's resignation after his conviction for income tax evasion, President Nixon nominated Ford for the vice presidency, and Congress confirmed him under the provisions of the Twenty-fifth Amendment. He became president upon Nixon's resignation in August 1974.

90. The statistics reported in this paragraph are from Watson and Stookey, *Shaping America,* 52.

91. Abraham, *Justices, Presidents, and Senators,* 276.

92. Holly Idelson, "Clinton's Choice of Ginsburg Signals Moderation" (quotation at 1569).

93. Ibid.

94. Ibid., 1569, 1574.

95. Breyer Hearings, 269.

96. See, e.g., Gwen Ifill, "President Chooses Breyer, an Appeals Judge in Boston, for Blackmun's Court Seat," *New York Times,* May 14, 1994, A1; W. John Moore, "Ho Hum, It's Confirmation Hearings Time"; Holly Idelson, "Breyer's Liberal, Conservative Mix."

97. Idelson, "Breyer's Liberal, Conservative Mix," 1305.

98. Holly Idelson, "From 'Wealth of Talent.'"

99. Abraham, *Justices, Presidents, and Senators,* 216.

100. Ibid., 219.

101. For the advance warning or opposition to Haynsworth, see David A. Yalof, *Pursuit of Justices,* 106–7; and Warren Weaver, "Rights and Labor Leaders Oppose Court Nomination," *New York Times,* August 19, 1969, 27.

102. Abraham, *Justices, Presidents, and Senators,* 10. The story of the stock transaction is told in "Haynsworth Critics Rebutted in Report to His Supporters," *New York Times,* November 1, 1969, 16.

103. Richard Harris, *Decision* (quotation at 11).

104. Fred P. Graham, "Senators Are Told Carswell Was 'Insulting' to Negro Lawyers," *New York Times,* February 3, 1970, 15.

105. Fred P. Graham, "Carswell Denies He Tried to Balk Club's Integration," *New York Times,* January 28, 1970, 1; "The Tallahassee Transaction," *New York Times,* February 27, 1970, 36.

106. Abraham, *Justices, Presidents, and Senators,* 12.

107. *Congressional Record,* 91st Cong., 2d sess., vol. 116, 7498.

108. Ibid., 7487.

109. On abortion, see *Planned Parenthood v. Ashcroft,* 462 U.S. 476 (1983); and *Thornburgh v. American College of Obstetricians and Gynecologists,* 476 U.S. 747 (1986). On affirmative action, see *Regents of the University of California v. Bakke,* 438 U.S. 265 (1978); and *United States v. Paradise,* 480 U.S. 149 (1987).

110. Stuart Taylor Jr., "Powell Leaves High Court; Took Key Role on Abortion and on Affirmative Action," *New York Times,* June 27, 1987, 1.

111. These Gallup poll figures are in Watson and Stookey, *Shaping America,* 52.

112. The story of the Reagan Administration's internal deliberations leading up to the Bork nomination is told in David Yalof, *Pursuit of Justices,* 156–60.

113. Ibid., 159.

114. Gary J. Simson, "Mired in the Confirmation Mess" (quotations at 1040, 1051–52).

115. Steven V. Roberts, "Reagan Vows New Appointment as Upsetting to His Foes as Bork's," *New York Times,* October 14, 1987, A1.

116. Ginsburg had argued only one case in court in his entire career. Yalof, *Pursuit of Justices,* 163.

117. Stuart Taylor Jr., "Youthful Conservative Judge," *New York Times,* October 30, 1987, D23.

118. Tamar Jacoby et al., "Spoiling for a Second Round."

119. Yalof, *Pursuit of Justices,* 163.

120. Ibid.

121. Joel Brinkley, "President Selects Appellate Judge to Become Justice," *New York Times,* October 30, 1987, A1.

122. When Thomas was asked by Kenneth Duberstein, the former chief of staff in the Reagan White House and the figure tapped by the Bush Administration to shepherd Thomas's nomination through the Senate, whether anything in his past might derail his nomination, Thomas cited only his Vietnam-era draft deferment and his apparently infrequent use of marijuana while a student years before. Administration officials had earlier investigated a rumor that Thomas had abused his first wife and had found no support for it. Jane Mayer and Jill Abramson, *Strange Justice,* 26–27.

123. Timothy Phelps and Helen Winternitz, *Capitol Games,* 227–36; and Mayer and Abramson, *Strange Justice,* 250–57.

124. See Malcolm Gladwell, "The Practical Idealist," *Washington Post National Weekly Edition,* July 4–10, 1994, 6–7; and Neil A. Lewis, "Breyer Is Challenged on Apparent Conflict on Eve of Hearing," *New York Times,* July 21, 1994, A11.

125. "Sharp Questions for Judge Breyer," July 10, 1994, sec. 4, p. 18.

126. Breyer Report, 12–14.

127. Breyer Hearings, 400.

128. Twentieth Century Fund Task Force on Judicial Selection, *Judicial Roulette* (quotation at 9–10, emphasis in the original).

129. Ibid., 10.

130. Carter, *Confirmation Mess,* 17, 194.

131. Ibid., 194.

132. Ibid., 18.

133. David A. Strauss and Cass R. Sunstein, "The Senate, the Constitution," 1518.

134. Ibid.

135. Stephanie B. Goldberg, "What's the Alternative?", 41–42.

136. Ibid., 43.

137. Watson and Stookey, *Shaping America,* 21.

138. From the administration of Warren Harding through that of John F. Kennedy, an average of twenty-three days elapsed between the announcement of a Supreme Court nomination and the Senate's confirmation vote. Setting aside the long-delayed confirmations of four Eisenhower nominees, the Senate spent an average of only fifteen days reviewing the nominations of that period. By contrast, President Bill Clinton's widely acclaimed, "consensual" nominations of Ruth Bader Ginsburg and Stephen Breyer took seven and eleven weeks, respectively, to pass through the Senate. During that time, congressional staffers, senators, FBI personnel, and numerous interest groups and reporters sifted through volumes of material on the nominees. New York Times, *New York Times Index,* vols. 1921–63, 1993–94.

139. This account of Rutledge's confirmation travails is taken from Maltese, *Selling,* 26–31 (quotation at 30).

140. Ibid., 31.

141. The *New York Times,* for instance, found "deeply disturbing" Black's "almost complete lack of judicial experience and his failure to show . . . any trace of a genuinely judicial temperament. His partisanship . . . has been more intense than any far-sighted person could desire . . . he has been willing as a member of the Senate to trample on private rights on more than one occasion and to override the traditional safeguards of individual liberty." *New York Times,* "The New Justice," August 18, 1937, 18. The *Washington Post* likewise editorialized against Black's "combined lack of training . . . and extreme partisanship." Quoted in Abraham, *Justices, Presidents, and Senators,* 162.

142. This account of Black's confirmation is taken from Abraham, *Justices, Presidents, and Senators,* 160–64; "Committee Upholds Black, 13 to 4, in Stormy Session," *New York Times,* August 17, 1937, 1; "Black Confirmed by Senate, 63–16; Debate Is Bitter," *New York Times,* August 18, 1937, 1.

143. Abraham, *Justices, Presidents, and Senators,* appendix A, 369–72.

144. "Chief Confidant to Chief Justice," *Time,* July 5, 1968, 12–17; Fred P. Graham, "Many-Sided Justice Fortas."

145. Harris, *Decision,* 26–27.

146. In fairness to Carter, he seems uncertain whether television brings us "gossip" or something more worthwhile. After quoting approvingly a television executive who states that "We get our gossip from television," Carter writes: "Well, of course! . . . You can call it 'gossip' or you can call it 'the opportunity for the American people to be informed on the character and fitness of those who would serve them in public office.' But whatever you call it . . . it fulfills our need to be involved." *Confirmation Mess,* 17–18.

147. A detailed account of this episode is in Chapter 5.

148. Mayer and Abramson, *Strange Justice,* 251–52.

149. Phelps and Winternitz, *Capitol Games*, 227.

150. Mayer and Abramson, *Strange Justice*, 350; Paul Simon, *Advice and Consent*, 121.

151. Watson and Stookey, *Shaping America*, 116, 145, 154–55.

152. Walter Berns, quoted in Twentieth Century Fund Task Force on Judicial Selection, *Judicial Roulette*, 10.

153. Burger Hearings.

154. New York Times, *New York Times Index*, vols. 1981–94.

155. Watson and Stookey, *Shaping America*, 148–55.

156. See, e.g., Carter, *Confirmation Mess*, 6; Paul A. Freund, "Appointment of Justices," 1163; Eugene W. Hickok Jr., "Senate," 50; Strauss and Sunstein, "The Senate, the Constitution," 1518–19; and Twentieth Century Fund Task Force on Judicial Selection, *Judicial Roulette*, 9.

157. A copy of this memo to Justice Robert Jackson, written while Rehnquist clerked for Jackson, and an unpublished memo on *Brown* authored by Jackson himself, are in David M. O'Brien, *Constitutional Law and Politics: Civil Rights and Civil Liberties*, 2:1381–82 and 2:1382–87.

158. Neil A. Lewis, "Ginsburg's Hearings End in a Secluded Meeting," *New York Times*, July 24, 1993, A26.

159. For example, in Goldberg, "What's the Alternative?"

160. As noted in this chapter, however, Strauss and Sunstein have cited the "reliance on general appearance before the cameras" in Souter's case. "The Senate, the Constitution," 1518.

161. Kathleen Frankovic and Joyce Gelb, "Public Opinion and the Thomas Nomination."

162. Overby et al., "Courting Constituents?"

163. See Chapter 5 on this point.

164. Richard Morin, "Harassment Consensus Grows: Polls Find Greater Awareness of Misconduct," *Washington Post*, December 18, 1992, A1. See also Chapter 5.

4. THE CONFIRMATION PROCESS AND THE QUALITY OF JUSTICES

1. Bruce Fein, "A Court of Mediocrity," *ABA Journal*, October 1991, 75.

2. Ibid., 74.

3. Ibid., 74–79; Robert H. Bork, *Tempting of America*, 347; Terry Eastland, "Bush and the Politics of Race," *New York Times*, July 3, 1991, A19; Stuart Taylor Jr., "Supreme Disappointment," quoting Michael McConnell at 77.

4. E.g., Stephen L. Carter, "Confirmation Mess, Revisited"; Abner Mikva, "How Should We Select Our Judges?"; Taylor, "Supreme Disappointment."

5. David Schultz, "Why No More Giants on the Supreme Court"; Mark Silverstein, *Judicious Choices*, 160–71.

6. Silverstein, *Judicious Choices*, 71.

7. Ibid., 4.

8. Ibid., 162–63.

9. Ibid., 171.

10. George L. Watson and John A. Stookey, *Shaping America,* 222.

11. Robert C. Bradley, "Who Are the Great Justices?"

12. American Bar Association, *Official American Bar Association Guide to Approved Law Schools.*

13. In an earlier survey the author conducted entirely by surface mail, the response rate was barely above 30 percent.

14. Only 12 percent (14 of 121) of judges surveyed by Bradley responded to his survey. The response rate for attorneys was 23 percent. Bradley, "Who Are the Great Justices?", 13, 15, 16.

15. Ibid., 20. The top three criteria cited by scholars were (1) "intellectual ability," (2) "writing ability," and (3) "leadership." "Enhance Court's power" was fourth, and "impact on law" (similar to leadership on the Court) was fifth.

16. Stephen L. Carter, *Confirmation Mess,* 65–68.

17. 347 U.S. 483.

18. Henry J. Abraham, *Justices, Presidents, and Senators,* 189–250; Carter, *Confirmation Mess,* 65–68.

19. Stewart's confirmation was delayed by four months, mainly by Southern senators who surmised correctly that he supported *Brown v. Board of Education.* Abraham, *Justices, Presidents, and Senators,* 205.

20. Burger Hearings.

21. These lists are, in chronological order, Roscoe Pound, *Formative Era,* 30–31; Felix Frankfurter, "Supreme Court"; John P. Frank, *Marble Palace,* 43–44; George R. Currie, "Judicial All-Star Nine"; Stuart S. Nagel, "Characteristics of Supreme Court Greatness"; Sidney H. Asch, *Supreme Court*; Albert P. Blaustein and Roy M. Mersky, *First One Hundred Justices;* Bernard Schwartz, "Judicial Ten"; James E. Hambleton, "All-Time All-Star All-Era"; Bradley, "Who Are the Great Justices?", 1–32.

22. The four are: Blaustein and Mersky, *First One Hundred Justices;* and Bradley, "Who Are the Great Justices?", who administered his survey to three separate groups—scholars, lawyers, and judges.

23. The mean scores for the five periods were: 1901–20, 2.27; 1921–40, 2.69; 1941–60, 2.36; 1961–80, 2.49; 1981–99, 2.53. Despite the observable differences, no period was statistically distinguishable from any other below the 0.19 confidence level (for the 1901–20 and 1921–40 periods).

24. The mean from Burger to Breyer is 2.54; for the earlier group 2.44. The *t*-statistic between the groups is 0.61, the probability value .5465.

25. This account of Burger's nomination and summary of his performance on the Court are taken from Abraham, *Justices, Presidents, and Senators,* 9–10, 252–58; Fred P. Graham, "Burger's Down-to-Earth Qualities May Spur Confirmation," *New York Times,* May 25, 1969, 55; Robert E. Semple Jr., "Warren E. Burger Named Chief Justice by Nixon; Now on Appeals Bench," *New York Times,* May 22, 1969, 1; Bernard Schwartz, *History of the Supreme Court,* 311–14; Sidney E. Zion, "Nixon's Nominee for the Post of Chief Justice," *New York Times,* May 22, 1969, 36. See also Edward A. Tamm and Paul C. Reardon, "Warren Burger," 447–521.

26. Zion, "Nixon's Nominee," 36.

27. Ibid.

28. The six past presidents of the ABA present to testify if called at Burger's confirmation hearing (including then-attorney Lewis Powell) and two others who supported the nominee by telegram are at Burger Hearings, 1–2. On Burger's amiable personal nature and legal ability, see the comments of Robert McKay, dean of the New York University Law School, in Zion, "Nixon's Nominee," and unidentified lawyers and "observers" in Graham, "Burger's Down-to-Earth Qualities."

29. Burger Hearings, 1.

30. These matters are discussed in the following chapter.

31. Charles M. Cameron, Albert D. Cover, and Jeffrey A. Segal, "Senate Voting"; for evidence of this in Antonin Scalia's case, see Stephen Roberts, "Selection Praised by GOP Senators," *New York Times,* June 18, 1986, A32.

32. Schultz, "Why No More Giants"; Silverstein, *Judicious Choices.*

33. Silverstein, *Judicious Choices,* 171.

34. Identifying no current justices as great are: Frank, *Marble Palace* (1958); Currie, "Judicial All-Star Nine" (1964); Blaustein and Mersky, *First One Hundred Justices* (1978); Schwartz, "Judicial Ten" (1979); Hambleton, "All-Time All-Star All-Era" (1983); and two surveys (one of scholars and one of judges) by Bradley, "Who Are the Great Justices?" (1993). Two lists that also identified no current justices as great were authored by Supreme Court justices, who may not have felt free to be candid: Charles Evans Hughes, *Supreme Court;* and Frankfurter, "Supreme Court" (1957).

35. Nagel, "Characteristics of Supreme Court Greatness," 957; Asch, *Supreme Court,* 189–217.

36. Bradley, "Who Are the Great Justices?", 16. The other was Cardozo, who was actually rated a great "judge" by Roscoe Pound, *Formative Era,* 4, 31.

37. David A. Yalof, *Pursuit of Justices,* 44–51.

38. Ibid., 55–61.

39. Paul Freund, "Appointment of Justices," 1163.

40. Steven Roberts, "The Supreme Court: Decisions in the Oval Office," *New York Times,* June 18, 1986, A32. For a list of Scalia's many well-known controversial views, see Stuart Taylor Jr., "More Vigor for the Right," *New York Times,* June 18, 1986, A1.

41. Scalia Hearings, 109 (remarks of Senator Joseph Biden).

42. Abraham, *Justices, Presidents, and Senators,* 295–97.

43. That moniker appears, among other places, in David A. Kaplan and Bob Cohn, "A Frankfurter, Not a Hot Dog."

44. Silverstein, *Judicious Choices,* 162.

45. Descriptions of Souter as such are Paul M. Barrett, "David Souter Emerges as Reflective Moderate on the Supreme Court," *Wall Street Journal,* February 2, 1994, 1; David J. Garrow, "Justice Souter Emerges"; Liza Weizman Hanks, "Justice Souter"; and Thomas M. Keck, "David H. Souter," esp. 210.

46. Fein, "A Court of Mediocrity," 74.

5. THE CONFIRMATION OF CLARENCE THOMAS

1. Larry Hugick, "One Night Before Vote" (quotations at 26).

2. Frank Newport, "Military Retains Top Position," 55. The fall in public confidence in the Supreme Court during 1991 may have reflected in part an across-the-board decline in public confidence in American institutions that year. See George Gallup and Frank Newport, "Confidence in Major U.S. Institutions."

3. David A. Yalof, *Pursuit of Justices,* 190, 192–95; Jane Mayer and Jill Abramson, *Strange Justice,* 11–14; Bill McAllister, "Judiciary Panel Votes 12–1 to Put Thomas on U.S. Bench; Don't Assume Way Is Clear to Supreme Court Seat, Democrats Warn," *Washington Post,* February 23, 1990, A21.

4. Maureen Dowd, "The Supreme Court: Conservative Black Judge, Clarence Thomas, Is Named to Marshall's Court Seat," *New York Times* July 2, 1991, A1.

5. Thomas's inexperience is detailed in Thomas Hearings, 82. Bush's remarks are in "The Supreme Court: Excerpts from News Conference Announcing Court Nominee," *New York Times,* July 2, 1991, A14.

6. George L. Watson and John A. Stookey, *Shaping America,* 110–11.

7. Thomas Hearings, September 10, 12, 13, and 16, 1991, pt. 1, 529.

8. Ibid., 531.

9. Ibid.

10. Thomas Hearings, pt. 1, 331–32, 447; quotation at 447.

11. Juan Williams, "EEOC Shifting Its Anti-Bias Policy; Agency to Pursue Individual Remedies, Fewer Class Actions," *Washington Post,* February 13, 1985, A1; U.S. House Committee on Education and Labor, Subcommittee on Employment Opportunities, *Equal Employment Opportunity Commission Policies.*

12. Thomas altered EEOC policy at least partly in order to hew to Reagan Administration policy. See Fred Barbash and Juan Williams, "Administration Prods EEOC on Quotas Brief," *Washington Post,* April 7, 1983, A1; Felicity Barringer, "EEOC Chief Criticizes Justice Department Job Plan," *Washington Post,* September 7, 1983, A15; Mayer and Abramson, *Strange Justice,* 120–21.

13. The decision was *Johnson v. Transportation Agency, Santa Clara County,* 480 U.S. 616 (1987), 657 (Scalia dissenting). Thomas's remark is in Thomas Hearings, pt. 1, 73, 289–92.

14. The statute is the Older Workers Benefit Protection Act, 104 Stat. 978 (1990). Senator John Melcher's (D-MT) claims that Thomas withheld accurate information from Congress are at *The EEOC's Performance in Enforcing the Age Discrimination in Employment Act,* 100th Cong., 2nd sess., June 23–24, 1988, 343; and in Jim Schachter, "900 Age Bias Cases Botched by U.S. Agency," *Los Angeles Times,* January 8, 1988, 1.

15. Quotation in U.S. House Select Committee on Aging, *Age Discrimination,* 72. Thomas blamed subordinates in 71–73, 101; and in Senate Committee, *EEOC's Performance,* 257, 268–71. Thomas's accusation that congressional Democrats had helped "mug" (underfund) his agency is in Schachter, "900 Age Bias Cases Botched," 1.

16. *AARP v. EEOC,* 655 F. Supp. 228 (1987) (quotations at 229, 240).

17. Robert P. Hey, "Age Bias in the Workplace," *Christian Science Monitor,* January 5, 1988, 1. The legislation was Older Workers Benefit Protection Act (1990).

18. Thomas's plea to Congress to "leave [the EEOC] alone" except to increase its budget, and his denunciation of the Senate's investigation into the lapsed age discrimination cases, are at U.S. House, Employment and Housing Subcommittee of the Committee on Government Operations, *EEOC's Reprisal Against District Director,* 99. His remarks on the propriety of oversight are at Thomas Hearings, pt. 2, 799–805; and Thomas Report, 61–62.

19. Thomas Hearings, pt. 1, 479. The comparison to Hoover is at "Clarence Thomas at the EEOC," DataLine, September 1991, available at: http://cyberwerks. com/dataline/profiles/cthomas.html. Congress's investigations into a second alleged case of retaliation by Thomas are in House Subcommittee, *EEOC's Reprisal* (1989), and U.S. Senate Special Committee on Aging, *EEOC Headquarters Officials Punish District Director.*

20. Clarence Thomas, "The Modern Civil Rights Movement: Can a Regime of Individual Rights and the Rule of Law Survive?" Speech at the Tocqueville Forum, Wake Forest University, April 18, 1988, 20. See also Thomas's remarks in Jim Schachter, "900 Age Bias Cases Botched," 1; Robert A. Rosenblatt, "Equal Jobs Chief Ordered to Give Age Bias Case Data," *Los Angeles Times,* February 25, 1988, 23; Robert A. Rosenblatt, "House Panel Told EEOC Botched 200 Age Discrimination Cases," *Los Angeles Times,* March 21, 1989, sec. 4, p. 1.

21. Thomas was asked in a *Reason* magazine interview, "Why do you think [the EEOC] should exist in a free society?" His full response was: "Well, in a free society I don't think there would be a need for it to exist. Had we lived up to our Constitution, had we lived up to the principles that we espoused, there would certainly be no need. There would have been no need for manumission either. Unfortunately, the reality was that, for political reasons or whatever, there was a need to enforce antidiscrimination laws, or at least there was a perceived need to do that. Why do you need a Department of Labor, why do you need a department of Commerce? You can go down the whole list—you don't need any of them, really." "*Reason* Interview: Clarence Thomas."

22. Thomas Report, 66–67.

23. Thomas Hearings, 129–31. The report was Working Group, *Family,* 10–12.

24. U.S. Senate Committee on the Judiciary, *Confirmation Hearings on Federal Appointments,* 101st Cong., 2nd sess., February 6, 21, and 27, 1990, 399–401, 458–60 (quotations at 399, 400, 458, 459).

25. Thomas Hearings, pt. 2, 668, 686.

26. "Speech by Clarence Thomas Before the Pacific Research Institute," San Francisco, CA, August 10, 1987 (quotation at 16), cited in Thomas Report, 32, 84.

27. "Speech by Clarence Thomas to the ABA Business Law Section," August 11, 1987, 9, cited in Thomas Report, 32, 84.

28. Ibid.

29. "Speech by Clarence Thomas Before the Pacific Research Institute," 11.

30. Thomas's many pronouncements on natural law are in Thomas Hearings, pt. 1, 117–26.

31. "Speech by Clarence Thomas Before the Heritage Foundation," Washington, D.C., June 18, 1987, 22. The article was Lewis Lehrman, "Declaration of Independence."

32. Thomas Hearings, pt. 1, 118; ibid., pt. 2, 826–27; Thomas Report, 61–63, 84–85.

33. "Speech to the Federalist Society, University of Virginia," 9 (emphasis in the original). Similar remarks are in "Speech Before the Cato Institute," October 2, 1987, 13; "Speech at the Tocqueville Forum," 21.

34. Thomas said of congressional Democrats attempting oversight of the EEOC: "In obscure meetings [they] browbeat, threaten, and harass agency heads to follow their lead" and then produce "press releases to show what a fine job" they have done. Speech at the Tocqueville Forum, 21. Thomas wrote in a speech he never delivered that as EEOC head he had been "defiant in the face of some petty despots in Congress." Prepared text, "Speech to the Federalist Society," Harvard University, April 7, 1988, 13. See also Thomas Report, 63–64, 84–86.

35. Juan Williams, "Question of Fairness."

36. Clarence Thomas, "Thomas Sowell" (quotation at 15).

37. Thomas Hearings, pt. 1, 449–51; Juan Williams, "EEOC Chairman Blasts Black Leaders," Washington Post, October 25, 1984, A7; and Thomas Report, 75–76.

38. Clarence Thomas, "Equal Employment Opportunity Commission."

39. Clarence Thomas, "Civil Rights as a Principle" (quotations at 398, 399).

40. Ruth Marcus, "Nominee Thomas Distances Himself from Farrakhan," Washington Post, July 13, 1991, A7.

41. Thomas Hearings, pt. 1, 432.

42. "Speech by Clarence Thomas Before the Pacific Research Institute," 8–9 (emphasis in the original).

43. Ibid., 9.

44. Ibid., 8.

45. Ibid.

46. Thomas Hearings, pt. 1, 431.

47. Thomas Hearings, pt. 2, 668; Timothy Phelps and Helen Winternitz, Capitol Games, 67–68; Mayer and Abramson, Strange Justice, 72.

48. David Bernstein, "Economic Regulation and Discrimination."

49. Patrick Monaghan, "Substantively Due-Processing" (quotations at 46, 53).

50. Vincent P. Miceli, The Antichrist (Harrison, NY: Roman Catholic Books, 1981), reviewed by John M. Snyder in Lincoln Review.

51. Phelps and Winternitz, Capitol Games, 65.

52. E.g., Clarence Thomas, "Thomas Sowell"; Clarence Thomas, "You Can't Give What You Don't Have."

53. Phelps and Winternitz, Capitol Games, 116–17, 146.

54. ALPO Petfoods v. Ralston Purina, 286 U.S. App. D.C. 192; 913 F.2nd 958 (1990). Opposing views on Thomas's participation in the case are Monroe Freedman,

"Ethics of Clarence Thomas"; Ronald D. Rotunda, "Resolving Doubts about Clarence Thomas."

55. *U.S. v. North,* 287 U.S. App. D.C. 146; 920 F.2d 940 (1990).

56. "Code of Conduct for United States Judges" esp. canons 1, 3, 5, and 7. Available at: http://www.utd.uscourts.gov/judges/judges_code.html.

57. The strategy is described in Mayer and Abramson, *Strange Justice,* 29–30, 178–82, 184, 189–90; Phelps and Winternitz, *Capitol Games,* 144, 75–76; and Linda Diebel, "Black Judge Describes His Struggles," *Toronto Star,* September 11, 1991, A17. At an awards dinner for Thomas in 2001, Robert Bork called Thomas's supposed roots in Pin Point "a public relations gimmick": http://www.aei.org/news/newsID.15213/news_detail.asp.

58. "Clarence Thomas Rises from Poverty to Supreme Court Nominee." A superb description of the many activities undertaken to boost public and senatorial support for Thomas in 1991 is Mayer and Abramson, *Strange Justice,* 173–201; Phelps and Winternitz, *Capitol Games,* 126–47.

59. "Sexual Harassment Claim on Thomas Surfaces," *Los Angeles Times,* October 6, 1991, A14; Mayer and Abramson, *Strange Justice,* 21–24, 316–17.

60. Phelps and Winternitz, *Capitol Games,* 288–89.

61. Edwin Chen and Douglas Frantz, "Support for Thomas Holds Despite Charges," *Los Angeles Times,* October 8, 1991, 1; Bob Dart, "The Clarence Thomas Vote: Showdown Today; Vote Likely, but Many Press for Further Delay," *Atlanta Journal and Constitution,* October 8, 1991, 1.

62. Mayer and Abramson, *Strange Justice,* 282–86.

63. Quotation in Jillian Dickert, "Privacy and Publicity," pt. 2, 9.

64. Linda Greenhouse, "Thomas Sworn In as 106th Justice," *New York Times,* October 23, 1991, A18; Mayer and Abramson, *Strange Justice,* 349–50; Phelps and Winternitz, *Capitol Games,* xiii–xvii.

65. John C. Danforth, *Resurrection,* 27, 147.

66. Professions of candor are in Thomas Hearings, pt. 1, 13–14, 16–17, 108, 179, 370. His disavowals on property rights are at 111–15, 173, 396, 425–33; on the Ninth Amendment, 226, 255, 374, 383–84; on congressional oversight, 232, 382–83; on privacy, 129–30, 184–86, 255; on entitlements, 141–43, 380; on women and minorities in the professions, 144–45, 205; on affirmative action, 234–36, 262–63, 289–91, 354–56; on the need for the EEOC, 140–41; on civil rights leaders, 109, 449–51; on natural law, 111–15, 128–29, 146–47, 179–80, 218–19, 471–74; on voting rights, 410–12; on the special prosecutor law, 286–89, 350–52; on the proliferation of rights, 143–44; on Congress, 264; on Oliver North, 382–83.

67. E.g., on his disavowal of natural law in constitutional interpretation, see Thomas Hearings, pt. 1, 111–12, 238–43; on natural law and abortion, 147–48; on natural law and economic rights, 111; on his hope that a dissenting opinion by Justice Scalia would guide lower courts, 292; on his agreement with William Simon's views on collectivism, 430–34.

68. Thomas Hearings, pt. 1, 143–44, 171, 203, 224, 226, 231, 232, 264, 266, 267, 352–53, 387–88, 482–83, 494 (quotations at 203).

69. Ibid., 222–23 (quotation at 222).

70. Ibid., 253, 381–82, 481; Timothy M. Phelps, "Thomas Denies Knowing S. Africa Tie," *Newsday,* September 12, 1991, 17.

71. Danforth, *Resurrection,* 27, 147.

72. E.g., Joan Biskupic, "Thomas Hearings Illustrate Politics of the Process"; David Margolick, "Questions to Thomas Fall Short of the Mark," *New York Times,* September 15, 1991, sec. 4, p. 1.

73. These expressions of disbelief are in Thomas Hearings, pt. 1, 178, 452, 481–82, 236, 494.

74. Ibid., 493, 494. See also Thomas Report, 90.

75. Thomas Hearings, pt. 4 (quotations at 168, 186).

76. Ibid., 186 (all quotations).

77. Ibid., 187–88.

78. On the purported lack of corroboration, see ibid., 185, 186, 187; on Hill as the lone accuser, ibid., 185; on Angela Wright, see Adam Clymer, "The Thomas Nomination: Conflict Emerges over a 2d Witness," *New York Times,* October 11, 1991, A1.

79. The exchange with Hatch is at Thomas Hearings, pt. 4, 199–203; the claims of "lynching" at 10, 157, 158, 161, 202.

80. Phelps and Winternitz, Capitol Games, 169, 187–88; Mayer and Abramson, *Strange Justice,* 213–15; Danforth, *Resurrection,* 84; Paul Simon, *Advice and Consent,* 118; E. J. Dionne Jr., "On Once and Future Supreme Court Nominations," *Washington Post,* June 19, 1992, A25.

81. Mayer and Abramson, *Strange Justice,* 239–40.

82. Walter V. Robinson, "Files Suggest Illicit Thomas Travel; Vouchers Cover Time as EEOC Chairman," *Boston Globe,* September 7, 1991, 1; Phelps and Winternitz, *Capitol Games,* 189–90.

83. Thomas Hearings, pt. 1, 580; and pt. 2, 244.

84. Ibid., pt. 2, 572.

85. Jillian Dickert, "Privacy and Publicity," pt. 1, 13–14; Mayer and Abramson, *Strange Justice,* 237–38.

86. A Democratic senator later said he would be shocked if no one warned Thomas. Mayer and Abramson, *Strange Justice,* 246.

87. *Congressional Record,* 102nd Cong., 1st sess. (September 27, 1991), 137: S13869.

88. Ibid., S13865, S13868.

89. Ibid., S13869.

90. Dickert, "Privacy and Publicity," pt. 1, 18.

91. Senate, Biden, S13869.

92. Federal News Service, Senate Judiciary Committee Hearing on the Supreme Court Nomination of Judge Clarence Thomas, September 27, 1991.

93. See, e.g., the remarks of White House Spokesman Marlin Fitzwater in Dickert, "Privacy and Publicity," pt. 2, 1; Senate, Senator Hatch of Utah speaking on the nomination of Clarence Thomas, 102nd Cong., 1st sess., *Congressional Record* (October 7, 1981): 137, S14451.

94. Dickert, "Privacy and Publicity," pt. 2, 6.

95. Danforth, *Resurrection*, 84.

96. Mayer and Abramson, *Strange Justice*, 271.

97. Thomas Hearings, pt. 4, 10, 157, 158, 161, 202.

98. Ibid., 252.

99. Ibid., 184, 185, 187.

100. Ibid., 267.

101. Biden's failure to respond to Senator Alan Simpson's innuendo on Hill's "character" and "proclivities" is at Thomas Hearings, pt. 4, 253–54; to Senator Thurmond's questioning of her mental health and purported professional resentments and romantic disappointments with Thomas, 227; to similar allegations by others, 354–60; to Simpson and Specter's questioning of her mental health, 373–75, 384–86. After Specter charged Hill with "perjury," Biden let him question Thomas for four uninterrupted pages in the official transcript before responding laboriously and then being sidetracked by other issues; 230–38. Biden's regret is in Dionne, "On Once and Future," A25.

102. Thomas Hearings, pt. 4, 3, 305.

103. Ibid., 181, 205, 207, 378.

104. Ibid., 133.

105. Ibid., 267.

106. Ibid., 367.

107. Ibid., 4, 189, 268.

108. Ibid., 188–89, 246, 271–72.

109. Dionne, "On Once and Future," A25.

110. Wright's statement is in Thomas Hearings, pt. 4, 442–511, the listed particulars at 452–58, 460, 478–79, 459, 496–97, 478, 472; Jourdain's statement is at 512–51.

111. Mayer and Abramson, *Strange Justice*, 327–28.

112. Thomas Hearings, pt. 4, 1022–24, quotations at 1023, 1024.

113. Mayer and Abramson, *Strange Justice*, 330–31, 335–36.

114. Michael Wines, "The Thomas Nomination: Stark Conflict Marks Accounts Given by Thomas and Professor," *New York Times*, October 10, 1991, B14; also Steven V. Roberts, Jeannye Thornton, and Ted Gest, "Crowning Thomas Affair."

115. Florence George Graves, "The Other Woman: Remember Angela Wright? Neither Do Most People. Her Testimony Might Have Changed History." *Washington Post*, October 9, 1994, F1, at F9; Mayer and Abramson, *Strange Justice*, 342.

116. Quotation in Graves, "Other Woman," F9; Mayer and Abramson, *Strange Justice*, 343; Biden's account is supported by an aide in Dickert, "Privacy and Publicity," pt. 2, 13.

117. Wright had also been fired from a job in the office of a congressman and had resigned rather than be fired at the Agency for International Development, where she accused her boss of racism. Mayer and Abramson, *Strange Justice*, 325.

118. Mayer and Abramson, *Strange Justice*, 331–32, 340–42; Phelps and Winternitz, *Capitol Games*, 362–64; quotation in Graves, "Other Woman," F9.

119. Graves, "Other Woman," F9.

120. Mayer and Abramson, *Strange Justice,* 340, 343–45; Graves, "Other Woman," F9.

121. Graves, "Other Woman," F8–F9; Mayer and Abramson, *Strange Justice,* 342–43; Simon, *Advice and Consent,* 118.

122. Quotation in Dickert, "Privacy and Publicity," pt. 2, 14. The *New York Times'* brief excerpts were the most extensive excerpts published: "The Thomas Nomination: Excerpts from an Interview with Another Thomas Accuser," *New York Times,* October 15, 1991, A21.

123. Thomas Hearings, pt. 2, 668; Phelps and Winternitz, *Capitol Games,* 67–68; Mayer and Abramson, *Strange Justice,* 72.

124. Thomas Hearings, pt. 1, 263–65.

125. Ibid., 382–83.

126. Republican Arlen Specter of Pennsylvania, who learned of the matter from DeConcini, also read these materials. Dickert, "Privacy and Publicity," pt. 1, 15–16.

127. Dickert, "Privacy and Publicity," pt. 2, 2.

128. E.g., Thomas Hearings, pt. 4, 308, 424–25.

129. Ibid., 161.

130. Ibid., 253.

131. Ibid., 307, 330–31, 332–33.

132. Thomas's response to Leahy is in ibid., 195.

133. Ibid., 578.

134. Jack Nelson, "News Analysis: Democrats Failed to Protect Hill from GOP; Some Leading Members of Party Are Outraged," *Los Angeles Times,* October 15, 1991, A7.

135. Thomas Hearings, pt. 4, 160, 256, 264. The debate is at 246.

136. Anita Hill, *Speaking Truth,* 131–36; Counsel, Pursuant to Senate Resolution 202, 102nd Cong., 2nd sess., May 13, 1992, 13.

137. Dickert, "Privacy and Publicity," pt. 1, 28; Mayer and Abramson, *Strange Justice,* 221–28; quotation in Hill, *Speaking Truth,* 109.

138. Phelps and Winternitz, *Capitol Games,* 211.

139. Mayer and Abramson, *Strange Justice,* 232.

140. The events in this paragraph are taken from Counsel, 13–14; Mayer and Abramson, *Strange Justice,* 231–38; Phelps and Winternitz, *Capitol Games,* 146–47, 174–75.

141. Biden's account is in Counsel, pt. 1, 14; Mayer and Abramson, *Strange Justice,* 236–37; and Phelps and Winternitz, *Capitol Games,* 212–13. Hill's version of events is in Dickert, "Privacy and Publicity," pt. 2, 22; Hill, *Speaking Truth,* 112–13; Mayer and Abramson, *Strange Justice,* 237, 242.

142. Hill recounts her reluctance to confront Thomas in *Speaking Truth,* 112–13. Her request to Simon is in Simon, *Advice and Consent,* 104–5; Counsel, 20; and Hill, *Speaking Truth,* 120. Characterizations of her naivete are Mayer and Abramson, *Strange Justice,* 232–33; Phelps and Winternitz, *Capitol Games,* 21.

143. The statement is in Counsel, pt. 2, 33–37.

144. Ibid., 22; Mayer and Abramson, *Strange Justice,* 253.

145. Counsel, 22–30; Mayer and Abramson, *Strange Justice,* 251–56; and Hill, *Speaking Truth,* 121–22.

146. Adam Clymer, "Senate's Futile Search for Safe Ground," *New York Times,* October 16, 1991, A1; Danforth, *Resurrection,* 49.

147. "Anita Hill News Conference," in Dickert, "Privacy and Publicity," pt. 2, 20–23 (quotation at 23).

148. Dickert, pt. 1, 15–16.

149. *Congressional Record,* 102nd Cong., 1st sess. (October 8, 1991), 137: S14539–40. Republican leader Robert Dole suggested a delay, but only because he could not muster fifty votes for the nomination; S14566.

150. Denunciations of the charges as politically motivated are by Senator Hatch, ibid., S14451; Danforth, S14455; Jake Garn, S14520; Christopher Bond, S14559; Steven Symms, S14564. For affirmations of Thomas's good character, see, e.g., Senator Mitch McConnell, S14477; Craig, S14566; Bond, S14566.

151. Ibid., Thurmond, S14466; Bond, S14559.

152. Danforth, *Resurrection,* 121.

153. *Congressional Record,* 102nd Cong., 1st sess. (October 7, 1991), 137: S14467; ibid. (October 8, 1991), 137: S14523.

154. Ibid., S14525 (Kerry), S14544 (Simpson).

155. Quotation at Thomas Hearings, pt. 4, 253; Transcript, *NBC Meet the Press,* October 13, 1991, 1.

156. Thomas Hearings, pt. 4, 64–67 (quotation at 64).

157. Ibid., 117–18.

158. Ibid., 117.

159. Ibid., 228–31 (quotation at 230).

160. Ibid., 104–5, 233, 235–36 (quotations at 104, 233).

161. Danforth, *Resurrection,* 202.

162. Ibid. (quotations at 202, 203).

163. Ibid., 161–62. Danforth mentions only "an alleged incident involving pubic hair"; 162. More complete accounts are Mayer and Abramson, *Strange Justice,* 310–14, 334–35; and Phelps and Winternitz, *Capitol Games,* 353.

164. Danforth, *Resurrection,* 175.

165. Ibid., 160.

166. Ibid., 161.

167. Ibid. (quotations at 166, 188).

168. Ibid. (quotations at 167, 165).

169. Ibid., 188–90.

170. Ibid., 205, 37–39 (quotation at 205).

171. Ibid., 38.

172. Thomas Hearings, pt. 4, 343–44, 348, 362–64, 382.

173. Danforth, *Resurrection,* 37, 74 (quotation at 37).

174. Ibid., 41.

175. Danforth's expressions of shame are in ibid., 82, 175; his self-justifications at 40–41, 206–7 (quotations at 206–7).

176. Mayer and Abramson, *Strange Justice,* 21.

177. Ibid., 179–80; Phelps and Winternitz, *Capitol Games,* 12–15, 28–30, 73–75.

178. Thomas Hearings, pt. 3, 19.

179. Phelps and Winternitz, *Capitol Games,* 30, 73–74; Mayer and Abramson, *Strange Justice,* 180, 182–85.

180. Timothy M. Phelps, "Thomas Seen Gaining Momentum," *Newsday,* July 25, 1991, 17.

181. Peter Applebome, "Dr. King's Rights Group Backs Court Nominee," *New York Times,* September 27, 1991, A15.

182. Ruth Marcus, "Anti-Bork Forces Find Thomas a Different Fight," *Washington Post,* August 3, 1991, A1.

183. On Southern Democrats' dependence on black voters, see Steven A. Holmes, "A Changed Landscape for Southern Democrats," *New York Times,* September 8, 1991, pt. 1, p. 22; on black public opinion, Joan Biskupic, "How the Thomas Nomination Differs."

184. A statement of this hope is Maya Angelou, "Support Clarence Thomas and Hope That He Can Be Won Over," *St. Petersburg Times,* August 27, 1991, 9A.

185. See, e.g., "Statement of Ms. Niara Sudarkasa" Thomas Hearings, pt. 2, 76–78.

186. James J. Kilpatrick, "The Liberal Lynch Mob Moves in on Thomas," *St. Petersburg Times,* August 7, 1991, 13A.

187. Orlando Patterson, "Race, Gender, and Liberal Fallacies" (quotation at 164).

188. On the importance of this argument, see Mayer and Abramson, *Strange Justice,* 184–85, 188.

189. An explication of this view is Manning Marable, "Clarence Thomas."

190. Jacquelyne Johnson Jackson, "Them Against Us" (quotation at 104).

191. Blacks questioning Thomas's qualifications were Christopher Edley (a Harvard law professor), "Straight Talk on the Quota Candidate," *St. Louis Post-Dispatch,* July 14, 1991, 3B; Julius Chambers, counsel for the NAACP Legal Defense Fund, at Thomas Hearings, pt. 2, 832–33, 896–98; William Lucy, president of the Coalition of Black Trade Unionists, Thomas Hearings, pt. 2, 882–83; John Hope Franklin, "Letter to Senator Biden," in Thomas Hearings, pt. 4, 783–84. The lone white exception was Erwin Griswold, former dean of Harvard Law School, at Thomas Hearings, pt. 2, 233–35. Blacks who pointed to Thomas's modest comfort in his grandparents' home and his many educational advantages were Edley, "Straight Talk," 3B; NAACP, "A Report on the Nomination of Judge Clarence Thomas as Associate Justice of the United States Supreme Court," in Thomas Hearings, pt. 3, 97, 112; Rev. Amos C. Brown, Thomas Hearings, pt. 3, 125; Morrison, "Introduction," xx–xxi.

192. Jackson's remarks are in Nelson, "News Analysis," A7; Franklin's in Marcus, "Thomas Hearings," A27; Byrd's in *Congressional Record,* 102nd Cong., 1st sess. (October 15, 1991), 137: S14633.

193. Jane Mansbridge and Katherine Tate, "Race Trumps Gender?"; Marian Lief Palley and Howard A. Palley, "Thomas Appointment," 473–76; Jane Flax, *American Dream.* Quantitative studies are L. Marvin Overby et al., "Courting Constituents?"; L. Marvin Overby and Beth M. Henschen, "Race Trumps Gender?". Senatorial testi-

mony to the importance of race is in Dickert, "Privacy and Publicity," pt. 2, 14; and R. W. Apple Jr., "The Thomas Confirmation: Senate Confirms Thomas, 52–48," *New York Times,* October 16, 1991, A1.

194. The unsuccessful efforts of the Reagan White House to portray the staunchly conservative Bork as a moderate are described in Mark Gitenstein, *Matters of Principle,* 69–71, 87–88, 99–101.

195. These senators' reluctance to probe the issue of sexual harassment is alleged in Mayer and Abramson, *Strange Justice,* 199–200, 204–5, 233, 235–37; and Phelps and Winternitz, *Capitol Games,* 124–26, 142, 187–88. Biden had been forced to end his 1988 campaign for president after he plagiarized a speech by a British Labour Party leader; 187–88. DeConcini was one of the "Keating Five"—senators who allegedly interceded with regulators investigating a fraudulent savings and loan owned by a major campaign contributor; 204. Kennedy was compromised by his embarrassing behavior on and after a night of drinking and partying earlier that year that ended with his nephew, William Kennedy Smith, charged with raping a woman in the Kennedy compound in Palm Beach; 142. Mike Cleary, "Kennedy Testifies in Probe of Rape Case Obstruction," *Los Angeles Times,* August 31, 1991, A22.

196. Television viewership figures are from John Carmody, "The TV Column," *Washington Post,* October 14, 1991, D10; Terry Blount, "Thomas Hearings Wreck CBS Weekend Ratings," *Houston Chronicle,* October 18, 1991, 2.

197. See note 193 above.

198. E.g., Thomas Hearings, pt. 2, 49 (testimony of Drew S. Days); and 249, 254–55 (testimony of Guido Calabresi).

199. Thomas's ideological wanderlust is in Neil Lewis, "Thomas's Journey on Path of Self-Help," *New York Times,* July 7, 1991, 12, and Mayer and Abramson, *Strange Justice,* 51, 118–19, 140–43. On race-conscious policies, see Phelps and Winternitz, *Capitol Games,* 97–101; and Mayer and Abramson, *Strange Justice,* 120–21. His criticisms of the Reagan Administration are in "Speech by Clarence Thomas Before the Heritage Foundation," 8–13. His remarks on racism are in Williams, "Question of Fairness," 72.

200. *Congressional Quarterly* reported that on October 4, 1991—two days before the Hill story broke—Thomas had the support of thirteen Democrats and at least forty-one Republicans. Joan Biskupic, "Thomas Picks Up Support."

201. Dickert, "Privacy and Publicity," pt. 1, 20.

202. Thomas Hearings, pt. 4, 2.

203. Ibid., 1.

204. Dickert, "Privacy and Publicity," pt. 1, 14.

205. Mayer and Abramson, *Strange Justice,* 136–40, 333–34.

206. Barbara Sinclair makes this point in "Senate Process."

207. Dickert, "Privacy and Publicity," pt. 2 (quotations at 8).

208. On greater awareness of sexual harassment, see, e.g., Richard Morin, "Harassment Consensus Grows; Poll Finds Greater Awareness of Misconduct," *Washington Post,* December 18, 1992, A1. Sexual harassment complaints filed with the EEOC and state agencies rose from 6,886 in 1991 to 10,532 in 1992, and 15,836 in 2000 (personal communication from the EEOC, July 23, 1999; see also http://

www.eeoc.gov/ stats/harass.html). On employment policies, see Simon, *Advice and Consent,* 123.

209. Simon, *Advice and Consent,* 123. On other nations, see Alan Riding, "Harassment or Flirting? Europe Tries to Decide," *New York Times,* November 3, 1992, A8.

210. Among the apologizers were Senators Simpson, Metzenbaum, and Kennedy. Some commentators suggested that public apologies actually increase support for elected figures. Gwen Ifill, "Washington Talk; Old Political Tool Takes on a New Role," *New York Times,* October 29, 1991, A18.

211. A large number of open seats also helped produce this result. "The Transition: Women on the Ballot; Female Ranks in Elected Jobs," *New York Times,* November 8, 1992, 28.

212. Overby and Henschen, "Race Trumps Gender?"; Overby et al., "Courting Constituents?"; Apple, "The Thomas Confirmation."

6. UNREVEALING INQUIRIES: ARE NOMINEES ALL THAT STEALTHY?

1. Laurence H. Tribe, *God Save This Honorable Court,* 76.

2. Henry J. Abraham, *Judicial Process,* 73.

3. Nina Totenberg, "Confirmation Process," 1228.

4. Bruce A. Ackerman, "Transformative Appointments."

5. William H. Rehnquist, "The Making of a Supreme Court Justice" (quotation at 8).

6. L. A. Powe, "The Senate and the Court" (quotation at 893).

7. Grover Rees III, "Questions for Supreme Court Nominees" (quotation at 962–63).

8. Elena Kagan, "Confirmation Messes" (quotation at 920).

9. In its Report on Ruth Bader Ginsburg's 1993 nomination, the Senate Judiciary Committee stated that it was not "fully satisfied with the responsiveness of Judge Ginsburg's answers" to senators' questions and that it had "not been fully satisfied for many years" by nominees' testimony. Ginsburg Report, "Statement of Senator William Cohen," 48–49. See also the complaints of senators in Chapter 2.

10. U.S. Senate Committee on the Judiciary, *Nomination of William H. Rehnquist,* 25–28.

11. Souter Hearings, 70–74, 214–15.

12. Thomas Report (quotations at 9, 58).

13. Bork Hearings, 464.

14. Thomas Report, 107.

15. Bork Hearings, 464.

16. For a discussion of this means of avoiding more revealing testimony, see Chapter 2.

17. How he did so is discussed with considerable anger by several Democratic senators in Thomas Report.

18. John C. Danforth, *Resurrection,* 27.

19. Responding to questions about a speech he had given, nominee Antonin Scalia confessed his unease with strict adherence to the Founders' intent but told Senator Joseph Biden, "You are right . . . in suspecting me to be more inclined to the original meaning than I am to a phrase like 'living Constitution.'" Scalia Hearings, 48–49. Robert Bork told the Committee that the "only legitimate way" for judges to "find the law" is "by attempting to discern what those who made the law intended. The intentions of the lawmakers govern" (Bork Hearings, 103–4). Anthony Kennedy told the Committee, "The doctrine of original intent does not tell us how to decide a case. . . . I just did not think that original intent was very helpful as a methodology . . . because it just restates the question" (Kennedy Hearings, 140). David Souter testified that in applying a constitutional provision the judge's task is to identify "the principle that was intended to be applied" rather than the specific, original meaning of the provision (Souter Hearings, 128–29, 303). Ruth Bader Ginsburg expounded eloquently on the need to interpret constitutional provisions not merely according to "what [the Founders] might have intended immediately for their day" but rather by the Founders' "larger expectation that the Constitution would govern . . . not for the passing hour but for the expanding future" (Ginsburg Hearings, 127).

20. Souter Hearings, 200–202, rejecting the view of Chief Justice Rehnquist and Justice Scalia that unenumerated rights are protected only at "the most specific level at which a relevant tradition protecting . . . the asserted right can be identified" (quotation from *Michael H. v. Gerald D.,* 491 U.S. 110 [1989], 127, n. 6); Breyer Hearings, 223, asserting the need to consider "[t]he needs of the country [in the present day] for whatever conditions that will permit the dignity" of the individual.

21. Antonin Scalia indicated grave doubts about the value of legislative history as a guide to congressional intent (Scalia Hearings, 65–68). Stephen Breyer explicitly rejected Scalia's view (Breyer Hearings, 267, 296). Ruth Bader Ginsburg looked to legislative history with "hopeful skepticism" that she would "find something genuinely helpful there" (Ginsburg Hearings, 224). David Souter told senators that a judge should be guided by "an intent which can be attributed to the institution itself . . . not merely the statement of one committee member or committee staffer or one person on the floor, but in fact to an institution or to a sufficiently large enough number of the members of that institution, so that we can say they probably really do stand as surrogates for all those who voted for it" (Souter Hearings, 131).

22. David Souter told the Judiciary Committee that the unenumerated rights referred to by the Ninth Amendment were not limited to those provided for in the existing state constitutions and laws of the time, as Robert Bork had testified (Bork Hearings, 248–49; Souter Hearings, 55). A view similar to Souter's was also expressed by Stephen Breyer (Breyer Hearings, 166, 222–23).

23. Bork Hearings, 119, 254–57, 316, 330–31, 391–96 (rejecting the multitiered analysis in favor of the reasonable basis test); Kennedy Hearings, 118–20, and Thomas Hearings, 202–5 (accepting multiple tiers).

24. Ginsburg Report, 27.

25. Contrast the views of Antonin Scalia in Scalia Hearings, 48–49, with those of Ruth Bader Ginsburg in Ginsburg Hearings, 118–19, 126–27.

26. See, e.g., David Souter in Souther Hearings, 142, and Ruth Bader Ginsburg in Ginsburg Hearings, 168, 171.

27. George Watson and John Stookey, "Supreme Court Confirmation Hearings."

28. Jeffrey A. Segal, Albert D. Cover, and Charles M. Cameron, "Role of Ideology," 497–98.

29. Jeffrey A. Segal and Harold J. Spaeth, *Attitudinal Model.*

30. This list excludes Robert Bork, whose views were quite well known, and Douglas Ginsburg, whose views, as described in Chapter 3, were less well known. Many of the statistics quoted in this section on the justices' voting patterns are from two sources: Thomas R. Hensley, Christopher E. Smith, and Joyce A. Baugh, *Changing Supreme Court;* and Thomas R. Hensley, Christopher E. Smith, and Joyce A. Baugh, *Supreme Court Update: 2001* (unpublished manuscript, January 2002). I follow them in defining a "conservative" decision as one "rejecting individuals' claims of improper government interference with constitutionally protected rights" or, in civil rights, rejecting the position of the litigant that is trying to promote greater equality for racial minorities or women. *Changing Supreme Court,* 3; personal communication from Thomas R. Hensley, June 22, 1998.

31. For insight into Rehnquist's views in 1971, see Henry J. Abraham, *Justices and Presidents,* 320–21; and Fred P. Graham, "Rehnquist's Statements Indicate He Would Be an Activist Pressing Conservative Views," *New York Times,* November 3, 1971, 1.

32. For a review of Rehnquist's jurisprudence as an associate justice and his 1986 confirmation as chief justice, see Abraham, *Justices and Presidents,* 320–26, 350. The quotation is at 350.

33. Hensley, Smith, and Baugh, *Supreme Court Update,* 18, table 1.4 of unpublished manuscript.

34. For an account of Rehnquist's personal campaign to revise the Court's federalism jurisprudence, see David J. Garrow, "Rehnquist Reins."

35. Stuart Taylor Jr., "More Vigor for the Right," *New York Times,* June 18, 1986, A1 (quotation at A31).

36. For a statistical summary of Scalia's voting in civil rights and liberties cases, see Hensley, Smith, and Baugh, *Supreme Court Update,* 18, 22 (tables 1.4, 1.8 of unpublished manuscript). John M. Scheb II and Terry M. Bowen identify Scalia as the Court's most conservative member for six of the eight terms from 1986 to 1993: "Ideology on the Rehnquist Court," 519 (table 2). Richard Brisbin identifies Scalia as the Rehnquist Court's second most conservative justice: *Justice Antonin Scalia,* 63–65.

37. Neil A. Lewis, "Thomas's Journey on Path of Self-Help," *New York Times,* July 7, 1991, 12.

38. Thomas Report, 58.

39. Ibid., 9.

40. Thomas Hearings, pt. 1, 118; ibid., pt. 2, 826–27; Thomas Report, 61–63, 84–85.

41. Speech to the Federalist Society, University of Virginia, 9; also speech

before the Cato Institute, October 2, 1987, 13; and speech at the Tocqueville Forum, 21.

42. Juan Williams, "Question of Fairness"; Clarence Thomas, "Thomas Sowell," 15; "*Reason* Interview: Clarence Thomas."

43. Thomas Hearings, pt. 1, 449–51; Juan Williams, "EEOC Chairman Blasts Black Leaders," *Washington Post,* October 25, 1984, A7; and Thomas Report, 75–76.

44. Ibid., 11.

45. Ibid., 42–46.

46. Hensley, Smith, and Baugh, *Supreme Court Update,* 18–24 (tables 1.4–1.10 of unpublished manuscript). Hensley, Smith, and Baugh, *Changing Supreme Court,* 88 (tables 3.9, 3.10). A balanced overview of the record of this controversial justice, concluding that "Justice Thomas has established a consistent and predictable voting record as a dependable member of the Court's most conservative wing," is Christopher E. Smith, "Clarence Thomas." For expressions of dismay over Thomas's performance by opponents (and some reluctant supporters) of his nomination to the Court, see A. Leon Higginbotham Jr., "Justice Clarence Thomas."

47. John M. Crewdson, "Nominee for High Court: A Record Defying Labels," *New York Times,* July 12, 1981, 1.

48. O'Connor's record as a state senator is described in ibid.

49. Linda Greenhouse, "O'Connor Hearings Open on a Note of Friendship," *New York Times,* September 10, 1981, B14.

50. Kennedy and Powell's scores were 38 percent and 39 percent, respectively. The scores of all these justices are in Hensley, Smith, and Baugh, *Supreme Court Update,* 18 (table 1.4 of unpublished manuscript).

51. O'Connor favored procedural protections in only 29 percent of criminal justice cases between 1986 and 1994, barely above Justice Scalia's 26 percent. Hensley, Smith, and Baugh, *Changing Supreme Court,* 89 (table 3.11).

52. On race-based redistricting to increase the number of minority elected officials, see *Shaw v. Reno,* 509 U.S. 630 (1993); *Miller v. Johnson,* 515 U.S. 900 (1995); *Shaw v. Hunt,* 517 U.S. 899 (1996); *Bush v. Vera,* 517 U.S. 952 (1996); and *Abrams v. Johnson,* 521 U.S. 74 (1997). On affirmative action, see *Richmond v. Croson,* 488 U.S. 469 (1989); *Adarand Constructors v. Pena,* 515 U.S. 200 (1995); *Gratz v. Bollinger,* 539 U.S. 244 (2003). But see *Grutter v. Bollinger,* 539 U.S. 306 (2003), upholding the affirmative action program at the University of Michigan Law School.

53. *New York v. U.S.,* 505 U.S. 144 (1992); *U.S. v. Lopez,* 514 U.S. 549 (1995), 568, O'Connor and Kennedy concurring; *Seminole Tribe v. Florida,* 517 U.S. 44 (1996); *Printz v. U.S.,* 521 U.S. 898 (1997); *Alden v. Maine,* 527 U.S. 706 (1999); *College Savings Bank v. Florida Prepaid,* 527 U.S. 666 (1999); *Florida Prepaid v. College Savings Bank,* 527 U.S. 627 (1999); *Kimel v. Florida Board of Regents,* 528 U.S. 62 (2000); *U.S. v. Morrison,* 529 U.S. 598 (2000); *Alabama v. Garrett,* 531 U.S. 356 (2001).

54. *Planned Parenthood v. Casey,* 505 U.S. 833 (1992).

55. *Lee v. Weisman,* 505 U.S. 577 (1992).

56. *Romer v. Evans,* 517 U.S. 620 (1996).

57. *Lawrence v. Texas,* 123 S. Ct. 2472 (2003).

58. Stuart Taylor, "At Top of List, Judge Fitting Centrist Mold," *New York Times,* November 10, 1987, A1.

59. Nadine Cohodas, "Kennedy Finds Bork an Easy Act to Follow," *Congressional Quarterly Weekly Report,* December 5, 1987, 2989–90.

60. Taylor, "At Top of List," D34 (quoting Michael McDonald).

61. Abraham, *Justices and Presidents,* 364.

62. From 1986 to 1994, Kennedy supported procedural protections just 29 percent of the time. Smith, Hensley, and Baugh, *Changing Supreme Court,* 89 (table 3.11). On his profederalism views, see *New York v. U.S.* (1992); *U.S. v. Lopez* (1995), 568, O'Connor and Kennedy concurring; *Seminole Tribe v. Florida* (1996); *Printz v. U.S.* (1997); *Alden v. Maine* (1999); *College Savings Bank v. Florida Prepaid* (1999); *Florida Prepaid v. College Savings Bank* (1999); *Kimel v. Florida Board of Regents* (2000); *U.S. v. Morrison* (2000); *Alabama v. Garrett* (2001); and *Nevada Dep't of Human Resources v. Hibbs,* 123 S. Ct. 1972 (2003), Kennedy dissenting at 1986.

63. See n. 52 above for Kennedy's votes with O'Connor on this issue, but also his dissents in the pro–affirmative action decision in *Grutter v. Bollinger* (2003), at 2365 (joining Chief Justice Rehnquist) and 2370 (writing for himself).

64. These decisions are, in order, *Texas v. Johnson,* 491 U.S. 397 (1989); *United States v. Eichman,* 496 U.S. 310 (1990); *Lee v. Weisman,* 505 U.S. 577 (1992); *Planned Parenthood v. Casey,* 505 U.S. 833 (1992); *U.S. Term Limits v. Thornton,* 514 U.S. 779 (1995); *Romer v. Evans,* 517 U.S. 620 (1996); *Lawrence v. Texas,* 123 S. Ct. 2472 (2003); *U.S. v. Playboy Entertainment Group,* 529 U.S. 803 (2000); *Ashcroft v. Free Speech Coalition,* 535 U.S. 234 (2002).

65. Jeffrey Rosen, "Agonizer"; Lawrence Friedman, "Limitations of Labeling"; "Is Anthony Kennedy a Conservative?" *New Republic,* June 17, 1996, 9. Earl M. Maltz finds that Kennedy has diverged "from conservative ideology on a substantial number of key issues . . . such as sex discrimination, abortion rights, the constitutional status of sexual orientation, and a variety of other issues." "Anthony Kennedy," 154.

66. Linda Greenhouse, "An 'Intellectual Mind,'" *New York Times,* July 24, 1990, A1; David Margolick, "Ascetic at Home, but Vigorous on Bench," *New York Times,* July 25, 1990, A1.

67. Joan Biskupic, "Bush's Nominees Lack Baggage that Reagan's Often Carried" (quotation at 3020).

68. See, e.g., William D. Bader, "Meditations on the Original"; Liza Weiman Hanks, "Justice Souter"; Liang Kan, "Theory of Justice Souter"; David J. Garrow, "Justice Souter Emerges"; and Thomas M. Keck, "David H. Souter," esp. 210.

69. Hensley, Smith, and Baugh, *Supreme Court Update,* 18 (table 1.4 of unpublished manuscript).

70. From the 1992 through 2000 terms, Souter's annual percentage of liberal votes on civil rights and liberties cases has exceeded the average of the Court by 11 to 33 points. Hensley, Smith, and Baugh, *Supreme Court Update,* 18 (table 1.4 of unpublished manuscript). Through the Court's 2000 term, Souter was a consistent

member of a "moderately liberal" voting "bloc" with Justices Ginsburg and/or Breyer and/or Stevens (ibid., 19–24, tables 1.5–1.10). See also Hensley, Smith, and Baugh, *Changing Supreme Court,* 88 (tables 3.9, 3.10).

71. *Planned Parenthood v. Casey,* 505 U.S. 833 (1992).

72. *Lawrence v. Texas* (2003).

73. E.g., *U.S. v. Lopez* (1995), 603 (Souter dissenting); *Seminole Tribe v. Florida* (1996), 100 (Souter dissenting); *Printz v. U.S.* (1997), 966 (Souter dissenting); *Alden v. Maine* (1999), 760 (Souter dissenting); *College Savings Bank v. Florida Prepaid* (1999), 693 (Souter dissenting); *Florida Prepaid v. College Savings Bank* (1999), 648 (Souter dissenting); *Kimel v. Florida Board of Regents* (2000), 92 (Souter dissenting); *U.S. v. Morrison* (2000), 627 (Souter dissenting); *Alabama v. Garrett* (2001), 376 (Souter dissenting); *Locke v. Davey,* 124 S. Ct. 1307 (2004) (Souter joining the majority).

74. See, for example, *Shaw v. Reno* (1993), 679 (Souter dissenting); *Miller v. Johnson* (1995), 934 (Souter dissenting); and *Bush v. Vera* (1996), 1045 (Souter dissenting); *Adarand Constructors v. Pena* (1995), 264 (Souter dissenting) *Gratz v. Bollinger* (2003), 2434, 2438 (Souter dissenting); *Grutter v. Bollinger* (2003), 2331 (Souter joining the majority).

75. E.g., *Agostini v. Felton,* 521 U.S. 203 (1997), 240, 255 (Souter dissenting); *Rosenberger v. University of Virginia,* 515 U.S. 819 (1995), 863 (Souter dissenting); *Good News Club v. Milford Central School,* 533 U.S. 98 (2001), 134 (Souter dissenting); *Zelman v. Simmons-Harris,* 536 U.S. 639 (2002), 686, 717 (Souter dissenting); *Locke v. Davey,* 124 S. Ct. 1307 (2004) (Souter joining the majority).

76. *Yee v. Escondido,* 503 U.S. 519 (1992); *Dolan v. Tigard,* 512 U.S. 374 (1994), 411 (Souter dissenting).

77. Keck, "David H. Souter," 185–215.

78. Hensley, Smith, and Baugh, *Supreme Court Update,* 18 (table 1.4 of unpublished manuscript).

79. Holly Idelson, "Clinton's Choice of Ginsburg Signals Moderation."

80. E.g., *U.S. v. Lopez* (1995), 615 (Ginsburg dissenting); *Seminole Tribe v. Florida* (1996), 100 (Ginsburg dissenting); *Printz v. U.S.* (1997), 947 (Ginsburg dissenting); *College Savings Bank v. Florida Prepaid* (1999), 693 (Ginsburg dissenting); *Alden v. Maine* (1999), 760 (Ginsburg dissenting); *Florida Prepaid v. College Savings Bank* (1999), 648 (Ginsburg dissenting); *Kimel v. Florida Board of Regents* (2000), 92 (Ginsburg dissenting); *U.S. v. Morrison* (2000), 628 (Ginsburg dissenting); *Alabama v. Garrett* (2001), 376 (Ginsburg dissenting).

81. E.g., *Rosenberger v. University of Virginia* (1995), 863 (Ginsburg dissenting); *Agostini v. Felton* (1997), 240, 255 (Ginsburg dissenting); *Good News Club v. Milford Central School* (2001), 134 (Ginsburg dissenting); *Zelman v. Simmons-Harris* (2002), 686 (Ginsburg dissenting).

82. Hensley, Smith, and Baugh, *Changing Supreme Court,* 88 (table 3.9); Hensley, Smith, and Baugh, *Supreme Court Update,* 19–24 (tables 1.5–1.10 of unpublished manuscript).

83. Hensley, Smith, and Baugh, *Supreme Court Update,* 18 (table 1.4 of unpublished manuscript).

84. Judith A. Baer, "Advocate on the Court," 223.

85. Jeffrey Rosen, "New Look of Liberalism," 62.

86. Baer, "Advocate on the Court," 234.

87. Ibid., 236, n. 22.

88. Idelson, "Clinton's Choice of Ginsburg Signals Moderation." Baer attributes these qualities to Ginsburg's "lack of creativity and vision"; "Advocate on the Court," 234.

89. Breyer Hearings, 269.

90. Stephen G. Breyer, "On the Uses of Legislative History."

91. See, e.g., Holly Idelson, "Breyer's Liberal, Conservative Mix"; Gwen Ifill, "President Chooses Breyer, an Appeals Judge in Boston, for Blackmun's Court Seat," *New York Times,* May 14, 1994, A1; W. John Moore, "Ho Hum, It's Confirmation Hearings Time."

92. See *U.S. v. Lopez* (1995), 615 (Breyer dissenting); *Seminole Tribe v. Florida* (1996), 100 (Breyer dissenting); *Printz v. U.S.* (1997), 970 (Breyer dissenting); *College Savings Bank v. Florida Prepaid* (1999), 693 (Breyer dissenting); *Alden v. Maine* (1999), 760 (Breyer dissenting); *Florida Prepaid v. College Savings Bank* (1999), 648 (Breyer dissenting); *Kimel v. Florida Board of Regents* (2000), 92 (Breyer dissenting); *U.S. v. Morrison* (2000), 628, 655 (Breyer dissenting); *Alabama v. Garrett* (2001), 376 (Breyer dissenting).

93. E.g., *Good News Club v. Milford Central School* (2001), 128 (Breyer concurring); *Mitchell v. Helms,* 530 U.S. 793 (2000), 836 (Breyer concurring). For a brief review of Breyer's record in these and similar cases, see Ken I. Kersch, "Synthetic Progressivism."

94. Hensley, Smith, and Baugh, *Changing Supreme Court,* 88 (table 3.10); Hensley, Smith, and Baugh, *Supreme Court Update,* 19–24 (tables 1.5–1.10 of unpublished manuscript).

95. Hensley, Smith, and Baugh, *Supreme Court Update,* 18 (table 1.4 of unpublished manuscript).

96. Kagan, "Confirmation Messes," 937.

97. Segal, Cover, and Cameron, "Role of Ideology," 497–98.

98. See, e.g., Kennedy Hearings, 88–91.

99. Many political school critics of the confirmation process have argued against such senatorial deference to the president's choice. For an analysis of their arguments, see Chapter 8.

100. For an account of the ideological opposition to Thomas, see Robert Suro, "Thomas's Foes, Off to Slow Start, Say Swaying Public Will Be Hard," *New York Times,* September 8, 1991, 1. For expressions of dismay over Justice Thomas's voting record, by opponents—and some reluctant supporters—of his nomination, see Higginbotham, "Justice Clarence Thomas."

101. See, e.g., *City of Akron v. Akron Center for Reproductive Health,* 462 U.S. 416 (1983) and *Thornburgh v. College of Obstetricians and Gynecologists,* 476 U.S. 747 (1986). In both these cases, Justice O'Connor attacked the trimester approach the Court adopted in *Roe* as insupportable. In *Webster v. Reproductive Health Services,* 492 U.S. 490 (1989), Justices Kennedy and O'Connor voted to uphold a state's ban

on the use of public employees and facilities for performing abortions and a requirement that doctors test the viability of a fetus that is twenty weeks old or more before
performing an abortion.

102. 505 U.S. 833. The three justices' defense of *Roe* on its own merits takes up
three pages (850–53), the argument for adhering to *stare decisis* ten pages (854–64),
and the argument for upholding the Court's institutional integrity five pages
(864–69).

103. For Kennedy and O'Connor's opinions on affirmative action, see above,
notes 52, 63. See also David M. O'Brien, *Constitutional Law and Politics: Civil
Rights and Liberties,* 2:1441–46 ff.

104. See Chapter 2 for a discussion of the limits on nominee testimony imposed
by the requirement that judges not compromise their impartiality in future cases by
stating overly specific views at confirmation hearings.

105. Legal scholars have remarked on the way Justice Souter's early published
opinions evidenced his attempts to work his way through the difficult questions of
constitutional interpretation. See, e.g., the remarks of Paul Gewirtz in Linda Greenhouse, "Souter Anchoring the Court's New Center," *New York Times,* July 3, 1992,
A1, at A16. His increasingly liberal voting record also bespeaks the evolution of his
views (Hensley, Smith, and Baugh, *Supreme Court Update,* 18, table 1.4 of unpublished manuscript). After Justice Souter's first term on the Court, he was described as
a "quiet, dependable vote" for the Court's conservative majority. Scott P. Johnson and
Christopher E. Smith, "David Souter's First Term," 243. He is now one of the more
vocal justices during oral argument and is, as described above, clearly a member of
the Court's nonconservative wing.

106. For expressions of this view by nominee Sandra Day O'Connor and other
nominees, see Chapter 2.

107. The case was *Laird v. Tatum,* 409 U.S. 824 (1972). It became a major issue
upon Rehnquist's nomination for chief justice in 1986.

108. Authors who deny the need for frequent recusals (but not for frequent opinions justifying justices' decisions to participate in matters about which they have
spoken) are Steven Lubet, "Confirmation Ethics," 253–59; and Albert P. Melone,
"Senate's Confirmation Role," 76–78.

109. Scalia's opinion is at *Cheney v. U.S. District Court,* 2004 U.S. Lexis 2008
(March 18, 2004). Conflicting views of legal ethicists are in Adam Liptak, "A Case
of Blind Justice Among a Bunch of Friends," *New York Times,* March 21, 2004, sec.
4, p. 5.

7. COURT PACKING AND AN ABERRANT COURT

1. Laurence H. Tribe, *God Save This Honorable Court,* 76.

2. Gary J. Simson, "Mired in the Confirmation Mess," 1044.

3. Nina Totenberg, "Confirmation Process," 1228.

4. Bruce Ackerman, "Transformative Appointments." For a statement of similar concerns, see Terri Jennings Peretti, "Restoring the Balance of Power."

5. Harold W. Stanley and Richard G. Niemi, *Vital Statistics*, 272–77. Of course, presidents only "nominate" justices, but in places I use the term *appoint* for convenience.

6. See S. Sidney Ulmer, "Supreme Court Appointments." Note that some of the figures in Ulmer's table 3 are incorrect. The figures given here have been recalculated from the formula for a Poisson distribution.

7. Henry J. Abraham, *Justices, Presidents, and Senators*, appendix C, 377–81.

8. Two other recent nominees have been something other than what the president truly desired. On the compromise nature of President Bill Clinton's nominations of Ruth Bader Ginsburg and Stephen Breyer, see Mark Silverstein and William Haltom, "You Can't Always Get What You Want"; John Anthony Maltese, *Selling*, 149–57.

9. The rejected nominee was Judge John J. Parker in 1930.

10. Fred P. Graham, "Carswell Denies He Tried to Balk Club's Integration," *New York Times*, January 28, 1970, 1; "The Tallahassee Transaction," *New York Times*, February 27, 1970, 36.

11. See Chapter 3.

12. Mark Silverstein, "The People, the Senate, and the Court," 52.

13. For a history of congressional actions in the 1970s aimed at correcting what members saw as an excess of presidential power at the expense of Congress, see James L. Sundquist, *Decline and Resurgence*.

14. New York Times, *New York Times Index*, vols. 9–50 (providing the nomination and confirmation dates for each justice appointed during this period). The confirmations of Eisenhower nominees Earl Warren, John Marshall Harlan II, William Brennan, and Potter Stewart were held up by a combination of Southern Democrats battling desegregation, conservative Republicans fearful of communism and "world government," and Senator William Langer of North Dakota, who opposed the nomination of anyone not from North Dakota (which has never been represented on the Supreme Court). See Abraham, *Justices, Presidents, and Senators*, 191–200.

15. Abraham reports that "Clearly, gender was *the* primary concern of the Reagan Administration in choosing Judge O'Connor" (emphasis in the original), although conservatism was also required. *Justices, Presidents, and Senators*, 284. Reagan also signaled the importance of gender when he called O'Connor "the most qualified woman" the administration could find. "Transcript of Remarks by Reagan and Nominee to High Court," *New York Times*, July 8, 1981, A12.

16. Bush's selection of Souter is in Abraham, *Justices, Presidents, and Senators*, 304–9. For the nomination of Ginsburg, see Thomas L. Friedman, "The 11th Hour Scramble: After Hoping for a 'Home Run' in Choosing a Justice, Clinton May Be Home Free," *New York Times*, June 15, 1993, A1. According to *Congressional Quarterly*, a "standing political imperative of avoiding a draining confirmation battle" dictated Clinton's choice of Breyer over Interior Secretary Bruce Babbitt, a more clearly liberal figure who would have encountered "stiff opposition" from Senate Republicans. Holly Idelson, "From 'Wealth of Talent'" (quotations at 1213, 1215).

17. Estimates of how frequently justices generally disappoint the president who nominated them range from less than 10 percent to more than 25 percent. See Henry

J. Abraham, "Can Presidents Really Pack the Supreme Court?" Abraham also notes President Truman's disappointment with Tom Clark, and President Eisenhower's disappointment with Earl Warren and William Brennan; 46. See also Kimberly A. Beuger and Christopher E. Smith, "Clouds in the Crystal Ball"; John B. Gates and Jeffrey B. Cohen, "Presidents, Supreme Court Justices" ; Edward V. Heck and Steven A. Shull, "Policy Preferences"; Terri Jennings Peretti, *In Defense of a Political Court,* 130–31; David W. Rohde and Harold J. Spaeth, *Supreme Court Decision Making,* 107–10; Robert Scigliano, *The Supreme Court and the Presidency,* 147.

18. Abraham, *Justices, Presidents, and Senators,* 191–97.

19. See Burger Hearings; U.S. Senate Committee on the Judiciary, *Nomination of Clement F. Haynsworth Jr.* (1969); U.S. Senate Committee on the Judiciary, *Nomination of G. Harrold Carswell* (1970); U.S. Senate Committee on the Judiciary, *Nomination of Harry A. Blackmun* (1970); U.S. Senate Committee on the Judiciary, *Nominations of William H. Rehnquist and Lewis F. Powell, Jr.* (1971).

20. See Jack M. Balkin and Sanford Levinson, "Understanding the Constitutional Revolution," 1073.

21. Ibid., 1085. The cases are *Shaw v. Reno,* 509 U.S. 630 (1993); *Miller v. Johnson,* 515 U.S. 900 (1995); *Shaw v. Hunt,* 517 U.S. 899 (1996); *Bush v. Vera,* 517 U.S. 952 (1996); *Abrams v. Johnson,* 521 U.S. 74 (1997).

22. The cases were, respectively, *Boerne v. Flores,* 521 U.S. 507 (1997); and *Dickerson v. U.S.,* 530 U.S. 428 (2000). The Rehnquist Court's claims of judicial supremacy, which sometimes quote the Warren Court, are discussed later in this chapter.

23. See Vincent Blasi, *Burger Court.*

24. David M. O'Brien, "Background Paper," 99. Archibald Cox has written that during the Reagan years, "extreme political conservatives" sought to engineer a conservative counterrevolution: *The Court and the Constitution,* 361. See also Herman Schwartz, *Packing the Courts.*

25. David A. Yalof, *Pursuit of Justices,* 188–95.

26. Ramesh Ponnuru, "Empty Souter."

27. Thomas R. Hensley, Christopher E. Smith, and Joyce A. Baugh, *Changing Supreme Court,* 3; personal communication from Thomas R. Hensley, June 22, 1998.

28. E.g., Thomas Geoghegan, "No Love Lost for Labor."

29. See, e.g., David Savage's account of how his and others' descriptions of the Rehnquist Court were contradicted by subsequent rulings. "Journalist's Perspective."

30. See Lino Graglia, "Order in the Court"; Steven Calabresi, "Out of Order."

31. Cass R. Sunstein, *One Case at a Time;* and (seeing the Rehnquist Court as mainly incrementalist), Ernest A. Young, "Judicial Activism," 1214–16.

32. E.g., Herman Schwartz, "Supreme Court's Federalism"; Balkin and Levinson, "Understanding the Constitutional Revolution"; and Stephen E. Gottlieb, *Morality Imposed.*

33. *Printz v. U.S.,* 521 U.S. 898 (1997).

34. *Alden v. Maine,* 527 U.S. 706 (1999). See also *New York v. U.S.,* 505 U.S. 144 (1992).

35. *Gregory v. Ashcroft,* 501 U.S. 452 (1991); *Seminole Tribe v. Florida,* 517

U.S. 44 (1996); *Alden v. Maine* (1999); *College Savings Bank v. Florida Prepaid*, 527 U.S. 666 (1999); *Florida Prepaid v. College Savings Bank*, 527 U.S. 627 (1999). *Kimel v. Florida*, 528 U.S. 62 (2000); *Alabama v. Garrett*, 531 U.S. 356 (2001).

36. *Gregory v. Ashcroft*, 457.

37. *Fed. Maritime Commiss'n v. S.C. Ports Authority*, 535 U.S. 743 (2002).

38. *Nevada Dep't of Human Resources v. Hibbs*, 538 U.S. 721 (2003).

39. *Solid Waste Agency v. U.S. Army Corps of Engineers*, 531 U.S. 159 (2001), 174; quotation from Clean Water Act (33 USCS 1344(a)).

40. *U.S. Term Limits v. Thornton*, 514 U.S. 779 (1995).

41. David M. O'Brien, *Constitutional Law and Politics: Struggles for Power and Governmental Accountability*, 1:660–64.

42. E.g., Richard H. Fallon Jr., "'Conservative' Paths."

43. Balkin and Levinson, "Understanding the Constitutional Revolution," 1058–59.

44. Ibid.

45. *Kimel v. Florida* (2000) (Stevens dissenting at 97); *Federal Maritime Administration v. South Carolina* (2002) (Breyer dissenting at 1881).

46. *O'Lone v. Shabazz*, 478 U.S. 342 (1987); *Lyng v. Northwest Indian Cemetery*, 485 U.S. 439 (1988); *Employment Division v. Smith*, 492 U.S. 872 (1990).

47. Respectively, *Church of the Lukumi Babalu v. Hialeah*, 508 U.S. 520 (1993); *Wooley v. Maynard*, 430 U.S. 705 (1977); and *McDaniel v. Paty*, 435 U.S. 618 (1978).

48. O'Brien, *Constitutional Law and Politics: Civil Rights and Civil Liberties*, 2:673.

49. These holdings were, in order, *Bowen v. Kendrick*, 487 U.S. 589 (1988); *Westside Community Schools v. Mergens*, 496 U.S. 226 (1990), *Lamb's Chapel v. Center Moriches School Dist.*, 508 U.S. 384 (1993), and *Good News Club v. Milford Central School*, 533 U.S. 98 (2001); *Agostini v. Felton*, 521 U.S. 203 (1997), overturning *Aguilar v. Felton*, 473 U.S. 402 (1985); *Zobrest v. Catalina Foothills School Dist.*, 509 U.S. 1 (1993); *Rosenberger v. University of Virginia*, 515 U.S. 819 (1995); and *Mitchell v. Helms*, 530 U.S. 793 (2000), overturning *Meek v. Pittenger*, 421 U.S. 349 (1975) and *Wolman v. Walter*, 433 U.S. 229 (1997).

50. *Zelman v. Simmons-Harris*, 536 U.S. 639 (2002).

51. *Locke v. Davey*, 124 S. Ct. 1307 (2004). An analysis of the holding is Ira C. Lupu and Robert W. Tuttle, "Hitting the Wall."

52. The decisions were, in order, *Texas Monthly v. Bullock*, 489 U.S. 1 (1989); *Edwards v. Aguillard*, 482 U.S. 578 (1987); *Kiryas Joel v. Grumet*, 512 U.S. 687 (1994); and *Lee v. Weisman*, 505 U.S. 577 (1992); *Santa Fe Independent School Dist. v. Doe*, 530 U.S. 290 (2000).

53. *County of Allegheny v. ACLU*, 492 U.S. 573 (1989).

54. The five 5–4 decisions favoring accommodation were *Bowen v. Kendrick* (1988); *Zobrest v. Catalina* (1993); *Rosenberger v. UVA* (1995); *Agostini v. Felton* (1997); and *Zelman v. Simmons-Harris* (2002). The two 5–4 decisions against accommodation were *Lee v. Weisman* (1992) and *County of Allegheny v. ACLU* (1989)—although in the latter case, the holding was actually mixed.

55. *Arizona v. Mauro*, 481 U.S. 520 (1987); *Pennsylvania v. Bruder*, 488 U.S. 9

(1988); *Duckworth v. Eagan,* 492 U.S. 195 (1989); *Michigan v. Harvey,* 494 U.S. 344 (1990); *Illinois v. Perkins,* 496 U.S. 292 (1990); *Davis v. U.S,* 512 U.S. 452 (1994); *Ohio v. Robinette,* 519 U.S. 33 (1996); *Texas v. Cobb,* 532 U.S. 162 (2001); *Brogan v. U.S.,* 522 U.S. 398 (1998); *McKune v. Lile,* 536 U.S. 24 (2002).

56. *O'Dell v. Netherland,* 521 U.S. 151 (1997); *Jones v. U.S.,* 527 U.S. 373 (1999).

57. *McClesky v. Zant,* 499 U.S. 467 (1991); *Coleman v. Thompson,* 501 U.S. 722 (1991); *Keeney v. Tampayo-Reyes,* 504 U.S. 1 (1992); *Brecht v. Abrahamson,* 507 U.S. 619 (1993); *Herrera v. Collins,* 506 U.S. 390 (1993); *Felker v. Turpin,* 518 U.S. 651 (1996) (*Felker* was decided unanimously, implying that the appointment of conservatives was not crucial in this case); *Calderon v. Thompson,* 523 U.S. 538 (1998); *Williams v. Taylor,* 529 U.S. 362 (2000).

58. *Pennsylvania v. Finley,* 481 U.S. 551 (1987); *Murray v. Giarratano,* 492 U.S. 1 (1989).

59. *Mickens v. Taylor,* 535 U.S. 162 (2002).

60. *U.S. v. Dixon,* 509 U.S. 688 (1993), overruling *Grady v. Corbin,* 495 U.S. 508 (1990); *Monge v. California,* 524 U.S. 721 (1998).

61. *Ewing v. California,* 538 U.S. 11 (2003); *Lockyer v. Andrade,* 538 U.S. 63 (2003).

62. *HUD v. Rucker,* 535 U.S. 125 (2002).

63. Authorizing greater seizures are *Caplin and Drysdale v. U.S.,* 491 U.S. 617 (1989); *U.S. v. Monsanto,* 491 U.S. 600 (1989); *Libretti v. U.S.,* 516 U.S. 29 (1995); *Bennis v. Michigan,* 516 U.S. 442 (1996); *U.S. v. Ursery,* 518 U.S. 267 (1996). Limiting seizures are *Alexander v. U.S.,* 509 U.S. 544 (1993); *Austin v. U.S.,* 509 U.S. 602 (1993); *U.S. v. A Parcel of Land,* 507 U.S. 111 (1993); *U.S. v. Good,* 510 U.S. 43 (1993).

64. *Griffin v. Wisconsin,* 483 U.S. 868 (1987); *New York v. Burger,* 482 U.S. 691 (1987); *O'Connor v. Ortega,* 480 U.S. 709 (1987); *U.S. v. Dunn,* 480 U.S. 294 (1987); *Illinois v. Krull,* 480 U.S. 340 (1987); *Colorado v. Bertine,* 479 U.S. 367 (1987); *Skinner v. Railway Labor Executives' Assn.,* 489 U.S. 602 (1989); *Treasury Employees v. Von Raab,* 489 U.S. 656 (1989); *U.S. v. Sokolow,* 490 U.S. 1 (1989); *California v. Hodari D.,* 499 U.S. 621 (1991); *Florida v. Bostick,* 501 U.S. 429 (1991); *Florida v. Jimeno,* 500 U.S. 248 (1991); *California v. Acevedo,* 500 U.S. 565 (1991); *Minnesota v. Dickerson,* 508 U.S. 366 (1993); *Arizona v. Evans,* 514 U.S. 1 (1995); *Vernonia School Dist. 47J v. Acton,* 515 U.S. 646 (1995); *Whren v. U.S.,* 517 U.S. 806 (1996); *Pennsylvania Board of Probation v. Scott,* 524 U.S. 357 (1998); *Wyoming v. Houghton,* 526 U.S. 295 (1999); *Minnesota v. Carter,* 525 U.S. 83 (1998); *Illinois v. Wardlow,* 528 U.S. 119 (2000); *Atwater v. Lago Vista,* 532 U.S. 318 (2001); *U.S. v. Knights,* 534 U.S. 112 (2001); *U.S. v. Arvizu,* 534 U.S. 266 (2002); *U.S. v. Drayton,* 536 U.S. 194 (2002); *Board of Education v. Earls,* 536 U.S. 822 (2002). The drug testing of students approved in *Vernonia* and *Earls* did not involve criminal sanctions against those identified as drug users.

65. *Payne v. Tennessee,* 501 U.S. 808 (1991). The precedents were *Booth v. Maryland,* 482 U.S. 496 (1987); and *South Carolina v. Gathers,* 490 U.S. 805 (1989).

66. Respectively, *Kansas v. Hendricks*, 521 U.S. 346 (1997); *Miller v. French*, 530 U.S. 327 (2000); *Stanford v. Kentucky*, 492 U.S. 361 (1989).

67. *Jacobson v. U.S.*, 503 U.S. 540 (1992).

68. *Williams v. Taylor*, 529 U.S. 362 (2000); *Alabama v. Shelton*, 535 U.S. 654 (2002); *Wiggins v. Smith*, 123 S. Ct. 2527 (2003).

69. *Ohio v. Reiner*, 532 U.S. 17 (2001); *Dickerson v. U.S.* (2000), 443.

70. *Hudson v. McMillian*, 502 U.S. 1 (1992); *Helling v. McKinney*, 509 U.S. 25 (1993); *Farmer v. Brennan*, 511 U.S. 825 (1994); *U.S. v. Bajakajian*, 524 U.S. 321 (1998).

71. *Dep't of Revenue v. Kurth Ranch*, 511 U.S. 767 (1994).

72. *Chicago v. Morales*, 527 U.S. 41 (1999).

73. *Stogner v. California*, 123 S. Ct. 2446 (2003).

74. *Richardson v. McKnight*, 521 U.S. 399 (1997); *Hope v. Pelzer*, 536 U.S. 730 (2002).

75. *Morgan v. Illinois*, 504 U.S. 719 (1992); *Sullivan v. Louisiana*, 508 U.S. 275 (1993); *Simmons v. South Carolina*, 512 U.S. 154 (1994); *Kyles v. Whitley*, 514 U.S. 419 (1995); *Cooper v. Oklahoma*, 517 U.S. 348 (1996); *Apprendi v. New Jersey*, 530 U.S. 466 (2000); *Penry v. Johnson*, 532 U.S. 782 (2001); *Kelly v. South Carolina*, 534 U.S. 246 (2002).

76. *Arizona v. Hicks*, 480 U.S. 321 (1987); *Chandler v. Miller*, 520 U.S. 305 (1997); *Knowles v. Iowa*, 525 U.S. 113 (1998); *Wilson v. Layne*, 526 U.S. 603 (1999); *Florida v. J.L.*, 529 U.S. 266 (2000); *Indianapolis v. Edmond*, 531 U.S. 32 (2000); *Bond v. U.S.*, 529 U.S. 334 (2000); *Kyllo v. U.S.*, 533 U.S. 27 (2001); *Ferguson v. Charleston*, 532 U.S. 67 (2001).

77. *Stringer v. Black*, 505 U.S. 222 (1992); *Withrow v. Williams*, 507 U.S. 680 (1993); *McFarland v. Scott*, 512 U.S. 849 (1994); *Garlotte v. Fordice*, 515 U.S. 39 (1995); *Lonchar v. Thomas*, 517 U.S. 314 (1996); *Lindh v. Murphy*, 521 U.S. 320 (1997); *Bousley v. U.S.*, 523 U.S. 614 (1998); *Hohn v. U.S.*, 524 U.S. 236 (1998); *Stewart v. Martinez-Villareal*, 523 U.S. 637 (1998); *Slack v. McDaniel*, 529 U.S. 473 (2000); *Williams v. Taylor*, 529 U.S. 420 (2000); *Miller-El v. Cockrell*, 537 U.S. 322 (2003). The immigration cases were *Zadvydas v. Davis*, 533 U.S. 678 (2001) and *INS v. St. Cyr*, 533 U.S. 289 (2001).

78. *Zadvydas v. Davis* (2001).

79. *Atkins v. Virginia*, 536 U.S. 304 (2002), overturning *Penry v. Lynaugh*, 492 U.S. 302 (1989).

80. *U.S. v. Lopez*, 514 U.S. 549 (1995).

81. 529 U.S. 598 (2000).

82. 529 U.S. 848 (2000).

83. *U.S. v. Lopez* (1995), 560–63, 568 (quotation at 568).

84. Ibid., 569–74 (quotation at 574).

85. Ibid., 564–65; *U.S. v. Morrison* (2000), 612–13.

86. Official Transcript, Proceedings Before the Supreme Court of the United States: *U.S. v. Lopez*, Case No. 93-1260, November 8, 1994, 6–7, 10, 13, 22–23.

87. *U.S. v. Lopez* (1995), 616–17.

88. Laurence H. Tribe, *American Constitutional Law,* 824.

89. Balkin and Levinson, "Understanding the Constitutional Revolution" (quotations at 1101).

90. See *U.S. v. Lopez* (1995) (Thomas concurring at 584–603); *Printz v. U.S.* (1997) (Thomas concurring at 946).

91. *Richmond v. Croson,* 488 U.S. 469 (1989); *Adarand v. Pena,* 515 U.S. 200 (1995). *Adarand* overturned *Metro Broadcasting v. FCC,* 497 U.S. 547 (1990).

92. *Richmond v. Croson* (1989), 493.

93. Ibid., 495.

94. Ibid., 499–505.

95. Ibid., 539–42, 551–52.

96. *University of California v. Bakke,* 438 U.S. 265 (1978).

97. 123 S. Ct. 2325 (2003).

98. Ibid., at 2341. *Gratz v. Bollinger,* 123 S. Ct. 2411 (2003) followed *Bakke*'s spirit by ruling out an admissions plan that awarded an automatic twenty-point bonus to applicants for undergraduate admissions.

99. *Grutter v. Bollinger,* 2347.

100. *McCleskey v. Kemp,* 481 U.S. 279 (1987); *U.S. v. Armstrong,* 517 U.S. 456 (1996).

101. *Shaw v. Reno* (1993); *Miller v. Johnson* (1995); *Shaw v. Hunt* (1996); *Bush v. Vera* (1996); *Abrams v. Johnson* (1997).

102. E.g., *Miller v. Johnson* (1995), 947–48 (Justice Ginsburg, dissenting); *Shaw v. Hunt* (1996), 946–51 (Justice Stevens, dissenting); *Bush v. Vera* (1996), 1057–62 (Justice Souter, dissenting).

103. *Lawyer v. Dep't of Justice,* 521 U.S. 567 (1997); *Hunt v. Cromartie,* 526 U.S. 1128 (1999); *Hunt v. Cromartie,* 532 U.S. 234 (2001).

104. *Georgia v. Ashcroft,* 123 S. Ct. 2498.

105. *Reno v. Bossier Parish,* 528 U.S. 320 (2000).

106. 42 U.S.C. 1973(c).

107. The principal cases were *Wards Cove Packing v. Atonio,* 490 U.S. 692 (1989); *Lorance v. AT&T,* 490 U.S. 900 (1989); *Martin v. Wilks,* 490 U.S. 755 (1989); *Patterson v. McLean Credit Union,* 491 U.S. 164 (1989); *EEOC v. Arabian American Oil Co.,* 499 U.S. 244 (1991).

108. *Kolstad v. ADA,* 527 U.S. 526 (1999).

109. *Desert Palace v. Costa,* 539 U.S. 90 (2003).

110. *Reeves v. Sanderson Plumbing,* 530 U.S. 133 (2000).

111. *EEOC v. Waffle House,* 534 U.S. 279 (2002).

112. *Amtrak v. Morgan,* 536 U.S. 101 (2002).

113. *Alexander v. Sandoval,* 532 U.S. 275 (2001).

114. Ibid., 295.

115. See, e.g., the cases following *Seminole Tribe* (1996), discussed above. Quotation from *Gonzaga Univ. v. Doe,* 536 U.S. 273 (2002), 325.

116. *Wisconsin v. Mitchell,* 508 U.S. 476 (1993); *Crawford-El v. Britton,* 523 U.S. 574 (1998).

117. *Clark v. Jeter,* 486 U.S. 456 (1988).

118. On age, see *Gregory v. Ashcroft,* 501 U.S. 452 (1991); on indigence, *M.L.B. v. S.L.J.,* 519 U.S. 102 (1996), 122; on mental retardation, *Heller v. Doe,* 509 U.S. 312 (1993).

119. *Toyota v. Williams,* 534 U.S. 184 (2002), 197.

120. On correctable impairments, see *Sutton v. United Airlines,* 527 U.S. 471 (1999); *Murphy v. United Parcel Service,* 527 U.S. 516 (1999), and *Albertson's v. Kirkingburg,* 527 U.S. 555 (1999).

121. *US Airways v. Barnett,* 535 U.S. 391 (2002).

122. 531 U.S. 356. They may still sue state officials for injunctive relief. In some cases, the federal government may sue a state on their behalf.

123. *Barnes v. Gorman,* 536 U.S. 181 (2002).

124. These decisions are, respectively, *Bragdon v. Abbott,* 524 U.S. 624 (1998); *PGA Tour v. Martin,* 532 U.S. 661 (2001); *Pennsylvania v. Yeskey,* 524 U.S. 206 (1998); *Olmstead v. L.C.,* 527 U.S. 581 (1999); *Cleveland v. Policy Management Systems,* 526 U.S. 795 (1999).

125. *Cedar Rapids v. Garrett,* 526 U.S. 66 (1999). The statute is 20 USCS 1401(a)(17).

126. *Board of Education of Oklahoma City v. Dowell,* 498 U.S. 237 (1991); *Freeman v. Pitts,* 503 U.S. 467 (1992); *Missouri v. Jenkins,* 515 U.S. 70 (1995).

127. David M. O'Brien, *Constitutional Law and Politics: Civil Rights and Liberties,* 2:1373.

128. *Batson v. Kentucky,* 476 U.S. 79 (1986); *Powers v. Ohio,* 499 U.S. 400 (1991); *Edmonson v. Leesville Concrete,* 500 U.S. 614 (1991); *Georgia v. McCollum,* 505 U.S. 42 (1992).

129. *Pennell v. San Jose,* 485 U.S. 1 (1988); *Yee v. Escondido,* 503 U.S. 519 (1992).

130. 483 U.S. 825 and 512 U.S. 374.

131. 512 U.S. 374, at 392.

132. 505 U.S. 1003 (1992).

133. 533 U.S. 606 (2001).

134. *Eastern Enterprises v. Apfel,* 524 U.S. 498 (1998).

135. *Phillips v. Washington Legal Foundation,* 524 U.S. 156 (1998).

136. *Brown v. Legal Foundation,* 538 U.S. 216 (2003).

137. *Tahoe-Sierra Preservation Council v. Tahoe Regional Planning Agency,* 535 U.S. 302 (2002).

138. Ibid., 320–23 (quotation at 322).

139. *Babbitt v. Sweet Home Chapter of Communities for a Great Oregon,* 515 U.S. 687 (1995).

140. 528 U.S. 167 (2000). The earlier decisions were *Lujan v. National Wildlife Federation,* 497 U.S. 871 (1990); *Lujan v. Defenders of Wildlife,* 504 U.S. 555 (1992); *Bennett v. Spear,* 520 U.S. 154 (1997); and *Steel Co. v. Citizens for a Better Environment,* 523 U.S. 83 (1998). For an assessment of these cases, see A. H. Barnett and Timothy D. Terrell, "Economic Observations."

141. *FDA v. Brown and Williamson,* 529 U.S. 120 (2000).

142. 531 U.S. 457 (2001), quotation at 472.

143. *Medtronic v. Lohr,* 518 U.S. 470 (1996).

144. *Amchem Products v. Windsor,* 521 U.S. 591 (1997).

145. *Norfolk and Western Ry. v. Ayers,* 538 U.S. 135 (2003).

146. *Ortiz v. Fibreboard Corp.,* 527 U.S. 815 (1999).

147. *Devlin v. Scardelletti,* 536 U.S. 1 (2002).

148. *State Farm v. Campbell,* 538 U.S. 408 (2003). The earlier cases were *Pacific Mutual v. Haslip,* 499 U.S. 1 (1991); *Honda Motor Co. v. Oberg,* 512 U.S. 211 (1995); *BMW v. Gore,* 517 U.S. 559 (1996); and *Cooper Industries v. Leatherman,* 532 U.S. 424 (2001).

149. *Daubert v. Merrell Dow,* 509 U.S. 579 (1993); *Kumho Tire v. Carmichael,* 526 U.S. 137 (1999).

150. *State Oil v. Khan,* 522 U.S. 3 (1997) and *Quality King Distributors v. L'Anza Research International,* 523 U.S. 135 (1998).

151. Eleanor Fox, "In Business We Trust."

152. *Morrison v. Olson,* 487 U.S. 654 (1988).

153. Charles Fried, *Order and Law,* 153–55.

154. 531 U.S. 457 (2001). Writing only for himself in a concurrence, Justice Thomas suggested that even the 1930s standard might have permitted unconstitutional delegations; 486–87.

155. 524 U.S. 417 (1998).

156. See, e.g., *Felker v. Turpin,* 518 U.S. 651 (1996); *Reno v. American-Arab Anti-Discrimination Committee,* 525 U.S. 471 (1999); *Williams v. Taylor,* 529 U.S. 362 (2000).

157. *INS v. St. Cyr* (2001); *Zadvydas v. Davis* (2001).

158. Respectively, *U.S. v. Morrison* (2000), 616; *Boerne v. Flores* (1997), 536; *Clinton v. Jones,* 520 U.S. 681 (1997), 703.

159. *Legal Services Corp. v. Velazquez,* 531 U.S. 533 (2001), 545; *Dickerson v. U.S.* (2000), 437; *Boerne v. Flores* (1997), 536.

160. *Nixon v. U.S.,* 506 U.S. 224 (1993), 238 (citing *Powell v. McCormack,* 395 U.S. 486 (1969), 521 and *Baker v. Carr,* 369 U.S. 186 (1962), 211); *Miller v. Johnson* (1995), 922 (citing *Baker v. Carr* (1962), 211); *U.S. v. Morrison* (2000), 616 (citing *Cooper v. Aaron,* 358 U.S. 1 (1958), 18).

161. 418 U.S. 683 (1974), 703.

162. Some criticisms of judicial supremacy are Akhil Reed Amar and Alan Hirsch, *For the People;* Louis Fisher and Neal Devins, *Political Dynamics;* Mark Tushnet, *Taking the Constitution Away from the Courts.* A defense of judicial supremacy is Larry Alexander and Frederick Schauer, "On Extrajudicial Constitutional Interpretation."

163. Michael C. Dorf and Barry Friedman, "Shared Constitutional Interpretation," 63.

164. Ruth Colker and James J. Brudney, "Dissing Congress." See also the remarks of Walter Dellinger in Warren Richey, "Court Rebounds from *Bush v. Gore,*" *Christian Science Monitor,* July 2, 2001, 1; Tony Mauro, "Difficult to Pin Label on This Court."

165. 531 U.S. 98 (2000). An article criticizing this decision and the Rehnquist Court's allegedly self-aggrandizing version of judicial supremacy is Rachel Barkow, "More Supreme Than the Court?"

166. See, e.g., *Kimel v. Florida* (2000); *Alabama v. Garrett* (2001).

167. *Meritor Savings Bank v. Vinson*, 477 U.S. 57 (1986).

168. *International Union, United Automobile, Aerospace & Agricultural Implement Workers of America, UAW v. Johnson Controls*, 499 U.S. 187 (1991).

169. *Harris v. Forklift Systems*, 510 U.S. 17 (1993); *Oncale v. Sundowner Off-shore Services*, 523 U.S. 75 (1998).

170. *Faragher v. Boca Raton*, 524 U.S. 775 (1998); *Burlington Ind. v. Ellerth*, 524 U.S. 742 (1998). Praise of the rulings by women's and employers' groups is in Linda Greenhouse, "Court Spells Out Rules for Finding Sex Harassment," *New York Times*, June 27, 1998, A1. Complaints by conservatives are in Larry Reibstein, "The End of 'See-No-Evil.'"

171. *Franklin v. Gwinnet County Public Schools*, 503 U.S. 60 (1992); *Gebser v. Lago Vista Independent School Dist.*, 524 U.S. 274 (1998).

172. *Davis v. Monroe County Board of Education*, 526 U.S. 629 (1999) (Justice Kennedy, dissenting, at 654).

173. *J.E.B. v. Alabama ex rel. T.B.*, 511 U.S. 127 (1994).

174. *U.S. v. Virginia*, 518 U.S. 515 (1996).

175. 505 U.S. 833 (1992). For the public's approval of *Casey*, see Frank Newport and Leslie McAneny, "Whose Court Is It Anyhow?"

176. *Stenberg v. Carhart*, 530 U.S. 914 (2000). O'Connor's concurrence is at 950–51.

177. *National Organization for Women v. Scheidler*, 510 U.S. 249.

178. *Scheidler v. National Organization for Women*, 537 U.S. 393.

179. *Madsen v. Women's Health Center*, 512 U.S. 753 (1994); *Schenck v. Pro-Choice Network of Western New York*, 519 U.S. 357 (1997); *Hill v. Colorado*, 530 U.S. 703 (2000).

180. These decisions are, respectively, *Swidler and Berlin v. U.S.*, 524 U.S. 399 (1998); *Jaffee v. Redmond*, 518 U.S. 1 (1996); *Cruzan v. Director, Missouri Dep't of Health*, 497 U.S. 261 (1990).

181. *Washington v. Glucksburg*, 521 U.S. 702 (1997). The Court rejected an equal protection argument for such a right in a companion case: *Vacco v. Quill*, 521 U.S. 793 (1997).

182. *Washington v. Glucksburg* (1997), at 736, Justice O'Connor concurring; Justice Stevens concurring at 741–42; and Justice Souter concurring at 782.

183. *Troxel v. Granville*, 530 U.S. 57 (2000).

184. 536 U.S. 273.

185. *Texas v. Johnson*, 491 U.S. 397 (1989); *U.S. v. Eichman*, 496 U.S. 310 (1990).

186. *Sable Communications v. FCC*, 492 U.S. 115 (1989), and *Simon and Schuster v. New York Crime Victims Board*, 502 U.S. 105 (1991).

187. *44 Liquormart v. Rhode Island*, 517 U.S. 484 (1996); *Greater New Orleans*

Broadcasting Ass'n v. U.S., 527 U.S. 173 (1999); *Lorillard Tobacco v. Reilly,* 533 U.S. 525 (2001); *Thompson v. Western States Medical Center,* 535 U.S. 357 (2002). Thomas's view is at *44 Liquormart* (1996), 518.

188. *Bartnicki v. Vopper,* 532 U.S. 514 (2001).

189. 521 U.S. 844 (1997).

190. Ibid., 887.

191. *Ashcroft v. Free Speech Coalition,* 535 U.S. 234 (2002).

192. *Denver Area Consortium v. FCC,* 518 U.S. 727 (1996).

193. *U.S. v. Playboy Entertainment Group,* 529 U.S. 803 (2000).

194. *R.A.V. v. City of St. Paul,* 505 U.S. 377 (1992).

195. *Virginia v. Black,* 538 U.S. 343 (2003).

196. *Buckley v. American Constitutional Law Foundation,* 525 U.S. 182 (1999); *Watchtower Bible Society v. Stratton,* 536 U.S. 150 (2002); *Legal Services Corp. v. Velazquez* (2001); *Republican Party of Minnesota v. White,* 536 U.S. 765 (2002).

197. *Nixon v. Shrink Missouri Government PAC,* 528 U.S. 377 (2000); *Colorado Republican Federal Campaign Committee v. FEC,* 518 U.S. 604 (1996); *FEC v. Beaumont,* 123 S. Ct. 2200 (2003). The Burger Court's holdings were in *Buckley v. Valeo,* 424 U.S. 1 (1976).

198. *FEC v. Colorado Republican Federal Campaign Committee,* 533 U.S. 431 (2001).

199. 124 S. Ct. 619 (2003).

200. Burt Neuborne, "First Amendment for the Rich?"

201. 524 U.S. 569 (1998).

202. Ibid., 581–83.

203. *Reno v. American-Arab Anti-Discrimination Committee* (1999).

204. 500 U.S. 173 (1991).

205. 539 U.S. 194 (2003).

206. "First Amendment for the Rich?"

207. *Romer v. Evans,* 517 U.S. 620 (1996).

208. 123 S. Ct. 2472.

209. 478 U.S. 186. *Lawrence* also struck antisodomy laws applying to heterosexuals.

210. *Lawrence v. Texas,* Justice O'Connor concurring at 2484.

211. *Hurley v. Irish-American Gay, Lesbian, and Bisexual Group of Boston,* 515 U.S. 557 (1995).

212. *Boy Scouts of America v. Dale,* 530 U.S. 640 (2000).

213. Thomas R. Hensley, Christopher E. Smith, and Joyce A. Baugh, *Supreme Court Update: 2001* (unpublished manuscript, January 2002), 18 (table 1.4).

214. *Vacco v. Quill* (1997); *Washington v. Glucksburg* (1997).

215. *Boerne v. Flores* (1997). The three dissenters did not question the majority's holding that Congress may not define a civil liberty more broadly than the Court. One dissenter, Justice O'Connor, explicitly accepted it; 655.

216. *HUD v. Rucker* (2002).

217. This classification is very clear from an examination of voting in civil rights

and liberties cases between 1986 and 2001. Hensley, Smith, and Baugh, *Supreme Court Update,* 11–13; 17, 18 (tables 1.3 and 1.4 of unpublished manuscript).

218. *Zelman v. Simmons-Harris* (2002).

219. Brannon P. Denning and Glenn H. Reynolds, "Rulings and Resistance."

220. *Grutter v. Bollinger* (2003), 2347, where the Court expressed its expectation that "the use of racial preferences will no longer be necessary" in another twenty-five years.

221. Hensley, Smith, and Baugh, *Supreme Court Update* (unpublished manuscript), 12.

222. See, e.g., Joan Biskupic, "O'Connor, the 'Go-to' Justice," *USA Today,* July 12, 2000, A1; Warren Richey, "A Defining Term for High Court," *Christian Science Monitor;* October 4, 1999, 1; David J. Garrow, "Rehnquist Reins"; Earl M. Maltz, "Anthony Kennedy"; Nancy Maveety, "Justice Sandra Day O'Connor."

223. Thomas, Hensley, and Baugh, *Supreme Court Update* (unpublished manuscript), 12–13; 19–24 (tables 1.5 through 1.10).

224. See "The Statistics" section of the annual "Leading [Supreme Court] Cases" article in the November issue of the *Harvard Law Review;* Hensley, Smith, and Baugh, *Supreme Court Update* (unpublished manuscript), 13, 25 (table 1.11); Lawrence Sirovich, "Pattern Analysis," 7433–34.

225. David O'Brien makes this point in "Charting the Rehnquist Court's Course," 988–89.

226. Geoghegan, "No Love Lost," 35–36.

227. O'Brien, *Constitutional Law and Politics: Struggle for Power and Governmental Accountability,* 1:167–72.

228. A step in this direction was *McMillian v. Monroe County,* 520 U.S. 781 (1997).

229. See Balkin and Levinson, "Understanding the Constitutional Revolution," 1057.

230. Even some of the Court's harshest critics describe its federalism decisions this way. Balkin and Levinson, "Understanding the Constitutional Revolution," 1058–59.

231. Justice O'Connor suggested a constitutional means of doing so in *Stenberg v. Carhart,* 950–51.

232. Then ten were Burger (1969), Blackmun (1970), Powell and Rehnquist (1972), Stevens (1975), O'Connor (1981), Scalia (1986), Kennedy (1988), Souter (1990), and Thomas (1991).

233. For Stewart and Powell's centrist records, see Abraham, *Justices, Presidents, and Senators,* 205–7 and 263–67, respectively.

234. See n. 8 above.

235. William H. Rehnquist, "Presidential Appointments to the Supreme Court," 319–30 (quotation at 320–21).

236. Ackerman, "Transformative Appointments"; Peretti, "Restoring the Balance of Power"; Totenberg, "Confirmation Process," 1228.

237. See Jeffrey J. Mondak and Shannon Ishiyama Smithey, "Dynamics of Public Support," and sources therein.

238. Ibid. See also David G. Barnum, "Supreme Court and Public Opinion"; Benjamin I. Page and Robert Y. Shapiro, "Effects of Public Opinion on Policy"; Thomas R. Marshall, *Public Opinion.* Marshall finds that High Court rulings are especially likely to agree with public opinion in times of "crisis," when public attentiveness to the Court is greatest; 83. Thomas R. Marshall and Joseph Ignagni, "Supreme Court and Public Support"; Kevin McGuire and James Stimson, "The Least Dangerous Branch Revisited"; William Mishler and Reginald S. Sheehan, "Supreme Court as a Countermajoritarian Institution." For the period 1981 to 1989, Mishler and Sheehan (their fig. 1) report a growing divergence between an index of the liberalism of the public mood, which seemingly became more liberal over those years, and an index of the liberalism of the Court's opinions, which became more conservative. An inspection of the two indices plotted against each other readily reveals, however, that this seeming divergence depends heavily on a sharp drop in the measured liberalism of the Court's decisions in 1988–89.

239. Alexander M. Bickel, *Least Dangerous Branch;* Robert G. McCloskey, *American Supreme Court.*

240. Gregory A. Caldeira and James L. Gibson, "Etiology of Public Support" (quotations at 659).

241. Data on public "confidence" in the Court from 1973 to June 2001 is in Frank Newport, "Military Retains Top Position," 55. The 2003 figure is from a CNN/Gallup/ *USAToday* poll taken in June 2003 and reported in http://nationaljournal.com/members/ polltrack/2003/national/03courts.htm.

242. Newport, "Military Retains Top Position," 55; CNN/Gallup/*USAToday* poll, available at: http://nationaljournal.com/members/polltrack/2003/national/03courts. htm.

243. Wendy W. Simmons, "Election Controversy Apparently Drove Partisan Wedge into Attitudes Towards Supreme Court," *Gallup Poll Releases,* January 16, 2001. Available at: http://www.gallup.com/poll/releases/pr010116.asp.

244. Newport, "Military Retains Top Position," 52.

245. Ibid., 54.

246. 505 U.S. 833 (1992), 855–56.

247. Newport and McAneny, "Whose Court Is It Anyhow?", 51.

248. Joseph Tanenhaus and Walter F. Murphy, "Patterns of Public Support," 31–33.

249. Richard G. Niemi, John Mueller, and Tom W. Smith, *Trends in Public Opinion,* 136.

250. Richard Morin, "Crime Time: The Fear, the Facts," *Washington Post,* January 30, 1994, C1.

251. *Atkins v. Virginia,* 316.

252. Five percent "somewhat disagree[d]" and 8 percent "completely disagree[d]." http://nationaljournal.com/members/polltrack/2003/issues/03homosexuality.htm.

253. "Race and Ethnicity," Question 39B.

254. CNN/*USA Today*/Gallup, available at: http://www.publicagenda.org/issues/ major_proposals_detail.cfm?issue_type=race&list=7.

255. The latter case is *Grutter v. Bollinger.*

256. Polls cited are by the Pew Research Center, May 2003, reported at http://nationaljournal.com/members/polltrack/2003/issues/03affirmativeaction.htm#1.

257. ABC News/*Washington Post* Poll, January 2003, reported at ibid.

258. Ibid. A similar result from a *Los Angeles Times* poll in 2003 is reported here as well.

259. *University of California v. Bakke* (1978).

260. *Gratz v. Bollinger* (2003).

261. The language is that of Tinsley E. Yarbrough, *Rehnquist Court,* 253.

262. For negative reaction to the flag-burning rulings, see Tamar Jacoby, Ann McDaniel, and Peter McKillup, "Fight for Old Glory." Nine years after the first flag-burning decision, 79 percent of respondents in an ABC News/*Washington Post* poll agreed that flag burning "should be illegal," but only 50 percent favored a constitutional amendment to outlaw it (http://pollingreport.com/civil.htm). Nearly forty years after the Supreme Court banned public school prayers in the early 1960s, Americans supported school prayer by a two-to-one margin; http://www.pollingreport.com/educatio.htm#Prayer. In a 1999 Gallup poll, respondents favored "a constitutional amendment to limit the number of terms which members of Congress and the U.S. Senate can serve" by a margin of 73 percent to 24 percent; http://www.pollingreport.com/congress.htm#Term.

263. In *U.S. v. Carlton,* Scalia, joined by Thomas, asserted that "The Due Process Clause guarantees no substantive rights, but only (as it says) process." 512 U.S. 26 (1994) (quotation at 40).

264. *Michael H. v. Gerald D.,* 491 U.S. 110 (1989) (plurality opinion by Scalia at 127); O'Connor and Kennedy's contrary view is at 132.

8. CONCLUSION: REFORMING A MACHINE THAT WOULD RUN OF ITSELF

1. George L. Watson and John A. Stookey, *Shaping America,* 15.

2. Ibid., 15–16.

3. Lee Epstein et al., *Supreme Court Compendium,* table 4-13, 327–28.

4. D. Grier Stephenson Jr., *Campaigns and the Court,* ix.

5. Watson and Stookey, *Shaping America,* 220–21.

6. Steven Brill, "Where Have All Our Leaders Gone?"; Michael J. Gerhardt, "Divided Justice"; Joerg W. Knipprath, "The Judicial Appointment Process," 180; William G. Ross, "Supreme Court Appointment Process," 998; Barbara Sinclair, "Senate Process."

7. Ruth Bader Ginsburg, "Confirming Supreme Court Justices."

8. Segal and Spaeth, *Attitudinal Model.*

9. Henry J. Abraham, "Can Presidents Really Pack the Supreme Court?"; Kimberly A. Beuger and Christopher E. Smith, "Clouds in the Crystal Ball"; John B. Gates and Jeffrey B. Cohen, "Presidents, Supreme Court Justices"; Edward V. Heck and Steven A. Shull, "Policy Preferences"; Terri Jennings Peretti, *In Defense of a Political Court,* 130–31; David W. Rohde and Harold J. Spaeth, *Supreme Court*

Decision Making, 107–10; Robert Scigliano, *The Supreme Court and the Presidency,* 147.

10. These suggestions are discussed later in this chapter.

11. E.g., Stuart Taylor Jr., "Supreme Disappointment"; David Strauss and Cass R. Sunstein, "The Senate, the Constitution," 1518; Howard C. Anawalt, "Choosing Justice," 58.

12. Senate, Senate Democratic Task Force on the Confirmation Process, "Report of the Task Force on the Confirmation Process" (hereafter "Task Force Report"), *Congressional Record* 102nd Cong., 2nd sess., 1992, 138: S895-S898; Senate, Senate Resolution 194, 102nd Cong., 1st sess., 1991 (resolution submitted by Senator Paul Simon, D-IL); Paul Simon, "Advice and Consent."

13. Dennis E. Curtis, "The Fake Trial," 1529; Glenn H. Reynolds, "Taking Advice Seriously," 1580; Strauss and Sunstein, "The Senate, the Constitution," 1514.

14. See, e.g., Ray Forrester, "A Call for Integrity," 18.

15. Ross, "Supreme Court Appointment Process," 1000–1002; Senate Resolution 194 (1991); Senate, "Task Force Report," S898; Paul Simon, "Advice and Consent"; Walter Dellinger in Neil Skene, "Advice and Consent."

16. Ross, "Supreme Court Appointment Process," 1001–3.

17. Fred Strasser and Marcia Coyle, "Task Force Calls for Nomination Cooperation," *National Law Journal,* February 17, 1992, 29.

18. On Bill Clinton's purported "obsession" with "quick and painless" confirmations, see David A. Yalof, *Pursuit of Justices,* 190, 196–205 (quotation at 190). On Clinton's consultations with senators before the nominations of Ruth Bader Ginsburg and Stephen Breyer, see, respectively, Yalof, *Pursuit of Justices,* 200, and Henry J. Abraham, *Justices, Presidents, and Senators,* 323. On Clinton's use of trial balloons, see Yalof, *Pursuit of Justices,* 197–99. On President George H. W. Bush's considerable sensitivity to confirmability, see Yalof, *Pursuit of Justices,* 190–96. On the Ford Administration's concern to avoid a confirmation fight and its consultations with senators before nominating John Paul Stevens, see Yalof, *Pursuit of Justices,* 128–30. On Richard Nixon's use of trial balloons, see Abraham, *Justices, Presidents, and Senators,* 14–15.

19. E.g., Strauss and Sunstein, "The Senate, the Constitution," 1519; Gary J. Simson, "Thomas's Supreme Unfitness," 657–58.

20. Thomas Hearings, pt. 1, 178, 236, 452, 481–82, 494.

21. Senate, "Task Force Report," S896.

22. Thomas Hearings, pt. 1, 110–29, 267–77.

23. On the use of murder boards in the case of Clarence Thomas, see Jane Mayer and Jill Abramson, *Strange Justice,* 211–12.

24. Jeffrey A. Segal, Albert D. Cover, and Charles M. Cameron, "Role of Ideology," 497–98; Segal and Spaeth, *Attitudinal Model.*

25. See above, n. 5.

26. In the floor debate on the Thomas nomination, several Democratic senators cited Thomas's refusal to answer questions candidly—in addition to his ideology—to justify their rejection of his nomination: Senator Gore, speaking on the nomination

of Judge Clarence Thomas, *Congressional Record,* 102nd Cong., 1st sess. (October 8, 1991), 137: S14533; Senator Bumpers, S14533–35; Senator Simon (October 15, 1991), S14641; Senator Kennedy, S14642; Senator Byrd, S14633–34. In March 2002, Democrats on the Judiciary Committee, citing the nominee's ideology, rejected President George W. Bush's nomination of federal district court judge Charles Pickering for a seat on the Fifth Circuit Court of Appeals. Neil A. Lewis, "Panel Rejects Bush Nominee for Judgeship," *New York Times,* March 15, 2002, A1. In September 2002, Democrats cited ideology to defeat Bush's nomination of Priscilla Owen for a seat on that same court. Neil A. Lewis, "Democrats Reject Bush Pick in Battle over Court Balance," *New York Times,* September 6, 2002, A1. In 2003, Democrats successfully filibustered the nomination of Miguel Estrada for the federal Appeals Court in Washington, partly on the ground that he was unwilling to answer questions at his confirmation hearing and partly on the ground of his ideology. Neil A. Lewis, "Stymied by Democrats in Senate, Bush Court Pick Finally Gives Up," *New York Times,* September 5, 2003, A1.

27. Calvin R. Massey, "Commentary on the Supreme Court Nomination Process," 14–16; Simson, "Thomas's Supreme Unfitness," at 649–51. These authors believe that simple legislation or a change in the Senate rules could effect this procedural reform. There is good reason to doubt this belief. Ross, "Supreme Court Appointment Process," 1039–40.

28. Carl Hulse, "The Supreme Court: Judicial Vacancies; GOP Pushes Easier Rule on Filibusters," *New York Times,* June 25, 2003, A22.

29. D. Grier Stephenson Jr. has expressed such a sentiment: "[J]ustices of the United States Supreme Court succeed as credible constitutional authorities to the extent that they are persuasive that it is the Constitution, not their individual preferences, that speaks." *Campaigns and the Court,* 239. Similarly, Abner Mikva: "When the Court is perceived to be apolitical, wise, and impartial, the people have evinced a willingness to abide by its decisions. But if the Court is viewed simply as a Congress in black robes, the Court's ability to perform its constitutional function is threatened." "How Should We Select Our Judges?", 555.

30. E.g., Strauss and Sunstein, "The Senate, the Constitution," 1519; Taylor, "Supreme Disappointment"; and Michael J. Gerhardt, "Divided Justice," 991–93.

31. William G. Ross, "Functions, Roles, and Duties" (quotation at 634).

32. On its existence, see John P. Frank, "Are the Justices Quasi-Legislators Now?", 921–22, and Simson, "Thomas's Supreme Unfitness," 652–53; on its origins, Richard D. Friedman, "Transformation in Senate Response."

33. See the remarks of Republican Senator Arlen Specter in Taylor, "Supreme Disappointment"; Democratic Senator Dennis DeConcini in Thomas Report, 95; Democratic Senator Wyche Fowler speaking on the nomination of Clarence Thomas, *Congressional Record,* 102nd Cong., 1st sess. (October 3, 1991), 137: S14297; and Republican Senator Jake Garn (October 8, 1991), S14520.

34. Souter also benefited from an ardent campaign on his behalf by his friend and former colleague in New Hampshire, the much respected Senator Warren Rudman.

35. Ruth Marcus, "Conservative Mindset: Careful Jurist; Nominee's Legal Opinions Offer No Insight into His Views on Abortion, Civil Rights," *Washington Post,* July 25, 1990, A6.

36. Stephenson, *Campaigns and the Court.*

37. Strauss and Sunstein, "The Senate, the Constitution," 1494.

38. Some may cite Douglas Ginsburg as a second example of this phenomenon, but Ginsburg's views were not nearly as clearly objectionable as those of Robert Bork.

39. Strauss and Sunstein, "The Senate, the Constitution," 1494; Laurence H. Tribe, *God Save This Honorable Court,* 132; and Taylor, "Supreme Disappointment," suggesting the Senate achieve "full parity with the president" in the High Court appointment process.

40. As Senator Arlen Specter (R-PA) stated during the Thomas confirmation, "I continue to [believe] that there is still deference owed by the Senate [to the president's choice]. But that may change if the Court . . . becomes too revisionist or too extreme." Taylor, "Supreme Disappointment."

41. Watson and Stookey, *Shaping America,* 120–21.

Selected Bibliography

Abraham, Henry J. "Can the President Really Pack the Supreme Court?" In *An Essential Safeguard: Essays on the United States Supreme Court and Its Justices,* edited by D. Grier Stephenson Jr., 37–49. New York: Greenwood Press, 1991.

———. *Justices and Presidents: A Political History of Appointments to the Supreme Court.* New York: Oxford University Press, 1992.

———. *Justices, Presidents, and Senators: A History of the U.S. Supreme Court Appointments from Washington to Clinton,* rev. ed. Lanham, MD: Rowman and Littlefield, 1999.

———. *The Judicial Process: An Introductory Analysis of the Courts of the United States, England, and France.* 6th ed. New York: Oxford University Press, 1993.

Ackerman, Bruce A. "Transformative Appointments." *Harvard Law Review* 101 (1988): 1164–84.

Alexander, Larry, and Frederick Schauer. "On Extrajudicial Constitutional Interpretation." *Harvard Law Review* 110 (1997): 1359–87.

Amar, Akhil Reed, and Alan Hirsch. *For the People: What the Constitution Really Says About Your Rights.* New York: Free Press, 1998.

American Bar Association. *Official American Bar Association Guide to Approved Law Schools.* New York: Macmillan, 1998.

Anawalt, Howard C. "Choosing Justice." *St. John's Journal of Legal Commentary* 7 (Fall 1991): 49–60.

Asch, Sidney H. *The Supreme Court and Its Great Justices.* New York: Arco, 1971.

Asher, Herbert B. *Presidential Elections and American Politics: Voters, Candidates, and Campaigns Since 1952.* San Diego: Harcourt Brace, 1992.

Bader, William D. "Meditations on the Original: James Madison, Framer with Common Law Intentions—Ramifications in the Contemporary Supreme Court." *Vermont Law Review* 20 (Fall 1995): 5–17.

Baer, Judith A. "Advocate on the Court: Ruth Bader Ginsburg and the Limits of Formal Equality." In *Rehnquist Justice: Understanding the Court Dynamic,* edited by Earl M. Maltz, 216–40. Lawrence: University Press of Kansas, 2003.

Balkin, Jack M., and Sanford Levinson. "Understanding the Constitutional Revolution." *Virginia Law Review* 87 (2001): 1045–109.

Barkow, Rachel. "More Supreme Than the Court? The Fall of the Political Question Doctrine and the Rise of Judicial Supremacy." *Columbia Law Review* 102 (2002): 237–336.

Barnett, A. H., and Timothy D. Terrell. "Economic Observations on Citizen-Suit Provisions of Environmental Legislation." *Duke Environmental Law and Policy Forum* 12 (2001): 1–38.

Barnum, David G. "The Supreme Court and Public Opinion: Judicial Decision Making in the Post–New Deal Period." *Journal of Politics* 47 (1985): 652–66.

Bernstein, David. "Economic Regulation and Discrimination." *Lincoln Review* (Spring 1990): 19–27.

Berry, Jeffrey M. *The Interest Group Society.* New York: Longman, 1997.

Beuger, Kimberly A., and Christopher E. Smith. "Clouds in the Crystal Ball: Presidential Expectations and the Unpredictable Behavior of Supreme Court Appointees." *University of Akron Law Review* 27 (1993): 115–40.

Bickel, Alexander M. *The Least Dangerous Branch: The Supreme Court at the Bar of Politics.* Indianapolis: Bobbs-Merrill, 1962.

Biskupic, Joan. "Bush's Nominees Lack Baggage That Reagan's Often Carried." *Congressional Quarterly Weekly Report,* September 22, 1990, 3019–20.

———. "How the Thomas Nomination Differs from the Bork Fight." *Congressional Quarterly Weekly Report,* August 3, 1991, 2169.

———. "Thomas Hearings Illustrate Politics of the Process." *Congressional Quarterly Weekly Report,* September 21, 1991, 2688–89.

———. "Thomas Picks Up Support as Senate Nears Vote." *Congressional Quarterly Weekly Report,* October 5, 1991, 2867.

Black, Charles L., Jr. "A Note on Senatorial Consideration of Supreme Court Nominees." *Yale Law Journal* 79 (1970): 657–64.

Blasi, Vincent, ed. *The Burger Court: The Counter-Revolution That Wasn't.* New Haven, CT: Yale University Press, 1983.

Blaustein, Albert P., and Roy M. Mersky. *The First One Hundred Justices.* Hamden, CT: Archon Books, 1978.

Bork Hearings. U.S. Senate Committee on the Judiciary. *Nomination of Robert H. Bork to Be Associate Justice of the Supreme Court of the United States: Hearings Before the Committee on the Judiciary.* Parts 1 to 5. 100th Cong., 1st sess., September 15, 16, 17, 18, 19, 21, 22, 23, 25, 28, 29, and 30, 1987.

Bork Report. U.S. Senate Committee on the Judiciary. *Nomination of Robert H. Bork to Be an Associate Justice of the United States Supreme Court: Report of the Committee on the Judiciary.* 100th Cong., 1st sess., 1987. S. Exec. Rept 100-7.

Bork, Robert H. *Slouching Towards Gomorrah: Modern Liberalism and American Decline.* New York: Regan Books, 1996.

———. *The Tempting of America: The Political Seduction of the Law.* New York: Simon and Schuster, 1990.

Bradley, Robert C. "Who Are the Great Justices and What Criteria Did They Meet?"

In *Great Justices of the U.S. Supreme Court,* edited by William D. Pederson and Norman W. Provizer, 1–32. New York: Peter Lang, 1993.

Breyer Hearings. U.S. Senate Committee on the Judiciary. *Nomination of Stephen G. Breyer to Be an Associate Justice of the Supreme Court of the United States: Hearings Before the Committee on the Judiciary.* 103rd Cong., 2nd sess., 12, 13, 14, and 15, 1994.

Breyer Report. U.S. Senate Committee on the Judiciary. *Nomination of Stephen G. Breyer to Be an Associate Justice of the United States Supreme Court: Report Together with Additional Views.* 103rd Cong., 2nd sess. 1994. S. Exec. Rept. 103-31.

Breyer, Stephen G. "On the Uses of Legislative History in Interpreting Statutes." *Southern California Law Review* 65 (1992): 845–74.

Brill, Steven. "Where Have All Our Leaders Gone?" *American Lawyer,* November 1991, 5.

Brisbin, Richard. *Justice Antonin Scalia and the Court's Conservative Revival.* Baltimore: Johns Hopkins University Press, 1997.

Bronner, Ethan. *Battle for Justice: How the Bork Nomination Shook America.* New York: Norton, 1989.

Burger Hearings. U.S. Senate Committee on the Judiciary. *Nomination of Warren E. Burger to Be Chief Justice of the United States: Hearings Before the Committee on the Judiciary.* 91st Cong., 1st sess., June 3, 1969.

Burns, James McGregor. *Roosevelt: The Lion and the Fox.* New York: Harcourt, Brace, 1956.

Calabresi, Steven. "Out of Order." *Policy Review,* September–October 1996, 14–21.

Caldeira, Gregory A., and James L. Gibson. "The Etiology of Public Support for the Supreme Court." *American Journal of Political Science* 36 (1992): 635–64.

Caldeira, Gregory, Marie Hojnacki, and John R. Wright, "The Lobbying Activities of Organized Interests in Federal Judicial Nominations." *Journal of Politics* 62 (2000): 51–69.

Cameron, Charles M., Albert D. Cover, and Jeffrey A. Segal. "Senate Voting on Supreme Court Nominees: A Neoinstitutional Model." *American Political Science Review* 84 (1990): 525–34.

Cannon, Carl M. "Hooked on Polls." *National Journal,* October 17, 1998, 2438–41.

Carter, Stephen L. "The Confirmation Mess." *Harvard Law Review* 101 (1988): 1185–201.

———. "The Confirmation Mess, Revisited." *Northwestern University Law Review* 84 (1990): 962–75.

———. *The Confirmation Mess: Cleaning Up the Federal Appointments Process.* New York, Basic Books, 1994.

"Clarence Thomas Rises from Poverty to Supreme Court Nominee." *Jet,* July 22, 1991, 5.

Colker, Ruth, and James J. Brudney. "Dissing Congress." *Michigan Law Review* 100 (2001): 80–145.

Comiskey, Michael. "The Usefulness of Senate Confirmation Hearings for Judicial

Nominees: The Case of Ruth Bader Ginsburg." *PS: Political Science and Politics* 27 (1994): 224–27.

Counsel. U.S. Senate. *Report of the Temporary Special Independent Counsel.* May 13, 1992. Parts 1 and 2. Document 102-20.

Cox, Archibald. *The Court and the Constitution.* Boston: Houghton Mifflin, 1987.

Currie, George R. "A Judicial All-Star Nine." *Wisconsin Law Review* (1964): 3–31.

Curtis, Dennis E. "The Fake Trial." *Southern California Law Review* 65 (March 1992): 1523–530.

Danforth, John C. *Resurrection: The Confirmation of Clarence Thomas.* New York: Viking, 1994.

Denning, Brannon P., and Glenn H. Reynolds. "Rulings and Resistance: The New Commerce Clause Jurisprudence Encounters the Lower Courts." *Arkansas Law Review* 55 (2003): 1253–311.

Dickert, Jillian. "Privacy and Publicity: The Senate Confirmation of Clarence Thomas." Pt. 1. Kennedy School of Government Case Program, no. C16-92-1118.0.

———. "Privacy and Publicity: The Senate Confirmation of Clarence Thomas." Pt. 2. Kennedy School of Government Case Program, no. C16-92-1118.1.

Dorf, Michael C., and Barry Friedman. "Shared Constitutional Interpretation." *Supreme Court Review* 61 (2000): 61–107.

Elling, Richard C. "Ideological Change in the U.S. Senate: Time and Electoral Responsibilities." *Legislative Studies Quarterly* 7 (February 1982): 75–92.

Epstein, Lee, and Jack Knight. *The Choices Justices Make.* Washington, DC: Congressional Quarterly, 1998.

Epstein, Lee, Jeffrey A. Segal, Harold J. Spaeth, and Thomas G. Walker. *The Supreme Court Compendium: Data, Decisions and Developments.* 2nd ed. Washington, DC: Congressional Quarterly, 1996.

Fallon, Richard H., Jr. "The 'Conservative' Paths of the Rehnquist Court's Federalism Decisions." *University of Chicago Law Review* 69 (2002): 429–94.

Farrand, Max, ed. *The Records of the Federal Convention of 1787.* Rev. ed. New Haven, CT: Yale University Press, 1937.

Fein, Bruce. "A Court of Mediocrity." *ABA Journal,* October 1991, 74–79.

———. "Commentary: A Circumscribed Senate Confirmation Role." *Harvard Law Review* 102 (1989): 672–87.

Felice, John D., and Herbert F. Weisberg. "The Changing Importance of Ideology, Party, and Region in Confirmation of Supreme Court Nominees, 1953–1988." *Kentucky Law Journal* 77 (1989): 509–31.

"First Amendment for the Rich?" *Nation,* October 9, 2000, 25.

Fisher, Louis. *Constitutional Dialogues: Interpretation as Political Process.* Princeton, NJ: Princeton University Press, 1988.

Fisher, Louis, and Neal Devins. *Political Dynamics of Constitutional Law.* St. Paul, MN: West, 1996.

Flax, Jane. *The American Dream in Black and White: The Clarence Thomas Hearings.* Ithaca, NY: Cornell University Press, 1998.

Forrester, Ray. "A Call for Integrity." *Hastings Constitutional Law Quarterly* 19 (Fall 1991): 17–22.

Fox, Eleanor. "In Business We Trust." *Nation,* October 9, 2000, 31–32.

Frank, John P. "Are the Justices Quasi-Legislators Now?" *Northwestern University Law Review* 84 (Spring/Summer 1990): 921–24.

———. *Marble Palace.* New York: Knopf, 1958.

Frankfurter, Felix. "The Supreme Court in the Mirror of Justices." *University of Pennsylvania Law Review* 105 (1957): 781–96.

Frankfurter, Felix, and James M. Landis. *The Business of the Supreme Court.* New York: Macmillan, 1928.

Frankovic, Kathleen, and Joyce Gelb. "Public Opinion and the Thomas Nomination." *PS: Political Science and Politics* 25 (September 1992): 481–85.

Freedman, Monroe. "The Ethics of Clarence Thomas; Failure to Recuse Makes Judge Unfit to Sit on Supreme Court." *Connecticut Law Tribune,* September 9, 1991, 22.

Freund, Paul A. "Appointment of Justices: Some Historical Perspectives." *Harvard Law Review* 101 (1988): 1146–63.

Fried, Charles. *Order and Law: Arguing the Reagan Revolution; A Firsthand Account.* New York: Simon and Schuster, 1991.

Friedman, Lawrence. "The Limitations of Labeling." *Ohio Northern University Law Review* 20 (1993): 225–62.

Friedman, Richard D. "The Transformation in Senate Response to Supreme Court Nominees: From Reconstruction to the Taft Administration and Beyond." *Cardozo Law Review* 5 (1983): 1–95.

———. "Tribal Myths: Ideology and the Confirmation of Supreme Court Nominations." *Yale Law Journal* 95 (1986): 1283–320.

Gallup, George, and Frank Newport. "Confidence in Major U.S. Institutions at All-time Low." *Gallup Poll Monthly,* October 1991, 36–40.

Garrow, David J. "Justice Souter Emerges." *New York Times Magazine,* September 25, 1994, 36–43 ff.

———. "The Rehnquist Reins." *New York Times Magazine,* October 6, 1996, 65–71 ff.

Gates, John B., and Jeffrey B. Cohen. "Presidents, Supreme Court Justices, and Racial Equality Cases: 1954–1984." *Political Behavior* 10 (1988): 22–36.

Gauch, James E. "The Intended Role of the Senate in Supreme Court Appointments." *University of Chicago Law Review* 56 (1989): 337–65.

Geoghegan, Thomas. "No Love Lost for Labor." *Nation,* October 9, 2000, 35–36.

Gerhardt, Michael J. "Divided Justice: A Commentary on the Nomination and Confirmation of Justice Thomas." *George Washington Law Review* 60 (April 1992): 969–96.

Ginsburg Hearings. U.S. Senate Committee on the Judiciary. *Nomination of Ruth Bader Ginsburg to Be an Associate Justice of the United States Supreme Court: Hearings Before the Committee on the Judiciary.* 103rd Cong., 1st sess., July 20, 21, 22, and 23, 1993.

Ginsburg Report. U.S. Senate Committee on the Judiciary. *Nomination of Ruth Bader Ginsburg to Be an Associate Justice of the United States Supreme Court: Report Together with Additional Views.* 103rd Cong., 1st sess., 1993. S. Exec. Rept. 103-6.

Ginsburg, Ruth Bader. "Confirming Supreme Court Justices: Thoughts on the Second Opinion Rendered by the Senate." *University of Illinois Law Review* (1988): 101–17.

Gitenstein, Mark. *Matters of Principle: An Insider's Account of America's Rejection of Robert Bork's Nomination to the Supreme Court.* New York: Simon and Schuster, 1992.

Goldberg, Stephanie B., ed. "'What's the Alternative?' A Roundtable on the Confirmation Process." *ABA Journal* 78 (1992): 41–45.

Gottlieb, Stephen E. *Morality Imposed: The Rehnquist Court and Liberty in America.* New York: New York University Press, 2000.

Graglia, Lino. "Order in the Court." *National Review,* November 24, 1997, 48–49.

Graham, Fred P. "The Many-Sided Justice Fortas." *New York Times Magazine,* June 4, 1967, 26–27 ff.

Griffin, Stephen M. "Has the Hour of Democracy Come Round at Last? The New Critique of Judicial Review." *Constitutional Commentary* 17 (2000): 683–701.

Gunther, Gerald. *Individual Rights in Constitutional Law.* Westbury, NY: Foundation Press, 1992.

Hambleton, James E. "The All-Time All-Star All-Era Supreme Court." *American Bar Association Journal* 69 (1983): 463–64.

Hamilton, Alexander, James Madison, and John Jay. *The Federalist.* London: Penguin, 1987.

Hanks, Liza Weizman. "Justice Souter: Defining 'Substantive Neutrality' in an Age of Religious Politics." *Stanford Law Review* 48 (1996): 903–35.

Harris, Joseph P. *The Advice and Consent of the Senate: A Study of the Confirmation of Appointments by the United States Senate.* Berkeley: University of California Press, 1953.

Harris, Richard. *Decision.* New York: Dutton, 1971.

Hatch, Orrin G. "The Politics of Picking Judges." *Journal of Law and Politics* 6 (1989): 35–53.

Heck, Edward V., and Steven A. Shull. "Policy Preferences of Justices and Presidents: The Case of Civil Rights." *Law and Policy Quarterly* 4 (1982): 327–38.

Hensley, Thomas R., Christopher E. Smith, and Joyce A. Baugh. *The Changing Supreme Court: Civil Rights and Liberties.* Minneapolis, MN: West, 1997.

Hickok, Eugene W., Jr., "The Senate: Advice and Consent and Judicial Selection." National Legal Center for the Public Interest: White Paper. Vol. 4, no. 3, August 1992.

Higginbotham, A. Leon, Jr. "Justice Clarence Thomas in Retrospect." *Hastings Law Journal* 45 (1994): 1405–33.

Hill, Anita. *Speaking Truth to Power.* New York: Doubleday, 1997.

Hughes, Charles Evans. *The Supreme Court of the United States.* New York: Columbia University Press, 1928.

Hugick, Larry. "One Night Before Vote, Support for Thomas Remains Strong." *Gallup Poll Monthly,* October 1991, 23–27.

Idelson, Holly. "Breyer's Liberal, Conservative Mix Seems to Assure Confirmation." *Congressional Quarterly Weekly Report,* May 21, 1994, 1305–7.

———. "Clinton's Choice of Ginsburg Signals Moderation." *Congressional Quarterly Weekly Report,* June 19, 1993, 1569–74.

———. "From 'Wealth of Talent,' Clinton Picks Breyer." *Congressional Quarterly Weekly Report,* May 14, 1994, 1213–15.

———. "Quiet Confirmation Expected." *Congressional Quarterly Weekly Report,* July 17, 1993, 1875.

Jackson, Jacquelyne Johnson. "'Them Against Us': Anita Hill vs. Clarence Thomas." In *Court of Appeal: The Black Community Speaks Out on the Racial and Sexual Politics of Thomas v. Hill,* edited by Robert Chrisman and Robert L. Allen, 99–105. New York: Ballantine, 1992.

Jacoby, Tamar, Ann McDaniel, and Peter McKillup. "A Fight for Old Glory." *Newsweek,* July 3, 1989, 18–20.

Jacoby, Tamar, et al. "Spoiling for a Second Round." *Newsweek,* November 9, 1987, 42–45.

Johnson Scott P., and Christopher E. Smith. "David Souter's First Term on the Supreme Court: The Impact of a New Justice." *Judicature* 75 (1992): 238–43.

Kagan, Elena. "Confirmation Messes, Old and New." *University of Chicago Law Review* 62 (1995): 919–42.

Kan, Liang. "A Theory of Justice Souter." *Emory Law Journal* 45 (1996): 1373–427.

Kaplan, David A., and Bob Cohn. "A Frankfurter, Not a Hot Dog." *Newsweek,* June 28, 1993, 29.

Keck, Thomas M. "David H. Souter: Liberal Constitutionalism and the Brennan Seat." In *Rehnquist Justice: Understanding the Court Dynamic,* edited by Earl M. Maltz, 185–215. Lawrence: University Press of Kansas, 2003.

Kennedy Hearings. U.S. Senate Committee on the Judiciary. *Nomination of Anthony M. Kennedy to Be Associate Justice of the Supreme Court of the United States: Hearings Before the Committee on the Judiciary.* 100th Cong., 1st sess., December 14, 15, and 16, 1987.

Kersch, Ken I. "The Synthetic Progressivism of Stephen G. Breyer." In *Rehnquist Justice: Understanding the Court Dynamic,* edited by Earl M. Maltz, 241–76. Lawrence: University Press of Kansas, 2003.

Keller, Bill. "Reagan's Son." *New York Times Magazine,* January 26, 2003, 26–42 ff.

Knipprath, Joerg W. "The Judicial Appointment Process: An Appeal for Moderation and Self-Restraint." *St. John's Journal of Legal Commentary* 7 (1991): 179–91.

Lehrman, Lewis. "The Declaration of Independence and the Right to Life: One Leads Unmistakably from the Other." *American Spectator,* April 1987, 21–23.

Lerner, Max. "Has the Senate Gone Too Far? Courting Rituals." *New Republic,* February 1, 1988, 16–18.

Lubet, Steven. "Confirmation Ethics: President Reagan's Nominees to the United States Supreme Court." *Harvard Journal of Law and Public Policy* 13 (1990): 229–62.

Lupu, Ira C., and Robert W. Tuttle. "Hitting the Wall: Religion Is Still Special Under the Constitution, Says the High Court." *Legal Times,* March 15, 2004, 68–70.

Maltese, John Anthony. *The Selling of Supreme Court Nominees.* Baltimore: Johns Hopkins University Press, 1995.

Maltz, Earl M. "Anthony Kennedy and the Jurisprudence of Respectable Conservatism." In *Rehnquist Justice: Understanding the Court Dynamic,* edited by Earl M. Maltz, 140–56. Lawrence: University Press of Kansas, 2003.

Mansbridge, Jane, and Katherine Tate. "Race Trumps Gender: The Thomas Nomination in the Black Community." *PS: Political Science and Politics* 25 (1992): 488–92.

Marable, Manning. "Clarence Thomas and the Crisis of Black Political Culture." In *Race-ing, Justice, En-gendering Power: Essays on Anita Hill, Clarence Thomas, and the Construction of Social Reality,* edited by Toni Morrison, 61–85. New York: Pantheon Books, 1992.

Marshall, Thomas R. *Public Opinion and the Supreme Court.* Boston: Allen & Unwin, 1988.

Marshall, Thomas R., and Joseph Ignagni. "Supreme Court and Public Support for Rights Claims." *Judicature* 78 (1994): 146–51.

Massaro, John. *Supremely Political: The Role of Ideology and Presidential Management in Unsuccessful Supreme Court Confirmations.* Albany: State University of New York Press, 1990.

Massey, Calvin R. "Commentary on the Supreme Court Nomination Process: Getting There; A Brief History of the Politics of Supreme Court Appointments." *Hastings Constitutional Law Quarterly* 19 (Fall 1991): 1–16.

Mauro, Tony. "Difficult to Pin Label on This Court." *Legal Intelligencer,* July 3, 2000, 4.

Maveety, Nancy. "Justice Sandra Day O'Connor: Accommodation and Conservatism." In *Rehnquist Justice: Understanding the Court Dynamic,* edited by Earl M. Maltz, 103–39. Lawrence: University Press of Kansas, 2003.

Mayer, Jane, and Jill Abramson. *Strange Justice: The Selling of Clarence Thomas.* Boston: Houghton Mifflin, 1994.

McCloskey, Robert G. *The American Supreme Court.* Chicago: University of Chicago Press, 1960.

McGuire, Kevin, and James Stimson, "The Least Dangerous Branch Revisited: New Evidence on Supreme Court Responsiveness to Public Preferences." Paper delivered at the 58th Annual Meeting of the Midwest Political Science Association, Chicago, IL, April 27–30, 2000.

McHargue, Daniel. "Appointments to the Supreme Court of the United States: The Factors That Have Affected Appointments, 1789–1932." PhD thesis, UCLA, 1949.

Melone, Albert P. "The Senate's Confirmation Role in Supreme Court Nominations and the Politics of Ideology Versus Impartiality." *Judicature* 75 (1991): 68–79.

Mikva, Abner. "How Should We Select Our Judges in a Free Society?" *Southern Illinois University Law Journal* 16 (1992): 547–56.

Mishler, William, and Reginald S. Sheehan. "The Supreme Court as a Counter-majoritarian Institution? The Impact of Public Opinion on Supreme Court Decisions." *American Political Science Review* 87 (1993): 87–101.

Monaghan, Patrick. "'Substantively Due-Processing' the Black Population." *Lincoln Review* (Summer 1983): 45–59.

Mondak, Jeffrey J., and Shannon Ishiyama Smithey. "The Dynamics of Public Support for the Supreme Court." *Journal of Politics* 59 (1997): 1114–42.

Moore, John. "Ho Hum, It's Confirmation Hearings Time." *National Journal,* July 9, 1994, 1627–28.

Morrison, Toni. "Introduction: Friday on the Potomac." In *Raceing Justice, Engendering Power: Essays on Anita Hill, Clarence Thomas, and the Construction of Social Reality,* edited by Toni Morrison, vii–xxx. New York: Pantheon Books, 1992.

Murphy, Walter F. *Congress and the Court: A Case Study in the American Political Process.* Chicago: University of Chicago Press, 1962.

Murphy, Walter F., James E. Fleming, and Sotirios A. Barber. *American Constitutional Interpretation.* 2nd ed. Westbury, NY: Foundation Press, 1995.

Nagel, Stuart S. "Characteristics of Supreme Court Greatness." *Journal of the American Bar Association* 56 (1970): 957–59.

Neuborne, Burt. "First Amendment for the Rich?" *Nation,* October 9, 2000, 25–26.

Neustadt, Richard E. *Presidential Power: The Politics of Leadership from FDR to Carter.* New York: Wiley, 1980.

New York Times. *New York Times Index.* Vols. 9–50. New York: New York Times, 1921–62.

Newport, Frank. "Military Retains Top Position in Americans' Confidence Ratings." *Gallup Poll Monthly,* June 2001, 52–55.

Newport, Frank, and Leslie McAneny. "Whose Court Is It Anyhow? O'Connor, Kennedy, Souter Position Reflects Views of Most Americans." *Gallup Poll Monthly,* July 1992, 51–53.

Niemi, Richard G., John Mueller, and Tom W. Smith. *Trends in Public Opinion: A Compendium of Survey Data.* New York: Greenwood, 1989.

O'Brien, David M. "Background Paper." In *Judicial Roulette: Report of the Twentieth Century Fund Task Force on Judicial Selection,* 13–145. New York: Priority Press, 1988.

———. "Charting the Rehnquist Court's Course: How the Center Folds, Holds, and Shifts." *New York Law School Law Review* 40 (1996): 981–98.

———. *Constitutional Law and Politics: Civil Rights and Civil Liberties.* 5th ed. 2 vols. New York: Norton, 2003.

———. *Constitutional Law and Politics: Struggles for Power and Governmental Accountability.* 4th ed. New York: Norton, 2000.

———. *Storm Center: The Supreme Court in American Politics.* 5th ed. New York: Norton, 2000.

O'Connor, Karen, and Larry J. Sabato. *American Government: Continuity and Change.* New York: Longman, 2002.

O'Connor Hearings. U.S. Senate Committee on the Judiciary. *Nomination of Sandra*

Day O'Connor: Hearings Before the Committee on the Judiciary. 97th Cong., 1st sess., September 9, 10, and 11, 1981.

Opinion Research Service. *American Public Opinion Index.* Louisville, KY: Opinion Research Service, 1988.

Overby, L. Marvin, Beth M. Henschen, Julie Strauss, and Michael H. Walsh. "Courting Constituents? An Analysis of the Senate Confirmation Vote on Judge Clarence Thomas." *American Political Science Review* 86 (1992): 997–1003.

Overby, L. Marvin, and Beth M. Henschen. "Race Trumps Gender? Women, African-Americans, and the Senate Confirmation of Justice Clarence Thomas." *American Politics Quarterly* 20 (1994): 62–73.

Page, Benjamin I., and Robert Y. Shapiro. "Effects of Public Opinion on Policy." *American Political Science Review* 77 (1983): 175–90.

Palley, Marian Lief, and Howard A. Palley. "The Thomas Appointment: Defeats and Victories for Women." *PS: Political Science and Politics* 25 (1992): 473–76.

Parks, Daniel J. "Partisan Voting Holds Steady." *CQ Weekly Report,* December 11, 1999, 2975–78.

Patterson, Orlando. "Race, Gender, and Liberal Fallacies." *Court of Appeal: The Black Community Speaks Out on the Racial and Sexual Politics of Thomas v. Hill,* edited by Robert Chrisman and Robert L. Allen, 160–64. New York: Ballantine, 1992.

Peretti, Terri Jennings. *In Defense of a Political Court.* Princeton, NJ: Princeton University Press, 1999.

———. "Restoring the Balance of Power: The Struggle for Control of the Supreme Court." *Hastings Constitutional Law Quarterly* 20 (1992): 69–104.

Phelps, Timothy, and Helen Winternitz. *Capitol Games: The Inside Story of Clarence Thomas, Anita Hill, and a Supreme Court Nomination.* New York: Hyperion, 1992.

Plano, Jack C., Robert E. Riggs, and Helenan Robin. *The Dictionary of Political Analysis.* 2nd ed. Santa Barbara, CA: ABC-CLIO, 1982.

Ponnuru, Ramesh. "Empty Souter." *National Review,* September 11, 1995, 24–25.

Pound, Roscoe. *The Formative Era of American Law.* Boston: Little, Brown, 1938.

Powe, L. A. "The Senate and the Court: Questioning a Nominee." *Texas Law Review* 54 (1976): 891–901.

"*Reason* Interview: Clarence Thomas." *Reason,* November 1987, 31–32.

Rees, Grover, III. "Questions for Supreme Court Nominees at Confirmation Hearings: Excluding the Constitution." *Georgia Law Review* 17 (1983): 913–67.

Rehnquist, William H. "The Making of a Supreme Court Justice." *Harvard Law Record,* October 8, 1959, 7–10.

———. "Presidential Appointments to the Supreme Court." *Constitutional Quarterly* 2 (1985): 319–30.

Reibstein, Larry. "The End of 'See-No-Evil.'" *Newsweek,* July 6, 1998, 36–38.

Reynolds, Glenn H. "Taking Advice Seriously: An Immodest Proposal for Reforming the Confirmation Process." *Southern California Law Review* 65 (March 1992): 1577–82.

Rieselbach, Leroy N. *Congressional Reform.* Washington, DC: Congressional Quarterly, 1986.

Roberts, Steven V., Jeannye Thornton, and Ted Gest. "The Crowning Thomas Affair." *U.S. News and World Report,* September 16, 1991, 24.

Rohde, David, and Harold Spaeth. *Supreme Court Decision Making.* San Francisco: Freeman, 1976.

Rosen, Jeffrey. "The Agonizer." *New Yorker,* November 11, 1996, 85–87.

———. "The New Look of Liberalism on the Court." *New York Times Magazine,* October 5, 1997, 60–65 ff.

Ross, William G. "The Functions, Roles, and Duties of the Senate in the Supreme Court Appointment Process." *William and Mary Law Review* 28 (Summer 1987): 633–82.

———. "The Questioning of Supreme Court Nominees at Senate Confirmation Hearings: Proposals for Accommodating the Needs of the Senate and Ameliorating the Fears of the Nominees." *Tulane Law Review* 62 (1987): 109–74.

———. "The Supreme Court Appointment Process: A Search for a Synthesis." *Albany Law Review* 57 (Spring 1994): 993–1042.

Rotunda, Ronald D. "Resolving Doubts About Clarence Thomas; Liberals Judge Nominee Under Ethical Double Standard." *Recorder,* September 10, 1991, 5.

Savage, David. "A Journalist's Perspective." In *The Rehnquist Court: A Retrospective,* edited by Martin H. Belsky, 159–66. Oxford: Oxford University Press, 2002.

Scalia Hearings. U.S. Senate Committee on the Judiciary. *Nomination of Judge Antonin Scalia: Hearings Before the Committee on the Judiciary.* 99th Cong., 2nd sess., August 5 and 6, 1986.

Scheb, John M. II, and Terry M. Bowen. "Ideology on the Rehnquist Court." *Southeastern Political Review* 23 (1995): 515–23.

Schultz, David. "Why No More Giants on the Supreme Court: The Personalities and the Times." In *Leaders of the Pack: Polls and Case Studies of Great Supreme Court Justices,* edited by William D. Pederson and Norman W. Provizer, 262–74. New York: Peter Lang, 2003.

Schwartz, Bernard. *A History of the Supreme Court.* New York: Oxford University Press, 1993.

———. "The Judicial Ten: America's Greatest Judges." *Southern Illinois University Law Review* 1979 (1979): 405–47.

Schwartz, Herman. *Packing the Courts: The Conservative Campaign to Rewrite the Constitution.* New York: Scribner, 1988.

———. "The Supreme Court's Federalism: Fig Leaf for Conservatives." *Annals of the American Academy of Political and Social Science* 574 (2001): 119–31.

Scigliano, Robert G. *The Supreme Court and the Presidency.* New York: Free Press, 1971.

Segal, Jeffrey A., Albert D. Cover, and Charles M. Cameron. "The Role of Ideology in Senate Confirmation of Supreme Court Justices." *Kentucky Law Journal* 77 (1989): 485–507.

Segal, Jeffrey A., and Harold J. Spaeth. *The Supreme Court and the Attitudinal Model.* New York: Cambridge University Press, 1993.

"The Senate and Executive Branch Appointments: An Obstacle Course on Capitol Hill?" *Brookings Review* 19 (Spring 2001): 32–36.

Silverstein, Mark. *Judicious Choices: The New Politics of Supreme Court Confirmations.* New York: Norton, 1994.

———. "The People, the Senate, and the Court: The Democratization of the Judicial Confirmation System." *Constitutional Commentary* 9 (1992): 41–58.

Silverstein, Mark, and William Haltom. "You Can't Always Get What You Want: Reflections on the Ginsburg and Breyer Nominations." *Journal of Law and Politics* 12 (1996): 459–79.

Simon, Paul. "Advice and Consent: The Senate's Role in the Judicial Nomination Process." *St. John's Journal of Legal Commentary* 7 (1991): 41–80.

———. *Advice and Consent: Clarence Thomas, Robert Bork and the Intriguing History of the Supreme Court's Nomination Battles.* Washington, DC: National Press Books, 1992.

Simson, Gary J. "Better Way to Choose Supremes." *National Law Journal,* March 21, 1994, A19–20.

———. "Mired in the Confirmation Mess." *University of Pennsylvania Law Review* 143 (1995): 1035–63.

———. "Thomas's Supreme Unfitness—A Letter to the Senate on Advice and Consent." *Cornell Law Review* 78 (1993): 619–63.

Sinclair, Barbara. "Senate Process, Congressional Politics, and the Thomas Nomination." *PS: Political Science and Politics* 25 (1992): 477–80.

———. *The Transformation of the U.S. Senate.* Baltimore: Johns Hopkins, 1989.

Sirovich, Lawrence. "A Pattern Analysis of the Second Rehnquist U.S. Supreme Court." *Proceedings of the National Academy of Sciences USA* (2003): 7432–37.

Skene, Neil. "'Advice and Consent': Atrophying Power," *CQ Weekly Report,* October 5, 1991.

Smith, Christopher E. "Clarence Thomas: A Distinctive Justice." *Seton Hall Law Review* 28 (1997): 1–28.

Snyder, John M. Review of *The Antichrist,* by Vincent P. Miceli. *Lincoln Review* (Winter 1986): 71–74.

Songer, Donald R. "The Relevance of Policy Values for the Confirmation of Supreme Court Nominees." *Law and Society Review* 13 (Summer 1979): 927–48.

Souter Hearings. U.S. Senate Committee on the Judiciary. *Nomination of David H. Souter to Be Associate Justice of the Supreme Court of the United States: Hearings Before the Committee on the Judiciary.* 101st Cong., 2nd sess., September 13, 14, 17, 18, and 19, 1990.

Stanley, Harold W., and Richard G. Niemi. *Vital Statistics on American Politics.* 5th ed. Washington, DC: Congressional Quarterly, 1995.

Stephenson, D. Grier, Jr. *Campaigns and the Court: The U.S. Supreme Court in Presidential Elections.* New York: Columbia University Press, 1999.

Strasser, Fred, and Marcia Coyle, "Task Force Calls for Nomination Cooperation." *National Law Journal,* February 17, 1992, 29.

Strauss, David, and Cass R. Sunstein. "The Senate, the Constitution, and the Confirmation Process." *Yale Law Journal* 101 (1992): 1491–524.

Sullivan, Kathleen M. "Constitutional Amendmentitis." *American Prospect,* 23 (Fall 1995): 20–27.

Sundquist, James L. *The Decline and Resurgence of Congress.* Washington, DC: Brookings, 1981.

Sunstein, Cass R. *One Case at a Time: Judicial Minimalism on the Supreme Court.* Cambridge, MA: Harvard University Press, 1999.

Tamm, Edward A., and Paul C. Reardon. "Warren Burger and the Administration of Justice." *Brigham Young University Law Review* 3 (1981): 447–521.

Tanenhaus, Joseph, and Walter F. Murphy. "Patterns of Public Support." *Journal of Politics* 43 (1981): 24–39.

Taylor, Stuart, Jr. "The Senate Should Claim Full Parity with the President in Selecting Future Justices." *American Lawyer,* November 1991, 5.

———. "Supreme Disappointment; What's Really Wrong with the Way We Choose Supreme Court Justices." *American Lawyer,* November 1991, 5 ff.

Thomas Hearings. U.S. Senate Committee on the Judiciary. *Nomination of Judge Clarence Thomas to Be Associate Justice of the Supreme Court: Hearings Before the Committee on the Judiciary.* 102nd Cong., 1st sess. Parts 1–5. September 10, 11, 12, 13, 16, 17, 19, 20, 23, and October 11, 12, and 13, 1991.

Thomas Report. U.S. Senate Committee on the Judiciary. *Nomination of Clarence Thomas to Be an Associate Justice of the Supreme Court: Report Together with Additional and Supplemental Views.* 102nd Cong., 1st sess., 1991. S. Exec. Rept. 102-15.

Thomas, Clarence. "Civil Rights as a Principle Versus Civil Rights as an Interest." In *Assessing the Reagan Years,* edited by David Boaz, 391–402. Washington, DC: Cato Institute, 1988.

———. "The Equal Employment Opportunity Commission: Reflections on a New Philosophy." *Stetson Law Review* 15 (1985): 29–36.

———. "Thomas Sowell and the Heritage of Lincoln." *Lincoln Review* (Winter 1987–88): 7–19.

———. "You Can't Give What You Don't Have." *Lincoln Review* (Spring 1991): 11–19.

"Too Much Talk." *American Bar Association Journal,* July 1993, 43.

Totenberg, Nina. "The Confirmation Process and the Public: To Know or Not to Know." *Harvard Law Review* 101 (1988): 1213–29.

Tribe, Laurence H. *American Constitutional Law.* New York: Foundation Press, 2000.

———. *God Save This Honorable Court.* New York: Random House, 1985.

Tushnet, Mark. *Taking the Constitution away from the Courts.* Princeton, NJ: Princeton University Press, 2000.

Twentieth Century Fund Task Force on Judicial Selection. *Judicial Roulette: Report of the Twentieth Century Fund Task Force on Judicial Selection.* With Background Paper by David M. O'Brien. New York: Priority Press, 1988.

Ulmer, S. Sidney. "Supreme Court Appointments as a Poisson Distribution." *American Journal of Political Science* 26 (1982): 113–16.

U.S. House Employment and Housing Subcommittee of the Committee on Government Operations. *EEOC's Reprisal Against District Director for Testimony Before Congress on Age Discrimination Charges: Hearing Before the Employment and Housing Subcommittee.* 101st Cong., 1st sess., March 20, 1989.

U.S. House Select Committee on Aging. *Age Discrimination: Quality of Enforcement: Hearing Before the Select Committee on Aging.* 100th Cong., 2nd sess., January 28, 1988.

U.S. House Committee on Education and Labor, Subcommittee on Employment Opportunities. *Equal Employment Opportunity Commission Policies Regarding Goals and Timetables in Litigation Remedies.* 99th Cong., 2nd sess., March 11 and 13, 1986.

U.S. Senate Committee on the Judiciary. *Nomination of Clement F. Haynsworth Jr. to Be an Associate Justice of the United States Supreme Court: Hearings Before the Senate Judiciary Committee.* 91st Cong., 1st sess., 1969.

———. *Nomination of G. Harrold Carswell to Be an Associate Justice of the United States Supreme Court: Hearings Before the Senate Judiciary Committee.* 91st Cong., 2nd sess., 1970.

———. *Nomination of Harry A. Blackmun to Be an Associate Justice of the United States Supreme Court: Hearings Before the Senate Judiciary Committee.* 91st Cong., 2nd sess., 1970.

———. *Nomination of Thurgood Marshall, of New York, to Be an Associate Justice of the United States Supreme Court.* 90th Cong., 1st sess., July 13, 14, 18, 19, and 24, 1967.

———. *Nomination of William H. Rehnquist to Be Chief Justice of the United States: Report, from the Committee on the Judiciary, Together with Additional, Minority, and Supplemental Views.* 99th Cong., 2nd sess., 1986. S. Exec. Rept. 99-18.

———. *Nominations of Abe Fortas and Homer Thornberry: Hearings Before the Committee on the Judiciary.* Parts 1 and 2. 90th Cong., 2nd sess., July 11, 12, 16, 17, 18, 19, 20, 22, and 23, and September 13 and 16, 1968.

———. *Nominations of William H. Rehnquist and Lewis F. Powell, Jr., to Be Associate Justices of the United States Supreme Court: Hearings Before the Senate Judiciary Committee.* 92nd Cong., 1st sess., 1971.

U.S. Senate Special Committee on Aging. *EEOC Headquarters Officials Punish District Director for Exposing Headquarters Mismanagement: A Majority Staff Report.* 100th Cong., 2nd sess., 1988. S. Rept. 100-162.

Vieira, Norman, and Leonard E. Gross. "The Appointments Clause: Judge Bork and the Role of Ideology in Judicial Confirmations." *Journal of Legal History* 11 (1990): 311–52.

Vile, John R. *Rewriting the United States Constitution: An Examination of Proposals from Reconstruction to the Present.* New York: Praeger, 1991.

Warren, Charles. *The Supreme Court in United States History.* Boston: Little Brown, 1923.

Watson, George L., and John A. Stookey. *Shaping America: The Politics of Supreme Court Appointments.* New York: Harper Collins, 1995.

———. "Supreme Court Confirmation Hearings: A View from the Senate." *Judicature* 71 (1988): 186–93.

Williams, Juan. "A Question of Fairness." *Atlantic Monthly,* February 1987, 70–82.

Working Group. *The Family: Preserving America's Future; A Report to the President from the White House Working Group on the Family.* Washington, DC: The Working Group, 1986.

Yalof, David A. *Pursuit of Justices: Presidential Politics and the Selection of Supreme Court Nominees.* Chicago: University of Chicago Press, 1999.

Yarbrough, Tinsley E. *The Rehnquist Court and the Constitution.* New York: Oxford University Press, 2000.

Young, Ernest A. "Judicial Activism and Conservative Politics." *Colorado Law Review* 73 (2002): 1139–216.

Index